DATA SCIENCE
FUNDAMENTALS
Pocket Primer

Oswald Campesato

MERCURY LEARNING AND INFORMATION

Dulles, Virginia
Boston, Massachusetts
New Delhi

Publisher: David Pallai
MERCURY LEARNING AND INFORMATION
22841 Quicksilver Drive
Dulles, VA 20166
info@merclearning.com
www.merclearning.com
800-232-0223

O. Campesato. *Data Science Fundamentals Pocket Primer.*
ISBN: 978-1-68392-733-4

The publisher recognizes and respects all marks used by companies, manufacturers, and developers as a means to distinguish their products. All brand names and product names mentioned in this book are trademarks or service marks of their respective companies. Any omission or misuse (of any kind) of service marks or trademarks, etc. is not an attempt to infringe on the property of others.

Library of Congress Control Number: 2021937777

212223321 This book is printed on acid-free paper in the United States of America.

Our titles are available for adoption, license, or bulk purchase by institutions, corporations, etc. For additional information, please contact the Customer Service Dept. at 800-232-0223(toll free).

All of our titles are available in digital format at academiccourseware.com and other digital vendors. Companion files (figures and code listings) for this title are available by contacting info@merclearning. com. The sole obligation of MERCURY LEARNING AND INFORMATION to the purchaser is to replace the disc, based on defective materials or faulty workmanship, but not based on the operation or functionality of the product.

I'd like to dedicate this book to my parents–
may this bring joy and happiness into their lives.

Contents

Chapter 10 Data Visualization 379

Index 419

Preface

WHAT IS THE PRIMARY VALUE PROPOSITION FOR THIS BOOK?

This book contains a fast-paced introduction to as much relevant information about data analytics as possible that can be reasonably included in a book of this size. Please keep in mind the following point: *this book is intended to provide you with a broad overview of many relevant technologies.*

As such, you will be exposed to a variety of features of NumPy and Pandas, how to write regular expressions (with an accompanying chapter), and how to perform many data cleaning tasks. Keep in mind that some topics are presented in a cursory manner, which is for two main reasons. First, it's important that you be exposed to these concepts. In some cases, you will find topics that might pique your interest, and hence motivate you to learn more about them through self-study; in other cases, you will probably be satisfied with a brief introduction. In other words, you can decide whether to delve into more detail regarding the topics in this book.

Second, a full treatment of all the topics that are covered in this book would significantly increase the size of this book.

However, it's important for you to decide if this approach is suitable for your needs and learning style. If not, you can select one or more of the plethora of data analytics books that are available.

THE TARGET AUDIENCE

This book is intended primarily for people who have worked with Python and are interested in learning about several important Python libraries, such as NumPy and Pandas.

This book is also intended to reach an international audience of readers with highly diverse backgrounds. While many readers know how to read

English, their native spoken language is not English. Consequently, this book uses standard English rather than colloquial expressions that might be confusing to those readers. As you know, many people learn by different types of imitation, which includes reading, writing, or hearing new material. This book takes these points into consideration to provide a comfortable and meaningful learning experience for the intended readers.

WHAT WILL I LEARN FROM THIS BOOK?

The first chapter contains a quick tour of basic Python 3, followed by a chapter that introduces you to data types and data cleaning tasks, such as working with datasets that contain different types of data and how to handle missing data. The third and fourth chapters introduce you to NumPy and Pandas (and many code samples).

The fifth chapter contains fundamental concepts in probability and statistics, such as mean, mode, and variance and correlation matrices. You will also learn about Gini impurity, entropy, and KL-divergence. You will also learn about eigenvalues, eigenvectors, and PCA (Principal Component Analysis).

The sixth chapter of this book delves into Pandas, followed by Chapter 7 about R programming. Chapter 8 covers regular expressions and provides with plenty of examples. Chapter 9 discusses both SQL and NoSQL, and then Chapter 10 discusses data visualization with numerous code samples for Matplotlib, Seaborn, and Bokeh.

WHY ARE THE CODE SAMPLES PRIMARILY IN PYTHON?

Most of the code samples are short (usually less than one page and sometimes less than half a page), and if need be, you can easily and quickly copy/paste the code into a new Jupyter notebook. For the Python code samples that reference a CSV file, you do not need any additional code in the corresponding Jupyter notebook to access the CSV file. Moreover, the code samples execute quickly, so you won't need to avail yourself of the free GPU that is provided in Google Colaboratory.

If you do decide to use Google Colaboratory, you can avail yourself of many useful features of Colaboratory (e.g., the upload feature to upload existing Jupyter notebooks). If the Python code references a CSV file, make sure that you include the appropriate code snippet (as explained in Chapter 1) to access the CSV file in the corresponding Jupyter notebook in Google Colaboratory.

DO I NEED TO LEARN THE THEORY PORTIONS OF THIS BOOK?

Once again, the answer depends on the extent to which you plan to become involved in data analytics. For example, if you plan to study machine learning, then you will probably learn how to create and train a model, which is a task that is performed after data cleaning tasks. In general, you will probably need to learn everything that you encounter in this book if you are planning to become a machine learning engineer.

WHY DOES THIS BOOK INCLUDE SKLEARN MATERIAL?

The Sklearn material in this book is minimalistic because this book is not about machine learning. The Sklearn material is located in Chapter 6, where you will learn about some of the Sklearn built-in datasets. If you decide to delve into machine learning, you will have already been introduced to some aspects of Sklearn.

WHY IS A REGEX CHAPTER INCLUDED IN THIS BOOK?

Regular expressions are supported in multiple languages (including Java and JavaScript) and they enable you to perform complex tasks with very compact regular expressions. Regular expressions can seem arcane and too complex to learn in a reasonable amount of time. Chapter 2 contains some Pandas-based code samples that use regular expressions to perform tasks that might otherwise be more complicated.

If you plan to use Pandas extensively or you plan to work on NLP-related tasks, then the code samples in this chapter will be very useful for you because they are more than adequate for solving certain types of tasks, such as removing HTML tags. Moreover, your knowledge of RegEx will transfer instantly to other languages that support regular expressions.

GETTING THE MOST FROM THIS BOOK

Some programmers learn well from prose, others learn well from sample code (and lots of it), which means that there's no single style that can be used for everyone.

Moreover, some programmers want to run the code first, see what it does, and then return to the code to delve into the details (and others use the opposite approach).

Consequently, there are various types of code samples in this book: some are short, some are long, and other code samples "build" from earlier code samples.

WHAT DO I NEED TO KNOW FOR THIS BOOK?

Current knowledge of Python 3.x is the most helpful skill. Knowledge of other programming languages (such as Java) can also be helpful because of the exposure to programming concepts and constructs. The less technical knowledge that you have, the more diligence will be required to understand the various topics that are covered.

If you want to be sure that you can grasp the material in this book, glance through some of the code samples to get an idea of how much is familiar to you and how much is new for you.

DOESN'T THE COMPANION FILES OBVIATE THE NEED FOR THIS BOOK?

The companion files contains all the code samples to save you time and effort from the error-prone process of manually typing code into a text file. In addition, there are situations in which you might not have easy access to the companion files. Furthermore, the code samples in the book provide explanations that are not available on the companion files.

DOES THIS BOOK CONTAIN PRODUCTION-LEVEL CODE SAMPLES?

The primary purpose of the code samples in this book is to show you Python-based libraries for solving a variety of data-related tasks in conjunction with acquiring a rudimentary understanding of statistical concepts. Clarity has higher priority than writing more compact code that is more difficult to understand (and possibly more prone to bugs). If you decide to use any of the code in this book in a production website, you should subject that code to the same rigorous analysis as the other parts of your code base.

WHAT ARE THE NON-TECHNICAL PREREQUISITES FOR THIS BOOK?

Although the answer to this question is more difficult to quantify, it's important to have strong desire to learn about data science, along with the motivation and discipline to read and understand the code samples.

HOW DO I SET UP A COMMAND SHELL?

If you are a Mac user, there are three ways to do so. The first method is to use Finder to navigate to Applications > Utilities and then double click on the Utilities application. Next, if you already have a command shell available, you can launch a new command shell by typing the following command:

```
open /Applications/Utilities/Terminal.app
```

A second method for Mac users is to open a new command shell on a Macbook from a command shell that is already visible simply by clicking command+n in that command shell, and your Mac will launch another command shell.

If you are a PC user, you can install Cygwin (which is open source: *https://cygwin.com/*) that simulates bash commands, or use another toolkit such as MKS (a commercial product). Please read the online documentation that describes the download and installation process. Note that custom aliases are not automatically set if they are defined in a file other than the main start-up file (such as *.bash_login*).

COMPANION FILES

All the code samples and figures in this book may be obtained by writing to the publisher at *info@merclearning.com*.

WHAT ARE THE NEXT STEPS AFTER FINISHING THIS BOOK?

The answer to this question varies widely, mainly because the answer depends heavily on your objectives. If you are interested primarily in NLP, then you can learn more advanced concepts, such as attention, transformers, and the BERT-related models.

If you are primarily interested in machine learning, there are some subfields of machine learning, such as deep learning and reinforcement learning (and deep reinforcement learning) that might appeal to you. Fortunately, there are many resources available, and you can perform an Internet search for those resources. One other point: the aspects of machine learning for you to learn depend on who you are. The needs of a machine learning engineer, data scientist, manager, student, or software developer are all different.

Oswald Campesato
April 2021

## CHAPTER 1

WORKING WITH DATA

This chapter introduces you to data types, how to scale data values, and various techniques for handling missing data values. If most of the material in this chapter is new to you, be assured that it's not necessary to understand everything in this chapter. It's still a good idea to read as much material as you can absorb, and perhaps return to this chapter again after you have completed some of the other chapters in this book.

The first part of this chapter contains an overview of different types of data and an explanation of how to normalize and standardize a set of numeric values by calculating the mean and standard deviation of a set of numbers. You will see how to map categorical data to a set of integers and how to perform one-hot encoding.

The second part of this chapter discusses missing data, outliers, and anomalies, as well as some techniques for handling these scenarios. The third section discusses imbalanced data and the use of SMOTE (Synthetic Minority Over-sampling Technique) to deal with imbalanced classes in a dataset.

The fourth section discusses ways to evaluate classifiers such as LIME and ANOVA. This section also contains details regarding the bias-variance trade-off and various types of statistical bias.

WHAT ARE DATASETS?

In simple terms, a dataset is a source of data (such as a text file) that contains rows and columns of data. Each row is typically called a *data point*, and each column is called a *feature*. A dataset can be in a range of formats: CSV (comma separated values), TSV (tab separated values), Excel spreadsheet, a table in an RDMBS (Relational Database Management Systems), a document in a NoSQL database, or the output from a Web service. Someone needs to analyze the dataset to determine which features are the most important and which features can be safely ignored to train a model with the given dataset.

A dataset can vary from very small (a couple of features and 100 rows) to very large (more than 1,000 features and more than one million rows). If you are unfamiliar with the problem domain, then you might struggle to determine the most important features in a large dataset. In this situation, you might need a domain expert who understands the importance of the features, their inter-dependencies (if any), and whether the data values for the features are valid. In addition, there are algorithms (called dimensionality reduction algorithms) that can help you determine the most important features. For example, PCA (Principal Component Analysis) is one such algorithm, which is discussed in more detail in Chapter 2.

Data Preprocessing

Data preprocessing is the initial step that involves validating the contents of a dataset, which involves making decisions about missing data, duplicate data, and incorrect data values:

- dealing with missing data values
- cleaning "noisy" text-based data
- removing HTML tags
- removing emoticons
- dealing with emojis/emoticons
- filtering data
- grouping data
- handling currency and date formats (i18n)

Cleaning data is done before data wrangling that involves removing unwanted data as well as handling missing data. In the case of text-based data, you might need to remove HTML tags and punctuation. In the case of numeric data, it's less likely (though still possible) that alphabetic characters are mixed together with numeric data. However, a dataset with numeric features might have incorrect values or missing values (discussed later). In addition, calculating the minimum, maximum, mean, median, and standard deviation of the values of a feature obviously pertain only to numeric values.

After the preprocessing step is completed, *data wrangling* is performed, which refers to transforming data into a new format. You might have to combine data from multiple sources into a single dataset. For example, you might need to convert between different units of measurement (such as date formats or currency values) so that the data values can be represented in a consistent manner in a dataset.

Currency and date values are part of *i18n* (internationalization), whereas *l10n* (localization) targets a specific nationality, language, or region. Hard-coded values (such as text strings) can be stored as resource strings in a file called a *resource bundle*, where each string is referenced via a code. Each language has its own resource bundle.

DATA TYPES

Explicit data types exist in many programming languages, such as C, C++, Java, and TypeScript. Some programming languages, such as JavaScript and awk, do not require initializing variables with an explicit type: the type of a variable is inferred dynamically via an implicit type system (i.e., one that is not directly exposed to a developer).

In machine learning, datasets can contain features that have different types of data, such as a combination of one or more of the following:

- numeric data (integer/floating point and discrete/continuous)
- character/categorical data (different languages)
- date-related data (different formats)
- currency data (different formats)
- binary data (yes/no, 0/1, and so forth)
- nominal data (multiple unrelated values)
- ordinal data (multiple and related values)

Consider a dataset that contains real estate data, which can have as many as thirty columns (or even more), often with the following features:

- the number of bedrooms in a house: numeric value and a discrete value
- the number of square feet: a numeric value and (probably) a continuous value
- the name of the city: character data
- the construction date: a date value
- the selling price: a currency value and probably a continuous value
- the "for sale" status: binary data (either "yes" or "no")

An example of nominal data is the seasons in a year. Although many (most?) countries have four distinct seasons, some countries have two distinct seasons. However, keep in mind that seasons can be associated with different temperature ranges (summer versus winter). An example of ordinal data is an employee's pay grade: 1=entry level, 2=one year of experience, and so forth. Another example of nominal data is a set of colors, such as {Red, Green, Blue}.

An example of binary data is the pair {Male, Female}, and some datasets contain a feature with these two values. If such a feature is required for training a model, first convert {Male, Female} to a numeric counterpart, such as {0,1}. Similarly, if you need to include a feature whose values are the previous set of colors, you can replace {Red, Green, Blue} with the values {0,1,2}. Categorical data is discussed in more detail later in this chapter.

PREPARING DATASETS

If you have the good fortune to inherit a dataset that is in pristine condition, then data cleaning tasks (discussed later) are vastly simplified: in fact, it might not be necessary to perform *any* data cleaning for the dataset. On the other hand, if you need to create a dataset that combines data from multiple datasets that contain different formats for dates and currency, then you need to perform a conversion to a common format.

If you need to train a model that includes features that have categorical data, then you need to convert that categorical data to numeric data. For instance, the Titanic dataset contains a feature called "sex," which is either male or female. As you will see later in this chapter, Pandas makes it extremely simple to "map" male to 0 and female to 1.

Discrete Data Versus Continuous Data

Discrete data is a set of values that can be counted, whereas *continuous data* must be measured. Discrete data can "reasonably" fit in a drop-down list of values, but there is no exact value for making such a determination. One person might think that a list of 500 values is discrete, whereas another person might think it's continuous.

For example, the list of provinces of Canada and the list of states of the United States are discrete data values, but is the same true for the number of countries in the world (roughly 200) or for the number of languages in the world (more than 7,000)?

On the other hand, values for temperature, humidity, and barometric pressure are considered continuous. Currency is also treated as continuous, even though there is a measurable difference between two consecutive values. The smallest unit of currency for U.S. currency is one penny, which is 1/100th of a dollar (accounting-based measurements use the "mil," which is 1/1,000th of a dollar).

Continuous data types can have subtle differences. For example, someone who is 200 centimeters tall is twice as tall as someone who is 100 centimeters tall; the same is true for 100 kilograms versus 50 kilograms. However, temperature is different: 80 degrees Fahrenheit is not twice as hot as 40 degrees Fahrenheit.

Furthermore, keep in mind that the meaning of the word "continuous" in mathematics is not necessarily the same as continuous in machine learning. In the former, a continuous function (let's say in the 2D Euclidean plane) can have an uncountably infinite number of values. On the other hand, a feature in a dataset that can have more values than can be "reasonably" displayed in a drop-down list is treated *as though* it's a continuous variable.

For instance, values for stock prices are discrete: they must differ by at least a penny (or some other minimal unit of currency), which is to say, it's meaningless to say that the stock price changes by one-millionth of a penny. However, since there are so many possible stock values, it's treated as a continuous variable. The same comments apply to car mileage, ambient temperature, and barometric pressure.

"Binning" Continuous Data

The concept of *binning* refers to subdividing a set of values into multiple intervals, and then treating all the numbers in the same interval as though they had the same value.

As a simple example, suppose that a feature in a dataset contains the age of people in a dataset. The range of values is approximately between 0 and 120, and we could bin them into 12 equal intervals, where each consists of 10 values: 0 through 9, 10 through 19, 20 through 29, and so forth.

However, partitioning the values of people's ages as described in the preceding paragraph can be problematic. Suppose that person A, person B, and person C are 29, 30, and 39, respectively. Then person A and person B are probably more similar to each other than person B and person C, but because of the way in which the ages are partitioned, B is classified as closer to C than to A. In fact, binning can increase Type I errors (false positive) and Type II errors (false negative), as discussed in the following blog post (along with some alternatives to binning):

https://medium.com/@peterflom/why-binning-continuous-data-is-almost-always-a-mistake-ad0b3a1d141f.

As another example, using quartiles is even more coarse-grained than the earlier age-related binning example. The issue with binning pertains to the consequences of classifying people in different bins, even though they are in close proximity to each other. For instance, some people struggle financially because they earn a meager wage, and they are disqualified from financial assistance because their salary is higher than the cutoff point for receiving any assistance.

Scaling Numeric Data via Normalization

A range of values can vary significantly, and it's important to note that they often need to be scaled to a smaller range, such as values in the range $[-1,1]$ or $[0,1]$, which you can do via the `tanh` function or the `sigmoid` function, respectively.

For example, measuring a person's height in terms of meters involves a range of values between 0.50 meters and 2.5 meters (in the vast majority of cases), whereas measuring height in terms of centimeters ranges between 50 centimeters and 250 centimeters: these two units differ by a factor of 100. A person's weight in kilograms generally varies between 5 kilograms and 200 kilograms, whereas measuring weight in grams differs by a factor of 1,000. Distances between objects can be measured in meters or in kilometers, which also differ by a factor of 1,000.

In general, use units of measure so that the data values in multiple features belong to a similar range of values. In fact, some machine learning algorithms require scaled data, often in the range of $[0,1]$ or $[-1,1]$. In addition to the tanh and sigmoid functions, there are other techniques for scaling data, such as standardizing data (such as the Gaussian distribution) and normalizing data (linearly scaled so that the new range of values is in [0,1]).

The following examples involve a floating point variable X with different ranges of values that will be scaled so that the new values are in the interval [0,1].

- Example 1: If the values of X are in the range [0,2], then X/2 is in the range [0,1].
- Example 2: If the values of X are in the range [3,6], then X–3 is in the range [0,3], and (X–3)/3 is in the range [0,1].
- Example 3: If the values of X are in the range [−10,20], then X +10 is in the range [0,30], and (X +10)/30 is in the range of [0,1].

In general, suppose that X is a random variable whose values are in the range [a,b], where a < b. You can scale the data values by performing two steps:

```
Step 1: X-a is in the range [0,b-a]
Step 2: (X-a)/(b-a) is in the range [0,1]
```

If X is a random variable that has the values {x1, x2, x3, . . ., xn}, then the formula for normalization involves mapping each xi value to (xi − min)/(max − min), where min is the minimum value of X and max is the maximum value of X.

As a simple example, suppose that the random variable x has the values {-1, 0, 1}. Then min and max are 1 and −1, respectively, and the normalization of {-1, 0, 1} is the set of values { (-1-(-1))/2, (0-(-1))/2, (1-(-1))/2}, which equals {0, 1/2, 1}.

Scaling Numeric Data via Standardization

The standardization technique involves finding the mean mu and the standard deviation sigma, and then mapping each xi value to (xi − mu)/sigma. Recall the following formulas:

```
mu = [SUM (x) ]/n
variance(x) = [SUM (x - xbar)*(x - xbar)]/n
sigma = sqrt(variance)
```

As a simple illustration of standardization, suppose that the random variable X has the values {−1, 0, 1}. Then mu and sigma are calculated as follows:

```
mu        = (SUM xi)/n = (-1 + 0 + 1)/3 = 0
variance  = [SUM (xi- mu)^2]/n
          = [(-1-0)^2 + (0-0)^2 + (1-0)^2]/3
          = 2/3
sigma     = sqrt(2/3) = 0.816 (approximate value)
```

Hence, the standardization of {-1, 0, 1} is {-1/0.816, 0/0.816, 1/0.816}, which in turn equals the set of values {-1.2254, 0, 1.2254}.

As another example, suppose that the random variable X has the values {-6, 0, 6}. Then mu and `sigma` are calculated as follows:

```
mu        = (SUM xi)/n = (-6 + 0 + 6)/3 = 0

variance = [SUM (xi- mu)^2]/n
         = [(-6-0)^2 + (0-0)^2 + (6-0)^2]/3
         = 72/3
         = 24

sigma     = sqrt(24) = 4.899 (approximate value)
```

Hence, the standardization of {-6, 0, 6} is {-6/4.899, 0/4.899, 6/4.899}, which in turn equals the set of values {-1.2247, 0, 1.2247}.

In the preceding two examples, the mean equals 0 in both cases, but the variance and standard deviation are significantly different. The normalization of a set of values *always* produces a set of numbers between 0 and 1.

On the other hand, the standardization of a set of values can generate numbers that are less than -1 and greater than 1: this will occur when `sigma` is less than the minimum value of every term |mu - xi|, where the latter is the absolute value of the difference between mu and each xi value. In the preceding example, the minimum difference equals 1, whereas `sigma` is 0.816, and therefore the largest standardized value is greater than 1.

What to Look for in Categorical Data

This section contains suggestions for handling inconsistent data values, and you can determine which ones to adopt based on any additional factors that are relevant to your particular task. For example, consider dropping columns that have very low cardinality (equal to or close to 1), as well as numeric columns with zero or very low variance.

Next, check the contents of categorical columns for inconsistent spellings or errors. A good example pertains to the gender category, which can consist of a combination of the following values:

```
male
Male
female
Female
m
f
M
F
```

The preceding categorical values for gender can be replaced with two categorical values (unless you have a valid reason to retain some of the other values). Moreover, if you are training a model whose analysis involves a single gender, then you need to determine which rows (if any) of a dataset must be excluded. Also check categorical data columns for redundant or missing white spaces.

Check for data values that have multiple data types, such as a numerical column with numbers as numerals and some numbers as strings or objects. Ensure there are consistent data formats: numbers as integers or floating numbers. Ensure that dates have the same format (for example, do not mix mm/dd/yyyy date formats with another date format, such as dd/mm/yyyy).

Mapping Categorical Data to Numeric Values

Character data is often called *categorical data*, examples of which include people's names, home or work addresses, and email addresses. Many types of categorical data involve short lists of values. For example, the days of the week and the months in a year involve seven and twelve distinct values, respectively. Notice that the days of the week have a relationship: each day has a previous day and a next day, and similarly for the months of a year.

On the other hand, the colors of an automobile are independent of each other. The color red is not "better" or "worse" than the color blue. However, cars of a certain color can have a statistically higher number of accidents, but we won't address that issue here.

There are several well-known techniques for mapping categorical values to a set of numeric values. A simple example where you need to perform this conversion involves the gender feature in the Titanic dataset. This feature is one of the relevant features for training a machine learning model. The gender feature has {M, F} as its set of possible values. As you will see later in this chapter, Pandas makes it very easy to convert the set of values {M,F} to the set of values {0,1}.

Another mapping technique involves mapping a set of categorical values to a set of consecutive integer values. For example, the set {Red, Green, Blue} can be mapped to the set of integers {0,1,2}. The set {Male, Female} can be mapped to the set of integers {0,1}. The days of the week can be mapped to {0,1,2,3,4,5,6}. Note that the first day of the week depends on the country (in some cases it's Sunday, and in other cases it's Monday).

Another technique is called *one-hot encoding*, which converts each value to a *vector*. Thus, {Male, Female} can be represented by the vectors [1,0] and [0,1], and the colors {Red, Green, Blue} can be represented by the vectors [1,0,0], [0,1,0], and [0,0,1]. If you vertically "line up" the two vectors for gender, they form a 2×2 identity matrix, and doing the same for the colors will form a 3×3 identity matrix as shown here:

```
[1,0,0]
[0,1,0]
[0,0,1]
```

If you are familiar with matrices, you probably noticed that the preceding set of vectors looks like the 3×3 identity matrix. In fact, this technique generalizes in a straightforward manner. Specifically, if you have n distinct categorical values, you can map each of those values to one of the vectors in an nxn identity matrix.

As another example, the set of titles {"Intern", "Junior", "Mid-Range", "Senior", "Project Leader", "Dev Manager"} has a hierarchical relationship in terms of their salaries (which can also overlap, but we won't address that now).

Another set of categorical data involves the season of the year: {"Spring", "Summer", "Autumn", "Winter"}, and while these values are generally independent of each other, there are cases in which the season is significant. For example, the values for the monthly rainfall, average temperature, crime rate, or foreclosure rate can depend on the season, month, week, or day of the year.

If a feature has a large number of categorical values, then one-hot encoding will produce many additional columns for each data point. Since the majority of the values in the new columns equal 0, this can increase the sparsity of the dataset, which in turn can result in more overfitting and hence adversely affect the accuracy of machine learning algorithms that you adopt during the training process.

Another solution is to use a sequence-based solution in which N categories are mapped to the integers 1, 2, . . . , N. Another solution involves examining the row frequency of each categorical value. For example, suppose that N equals 20, and there are three categorical values that occur in 95% of the values for a given feature. You can try the following:

1. Assign the values 1, 2, and 3 to those three categorical values.
2. Assign numeric values that reflect the relative frequency of those categorical values.
3. Assign the category "OTHER" to the remaining categorical values.
4. Delete the rows whose categorical values belong to the 5%.

Working with Dates

The format for a calendar date varies among different countries, and this belongs to something called the *localization* of data (not to be confused with i18n, which is data internationalization). Some examples of date formats are shown as follows (and the first four are probably the most common):

```
MM/DD/YY
MM/DD/YYYY
DD/MM/YY
DD/MM/YYYY
YY/MM/DD
M/D/YY
D/M/YY
YY/M/D
MMDDYY
DDMMYY
YYMMDD
```

If you need to combine data from datasets that contain different date formats, then converting the disparate date formats to a single common date format will ensure consistency.

Working with Currency

The format for currency depends on the country, which includes different interpretations for a "," and "." in the currency (and decimal values in general). For example, 1,124.78 equals "one thousand one hundred twenty-four point seven eight" in the United States, whereas 1.124,78 has the same meaning in Europe (i.e., the "." symbol and the "," symbol are interchanged).

If you need to combine data from datasets that contain different currency formats, then you probably need to convert all the disparate currency formats to a single common currency format. There is another detail to consider: currency exchange rates can fluctuate on a daily basis, which in turn can affect the calculation of taxes, and late fees. Although you might be fortunate enough where you won't have to deal with these issues, it's still worth being aware of them.

MISSING DATA, ANOMALIES, AND OUTLIERS

Although missing data is not directly related to checking for anomalies and outliers, in general you will perform all three of these tasks. Each task involves a set of techniques to help you perform an analysis of the data in a dataset, and the following subsections describe some of those techniques.

Missing Data

How you decide to handle missing data depends on the specific dataset. Here are some ways to handle missing data (the first three techniques are manual techniques, and the other techniques are algorithms):

1. Replace missing data with the mean/median/mode value.
2. Infer ("impute") the value for missing data.
3. Delete rows with missing data.
4. Isolation forest (tree-based algorithm).
5. Use the minimum covariance determinant.
6. Use the local outlier factor.
7. Use the one-class SVM (Support Vector Machines).

In general, replacing a missing numeric value with zero is a risky choice: this value is obviously incorrect if the values of a feature are between 1,000 and 5,000. For a feature that has numeric values, replacing a missing value with the average value is better than the value zero (unless the average equals zero); also consider using the median value. For categorical data, consider using the mode to replace a missing value.

If you are not confident that you can impute a "reasonable" value, consider excluding the row with a missing value, and then train a model with the imputed value and the deleted row.

One problem that can arise after removing rows with missing values is that the resulting dataset is too small. In this case, consider using SMOTE, which is discussed later in this chapter, to generate synthetic data.

Anomalies and Outliers

In simplified terms, an outlier is an abnormal data value that is outside the range of "normal" values. For example, a person's height in centimeters is typically between 30 centimeters and 250 centimeters. Hence, a data point (e.g., a row of data in a spreadsheet) with a height of 5 centimeters or a height of 500 centimeters is an outlier. The consequences of these outlier values are unlikely to involve a significant financial or physical loss (though they could adversely affect the accuracy of a trained model).

Anomalies are also outside the "normal" range of values (just like outliers), and they are typically more problematic than outliers: anomalies can have more severe consequences than outliers. For example, consider the scenario in which someone who lives in California suddenly makes a credit card purchase in New York. If the person is on vacation (or a business trip), then the purchase is an outlier (it's outside the typical purchasing pattern), but it's not an issue. However, if that person was in California when the credit card purchase was made, then it's more likely to be credit card fraud, as well as an anomaly.

Unfortunately, there is no simple way to decide how to deal with anomalies and outliers in a dataset. Although you can exclude rows that contain outliers, keep in mind that doing so might deprive the dataset—and therefore the trained model—of valuable information. You can try modifying the data values (described as follows), but again, this might lead to erroneous inferences in the trained model. Another possibility is to train a model with the dataset that contains anomalies and outliers, and then train a model with a dataset from which the anomalies and outliers have been removed. Compare the two results and see if you can infer anything meaningful regarding the anomalies and outliers.

Outlier Detection

Although the decision to keep or drop outliers is your decision to make, there are some techniques available that help you detect outliers in a dataset. This section contains a short list of some techniques, along with a very brief description and links for additional information.

Perhaps *trimming* is the simplest technique (apart from dropping outliers), which involves removing rows whose feature value is in the upper 5% range or the lower 5% range. *Winsorizing* the data is an improvement over trimming. Set the values in the top 5% range equal to the maximum value in the 95th percentile, and set the values in the bottom 5% range equal to the minimum in the 5th percentile.

The *Minimum Covariance Determinant* is a covariance-based technique, and a Python-based code sample that uses this technique can be found online:

https://scikit-learn.org/stable/modules/outlier_detection.html.

The *Local Outlier Factor* (LOF) technique is an unsupervised technique that calculates a local anomaly score via the kNN (k Nearest Neighbor) algorithm. Documentation and short code samples that use LOF can be found online:

https://scikit-learn.org/stable/modules/generated/sklearn.neighbors.LocalOut-lierFactor.html.

Two other techniques involve the Huber and the Ridge classes, both of which are included as part of `Sklearn`. The Huber error is less sensitive to outliers because it's calculated via linear loss, similar to MAE (Mean Absolute Error). A code sample that compares Huber and Ridge can be found online:

https://scikit-learn.org/stable/auto_examples/linear_model/plot_huber_vs_ridge.html.

You can also explore the Theil-Sen estimator and RANSAC, which are "robust" against outliers, and additional information can be found online:

https://scikit-learn.org/stable/auto_examples/linear_model/plot_theilsen.html and *https://en.wikipedia.org/wiki/Random_sample_consensus.*

Four algorithms for outlier detection are discussed at the following site:

https://www.kdnuggets.com/2018/12/four-techniques-outlier-detection.html.

One other scenario involves "local" outliers. For example, suppose that you use kMeans (or some other clustering algorithm) and determine that a value is an outlier with respect to one of the clusters. While this value is not necessarily an "absolute" outlier, detecting such a value might be important for your use case.

What Is Data Drift?

The value of data is based on its accuracy, its relevance, and its age. Data drift refers to data that has become less relevant over time. For example, online purchasing patterns in 2010 are probably not as relevant as data from 2020 because of various factors (such as the profile of different types of customers). Keep in mind that there might be multiple factors that can influence data drift in a specific dataset.

Two techniques are domain classifier and the black-box shift detector, both of which can be found online:

https://blog.dataiku.com/towards-reliable-mlops-with-drift-detectors.

WHAT IS IMBALANCED CLASSIFICATION?

Imbalanced classification involves datasets with imbalanced classes. For example, suppose that class A has 99% of the data and class B has 1%. Which classification algorithm would you use? Unfortunately, classification algorithms don't work well with this type of imbalanced dataset. Here is a list of several well-known techniques for handling imbalanced datasets:

- Random resampling rebalances the class distribution.
- Random oversampling duplicates data in the minority class.
- Random undersampling deletes examples from the majority class.
- SMOTE

Random resampling transforms the training dataset into a new dataset, which is effective for imbalanced classification problems.

The *random undersampling* technique removes samples from the dataset, and involves the following:

- randomly remove samples from the majority class
- can be performed with or without replacement
- alleviates imbalance in the dataset
- may increase the variance of the classifier
- may discard useful or important samples

However, random undersampling does not work so well with a dataset that has a 99%/1% split into two classes. Moreover, undersampling can result in losing information that is useful for a model.

Instead of random undersampling, another approach involves generating new samples from a minority class. The first technique involves oversampling examples in the minority class and duplicate examples from the minority class.

There is another technique that is better than the preceding technique, which involves the following:

- synthesizing new examples from a minority class
- a type of data augmentation for tabular data
- generating new samples from a minority class

Another well-known technique is called SMOTE, which involves data augmentation (i.e., synthesizing new data samples) well before you use a classification algorithm. SMOTE was initially developed by means of the kNN algorithm (other options are available), and it can be an effective technique for handling imbalanced classes.

Yet another option to consider is the Python package `imbalanced-learn` in the `scikit-learn-contrib` project. This project provides various resampling techniques for datasets that exhibit class imbalance. More details are available online:

https://github.com/scikit-learn-contrib/imbalanced-learn.

WHAT IS SMOTE?

SMOTE is a technique for synthesizing new samples for a dataset. This technique is based on linear interpolation:

Step 1: Select samples that are close in the feature space.
Step 2: Draw a line between the samples in the feature space.
Step 3: Draw a new sample at a point along that line.

A more detailed explanation of the SMOTE algorithm is here:

• Select a random sample "a" from the minority class.
• Now find k nearest neighbors for that example.
• Select a random neighbor "b" from the nearest neighbors.
• Create a line L that connects "a" and "b."
• Randomly select one or more points "c" on line L.

If need be, you can repeat this process for the other (k–1) nearest neighbors to distribute the synthetic values more evenly among the nearest neighbors.

SMOTE Extensions

The initial SMOTE algorithm is based on the kNN classification algorithm, which has been extended in various ways, such as replacing kNN with SVM. A list of SMOTE extensions is shown as follows:

• selective synthetic sample generation
• Borderline-SMOTE (kNN)
• Borderline-SMOTE (SVM)
• Adaptive Synthetic Sampling (ADASYN)

More information can be found online:

https://en.wikipedia.org/wiki/Oversampling_and_undersampling_in_data_analysis.

ANALYZING CLASSIFIERS (OPTIONAL)

This section is marked optional because its contents pertain to machine learning classifiers, which are not the focus of this book. However, it's still worthwhile to glance through the material, or perhaps return to this section after you have a basic understanding of machine learning classifiers.

Several well-known techniques are available for analyzing the quality of machine learning classifiers. Two techniques are LIME and ANOVA, both of which are discussed in the following subsections.

What is LIME?

LIME is an acronym for Local Interpretable Model-Agnostic Explanations. LIME is a model-agnostic technique that can be used with machine learning models. The methodology of this technique is straightforward: make small random changes to data samples and then observe the manner in which predictions change (or not). The approach involves changing the data just a little and then observing what happens to the output.

By way of contrast, consider food inspectors who test for bacteria in truckloads of perishable food. Clearly, it's infeasible to test every food item in a truck (or a train car), so inspectors perform "spot checks" that involve testing randomly selected items. Instead of sampling data, LIME makes small changes to input data in random locations and then analyzes the changes in the associated output values.

However, there are two caveats to keep in mind when you use LIME with input data for a given model:

1. The actual changes to input values are model-specific.
2. This technique works on input that is interpretable.

Examples of interpretable input include machine learning classifiers (such as trees and random forests) and NLP techniques such as BoW (Bag of Words). Non-interpretable input involves "dense" data, such as a word embedding (which is a vector of floating point numbers).

You could also substitute your model with another model that involves interpretable data, but then you need to evaluate how accurate the approximation is to the original model.

What is ANOVA?

ANOVA is an acronym for *analysis of variance*, which attempts to analyze the differences among the mean values of a sample that's taken from a population. ANOVA enables you to test if multiple mean values are equal. More importantly, ANOVA can assist in reducing Type I (false positive) errors and Type II errors (false negative) errors. For example, suppose that person A is diagnosed with cancer and person B is diagnosed as healthy, and that both diagnoses are incorrect. Then the result for person A is a false positive whereas the result for person B is a false negative. In general, a test result of false positive is preferable to a test result of false negative.

ANOVA pertains to the design of experiments and hypothesis testing, which can produce meaningful results in various situations. For example, suppose that a dataset contains a feature that can be partitioned into several "reasonably" homogenous groups. Next, analyze the variance in each group and perform comparisons with the goal of determining different sources of variance for the values of a given feature.

More information about ANOVA is available online:

https://en.wikipedia.org/wiki/Analysis_of_variance.

THE BIAS-VARIANCE TRADE-OFF

This section is presented from the viewpoint of machine learning, but the concepts of bias and variance are highly relevant outside of machine learning, so it's probably still worthwhile to read this section as well as the previous section.

Bias in machine learning can be due to an error from wrong assumptions in a learning algorithm. High bias might cause an algorithm to miss relevant relations between features and target outputs (underfitting). Prediction bias can occur because of "noisy" data, an incomplete feature set, or a biased training sample.

Error due to bias is the difference between the expected (or average) prediction of your model and the correct value that you want to predict. Repeat the model building process multiple times, gather new data each time, and perform an analysis to produce a new model. The resulting models have a range of predictions because the underlying datasets have a degree of randomness. Bias measures the extent to which the predictions for these models deviate from the correct value.

Variance in machine learning is the expected value of the squared deviation from the mean. High variance can/might cause an algorithm to model the random noise in the training data (aka overfitting), rather than the intended outputs. Moreover, adding parameters to a model increases its complexity, increases the variance, and decreases the bias.

The point to remember is that dealing with bias and variance involves dealing with underfitting and overfitting.

Error due to variance is the variability of a model prediction for a given data point. As before, repeat the entire model building process, and the variance is the extent to which predictions for a given point vary among different "instances" of the model.

If you have worked with datasets and performed data analysis, you already know that finding well-balanced samples can be difficult or highly impractical. Moreover, performing an analysis of the data in a dataset is vitally important, yet there is no guarantee that you can produce a dataset that is 100% "clean."

A *biased statistic* is a statistic that is systematically different from the entity in the population that is being estimated. In more casual terminology, if a data sample "favors" or "leans" toward one aspect of the population, then the sample has bias. For example, if you prefer movies that are comedies more so than any other type of movie, then clearly you are more likely to select a comedy instead of a dramatic movie or a science fiction movie. Thus, a frequency graph of the movie types in a sample of your movie selections will be more closely clustered around comedies.

On the other hand, if you have a wide-ranging set of preferences for movies, then the corresponding frequency graph will be more varied, and therefore have a larger spread of values.

As a simple example, suppose that you are given an assignment that involves writing a term paper on a controversial subject that has many opposing viewpoints. Since you want a bibliography that supports your well-balanced term paper that takes into account multiple viewpoints, your bibliography will contain a wide variety of sources. In other words, your bibliography will have a larger variance and a smaller bias. On the other hand, if most (or all) the references in your bibliography espouse the same point of view, then you will have a smaller variance and a larger bias (it's just an analogy, so it's not a perfect counterpart to bias vs. variance).

The bias-variance trade-off can be stated in simple terms. In general, reducing the bias in samples can increase the variance, whereas reducing the variance tends to increase the bias.

Types of Bias in Data

In addition to the bias-variance trade-off that is discussed in the previous section, there are several types of bias, some of which are listed as follows:

- Availability Bias
- Confirmation Bias
- False Causality
- Sunk Cost Fallacy
- Survivorship Bias

Availability bias is akin to making a "rule" based on an exception. For example, there is a known link between smoking cigarettes and cancer, but there are exceptions. If you find someone who has smoked three packs of cigarettes on a daily basis for four decades and is still healthy, can you assert that smoking does not lead to cancer?

Confirmation bias refers to the tendency to focus on data that confirms one's beliefs and simultaneously ignore data that contradicts a belief.

False causality occurs when you incorrectly assert that the occurrence of a particular event causes another event to occur as well. One of the most well-known examples involves ice cream consumption and violent crime in New York during the summer. Since more people eat ice cream in the summer, that "causes" more violent crime, which is a false causality. Other factors, such as the increase in temperature, may be linked to the increase in crime. However, it's important to distinguish between correlation and causality. The latter is a much stronger link than the former, and it's also more difficult to establish causality instead of correlation.

Sunk cost refers to something (often money) that has been spent or incurred that cannot be recouped. A common example pertains to gambling at a casino. People fall into the pattern of spending more money in order to recoup a substantial amount of money that has already been lost. While there are cases in which people do recover their money, in many (most?) cases people simply incur an even greater loss because they continue to spend their money. Hence the expression, "it's time to cut your losses and walk away."

Survivorship bias refers to analyzing a particular subset of "positive" data while ignoring the "negative" data. This bias occurs in various situations, such as being influenced by individuals who recount their rags-to-riches success story ("positive" data) while ignoring the fate of the people (which is often a very high percentage) who did not succeed (the "negative" data) in a similar quest. So, while it's certainly possible for an individual to overcome many difficult obstacles in order to succeed, is the success rate one in one thousand (or even lower)?

SUMMARY

This chapter started with an explanation of datasets, a description of data wrangling, and details regarding various types of data. Then you learned about techniques for scaling numeric data, such as normalization and standardization. You saw how to convert categorical data to numeric values, and how to handle dates and currency.

Then you learned some of the nuances of missing data, anomalies, and outliers, and techniques for handling these scenarios. You also learned about imbalanced data and evaluating the use of SMOTE to deal with imbalanced classes in a dataset. In addition, you learned about classifiers using two techniques, LIME and ANOVA. Finally, you learned about the bias-variance trade-off and various types of statistical bias.

## CHAPTER 2

INTRO TO PROBABILITY AND STATISTICS

This chapter introduces you to data types, how to scale data values, and various techniques for handling missing data values. If most of the material in this chapter is new to you, be assured that it's not necessary to understand everything in this chapter. It's still a good idea to read as much material as you can absorb, and perhaps return to this chapter again after you have completed some of the other chapters in this book.

This chapter introduces you to concepts in probability as well as a wide assortment of statistical terms and algorithms.

The first section of this chapter starts with a discussion of probability, how to calculate the expected value of a set of numbers (with associated probabilities), the concept of a random variable (discrete and continuous), and a short list of some well-known probability distributions.

The second section of this chapter introduces basic statistical concepts, such as mean, median, mode, variance, and standard deviation, along with simple examples that illustrate how to calculate these terms. You will also learn about the terms RSS, TSS, R^2, and F1 score.

The third section of this chapter introduces the Gini impurity, entropy, perplexity, cross-entropy, and KL divergence. You will also learn about skewness and kurtosis.

The fourth section explains covariance and correlation matrices and how to calculate eigenvalues and eigenvectors.

The fifth section explains PCA (Principal Component Analysis), which is a well-known dimensionality reduction technique. The final section introduces you to Bayes' Theorem.

WHAT IS A PROBABILITY?

If you have ever performed a science experiment in one of your classes, you might remember that measurements have some uncertainty. In general, we assume that there is a correct value, and we endeavor to find the best estimate of that value.

When we work with an event that can have multiple outcomes, we try to define the probability of an outcome as the chance that it will occur, which is calculated as follows:

```
p(outcome) = # of times outcome occurs/(total number of outcomes)
```

For example, in the case of a single balanced coin, the probability of tossing a head H equals the probability of tossing a tail T:

```
p(H) = 1/2 = p(T)
```

The set of probabilities associated with the outcomes {H, T} is shown in the set P:

```
P = {1/2, 1/2}
```

Some experiments involve replacement while others involve non-replacement. For example, suppose that an urn contains 10 red balls and 10 green balls. What is the probability that a randomly selected ball is red? The answer is 10/(10+10) = 1/2. What is the probability that the second ball is also red?

There are two scenarios with two different answers. If each ball is selected with replacement, then each ball is returned to the urn after selection, which means that the urn always contains 10 red balls and 10 green balls. In this case, the answer is 1/2 * 1/2 = 1/4. In fact, the probability of any event is independent of all previous events.

On the other hand, if balls are selected without replacement, then the answer is 10/20 * 9/19. As you undoubtedly know, card games are also examples of selecting cards without replacement.

One other concept is called *conditional probability*, which refers to the likelihood of the occurrence of event E1 given that event E2 has occurred. A simple example is the following statement:

```
"If it rains (E2), then I will carry an umbrella (E1)."
```

Calculating the Expected Value

Consider the following scenario involving a well-balanced coin: Whenever a head appears, you earn $1 and whenever a tail appears, you earn $1 dollar. If you toss the coin 100 times, how much money do you expect to earn? Since you will earn $1 regardless of the outcome, the expected value (in fact, the guaranteed value) is $100.

Now consider this scenario: whenever a head appears, you earn $1 and whenever a tail appears, you earn 0 dollars. If you toss the coin 100 times, how much money do you expect to earn? You probably determined the value 50 (which is the correct answer) by making a quick mental calculation. The more formal derivation of the value of E (the expected earning) is here:

```
E = 100 *[1 * 0.5 + 0 * 0.5] = 100 * 0.5 = 50
```

The quantity **1** * 0.5 + **0** * 0.5 is the amount of money you expected to earn during each coin toss (half the time you earn $1 and half the time you earn 0 dollars), and multiplying this number by 100 is the expected earning after 100 coin tosses. Note that you might never earn $50: the actual amount that you earn can be any integer between 1 and 100, inclusive.

As another example, suppose that you earn $3 whenever a head appears, and you *lose* $1.50 whenever a tail appears. Then the expected earning E after 100 coin tosses is shown here:

```
E = 100 *[3 * 0.5 - 1.5 * 0.5] = 100 * 1.5 = 150
```

We can generalize the preceding calculations as follows. Let P = {p1,...,pn} be a probability distribution, which means that the values in P are non-negative and their sum equals 1. In addition, let R = {R1,...,Rn} be a set of rewards, where reward Ri is received with probability pi. Then the expected value E after N trials is shown here:

```
E = N * [SUM pi*Ri]
```

In the case of a single balanced die, we have the following probabilities:

```
p(1) = 1/6
p(2) = 1/6
p(3) = 1/6
p(4) = 1/6
p(5) = 1/6
p(6) = 1/6
P = { 1/6, 1/6, 1/6, 1/6, 1/6, 1/6}
```

As a simple example, suppose that the earnings are {3, 0, -1, 2, 4, -1} when the values 1, 2, 3, 4, 5, and 6, respectively, appear when tossing the single die. Then after 100 trials our expected earnings are calculated as follows:

```
E = 100 * [3 + 0 + -1 + 2 + 4 + -1]/6 = 100 * 3/6 = 50
```

In the case of two balanced dice, we have the following probabilities of rolling 2, 3, ... or 12:

```
p(2) = 1/36
p(3) = 2/36
...
p(12) = 1/36
P = {1/36,2/36,3/36,4/36,5/36,6/36,5/36,4/36,3/36,2/36,1/36}
```

RANDOM VARIABLES

A random variable is a variable that can have multiple values and where each value has an associated probability of occurrence. For example, if we let X be a random variable whose values are the outcomes of tossing a well-balanced die, then the values of X are the numbers in the set {1,2,3,4,5,6}. Moreover, each of those values can occur with equal probability (which is 1/6).

In the case of two well-balanced dice, let X be a random variable whose values can be any of the numbers in the set {2,3,4, . . . , 12}. Then the associated probabilities for the different values for X are listed in the previous section.

Discrete versus Continuous Random Variables

The preceding section contains examples of *discrete* random variables because the list of possible values is either finite or countably infinite (such as the set of integers). As an aside, the set of rational numbers is also countably infinite, but the set of irrational numbers and also the set of real numbers are both uncountably infinite (proofs are available online). As pointed out earlier, the associated set of probabilities must form a probability distribution, which means that the probability values are non-negative and their sum equals 1.

A *continuous* random variable is a variable whose values can be *any* number in an interval, which can be an uncountably infinite number of values. For example, the amount of time required to perform a task is represented by a continuous random variable.

A continuous random variable also has a probability distribution that is represented as a continuous function. The constraint for such a variable is that the area under the curve (which is sometimes calculated via a mathematical integral) equals 1.

Well-Known Probability Distributions

There are many probability distributions, and some of the well-known probability distributions are listed here:

- Gaussian distribution
- Poisson distribution
- Chi-squared distribution
- Binomial distribution

The Gaussian distribution is named after Karl F. Gauss, and it is sometimes called the normal distribution or the Bell curve. The Gaussian distribution is symmetric: The shape of the curve on the left of the mean is identical to the shape of the curve on the right side of the mean. As an example, the distribution of IQ scores follows a curve that is similar to a Gaussian distribution.

The frequency of traffic at a given point in a road follows a Poisson distribution (which is not symmetric). Interestingly, if you count the number of people who go to a public pool based on five-degree (Fahrenheit) increments of the temperature, followed by five-degree decrements in temperature, that set of numbers follows a Poisson distribution.

Perform an Internet search for each of the bullet items in the preceding list and you will find numerous articles that contain images and technical details about these (and other) probability distributions.

This concludes the brief introduction to probability, and the next section delves into the concepts of mean, median, mode, and standard deviation.

FUNDAMENTAL CONCEPTS IN STATISTICS

This section contains several subsections that discuss the mean, median, mode, variance, and standard deviation. Feel free to skim (or skip) this section if you are already familiar with these concepts. As a start point, let's suppose that we have a set of numbers X = {x1, ..., xn} that can be positive, negative, integer-valued, or decimal values.

The Mean

The *mean* of the numbers in the set X is the average of the values. For example, if the set X consists of {-10, 35, 75, 100}, then the mean equals (-10 + 35 + 75 + 100)/4 = 50. If the set X consists of {2, 2, 2, 2}, then the mean equals (2+2+2+2)/4 = 2. As you can see, the mean value is not necessarily one of the values in the set.

Keep in mind that the mean is sensitive to outliers. For example, the mean of the set of numbers {1,2,3,4} is 2.5, whereas the mean of the set of number {1,2,3,4,1000} is 202. Since the formulas for the variance and standard deviation involve the mean of a set of numbers, both of these terms are also more sensitive to outliers.

The Median

The *median* of the numbers (sorted in increasing or decreasing order) in the set X is the middle value in the set of values, which means that half the numbers in the set are less than the median and half the numbers in the set are greater than the median. For example, if the set X consists of {-10, 35, 75, 100}, then the median equals 55 because 55 is the average of the two numbers 35 and 75. As you can see, half the numbers are less than 55 and half the numbers are greater than 55. If the set X consists of {2, 2, 2, 2}, then the median equals 2.

By contrast, the median is much less sensitive to outliers than the mean. For example, the median of the set of numbers {1,2,3,4} is 2.5, and the median of the set of numbers {1,2,3,4,1000} is 3.

The Mode

The *mode* of the numbers (sorted in increasing or decreasing order) in the set X is the most frequently occurring value, which means that there can be more than one such value. If the set X consists of {2,2,2,2}, then the mode equals 2.

If X is the set of numbers {2,4,5,5,6,8}, then the number 5 occurs twice and the other numbers occur only once, so the mode equals 5.

If X is the set of numbers {2,2,4,5,5,6,8}, then the numbers 2 and 5 occur twice and the other numbers occur only once, so the mode equals 2 and 5. A set that has two modes is called *bimodal*, and a set that has more than two modes is called *multimodal*.

One other scenario involves sets that have numbers with the same frequency and they are all different. In this case, the mode does not provide meaningful information, and one alternative is to partition the numbers into subsets and then select the largest subset. For example, if set X has the values {1,2,15,16,17,25,35,50}, we can partition the set into subsets whose elements are in ranges that are multiples of ten, which results in the subsets {1,2}, {15,16,17}, {25}, {35}, and {50}. The largest subset is {15,16,17}, so we could select the number 16 as the mode.

As another example, if set X has the values {-10,35,75,100}, then partitioning this set does not provide any additional information, so it's probably better to work with either the mean or the median.

The Variance and Standard Deviation

The *variance* is the sum of the squares of the difference between the numbers in X and the mean mu of the set X, divided by the number of value in X, as shown here:

```
variance = [SUM (xi - mu)**2 ] / n
```

For example, if the set X consists of {-10,35,75,100}, then the mean equals (-10 + 35 + 75 + 100)/4 = 50, and the variance is computed as follows:

```
variance = [(-10-50)**2 + (35-50)**2 + (75-50)**2 + (100-50)**2]/4
         = [60**2 + 15**2 + 25**2 + 50**2]/4
         = [3600 + 225 + 625 + 2500]/4
         = 6950/4 = 1,737
```

The standard deviation std is the square root of the variance:

```
std = sqrt(1737) = 41.677
```

If the set X consists of {2,2,2,2}, then the *mean* equals (2+2+2+2)/4 = 2, and the variance is computed as follows:

```
variance = [(2-2)**2 + (2-2)**2 + (2-2)**2 + (2-2)**2]/4
         = [0**2 + 0**2 + 0**2 + 0**2]/4
         = 0
```

The standard deviation std is the square root of the variance:

```
std = sqrt(0) = 0
```

Population, Sample, and Population Variance

The population specifically refers to the entire set of entities in a given group, such as the population of a country, the people over 65 in the United States, or the number of first-year students in a university.

However, in many cases statistical quantities are calculated on samples instead of an entire population. Thus, a sample is a (much smaller) subset of the given population. See the central limit theorem regarding the distribution of the mean of a sample of a population (which need not be a population with a Gaussian distribution).

Here are some techniques for sampling data:

• Stratified sampling
• Cluster sampling
• Quota sampling

One other important point: The population variance is calculated by multiplying the sample variance by $n/(n-1)$, as shown here:

```
population variance = [n/(n-1)]*variance
```

Chebyshev's Inequality

Chebyshev's inequality provides a simple way to determine the minimum percentage of data that lies within k standard deviations. Specifically, this inequality states that for any positive integer k greater than 1, the amount of data in a sample that lies within k standard deviations is at least $1 - 1/k{**}2$. For example, if k = 2, then at least $1 - 1/2{**}2 = 3/4$ of the data must lie within 2 standard deviations.

The interesting part of this inequality is that it's been mathematically proven to be true; that is, it's not an empirical or heuristic-based result. An extensive description regarding Chebyshev's inequality (including some advanced mathematical explanations) is available online:

https://en.wikipedia.org/wiki/Chebyshev%27s_inequality.

What is a P-Value?

The null hypothesis states that there is no correlation between a dependent variable (such as y) and an independent variable (such as x). The p-value is used to reject the null hypothesis if the p-value is small enough (< 0.005), which indicates a higher significance. The threshold value for p is typically 1% or 5%.

There is no straightforward formula for calculating p-values, which are values that are always between 0 and 1. In fact, p-values are statistical quantities to evaluate the null hypothesis, and they are calculated by means of p-value tables or via spreadsheet/statistical software.

THE MOMENTS OF A FUNCTION (OPTIONAL)

The previous sections describe several statistical terms that are sufficient for the material in this book. However, several of those terms can be viewed from the perspective of different moments of a function.

In brief, the moments of a function are measures that provide information regarding the shape of the graph of a function. In the case of a probability distribution, the first four moments are defined as follows:

- The mean is the first central moment.
- The variance is the second central moment.
- The skewness (discussed later) is the third central moment.
- The kurtosis (discussed later) is the fourth central moment.

More detailed information (including the relevant integrals) regarding moments of a function is available online:

https://en.wikipedia.org/wiki/Moment_(mathematics)#Variance.

What is Skewness?

Skewness is a measure of the asymmetry of a probability distribution. A Gaussian distribution is symmetric, which means that its skew value is zero (it's not exactly zero, but close enough for our purposes). In addition, the skewness of a distribution is the third moment of the distribution.

A distribution can be skewed on the left side or on the right side. A *left-sided skew* means that the long tail is on the left side of the curve, with the following relationships:

```
mean < median < mode
```

A *right-sided skew* means that the long tail is on the right side of the curve, with the following relationships (compare with the left-sided skew):

```
mode < median < mean
```

If need be, you can transform skewed data to a normally distributed dataset using one of the following techniques (which depends on the specific use-case):

- Exponential transform
- Log transform
- Power transform

Perform an online search for more information regarding the preceding transforms and when to use each of these transforms.

What is Kurtosis?

Kurtosis is related to the skewness of a probability distribution, in the sense that both of them assess the asymmetry of a probability distribution. The kurtosis of a distribution is a scaled version of the fourth moment of the distribution, whereas its skewness is the third moment of the distribution. Note that the kurtosis of a univariate distribution equals 3.

If you are interested in learning about additional kurtosis-related concepts, you can perform an online search for information regarding the mesokurtic, leptokurtic, and platykurtic types of so-called "excess kurtosis."

DATA AND STATISTICS

This section contains various subsections that briefly discuss some of the challenges and obstacles that you might encounter when working with data-sets. This section and subsequent sections introduce you to the following concepts:

- Correlation versus causation
- The bias-variance tradeoff
- Types of bias
- The central limit theorem
- Statistical inferences

Keep in mind that statistics typically involves data *samples*, which are subsets of observations of a population. The goal is to find well-balanced samples that provide a good representation of the entire population.

Although this goal can be very difficult to achieve, it's also possible to achieve highly accurate results with a very small sample size. For example, the Harris poll in the United States has been used for decades to analyze political trends. This poll computes percentages that indicate the favorability rating of political candidates, and it's usually within 3.5% of the correct percentage values. What's remarkable about the Harris poll is that its sample size is a mere 4,000 people from the U.S. population, which is greater than 325,000,000 people.

Another aspect to consider is that each sample has a mean and variance, which do not necessarily equal the mean and variance of the actual population. However, the expected value of the sample mean and variance equal the mean and variance, respectively, of the population.

The Central Limit Theorem

Samples of a population have an interesting property. Suppose that you take a set of samples {S1, S3, ..., Sn} of a population and you calculate the mean of those samples, which is {m1, m2, ..., mn}. The Central Limit Theorem yields a remarkable result. Given a set of samples of a population and the mean value of those samples, the distribution of the mean values can be approximated by a Gaussian distribution. Moreover, as the number of samples increases, the approximation becomes more accurate.

Correlation versus Causation

In general, datasets have some features (columns) that are more significant in terms of their set of values, and some features only provide additional information that does not contribute to potential trends in the dataset. For example, the passenger names in the list of passengers on the Titanic are unlikely to affect the survival rate of those passengers, whereas the gender of the passengers is likely to be an important factor.

In addition, a pair of significant features may also be "closely coupled" in terms of their values. For example, a real estate dataset for a set of houses will contain the number of bedrooms and the number of bathrooms for each house in the dataset. As you know, these values tend to increase together and also decrease together. Have you ever seen a house that has ten bedrooms and one bathroom, or a house that has ten bathrooms and one bedroom? If you did find such a house, would you purchase that house as your primary residence?

The extent to which the values of two features change is called their correlation, which is a number between -1 and 1. Two "perfectly" correlated features have a correlation of 1, and two features that are not correlated have a correlation of 0. In addition, if the values of one feature decrease when the values of another feature increase, and vice versa, then their correlation is closer to -1 (and might also equal -1).

Causation between two features means that the values of one feature can be used to calculate the values of the second feature (within some margin of error).

Keep in mind this fundamental point about machine learning models: They can provide correlation, but they cannot provide causation.

Statistical Inferences

Statistical thinking relates to processes and statistics, whereas statistical inference refers to the process by which inferences are made regarding a population. Those inferences are based on statistics that are derived from samples of the population. The validity and reliability of those inferences depend on random sampling in order to reduce bias. There are various metrics that you can calculate to help you assess the validity of a model that has been trained on a particular dataset.

STATISTICAL TERMS – RSS, TSS, R^2, AND F1 SCORE

Statistics is extremely important in machine learning, so it's not surprising that many concepts are common to both fields. Machine learning relies on a number of statistical quantities in order to assess the validity of a model, some of which are listed here:

- RSS
- TSS
- R^2

The term RSS is the "residual sum of squares" and the term TSS is the "total sum of squares." Moreover, these terms are used in regression models.

As a starting point so we can simplify the explanation of the preceding terms, suppose that we have a set of points { (x1,y1) , . . . , (xn,yn) } in the Euclidean plane. In addition, let's define the following quantities:

(x,y) is any point in the dataset.
y is the y-coordinate of a point in the dataset.
y_ is the mean of the y-values of the points in the dataset.
y_hat is the y-coordinate of a point on a best-fitting line.

Just to be clear, (x,y) is a point in the *dataset*, whereas (x,y_hat) is the corresponding point that lies on the *best fitting line*. With these definitions in mind, the definitions of RSS, TSS, and R^2 are listed here (n equals the number of points in the dataset):

```
RSS = Iy - y_hat)**2/n
TSS = (y - y_bar)**2/n
R^2 = 1 - RSS/TSS
```

We also have the following inequalities involving RSS, TSS, and R^2:

```
0 <= RSS
RSS <= TSS
0 <= RSS/TSS <= 1
0 <= 1 - RSS/TSS <= 1
0 <= R^2 <= 1
```

When RSS is close to 0, then RSS/TSS is also close to zero, which means that R^2 is close to 1. Conversely, when RSS is close to TSS, then RSS/TSS is close to 1, and R^2 is close to 0. In general, a larger R^2 is preferred (i.e., the model is closer to the data points), but a lower value of R^2 is not necessarily a bad score.

What is an F1 Score?

In machine learning, an F1 score is for models that are evaluated on a feature that contains categorical data, and the p-value is useful for machine learning in general. An *F1* score is a measure of the accuracy of a test, and it's defined as the harmonic mean of precision and recall. Here are the relevant formulas, where p is the precision and r is the recall:

```
p = (# of correct positive results)/(# of all positive results)
r = (# of correct positive results)/(# of all relevant samples)

F1-score  = 1/[((1/r) + (1/p))/2]
          = 2*[p*r]/[p+r]
```

The best value of an F1 score is 1 and the worst value is 0. Keep in mind that an F1 score is for categorical classification problems, whereas the R^2 value is typically for regression tasks (such as linear regression).

GINI IMPURITY, ENTROPY, AND PERPLEXITY

These concepts are useful for assessing the quality of a machine learning model, and the latter pair are useful for dimensionality reduction algorithms.

Before we discuss the details of the Gini impurity, suppose that P is a set of non-negative numbers {p1, p2, ..., pn} such that the sum of all the numbers in the set P equals 1. Under these two assumptions, the values in the set P comprise a probability distribution, which we can represent with the letter p.

Now suppose that the set K contains a total of M elements, with k1 elements from class S1, k2 elements from class S2, . . . , and kn elements from class Sn. Compute the fractional representation for each class as follows:

```
p1 = k1/M, p2 = k2/M, . . ., pn = kn/M
```

As you can surmise, the values in the set {p1, p2, ..., pn} form a probability distribution. We're going to use the preceding values in the following subsections.

What is the Gini Impurity?

The Gini impurity is defined as follows, where {p1,p2,...,pn} is a probability distribution:

```
Gini = 1 - [p1*p1 + p2*p2 + . . . + pn*pn]
     = 1 - SUM pi*pi (for all i, where 1<=i<=n)
```

Since each pi is between 0 and 1, then pi*pi   <= pi, which means that

```
1 = p1 + p2 + . . . + pn
 >= p1*p1 + p2*p2 + . . . + pn*pn
  = Gini impurity
```

Since the Gini impurity is the sum of the squared values of a set of probabilities, the Gini impurity cannot be negative. Hence, we have derived the following result:

```
0 <= Gini impurity <= 1
```

What is Entropy?

Entropy is a measure of the expected ("average") number of bits required to encode the outcome of a random variable. The calculation for the entropy H (the letter E is reserved for Einstein's formula) is defined via the following formula:

```
H = (-1)*[p1*log p1 + p2 * log p2 + . . . + pn * log pn]
  = (-1)* SUM [pi * log(pi)] (for all i, where 1<=i<=n)
```

Calculating Gini Impurity and Entropy Values

For our first example, suppose that we have two classes A and B and a cluster of 10 elements with 8 elements from class A and 2 elements from class B. Therefore, p1 and p2 are 8/10 and 2/10, respectively. We can compute the Gini score as follows:

```
Gini = 1 - [p1*p1 + p2*p2]
     = 1 - [64/100 + 04/100]
     = 1 - 68/100
     = 32/100
     = 0.32
```

We can also calculate the entropy for this example as follows:

```
Entropy = (-1)*[p1 * log p1 + p2 * log p2]
        = (-1)*[0.8 * log 0.8 + 0.2 * log 0.2]
        = (-1)*[0.8 * (-0.322) + 0.2 * (-2.322)]
        = 0.8 * 0.322 + 0.2 * 2.322
        = 0.7220
```

For our second example, suppose that we have three classes (A, B, and C) and a cluster of 10 elements with 5 elements from class A, 3 elements from class B, and 2 elements from class C. Therefore p1, p2, and p3 are 5/10, 3/10, and 2/10, respectively. We can compute the Gini score as follows:

```
Gini = 1 - [p1*p1 + p2*p2 + p3*p3]
     = 1 - [25/100 + 9/100 + 04/100]
     = 1 - 38/100
     = 62/100
     = 0.62
```

We can also calculate the entropy for this example as follows:

```
Entropy = (-1)*[p1 * log p1 + p2 * log p2]
        = (-1)*[0.5*log0.5 + 0.3*log0.3 + 0.2*log0.2]
        = (-1)*[-1 + 0.3*(-1.737) + 0.2*(-2.322)]
        = 1 + 0.3*1.737 + 0.2*2.322
        = 1.9855
```

In both examples the Gini impurity is between 0 and 1. However, while the entropy is between 0 and 1 in the first example, it's greater than 1 in the second example (which was the rationale for showing you two examples).

Keep in mind that a set whose elements belong to the same class has Gini impurity equal to 0 and also its entropy equal to 0. For example, if a set has 10 elements that belong to class S1, then:

```
Gini = 1 - SUM pi*pi
     = 1 - p1*p1
     = 1 - (10/10)*(10/10)
     = 1 - 1 = 0
Entropy = (-1)*SUM pi*log pi
        = (-1) * p1*log pi
```

```
= (-1) * (10/10) * log(10/10)
= (-1)*1*0  = 0
```

Multidimensional Gini Index

The Gini index is a one-dimensional index that works well because the value is uniquely defined. However, when working with multiple factors, we need a multidimensional index. Unfortunately, the multidimensional Gini index (MGI) is not uniquely defined. While there have been various attempts to define an MGI that has unique values, they tend to be nonintuitive and mathematically much more complex. More information about MGI is available online:

https://link.springer.com/chapter/10.1007/978-981-13-1727-9_5.

What is Perplexity?

Suppose that q and p are two probability distributions, and {x1, x2, ..., xN} is a set of sample values that is drawn from a model whose probability distribution is p. In addition, suppose that b is a positive integer (it's usually equal to 2). Now define the variable S as the following sum (logarithms are in base b not 10):

```
S = (-1/N) * [log q(x1) + log q(x2) + . . . + log q(xN)]
  = (-1/N) * SUM log q(xi)
```

The formula for the perplexity PERP of the model q is b raised to the power S, as shown here:

```
PERP = b^S
```

If you compare the formula for entropy with the formula for S, you can see that the formulas are similar, so the perplexity of a model is somewhat related to the entropy of a model.

CROSS-ENTROPY AND KL DIVERGENCE

Cross-entropy is useful for understanding machine learning algorithms and frameworks such as TensorFlow, which supports multiple APIs that involve cross-entropy. The KL divergence is relevant in machine learning, deep learning, and reinforcement learning.

As an interesting example, consider the credit assignment problem, which involves assigning credit to different elements or steps in a sequence. For example, suppose that users arrive at a Web page by clicking on a previous page, which was also reached by clicking on yet another Web page. Then on the final Web page users click on an ad. How much credit is given to the first and second Web pages for the selected ad? You might be surprised to discover that one solution to this problem involves the KL divergence.

What is Cross-Entropy?

The following formulas for logarithms are presented here because they are useful for the derivation of cross entropy in this section:

```
log (a * b) = log a + log b
log (a / b) = log a - log b
log (1 / b) = (-1) * log b
```

In a previous section, you learned that for a probability distribution P with values {p1,p2,... pn}, its entropy is H defined as follows:

```
H(P) = (-1)*SUM pi*log(pi)
```

Now let's introduce another probability distribution Q whose values are {q1,q2,..., qn}, which means that the entropy H of Q is defined as follows:

```
H(Q) = (-1)*SUM qi*log(qi)
```

Now we can define the cross-entropy CE of Q and P as follows (notice the log qi and log pi terms and recall the formulas for logarithms earlier in this section):

```
CE(Q,P) = SUM (pi*log qi) - SUM (pi*log pi)
        = SUM (pi*log qi - pi*log pi)
        = SUM pi*(log qi - log pi)
        = SUM pi*(log qi/pi)
```

What is KL Divergence?

Now that entropy and cross-entropy have been discussed, we can easily define the KL divergence of the probability distributions Q and P as follows:

```
KL(P||Q) = CE(P,Q) - H(P)
```

The definitions of entropy H, cross-entropy CE, and KL divergence in this chapter involve discrete probability distributions P and Q. However, these concepts have counterparts in continuous probability density functions. The mathematics involves the concept of a Lebesgue measure on Borel sets (which is beyond the scope of this book) that are described here:

https://en.wikipedia.org/wiki/Lebesgue_measure
https://en.wikipedia.org/wiki/Borel_set

In addition to the KL divergence, there is also the JS divergence, also called the Jenson-Shannon divergence, which was developed by Johan Jensen and Claude Shannon (who defined the formula for entropy). The JS divergence is based on the KL divergence, but it has some differences. The JS divergence is symmetric and a true metric, whereas the KL divergence is neither (as noted in Chapter 4). More information regarding the JS divergence is available online:

https://en.wikipedia.org/wiki/Jensen–Shannon_divergence.

What's Their Purpose?

The Gini impurity is often used to obtain a measure of the homogeneity of a set of elements in a decision tree. The entropy of that set is an alternative to its Gini impurity, and you will see both of these quantities used in machine learning models.

The perplexity value in NLP is one way to evaluate language models, which are probability distributions over sentences or texts. This value provides an estimate for the encoding size of a set of sentences.

Cross-entropy is used in various methods in the TensorFlow framework, and the KL divergence is used in various algorithms, such as the dimensionality reduction algorithm t-SNE. For more information about any of these terms, perform an online search and you will find numerous online tutorials that provide more detailed information.

COVARIANCE AND CORRELATION MATRICES

This section explains two important matrices: the covariance matrix and the correlation matrix. Although these are relevant for PCA (principal component analysis) that is discussed later in this chapter, these matrices are not specific to PCA, which is the rationale for discussing them in a separate section. If you are familiar with these matrices, feel free to skim through this section.

The Covariance Matrix

As a reminder, the statistical quantity called the variance of a random variable X is defined as follows:

```
variance(x) = [SUM (x – xbar)*(x-xbar)]/n
```

A covariance matrix C is an nxn matrix whose values on the main diagonal are the variance of the variables X1, X2, . . . , Xn. The other values of C are the covariance values of each pair of variables Xi and Xj.

The formula for the covariance of the variables X and Y is a generalization of the variance of a variable, and the formula is shown here:

```
covariance(X, Y) = [SUM (x – xbar)*(y-ybar)]/n
```

Notice that you can reverse the order of the product of terms (multiplication is commutative), and therefore the covariance matrix C is a symmetric matrix:

```
covariance(X, Y) = covariance(Y,X)
```

Suppose that a CSV file contains four numeric features, all of which have been scaled appropriately, and let's call them x1, x2, x3, and x4. Then the covariance matrix C is a 4×4 square matrix that is defined with the following entries (pretend that there are outer brackets on the left side and the right side to indicate a matrix):

$$\begin{bmatrix} \text{cov(x1, x1)} & \text{cov(x1, x2)} & \text{cov(x1, x3)} & \text{cov(x1, x4)} \\ \text{cov(x2, x1)} & \text{cov(x2, x2)} & \text{cov(x2, x3)} & \text{cov(x2, x4)} \\ \text{cov(x3, x1)} & \text{cov(x3, x2)} & \text{cov(x3, x3)} & \text{cov(x3, x4)} \\ \text{cov(x4, x1)} & \text{cov(x4, x2)} & \text{cov(x4, x3)} & \text{cov(x4, x4)} \end{bmatrix}$$

Note that the following is true for the diagonal entries in the preceding covariance matrix C:

```
var(x1,x1) = cov(x1,x1)
var(x2,x2) = cov(x2,x2)
var(x3,x3) = cov(x3,x3)
var(x4,x4) = cov(x4,x4)
```

In addition, C is a symmetric matrix, which is to say that the transpose of matrix C (rows become columns and columns become rows) is identical to the matrix C. The latter is true because (as you saw in the previous section) cov(x,y) = cov(y,x) for any feature x and any feature y.

Covariance Matrix: An Example

Suppose we have the two-column matrix A defined as follows:

$$A = \begin{matrix} x & y \\ \begin{bmatrix} 1 & 1 \\ 2 & 1 \\ 3 & 2 \\ 4 & 2 \\ 5 & 3 \\ 6 & 3 \end{bmatrix} \end{matrix} \quad \text{<= 6x2 matrix}$$

The mean x_bar of column x is (1+2+3+4+5+6)/6 = 3.5, and the mean y_bar of column y is (1+1+2+2+3+3)/6 = 2. Now subtract x_bar from column x and subtract y_bar from column y and we get matrix B, as shown here:

$$B = \begin{bmatrix} -2.5 & -1 \\ -1.5 & -1 \\ -0.5 & 0 \\ 0.5 & 0 \\ 1.5 & 1 \\ 2.5 & 1 \end{bmatrix} \quad \text{<= 6x2 matrix}$$

Let Bt indicate the transpose of the matrix B (i.e., switch columns with rows and rows with columns), which means that Bt is a 2×6 matrix, as shown here:

$$Bt = \begin{bmatrix} -2.5 & -1.5 & -0.5 & 0.5 & 1.5 & 2.5 \\ -1 & -1 & 0 & 0 & 1 & 1 \end{bmatrix}$$

The covariance matrix C is the product of Bt and B, as shown here:

$$C = Bt * B = \begin{bmatrix} 15.25 & 4 \\ 4 & 8 \end{bmatrix}$$

Note that if the units of measure of features x and y do not have a similar scale, then the covariance matrix is adversely affected. In this case, the solution is simple: use the correlation matrix, which defined in the next section.

The Correlation Matrix

As you learned in the preceding section, if the units of measure of features x and y do not have a similar scale, then the covariance matrix is adversely affected. The solution involves the correlation matrix, which equals the covariance values `cov(x,y)` divided by the standard deviation `stdx` and `stdy` of x and y, respectively, as shown here:

```
corr(x,y) = cov(x,y)/[stdx * stdy]
```

The correlation matrix no longer has units of measure, and we can use this matrix to find the eigenvalues and eigenvectors.

Now that you understand how to calculate the covariance matrix and the correlation matrix, you are ready for an example of calculating eigenvalues and eigenvectors, which are the topic of the next section.

Eigenvalues and Eigenvectors

According to a well-known theorem in mathematics (whose proof you can find online), the eigenvalues of a symmetric matrix are real numbers. Consequently, the eigenvectors of C are vectors in a Euclidean vector space (not a complex vector space).

Before we continue, a non-zero vector x' is an eigenvector of the matrix C if there is a non-zero scalar lambda such that `C*x' = lambda * x'`.

Now suppose that the eigenvalues of C are b1, b2, b3, and b4, in decreasing numeric order from left to right, and that the corresponding eigenvectors of C are the vectors w1, w2, w3, and w4. Then the matrix M that consists of the column vectors w1, w2, w3, and w4 represents the principal components.

CALCULATING EIGENVECTORS: A SIMPLE EXAMPLE

As a simple illustration of calculating eigenvalues and eigenvectors, suppose that the square matrix C is defined as follows:

$$\begin{bmatrix} 1 & 3 \\ 3 & 1 \end{bmatrix}$$

Let I denote the 2×2 identity matrix, and let b' be an eigenvalue of C, which means that there is an eigenvector x' such that:

```
C* x' = b' * x', or
(C-b*I)*x' = 0 (the right side is a 2x1 vector)
```

Since x' is non-zero, that means the following is true (where det refers to the determinant of a matrix):

$$\det(C - b*I) = \det \begin{bmatrix} 1 - b & 3 \\ 3 & 1 - b \end{bmatrix} = (1 - b) * (1 - b) - 9 = 0$$

We can expand the quadratic equation in the preceding line to get:

```
det(C-b*I)  =  (1-b)*(1-b)  -  9
            =  1 - 2*b + b*b  -  9
            =  -8 - 2*b + b*b
            =  b*b - 2*b - 8
```

Use the quadratic formula (or perform factorization by visual inspection) to determine that the solution for `det(C-b*I) = 0` is `b = -2` or `b = 4`. Next, substitute b = -2 into `(C-b*I)x' = 0` and we get the following result:

$$\begin{bmatrix} 1 - (-2) & 3 \\ 3 & 1 - (-2) \end{bmatrix} \begin{bmatrix} x1 \\ x2 \end{bmatrix} = \begin{bmatrix} 0 \\ 0 \end{bmatrix}$$

The preceding reduces to the following identical equations:

```
3*x1 + 3*x2 = 0
3*x1 + 3*x2 = 0
```

The general solution is `x1 = -x2`, and we can choose any non-zero value for x2, so let's set x2 = 1 (any non-zero value will do), which yields x1 = -1. Therefore, the eigenvector [-1, 1] is associated with the eigenvalue -2. In a similar fashion, if `x'` is an eigenvector whose eigenvalue is 4, then [1,1] is an eigenvector.

Notice that the eigenvectors [-1, 1] and [1,1] are orthogonal because their inner product is zero, as shown here:

```
[-1,1] * [1,1] = (-1)*1 + (1)*1 = 0
```

In fact, the set of eigenvectors of a square matrix (whose eigenvalues are real) are always orthogonal, regardless of the dimensionality of the matrix.

Gauss Jordan Elimination (Optional)

This simple technique enables you to find the solution to systems of linear equations "in place," which involves a sequence of arithmetic operations to transform a given matrix into an identity matrix.

The following example combines the Gauss-Jordan elimination technique (which finds the solution to a set of linear equations) with the "bookkeeper's method," which determines the inverse of an invertible matrix (its determinant is non-zero).

This technique involves two adjacent matrices: the left-side matrix is the initial matrix, and the right-side matrix is an identity matrix. Next, perform various linear operations on the left-side matrix to reduce it to an identity matrix: the matrix on the right side equals its inverse. For example, consider the following pair of linear equations whose solution is x = 1 and y = 2:

```
2*x + 2*y = 6
4*x - 1*y = 2
```

Step 1: Create a 2×2 matrix with the coefficients of x in column 1 and the coefficients of y in column two, followed by the 2×2 identity matrix, and finally a column from the numbers on the right of the equals sign:

$$\begin{bmatrix} 2 & 2 \\ 4 & -1 \end{bmatrix} \begin{bmatrix} 1 & 0 \\ 0 & 1 \end{bmatrix} \begin{bmatrix} 6 \\ 2 \end{bmatrix}$$

Step 2: Add (-2) times the first row to the second row:

$$\begin{bmatrix} 2 & 2 \\ 0 & -5 \end{bmatrix} \begin{bmatrix} 1 & 0 \\ -2 & 1 \end{bmatrix} \begin{bmatrix} 6 \\ -10 \end{bmatrix}$$

Step 3: Divide the second row by 5:

$$\begin{bmatrix} 2 & 2 \\ 0 & -1 \end{bmatrix} \begin{bmatrix} 1 & 0 \\ -2/5 & 1/5 \end{bmatrix} \begin{bmatrix} 6 \\ -10/5 \end{bmatrix}$$

Step 4: Add 2 times the second row to the first row:

$$\begin{bmatrix} 2 & 0 \\ 0 & -1 \end{bmatrix} \begin{bmatrix} 1/5 & 2/5 \\ -2/5 & 1/5 \end{bmatrix} \begin{bmatrix} 2 \\ -2 \end{bmatrix}$$

Step 5: Divide the first row by 2:

$$\begin{bmatrix} 1 & 0 \\ 0 & -1 \end{bmatrix} \begin{bmatrix} -2/10 & 2/10 \\ -2/5 & 1/5 \end{bmatrix} \begin{bmatrix} 1 \\ -2 \end{bmatrix}$$

Step 6: Multiply the second row by (-1):

$$\begin{bmatrix} 1 & 0 \\ 0 & 1 \end{bmatrix} \begin{bmatrix} -2/10 & 2/10 \\ 2/5 & -1/5 \end{bmatrix} \begin{bmatrix} 1 \\ 2 \end{bmatrix}$$

As you can see, the left-side matrix is the 2×2 identity matrix, the matrix in the middle is the inverse of the original matrix, and the rightmost column is the solution to the original pair of linear equations (x=1 and y=2).

PCA (PRINCIPAL COMPONENT ANALYSIS)

PCA is a linear dimensionality reduction technique for determining the most important features in a dataset. This section discusses PCA because it's a very popular technique that you will encounter frequently. Other techniques are more efficient than PCA, so it's worthwhile to learn other dimensionality reduction techniques, as well.

Keep in mind the following points regarding the PCA technique:
PCA is a variance-based algorithm.
PCA creates variables that are linear combinations of the original variables.
The new variables are all pair-wise orthogonal.
PCA can be a useful preprocessing step before clustering.
PCA is generally preferred for data reduction.

PCA can be useful for variables that are strongly correlated. If most of the coefficients in the correlation matrix are smaller than 0.3, PCA is not helpful. PCA provides some advantages: less computation time for training a model (for example, using only five features instead of 100 features), a simpler model, and the ability to render the data visually when two or three features are selected. Here is a key point about PCA:

PCA calculates the eigenvalues and the eigenvectors of the covariance (or correlation) matrix C.

If you have four or five components, you won't be able to display them visually, but you could select subsets of three components for visualization, and perhaps gain some additional insight into the dataset.

The PCA algorithm involves the following sequence of steps:

1. Calculate the correlation matrix (from the covariance matrix) C of a dataset.
2. Find the eigenvalues of C.
3. Find the eigenvectors of C.
4. Construct a new matrix that comprises the eigenvectors.

The covariance matrix and correlation matrix were explained in a previous section. You also saw the definition of eigenvalues and eigenvectors, along with an example of calculating eigenvalues and eigenvectors.

The eigenvectors are treated as column vectors that are placed adjacent to each other in decreasing order (from left to right) with respect to their associated eigenvectors.

PCA uses the variance as a measure of information: the higher the variance, the more important the component. In fact, PCA determines the eigenvalues and eigenvectors of a covariance matrix (discussed in a previous section) and constructs a new matrix whose columns are eigenvectors, ordered from left to right in a sequence that matches the corresponding sequence of eigenvalues: the leftmost eigenvector has the largest eigenvalue, the next eigenvector has the second-largest eigenvalue, and continuing on in this fashion until we reach the rightmost eigenvector (which has the smallest eigenvalue).

Alternatively, there is an interesting theorem in linear algebra: if C is a symmetric matrix, then there is a diagonal matrix D and an orthogonal matrix P (the columns are pair-wise orthogonal, which means their pair-wise inner product is zero), such that the following holds:

```
C = P * D * Pt (where Pt is the transpose of matrix P)
```

The diagonal values of D are eigenvalues, and the columns of P are the corresponding eigenvectors of the matrix C.

Fortunately, we can use NumPy and Pandas to calculate the mean, standard deviation, covariance matrix, correlation matrix, as well as the matrices D and P to determine the eigenvalues and eigenvectors.

Any positive definite square matrix has real-valued eigenvectors, which also applies to the covariance matrix C because it is a real-valued symmetric matrix.

The New Matrix of Eigenvectors

The previous section described how the matrices D and P are determined. The leftmost eigenvector of D has the largest eigenvalue, the next eigenvector has the second-largest eigenvalue, and so forth. This fact is very convenient: The eigenvector with the highest eigenvalue is the principal component of the dataset. The eigenvector with the second-highest eigenvalue is the second principal component, and so forth. You specify the number of principal components that you want via the n_components hyperparameter in the PCA class of Sklearn (discussed briefly in Chapter 7).

As a simple and minimalistic example, consider the following code block that uses PCA for a (somewhat contrived) dataset:

```
import numpy as np
from sklearn.decomposition import PCA
data = np.array([[-1,-1], [-2,-1], [-3,-2], [1,1], [2,1],
                 [3,2]])
pca = PCA(n_components=2)
pca.fit(X)
```

Note the trade-off here. We greatly reduce the number of components, which reduces the computation time and the complexity of the model, but we also lose some accuracy. However, if the unselected eigenvalues are small, we lose only a small amount of accuracy.

Now let's use the following notation:

NM denotes the matrix with the new principal components.
NMt is the transpose of NM.
PC is the matrix of the subset of selected principal components.
SD is the matrix of scaled data from the original dataset.
SDt is the transpose of SD.

Then the matrix NM is calculated via the following formula:

```
NM = PCt * SDt
```

Although PCA is a very nice technique for dimensionality reduction, keep in mind the following limitations of PCA:

less suitable for data with nonlinear relationships
less suitable for special classification problems

A related algorithm is called Kernel PCA, which is an extension of PCA that introduces a nonlinear transformation so you can still use the PCA approach.

WELL-KNOWN DISTANCE METRICS

There are several similarity metrics available, such as item similarity metrics, Jaccard (user-based) similarity, and cosine similarity (which is used to compare vectors of numbers). The following subsections introduce you to these similarity metrics.

Another well-known distance metric is the so-called *taxicab metric*, which is also called the *Manhattan distance metric*. Given two points A and B in a rectangular grid, the taxicab metric calculates the distance between two points by counting the number of "blocks" that must be traversed in order to reach B from A (the other direction has the same taxicab metric value). For example, if you need to travel two blocks north and then three blocks east in a rectangular grid, then the Manhattan distance is 5.

There are various other metrics available that you can learn about by searching Wikipedia. In the case of NLP, the most commonly used distance metric is calculated via the cosine similarity of two vectors, and it's derived from the formula for the inner ("dot") product of two vectors.

Pearson Correlation Coefficient

Pearson similarity is the Pearson coefficient between two vectors. Given random variables X and Y, and the following terms:

```
std(X)    = standard deviation of X
std(Y)    = standard deviation of Y
cov(X,Y) = covariance of X and Y
```

Then the Pearson correlation coefficient rho(X,Y) is defined as follows:

$$rho(X, Y) = \frac{cov(X, Y)}{std(X) * std(Y)}$$

Keep in mind that the Pearson coefficient is limited to items of the same type. More information about the Pearson correlation coefficient is online:

https://en.wikipedia.org/wiki/Pearson_correlation_coefficient.

Jaccard Index (or Similarity)

The Jaccard similarity is based on the number of users which have rated item A and B divided by the number of users who have rated either A or B. Jaccard similarity is based on unique words in a sentence and is unaffected by duplicates, whereas cosine similarity is based on the length of all word vectors (which changes when duplicates are added). The choice between cosine similarity and Jaccard similarity depends on whether or not word duplicates are important.

The following Python method illustrates how to compute the Jaccard similarity of two sentences:

```
def get_jaccard_sim(str1, str2):
  set1 = set(str1.split())
  set2 = set(str2.split())
```

```
set3 = set1.intersection(set2)
# (size of intersection) / (size of union):
return float(len(set3)) / (len(set1) + len(set2) - len(set3))
```

Jaccard similarity can be used in situations involving Boolean values, such as product purchases (true/false), instead of numeric values. More information is available online:

https://en.wikipedia.org/wiki/Jaccard_index.

Local Sensitivity Hashing (Optional)

If you are familiar with hash algorithms, you know that they are algorithms that create a hash table that associates items with a value. The advantage of hash tables is that the lookup time to determine whether or not an item exists in the hash table is constant. Of course, it's possible for two items to "collide," which means that they both occupy the same bucket in the hash table. In this case, a bucket can consist of a list of items that can be searched in more or less constant time. If there are too many items in the same bucket, then a different hashing function can be selected to reduce the number of collisions. The goal of a hash table is to minimize the number of collisions.

The local sensitivity hashing (LSH) algorithm hashes similar input items into the same "buckets." In fact, the goal of LSH is to maximize the number of collisions, whereas traditional hashing algorithms attempt to minimize the number of collisions.

Since similar items end up in the same buckets, LSH is useful for data clustering and nearest neighbor searches. Moreover, LSH is a dimensionality reduction technique that places data points of high dimensionality closer together in a lower-dimensional space, while simultaneously preserving the relative distances between those data points.

More details about LSH are online:

https://en.wikipedia.org/wiki/Locality-sensitive_hashing.

TYPES OF DISTANCE METRICS

Nonlinear dimensionality reduction techniques can also have different distance metrics. For example, linear reduction techniques can use the Euclidean distance metric (based on the Pythagorean theorem). However, you need to use a different distance metric to measure the distance between two points on a sphere (or some other curved surface). In the case of NLP, the cosine similarity metric is used to measure the distance between word embeddings (which are vectors of floating point numbers that represent words or tokens).

Distance metrics are used for measuring physical distances, and some well-known distance metrics are listed here:

- Euclidean distance
- Manhattan distance
- Chebyshev distance

The Euclidean algorithm also obeys the "triangle inequality," which states that for any triangle in the Euclidean plane, the sum of the lengths of any pair of sides must be greater than the length of the third side.

In spherical geometry, you can define the distance between two points as the arc of a great circle that passes through the two points (always selecting the smaller of the two arcs when they are different).

In addition to physical metrics, there are algorithms that implement the concept of "edit distance" (the distance between strings), as listed here:

- Hamming distance
- Jaro–Winkler distance
- Lee distance
- Levenshtein distance
- Mahalanobis distance metric
- Wasserstein metric

The Mahalanobis metric is based on an interesting idea. Given a point P and a probability distribution D, this metric measures the number of standard deviations that separate point P from distribution D. More information about Mahalanobis is available online:

https://en.wikipedia.org/wiki/Mahalanobis_distance.

In the branch of mathematics called topology, a metric space is a set for which distances between all members of the set are defined. Various metrics are available (such as the Hausdorff metric), depending on the type of topology.

The Wasserstein metric measures the distance between two probability distributions over a metric space X. This metric is also called the "earth mover's metric" for the following reason: Given two unit piles of dirt, it's the measure of the minimum cost of moving one pile on top of the other pile.

The KL divergence bears some superficial resemblance to the Wasserstein metric. However, there are some important differences between them. Specifically, the Wasserstein metric has the following properties:

1. It is a metric.
2. It is symmetric.
3. It satisfies the triangle inequality.

The KL divergence has the following properties:

1. It is not a metric (it's a divergence).
2. It is not symmetric: $KL(P,Q) \mathrel{!=} KL(Q,P)$.
3. It does not satisfy the triangle inequality.

Note that the JS divergence (which is based on the KL Divergence) is a true metric, which would enable a more meaningful comparison with other metrics (such as the Wasserstein metric):

https://stats.stackexchange.com/questions/295617/what-is-the-advantages-of-wasserstein-metric-compared-to-kullback-leibler-diverg.

More information is available online:

https://en.wikipedia.org/wiki/Wasserstein_metric.

WHAT IS BAYESIAN INFERENCE?

Bayesian inference is an important technique in statistics that involves statistical inference and Bayes' Theorem to update the probability for a hypothesis as more information becomes available. Bayesian inference is often called "Bayesian probability," and it's important in dynamic analysis of sequential data.

Bayes' Theorem

Given two sets A and B, let's define the following numeric values (all of them are between 0 and 1):

```
P(A) = probability of being in set A
P(B) = probability of being in set B
P(Both) = probability of being in A intersect B
P(A|B) = probability of being in A (given you're in B)
P(B|A) = probability of being in B (given you're in A)
```

Then the following formulas are also true:

```
P(A|B) = P(Both)/P(B)  (#1)
P(B|A) = P(Both)/P(A)  (#2)
```

Multiply the preceding pair of equations by the term that appears in the denominator and we get these equations:

```
P(B)*P(A|B) = P(Both)  (#3)
P(A)*P(B|A) = P(Both)  (#4)
```

Now set the left side of Equations (#3) and (#4) equal to each another and that gives us this equation:

```
P(B)*P(A|B) = P(A)*P(B|A)  (#5)
```

Divide both sides of Equation (#5) by P(B) to obtain this well-known equation:

```
P(A|B) = P(A)*P(A|B)/P(B)  (#6)
```

Some Bayesian Terminology

In the previous section, we derived the following relationship:

```
P(h|d) = (P(d|h) * P(h)) / P(d)
```

There is a name for each of the four terms in the preceding equation, discussed as follows.

First, the *posterior probability* is P(h|d), which is the probability of hypothesis h given the data d.

Second, P(d|h) is the probability of data d given that the hypothesis h was true.

Third, the *prior probability* of h is P(h), which is the probability of hypothesis h being true (regardless of the data).

Finally, P(d) is the probability of the data (regardless of the hypothesis)

We are interested in calculating the posterior probability of P(h|d) from the prior probability p(h) with P(D) and P(d|h).

What is MAP?

The maximum a posteriori (MAP) hypothesis is the hypothesis with the highest probability, which is the maximum probable hypothesis. This can be written as follows:

```
MAP(h) = max(P(h|d))
```

or:

```
MAP(h) = max((P(d|h) * P(h)) / P(d))
```

or:

```
MAP(h) = max(P(d|h) * P(h))
```

Why Use Bayes' Theorem?

Bayes' Theorem describes the probability of an event based on the prior knowledge of the conditions that might be related to the event. If we know the conditional probability, we can use the Bayes rule to find out the reverse probabilities. The previous statement is the general representation of the Bayes rule.

SUMMARY

This chapter started with a discussion of probability, expected values, and the concept of a random variable. Then you learned about some basic statistical concepts, such as mean, median, mode, variance, and standard deviation. Next, you learned about the terms RSS, TSS, R^2, and F1 score. In addition, you got an introduction to the concepts of skewness, kurtosis, Gini impurity, entropy, perplexity, cross-entropy, and KL divergence.

Next, you learned about covariance and correlation matrices and how to calculate eigenvalues and eigenvectors. Then you were introduced to the dimensionality reduction technique known as PCA (principal component analysis), after which you learned about Bayes' Theorem.

## CHAPTER 3

LINEAR ALGEBRA CONCEPTS

Linear algebra is a vast topic, and it's often introduced as an undergraduate course as well as a more advanced graduate course. Linear algebra is the subject of entire books, so this chapter provides only a foundation.

The first section includes a very brief description of linear algebra, and then describes vectors in the Euclidean plane. Next we discuss how to perform various operations, such as adding and subtracting vectors, as well as how to compute the inner ("dot") product of two vectors. Other topics include the magnitude ("norm") of vectors, unit vectors, orthogonal vectors, spanning sets of vectors, and a basis.

The second section introduces matrices and then discusses various types of matrices, such as diagonal matrices, symmetric matrices, and invertible matrices. We discuss how to multiply vectors and matrices. This section also contains an example of calculating the inverse of an invertible nxn matrix.

The third section provides the foundation for PCA (Principal Component Analysis). Specifically, we show how to create a covariance matrix and a correlation matrix from a dataset that contains a set of features. We include an example of calculating eigenvalues and eigenvectors to construct a matrix that consists of principal components. In addition, we discuss positive semi-definite matrices and positive definite matrices.

The fourth section discusses SVD (Singular Value Decomposition) and several algorithms that are associated with SVD. The final section briefly introduces complex numbers, which are relevant for the complex conjugate root theorem as well as complex matrices, and an example of a Hermitian matrix.

Two other details to keep in mind before you read this chapter. First, some of the material pertaining to matrices (such as Hermitian matrices) is more advanced than what is normally included in an introductory book. Second, the sections that discuss vectors use the letters i, j, and k to denote unit vectors. However, when discussing complex numbers, the letter i refers to the square root of -1. In the complex plane, the horizontal axis is the real axis and the vertical axis is the pure complex axis. However, the point (a,b) occupies the same physical position in the 2D Euclidean plane and the complex plane. The only difference is that the vertical axis of the latter is the pure complex axis.

WHAT IS LINEAR ALGEBRA?

In simplified terms, linear algebra is a branch of mathematics that involves vectors, matrices, and vector spaces. After we discuss various concepts pertaining to vectors, we investigate the *basis*, which consists of a set of vectors that can be combined to represent any vector in a vector space. The number of vectors in a basis equals the dimensionality of the vector space. For example, a basis for the Euclidean plane consists of two (non-collinear and) non-zero vectors, whereas a basis for a three-dimensional vector space consists of three non-zero (and non-planar) vectors.

WHAT ARE VECTORS?

Let's start with two-dimensional vectors in the plane, and later we can generalize to three-dimensional vectors and even beyond (i.e., n-dimensional vectors).

The vector **i**=[1,0] is a vector of length one whose left endpoint is the origin (0,0) and its right endpoint is (1,0). The vector **j**=[0,1] is a vector of length one whose left endpoint is the origin (0,0) and its right endpoint is (0,1). The vectors **i** and **j** are called unit vectors that are perpendicular or orthogonal to each other.

If you construct a matrix A whose three rows are the values in the vectors **i** and **j**, then the matrix A is the 2×2 identity matrix (which is discussed in the next section):

```
i=[1,0]
j=[0,1]
```

The Norm of a Vector

If the vector a=[a1,a2], then the magnitude or the norm of the vector a is denoted by ||a||, and it's defined via the Pythagorean theorem, as shown here:

```
||a|| = sqrt(a1*a1 + a2*a2)
```

The magnitude of every vector is never negative, and the only way that the vector a can have a magnitude of 0 is if the vector a=[0,0].

The Inner Product of Two Vectors

Now suppose that the vector a=[a1,a2] and the vector b=[b1,b2]. The *inner product* (also called the "dot product") of a and b is defined as follows:

```
a*b = a1*b1 + a2*b2
```

If we compute the inner product of the unit vectors i and j, we get the following result:

```
i*j = 1*0 + 0*1 = 0
```

In general, if two vectors a and b are compatible and orthogonal, then a*b = 0. The converse is also true, which we can summarize as follows:

Two non-zero vectors are orthogonal, if and only if, their inner product is zero.

The Cosine Similarity of Two Vectors

Another way to calculate the inner product of two vectors a and b is via the following formula, where "*" on the left side of the following formula denotes "inner product" and "*" on the right side of the following formula denotes arithmetic multiplication:

```
a*b = ||a|| * ||b|| * cos(a,b)
```

In the preceding formula, ||a|| and ||b|| are the magnitude of the vectors a and b, respectively, and cos(a,b) denotes the cosine of the angle between the vectors a and b.

If we divide by sides of the preceding formula by the term ||a||*||b||, we get the following formula:

```
cos(a*b) = a*b / [||a|| * ||b||]
```

The preceding formula is the *cosine similarity* of a pair of vectors, which is a number between -1 and 1 inclusive. The closer the cosine similarity is to 1, the more similar are the two vectors (draw them in the plane and you will see that it's true).

Incidentally, in NLP (Natural Language Processing), each word in a vocabulary or dictionary is represented by a *context vector*, which is a vector of floating point numbers. If two context vectors (we'll exclude the details of how such vectors are constructed) have a cosine similarity that is close to 1, then the corresponding words are likely to be similar. Moreover, if the cosine similarity is close to 0, then the corresponding words are likely to be dissimilar.

The use of the cosine similarity is a *heuristic*, which means that it's reasonable and at least minimally intuitive, but there is no rigorous mathematical proof that underlies the heuristic. Nevertheless, cosine similarity works surprisingly well, unless you need multiple context vectors for a given word that appears in multiple sentences.

Context vectors are the basis for the word2vec algorithm (created by Google in 2013). However, in 2017 Google also created the transformer architecture that has eclipsed earlier NLP techniques, including the word2vec algorithm.

Now let's discuss bases and spanning sets, both of which are discussed in the next section.

Bases and Spanning Sets

Every vector in the 2D plane can be expressed as a linear combination of the unit vectors i and j. The intuition underlying the previous statement is straightforward. For example, if the point C=(c1,c2) is an arbitrary point in the Euclidean plane, then there is a corresponding vector c=[c1,c2], which in turn can be expressed as follows:

```
c  = c1*i + c2*j
```

A set of linearly independent non-zero vectors is a basis if every vector can be expressed as a linear combination of those vectors. The vectors {i,j,k} form a basis for a three-dimensional Euclidean space.

A *spanning set* is a set of vectors that contains a basis. For example, in the 2D Euclidean space, the sets {i,j,i+j} and {i+j,2*i+3*j,j} and {i+j,2*i+3*j,j} are all spanning sets. This definition is apparent for the set {i,j,i+j} because we can simply drop the third vector, which then consists of {i,j}, and we know that the latter is a basis.

The other two sets are also spanning sets, even though they do not contain {i,j} as vectors because of the following result:

Any pair of non-zero and non-collinear vectors in the 2D Euclidean plane form a basis.

For example, the set {i+j, j} is a basis because we can express the basis vectors i and j as linear combinations of i+j and j as follows:

```
i = 1*(i+j) + (-1)*j
j = 0*(i+j) + 1*j
```

In a similar fashion, the vectors i and j can be expressed as a linear combination of the vectors in the set {i, 2*i+3*j}, which means that the latter set is a basis as well.

Three Dimensional Vectors and Beyond

In the case of three-dimensional vectors, we can extend everything in the earlier part of this section by working with the vectors **i**, **j**, and **k** that are defined as follows:

```
i=[1,0,0]
j=[0,1,0]
k=[0,0,1]
```

If you construct a matrix A whose three rows are the values in the vectors **i**, **j**, and **k**, then the matrix A is the 3×3 identity matrix (discussed in the next section).

The most general case involves an n-dimensional vector space, where n is an arbitrary positive integer. Define a set of n vectors U = {U1, U2, . . . , Un} as follows:

Uk = [uk1, uk2, . . . , ukn] where Ukk = 1 and all other components are 0, where k ranges from 1 to n inclusive. Then the set U forms a basis for an n-dimensional vector space. In fact, the vectors in U are pairwise orthogonal unit vectors.

WHAT ARE MATRICES?

In this chapter, we work with two-dimensional matrices. There are various types of well-known matrices. For example, a matrix with only zero values is the zero matrix. The nxn square matrix I with 1 on the main diagonal (from upper left to lower right) and 0 elsewhere is called the nxn *identity matrix*.

A matrix is a diagonal matrix if the only non-zero values are on the main diagonal. If all the diagonal values are zero, then the matrix is the zero matrix. If the diagonal values are equal, then the matrix is a multiple of the nxn identity matrix.

A matrix is a *symmetric matrix* if the matrix equals its own transpose. The transpose of matrix A is obtained by switching the rows of A into columns and the columns of A into rows. Any diagonal matrix is a symmetric matrix.

Add and Multiply Matrices

If a pair of matrices have the same dimensions (i.e., an equal number of rows and an equal number of columns), it's possible to add or subtract them. Specifically, if A=[aij] and B=[bij] are mxn matrices, then A-B=[aij-bij] and A+B=[aij+bij], where subtraction and addition are performed based on corresponding cell locations of A and B.

Moreover, A+B = B+A, whereas A-B != B-A unless A=B. Notice that the preceding properties are simply generalizations of scalar addition and scalar subtraction. Another way of stating the same properties is to say that the addition of matrices is commutative (or Abelian) whereas subtraction of matrices is not commutative.

The multiplication of two matrices involves a different constraint. If A=[aij] is an mxn matrix and B=[bij] is an nxp matrix, then A*B is an mxp matrix. Notice that the number of columns of A must equal the number of rows of B. In general, matrix multiplication is not commutative, even if A and B are both nxn matrices. One notable exception pertains to square matrices that are diagonal matrices.

The Determinant of a Square Matrix

Let's start with a 2×2 matrix A whose contents are shown below:

$$A = \begin{bmatrix} a11 & a12 \\ a21 & a22 \end{bmatrix}$$

The *determinant* of A is defined as follows:

```
det(A) = a11*a22 - a21*a12
```

According to a theorem (stated here without proof) in linear algebra, a 2×2 matrix A is invertible if and only if det(A) = 0.

The same result holds if A is an nxn matrix; however, the determinant of an nxn matrix (for n > 2) is more complex and we won't discuss the details in this chapter (check online if you really want to know the details).

WELL-KNOWN MATRICES

In addition to the identity matrix that was described in a previous section, there are several more well-known matrices that are given a name that depends on the additional properties of those matrices.

For example, an nxn matrix A is a *symmetric matrix* if A equals the transpose of A. Thus, if a[i,j] is the value in row i and row j, then a[i,j] = a[j,i]. As you can see, a symmetric matrix must be a square matrix.

An nxn matrix A is a *diagonal matrix* if any entry that does not lie on the main diagonal (from upper left to lower right) has the value 0. Thus, if a[i,j] is the value in row i and row j of matrix A, then a[i,j]=0 whenever i != j.

Note that it's possible for one or more diagonal entries a[i,i] to be 0. If all the diagonal elements are also 0, then A is a *zero matrix*.

In addition, trees and graphs can be represented by an nxn matrix A, which is called an *adjacency matrix*. Specifically, a[i,j]=1 when there is an edge *between* vertices i and j; otherwise, a[i,j]=0. Note that a[i,j]=a[j,i] in an undirected tree, which means that its adjacency matrix is symmetric.

A *directed* tree structure can also be represented by an adjacency matrix A where a[i,j]=1 when there is an edge *from* vertex i *to* vertex j; otherwise, a[i,j]=0.

An nxn matrix A is an *invertible matrix* if there is a matrix A^(-1), such that the product of A and A^(-1) is the nxn identity matrix.

An nxn matrix A is an *orthogonal matrix* if the product of A and its transpose At equals the identity matrix. If you compare this definition with the definition of an invertible matrix, then you can see that A^(-1) = At, which is to say, the inverse of matrix A equals the transpose of matrix A.

An nxn matrix A is a *unitary matrix* if the product of A and its conjugate equals the identity matrix. Recall that if the complex number z equals a+b*i for some pair of real numbers a and b, then the conjugate of z is a-b*i.

The conjugate transpose of a real-valued matrix A is the same as the transpose of A. If matrix A contains complex numbers, then the conjugate transpose of A is different from the transpose of A.

Lastly, the *Frobenius norm* of a matrix A is the A is the square root of the sum of the squares of the elements of A. Thus, the Frobenius norm of A is the square root of the sum of the terms a[i,j] * a[i,j], where a[i,j] ranges over all the elements of matrix A. The Frobenius norm of the nxn identity matrix I is sqrt(n) and the Frobenius norm of the nxn zero matrix Z is 0. Note that the Frobenius norm exists for both square matrices and non-square matrices.

Based on the preceding definitions, the nxn identity matrix I is symmetric, diagonal, invertible, equal to its transpose, orthogonal, and unitary. The nxn zero matrix z is symmetric, diagonal, and equal to its transpose, but does not have the other properties.

Properties of Orthogonal Matrices

This section contains a list of some properties of orthogonal matrices (described in the previous section):

1. Identity matrices are orthogonal matrices.
2. Orthogonal matrices are symmetric.
3. Orthogonal matrices consist of real numbers.
4. If A is an orthogonal matrix, then A^(-1) = At.
5. If A and B are orthogonal, then so is their product A*B.
6. The transpose of orthogonal matrix A is also orthogonal.
7. The inverse of orthogonal matrix A is also orthogonal.
8. The determinant of orthogonal matrix A is +1 or -1.
9. The eigenvalues of orthogonal matrix A are +1 or -1.

Only the first item in the preceding list was discussed in the previous section, and you can find formal proofs online for the other points.

Operations Involving Vectors and Matrices

Suppose that you want to calculate A*x, where A is an mxn matrix and x is a vector. From the discussion in the previous section regarding the product of two matrices A and B, the vector x plays the role of B, from which we can conclude that x is a column vector of dimensionality nx1. Moreover, the product A*x produces an mx1 column vector.

If you want to compute the product x*A, where A is an mxn array, then the only way that x can be compatible with A is for x to be a 1xm row vector. As a result, the product x*A is a 1xn row vector.

This section contains two more definitions. First, the nxn matrix A is called *positive definite*, if x * A * xt > 0 for any non-zero vector x. Second, the nxn matrix A is called *positive semi-definite* if x * A * xt >= 0 for any non-zero vector x.

At this point, we have all the definitions that we need to find the solution to a set of linear equations, which is the topic of the next section.

GAUSS JORDAN ELIMINATION (OPTIONAL)

An nxn square matrix A is invertible if there is a matrix A^(-1) such that A* A^(-1)=I (where the right side is the nxn identity matrix). The Gauss Jordan Elimination algorithm is a straightforward technique to find the solution to systems of linear equations "in place." The algorithm involves a sequence of arithmetic operations to transform a given matrix to an identity matrix and produce the inverse of the initial matrix.

The following example combines the Gauss-Jordan elimination technique (which finds the solution to a set of linear equations) with the "bookkeeper's method," which determines the inverse of an invertible matrix (its determinant is non-zero).

This technique involves two adjacent matrices: The left-side matrix is the initial matrix and the right-side matrix is an identity matrix. Next, perform various linear operations on the left-side matrix to reduce it to an identity matrix. The matrix on the right side equals its inverse. For example, consider the following pair of linear equations whose solution is x = 1 and y = 2:

```
2*x + 2*y = 6
4*x - 1*y = 2
```

Step 1: Create a 2×2 matrix with the coefficients of x in column 1 and the coefficients of y in column two, followed by the 2×2 identity matrix, and finally a column from the numbers on the right of the equals sign:

$$\begin{bmatrix} 2 & 2 \\ 4 & -1 \end{bmatrix} \begin{bmatrix} 1 & 0 \\ 0 & 1 \end{bmatrix} \begin{bmatrix} 6 \\ 2 \end{bmatrix}$$

Step 2: Add (-2) times the first row to the second row:

$$\begin{bmatrix} 2 & 2 \\ 0 & -5 \end{bmatrix} \begin{bmatrix} 1 & 0 \\ -2 & 1 \end{bmatrix} \begin{bmatrix} 6 \\ -10 \end{bmatrix}$$

Step 3: Divide the second row by 5:

$$\begin{bmatrix} 2 & 2 \\ 0 & -1 \end{bmatrix} \begin{bmatrix} -1 & 0 \\ -2/5 & 1/5 \end{bmatrix} \begin{bmatrix} 6 \\ -10/5 \end{bmatrix}$$

Step 4: Add 2 times the second row to the first row:

$$\begin{bmatrix} 2 & 0 \\ 0 & -1 \end{bmatrix} \begin{bmatrix} 1/5 & 2/5 \\ -2/5 & 1/5 \end{bmatrix} \begin{bmatrix} 2 \\ -2 \end{bmatrix}$$

Step 5: Divide the first row by 2:

$$\begin{bmatrix} 1 & 0 \\ 0 & -1 \end{bmatrix} \begin{bmatrix} -2/10 & 2/10 \\ -2/5 & 1/5 \end{bmatrix} \begin{bmatrix} 1 \\ -2 \end{bmatrix}$$

Step 6: multiply the second row by (-1):

$$\begin{bmatrix} 1 & 0 \\ 0 & 1 \end{bmatrix} \begin{bmatrix} -2/10 & 2/10 \\ 2/5 & -1/5 \end{bmatrix} \begin{bmatrix} 1 \\ 2 \end{bmatrix}$$

The left-side matrix is the 2×2 identity matrix, the right-side matrix is the inverse of the original matrix, and the right-most column is the solution to the original pair of linear equations (x=1 and y=2).

COVARIANCE AND CORRELATION MATRICES

This section explains two important matrices: the covariance matrix and the correlation matrix. Although these are relevant for PCA (Principal Component Analysis), these matrices are not specific to PCA, which is the rationale for discussing them in a separate section.

The Covariance Matrix

The statistical quantity called the variance of a random variable X is defined as follows:

```
variance(x) = [SUM (x - xbar)*(x-xbar)]/n
```

A *covariance matrix* C is an nxn matrix whose values on the main diagonal are the variance of the variables X1, X2, . . ., Xn. The other values of C are the covariance values of each pair of variables Xi and Xj.

The formula for the covariance of the variables X and Y is a generalization of the variance of a variable, and the formula is shown here:

```
covariance(X, Y) = [SUM (x - xbar)*(y-ybar)]/n
```

Notice that you can reverse the order of the product of terms (multiplication is commutative), and therefore the covariance matrix C is a symmetric matrix:

```
covariance(X, Y) = covariance(Y,X)
```

Suppose that a dataset contains four numeric features (all of which have been scaled appropriately), and let's call them x1, x2, x3, and x4. In addition, suppose that the matrix A is assigned the values in the dataset, which means that A has dimensionality nx4, where n is the number of rows in the dataset.

Then the covariance matrix C is the product of At * A, where At is the transpose of A, which means that C is a 4×4 square matrix whose elements are defined as follows:

$$
\begin{bmatrix}
\text{cov(x1,x1)} & \text{cov(x1,x2)} & \text{cov(x1,x3)} & \text{cov(x1,x4)} \\
\text{cov(x2,x1)} & \text{cov(x2,x2)} & \text{cov(x2,x3)} & \text{cov(x2,x4)} \\
\text{cov(x3,x1)} & \text{cov(x3,x2)} & \text{cov(x3,x3)} & \text{cov(x3,x4)} \\
\text{cov(x4,x1)} & \text{cov(x4,x2)} & \text{cov(x4,x3)} & \text{cov(x4,x4)}
\end{bmatrix}
$$

Note that the following is true for the diagonal entries in the preceding covariance matrix C:

```
var(x1,x1) = cov(x1,x1)
var(x2,x2) = cov(x2,x2)
var(x3,x3) = cov(x3,x3)
var(x4,x4) = cov(x4,x4)
```

Furthermore, C is a symmetric matrix, which is to say that the transpose of matrix C (rows become columns and columns become rows) is identical to the matrix C. The latter is true because (as you saw in the previous section) `cov(x,y) = cov(y,x)` for any feature x and any feature y.

Covariance Matrix: An Example

Suppose we have the two-column matrix A defined as follows:

$$A = \begin{array}{cc} x & y \\ \begin{bmatrix} 1 & 1 \\ 2 & 1 \\ 3 & 2 \\ 4 & 2 \\ 5 & 3 \\ 6 & 3 \end{bmatrix} \end{array} \Leftarrow \text{6x2 matrix}$$

The mean x_bar of column x is $(1+2+3+4+5+6)/6 = 3.5$, and the mean y_bar of column y is $(1+1+2+2+3+3)/6 = 2$. Now subtract x_bar from column x and subtract y_bar from column y and we get matrix B, as shown here:

$$B = \begin{bmatrix} -2.5 & -1 \\ -1.5 & -1 \\ -0.5 & 0 \\ 0.5 & 0 \\ 1.5 & 1 \\ 2.5 & 1 \end{bmatrix} \Leftarrow \text{6x2 matrix}$$

Let Bt indicate the transpose of the matrix B, which means that Bt is a 2×6 matrix, as shown here:

$$Bt = \begin{bmatrix} -2.5 & -1.5 & -0.5 & 0.5 & 1.5 & 2.5 \\ -1 & -1 & 0 & 0 & 1 & 1 \end{bmatrix}$$

The covariance matrix C is the product of Bt and B, as shown here:

$$C = Bt * B = \begin{bmatrix} 15.25 & 4 \\ 4 & 8 \end{bmatrix}$$

Note that if the units of measure of features x and y do not have a similar scale, then the values in the covariance matrix are "skewed"; however, the solution is simple: use the correlation matrix, which defined in the next section.

However, if the units of measure of features x and y do not have a similar scale, then the covariance matrix is adversely affected. The solution is simple: Use the correlation matrix, which defined in the next section.

The Correlation Matrix

As you learned in the preceding section, if the units of measure of features x and y do not have a similar scale, then the covariance matrix is adversely affected. The solution involves the *correlation matrix*, which equals the covariance values cov(x,y) divided by the standard deviation stdx and stdy of x and y, respectively, as shown here:

corr(x,y) = cov(x,y)/[stdx * stdy]

The correlation matrix no longer has units of measure, and we can use this matrix to find the eigenvalues and eigenvectors.

EIGENVALUES AND EIGENVECTORS

According to a well-known theorem in mathematics, the eigenvalues of a symmetric matrix are real numbers. Consequently, the eigenvectors of C are vectors in a Euclidean vector space (not a complex vector space).

A non-zero vector x' is an eigenvector of the matrix C if there is a non-zero scalar lambda such that C*x' = lambda * x'.

Now suppose that the eigenvalues of C are b1, b2, b3, and b4, in decreasing numeric order from left-to-right, and that the corresponding eigenvectors of C are the vectors w1, w2, w3, and w4. These vectors form the principal components of the new matrix.

Now that you understand how to calculate the covariance matrix and the correlation matrix, you are ready for an example of calculating eigenvalues and eigenvectors.

Calculating Eigenvectors: A Simple Example

As a simple illustration of calculating eigenvalues and eigenvectors, suppose that the square matrix C is defined as follows:

$$C = \begin{bmatrix} 1 & 3 \\ 3 & 1 \end{bmatrix}$$

Let I denote the 2×2 identity matrix, and let b' be an eigenvalue of C, which means that there is an eigenvector x' such that:

```
C*x' = b' * x', or
(C-b*I)x' = 0 (the right side is a 2x1 vector)
```

Since x' is non-zero, that means the following is true (where det refers to the *determinant* of a matrix):

$$\det(C-b*I) = \det \begin{bmatrix} 1-b & 3 \\ 3 & 1-b \end{bmatrix} = (1-b)*(1-b)-9 = 0$$

We can expand the quadratic equation in the preceding line to obtain the following:

```
det(C-b*I) = (1-b)*(1-b) - 9
           = 1 - 2*b + b*b - 9
           = -8 - 2*b + b*b
           = b*b - 2*b - 8
```

Use the quadratic formula (or perform factorization by visual inspection) to determine that the solution for det(C-b*I) = 0 is b = -2 or b = 4. Next, substitute b = -2 into (C-b*I)x' = 0 to obtain the following result:

$$\begin{bmatrix} 1-(-2) & 3 \\ 3 & 1-(-2) \end{bmatrix} \begin{bmatrix} x1 \\ x2 \end{bmatrix} \begin{bmatrix} 0 \\ 0 \end{bmatrix}$$

The preceding reduces to the following identical equations:
```
3*x1 + 3*x2 = 0
3*x1 + 3*x2 = 0
```
The general solution is $x1 = -x2$, and we can choose any non-zero value for x2, so let's set $x2 = 1$ (any other non-zero value will do), which yields $x1 = -1$. Therefore, the eigenvector [-1, 1] is associated with the eigenvalue -2. In a similar fashion, if x' is an eigenvector whose eigenvalue is 4, then [1,1] is an eigenvector.

Notice that the eigenvectors [-1, 1] and [1,1] are orthogonal because their inner product is zero, as shown here:

```
[-1,1] * [1,1] = (-1)*1 + (1)*1 = 0
```

In fact, the set of eigenvectors of a square matrix (whose eigenvalues are real) are always orthogonal, regardless of the dimensionality of the matrix.

WHAT IS PCA (PRINCIPAL COMPONENT ANALYSIS)?

PCA is a linear dimensionality reduction technique for determining the most important features in a dataset. This section discusses PCA because it's a very popular technique. Other techniques (such as SVD) are more efficient than PCA, so it's worthwhile to learn other dimensionality reduction techniques as well.

THE MAIN STEPS IN PCA

PCA involves a sequence of steps that you have seen in previous sections of this chapter. If you have a dataset D, perform the following steps:

• Create a matrix A from a subset of the features of a dataset.
• Initialize the matrix C as the product of A and A transpose.
• Compute the mean of each column in C and subtract these values from the columns.
• Calculate the eigenvalues of C.
• Calculate the eigenvectors of C.
• Create a matrix M of the principal components.

Keep in mind the following points regarding the PCA technique:

• PCA is a variance-based algorithm.
• PCA creates variables that are linear combinations of the original variables.
• The new variables are all pair-wise orthogonal.
• PCA can be a useful pre-processing step before clustering.
• PCA is generally preferred for data reduction.

PCA can be useful for variables that are strongly correlated. If most of the coefficients in the correlation matrix are smaller than 0.3, PCA is not helpful. PCA provides some advantages: less computation time for training a model (for example, using only five features instead of 100 features), a simpler model, and the ability to render the data visually when two or three features are selected. Here is a key point regarding PCA:

PCA calculates the eigenvalues and the eigenvectors of the covariance (or correlation) matrix C.

If you have four or five components, you won't be able to display them visually, but you could select subsets of three components for visualization, and perhaps gain some additional insight into the dataset.

The PCA algorithm involves the following sequence of steps:

1. Calculate the correlation matrix (from the covariance matrix) C of a dataset.
2. Find the eigenvalues of C.
3. Find the eigenvectors of C.
4. Construct a new matrix that comprises the eigenvectors.

The covariance matrix and correlation matrix were explained in a previous section. You also saw the definition of eigenvalues and eigenvectors, along with an example of calculating eigenvalues and eigenvectors.

The eigenvectors are treated as column vectors that are placed adjacent to each other in decreasing order (from left-to-right) with respect to their associated eigenvectors.

PCA uses the variance as a measure of information: the higher the variance, the more important the component. PCA determines the eigenvalues and eigenvectors of a covariance matrix (discussed in a previous section), and constructs a new matrix whose columns are eigenvectors, ordered from left-to-right based on the maximum eigenvalue in the left-most column, decreasing until the right-most eigenvector also has the smallest eigenvalue.

Alternatively, there is an interesting theorem in linear algebra: If C is a symmetric matrix, then there is a diagonal matrix D and an orthogonal matrix P (the columns are pair-wise orthogonal, which means their pair-wise inner product is zero), such that the following holds:

```
C = P * D * Pt (where Pt is the transpose of matrix P)
```

In fact, the diagonal values of D are eigenvalues, and the columns of P are the corresponding eigenvectors of the matrix C.

Fortunately, we can use NumPy and Pandas to calculate the mean, standard deviation, covariance matrix, correlation matrix, as well as the matrices D and P in order to determine the eigenvalues and eigenvectors.

Any positive definite square matrix has real-valued eigenvectors, which also applies to the covariance matrix C because it is a real-valued symmetric matrix.

The New Matrix of Eigenvectors

The previous section described how the matrices D and P are determined. The left-most eigenvector of D has the largest eigenvalue, the next eigenvector has the second-largest eigenvalue, and so forth. This fact is very convenient. The eigenvector with the highest eigenvalue is the principal component of the dataset. The eigenvector with the second-highest eigenvalue is the second principal component, and so forth. You specify the number of principal components that you want via the n_components hyperparameter in the PCA class of Sklearn.

As a simple and minimalistic example, consider the following code block that uses PCA for a (somewhat contrived) dataset:

```
import numpy as np
from Sklearn.decomposition import PCA
data = np.array([[-1,-1], [-2,-1], [-3,-2], [1,1], [2,1], [3,2]])
pca = PCA(n_components=2)
pca.fit(X)
```

Note the trade-off here. We greatly reduce the number of components, which reduces the computation time and the complexity of the model, but we also lose some accuracy. However, if the unselected eigenvalues are small, we lose only a small amount of accuracy.

Now let's define the variables NM, NMt, PC, SD, and SDt as follows:

NM denotes the matrix with the new principal components.
NMt is the transpose of NM.
PC is the matrix of the subset of selected principal components.
SD is the matrix of scaled data from the original dataset.
SDt is the transpose of SD.

Then the matrix NM can be expressed via the following formula:

```
NM = PCt * SDt
```

Although PCA is a very nice technique for dimensionality reduction, keep in mind the following limitations of PCA:

less suitable for data with non-linear relationships
less suitable for special classification problems

A related algorithm is called Kernel PCA, which is an extension of PCA that introduces a non-linear transformation so you can still use the PCA approach.

DIMENSIONALITY REDUCTION

The previous section described various types of feature selection techniques, whereas dimensionality reduction involves a transformation of the data (such as PCA) or a projection of the data. Some of the well-known algorithms that perform dimensionality reduction are listed here:

Principal component analysis (PCA)
Kernel PCA
Graph-based Kernel PCA
SVD (Singular Value Decomposition)
Non-negative Matrix Factorization (NMF)
Linear Discriminant Analysis (LDA)
Generalized Discriminant Analysis (GDA)
Isomap Embedding
Locally Linear Embedding
Modified Locally Linear Embedding
VAEs (Variational Autoencoders)

VAEs (the last item in the preceding list) are deep learning models that have a number of use cases. Although VAEs are beyond the scope of this book, a comparison of PCA and VAEs is available online:

https://towardsdatascience.com/dimensionality-reduction-pca-versus-autoen-coders-338fcaf3297d.

The following algorithms combine feature extraction and dimensionality reduction (some of which belong to both lists):

PCA
LDA
CCA
NMF

These algorithms can be used during a pre-processing step before using clustering or some other algorithm (such as kNN) on a dataset.

One other group of algorithms involves methods based on projections, which includes t-Distributed Stochastic Neighbor Embedding (t-SNE) as well as UMAP.

DIMENSIONALITY REDUCTION TECHNIQUES

In simplified terms, dimensionality reduction refers to reducing a high-dimensional vector space to a lower dimensional vector space. There are several techniques that perform dimensionality reduction (such as PCA in the previous section), as listed here:

PCA
SVD
LLE

UMAP
t-SNE
PHATE

The previous section discussed PCA because PCA is a common algorithm for dimensionality reduction in machine learning. The other algorithms in the preceding list are discussed in a high-level fashion in the following subsections.

Dimensionality reduction techniques belong to different categories, such as matrix factorization (PCA and SVD), model-based reduction (LDA), and manifold learning (SOM and t-SNE).

The Curse of Dimensionality

As you increase the number of dimensions in a dataset, the data points in the dataset tend to be farther apart, which in turn increases the possibility of overfitting. In a perfect world, the data points in a dataset are evenly distributed, but in reality, different features have different distributions. One feature might be almost constant, a second feature might have a Gaussian distribution, and a third feature might be bi-modal.

Nevertheless, many dimensionality reduction algorithms involve projecting data points in a dataset to a lower-dimensional space (the other technique is discussed later).

SVD (Singular Value Decomposition)

SVD is a technique in linear algebra that factors any mxn matrix A into the product of three matrices U, S, and V, as shown here:

```
A = U*S*Vt
```

The preceding formula is true for any matrix A (square, rectangular, invertible, or non-invertible), and the matrices U, S, and V are as follows:

```
U:  (mxm)  is orthogonal  (U*Ut = I)  with left singular vectors
V:  (nxn)  is orthogonal  (V*Vt = I)  with right singular vectors
S:  (mxn)  is diagonal with "singular values"
```

Recall that if B, C, and D are compatible matrices, then the following transpose rules are true:

```
(B*C)t = Ct * Bt
(B*C*D)t = Dt * Ct * Bt
```

Now we can determine the nature of the matrices U and V by computing At*A and A*At, as shown below:

```
At*A = (V*S*Ut)*(U*S*Vt) = V*S^2*Vt (because Ut*U = I)
```

In fact, V is the matrix of eigenvectors for At*A, and S^2 is the matrix of eigenvalues for At*A. Now let's compute A*At, as shown below:

```
A*At = (U*S*Vt)*(V*S*Ut) = U*S^2*Ut (because Vt*V = I)
```

Now U is the matrix of eigenvectors for A*At, and S^2 is the matrix of eigenvalues for At*A. Since S^2 is a diagonal matrix of eigenvalues, the diagonal matrix S consists of the square root of the eigenvalues.

There are some scalability and performance-related issues regarding SVD, as listed below:

complexity is O(m*n^2) when n < m (n x m matrix)
not scalable for millions of words/documents
difficult to incorporate new words/documents

One application of SVD is the decomposition of the ratings matrix in recommender systems into a product of three matrices. Another application of SVD pertains to gene expression, which is discussed online:

http://homepages.math.uic.edu/~friedlan/svdwvumerge.pdf.

There are several variants of SVD that might be of interest, and perhaps better suited to your particular needs. For example, Truncated SVD reduces dimensionality by selecting only the largest singular values, keeping the first t columns of U and V. Details for Truncated SVD as well as Thin SVD and Compact SVD are provided online: *https://en.wikipedia.org/wiki/Singular_value_decomposition*

Another variant of SVD is SVDpp (sometimes called SVD++), which is described online:

https://surprise.readthedocs.io/en/stable/matrix_factorization.html.

Finally, HybridSVD, PureSVD, SVDpp, and timeSVDpp are additional variations of SVD.

LLE (Locally Linear Embedding)

LLE is a non-linear dimensionality reduction technique that is based on the following two tasks:

1. Compute the linear distance of a datapoint to its nearest neighbor.
2. Attempt to determine a lower-dimensional representation of the data points such that the local relationships are preserved.

Thus, the motivating principle behind LLE is similar to that of t-SNE. An example of using Locally Linear Embedding with Sklearn is online:

https://scikit-learn.org/stable/modules/generated/Sklearn.manifold.Locally-LinearEmbedding.html.

UMAP

UMAP is an acronym for Uniform Manifold Approximation and Projection, and it's a nonlinear dimensionality reduction technique. Although it is similar to the t-SNE algorithm (discussed in the next section), UMAP makes the assumption that the data is uniformly distributed on a locally connected Riemannian manifold and that the Riemannian metric is locally constant or approximately locally constant. A detailed discussion regarding Riemannian metrics is available online:

https://arxiv.org/pdf/1212.2474.pdf.

t-SNE

The t-SNE (T-distributed Stochastic Neighbor Embedding) algorithm is a non-linear dimensionality reduction technique used in machine learning algorithms for visualization.

The goal of t-SNE is to perform the following:

1. map similar objects to nearby points
2. map dissimilar objects to more distant points

By way of analogy for item #1, imagine a triangle parallel to the horizontal axis, and split the triangle with a line parallel to the base.

The smaller triangle is a scaled version of the whole triangle, so it retains the same relative distances as the whole triangle.

The implementation of t-SNE involves two probability distributions: one for pairs of high-dimensional objects that performs #1, and another for pairs of low-dimensional objects that performs #2. The next step involves minimizing the KL (Kullback-Leibler) divergence for these two probability distributions.

Note that PCA is a much older technique (1930s) whereas t-SNE was developed more recently (2008). PCA performs linear dimension reduction that 1) maximizes variance and 2) preserves large pairwise distances. As a result, different data points will be moved farther apart in PCA, which might not work as well with non-linear data.

By contrast, t-SNE preserves small pairwise distances by means of an algorithm that calculates a similarity measure between data points in the high dimensional space as well as in the low dimensional space. In addition, t-SNE uses a cost function to optimize similarity measures.

PHATE

PHATE is an acronym for Potential of Heat-diffusion Affinity-based Transition Embedding. PHATE is a visualization and dimensionality reduction technique that resembles t-SNE. Both are sensitive to local and global relationships and attempt to preserve relationships among close objects and distant objects.

Note that this technique shows up in biological data, which is not discussed in this book. However, more information about PHATE is available online:

https://www.biorxiv.org/content/10.1101/120378v1.full.pdf.

LINEAR VERSUS NON-LINEAR REDUCTION TECHNIQUES

There is a difference between linear dimensionality reduction and non-linear dimensionality reduction algorithms. Before discussing those two types of algorithms, a mathematical definition is required.

Suppose that T is a mapping from vector space U to the vector space V (which can have different dimensions), denoted as T:U->V. Then T is a *linear transformation* if the following are both true for any vectors u1 and u2 in U and any real number a:

1. T(u1+u2) = T(u1) + T(u2)

2. T(a*u)   = a*T(u)

For example, rotating a vector in the plane or scaling a vector in the plane is a linear transformation. Shifting a vector in the plane is not a linear transformation if it does not preserve the origin: It's an *affine transformation*.

If the dimensions of U and V are the same and equal n, then a linear transformation T can be represented as an nxn invertible matrix (i.e., it has an inverse). If the dimension of V is lower than the dimension of U, then the linear transformation T involves a *projection*. If the dimension of V is higher than the dimension of U, then the transformation T involves an *embedding*.

For example, if T doubles the size of the components of vectors in two-dimensional Euclidean space, then T can be represented by the following matrix:

$$\begin{bmatrix} 2 & 0 \\ 0 & 2 \end{bmatrix}$$

If T halves the first component and triples the second component of vectors in two-dimensional space, then T can be represented by the following matrix:

$$\begin{bmatrix} 0.5 & 0 \\ 0 & 3 \end{bmatrix}$$

If T maps the vector of the form (x,y,z) to a vector of the form (x,y,0), then T is a projection, and T can be represented by the following matrix:

$$\begin{bmatrix} 1 & 0 & 0 \\ 0 & 1 & 0 \\ 0 & 0 & 0 \end{bmatrix}$$

Based on the definition of a linear transformation in the beginning of this section, PCA is a *linear* dimensionality reduction algorithm, whereas Kernel PCA is a *non-linear* dimensionality reduction algorithm.

Linear reduction involves computing a linear combination of features or performing a linear transformation. An example of the latter transforming a spanning set of vectors by a non-singular matrix. Specifically, suppose that set B's vectors {v1, v2, . . . , vn} are orthogonal and they form a basis for an n-dimensional vector space V. In addition, suppose that M is an nxn non-singular matrix (its determinant is non-zero). Then {Mv1, Mv2, . . ., Mvn} is a linear transformation of the basis B that also spans the vector space V.

By contrast, non-linear (NL) dimensionality reduction techniques perform non-linear transformations. However, in many cases, NL dimensionality reduction techniques are related to linear methods, and they tend to belong to one of two groups:

1. NL techniques that provide high-to-low mapping (or vice versa)
2. NL techniques that provide visualization

Mapping methods are used to perform an initial feature extraction step, after which machine learning algorithms can perform pattern recognition. On the other hand, NL techniques that provide visualization perform calculations involving the distance between objects.

COMPLEX NUMBERS (OPTIONAL)

Complex numbers exist in a complex plane, where the horizontal axis is the real axis and the vertical axis is the complex axis. Every point in the complex plane can be expressed in the form a+b*i, where a and b are real numbers and i is the square root of -1.

The sum and difference of a pair of complex numbers is calculated separately on the real portion and the complex portion of the two numbers. For example, if we have the complex numbers z1 = a1 + i*b1 and z2 = a2 + i*b2 then

```
z1+z2 = (a1+a2) + i*(b1+b2) and
z1-z2 = (a1+a2) - i*(b1+b2)
```

In addition, the product z1*z2 is computed as follows:

```
z1*z2 = (a1+b1*i) * (a2+b2*i)
      = a1*a2 + b1*b2*i*i + a1*b2*i + a2*b1*i
      = a1*a2 - b1*b2     + (a1*b2 + a2*b1)*I
```

Complex Numbers on the Unit Circle

A complex number z on the unit circle whose center is the origin can be expressed as follows:

```
z = cos(alpha) + i*sin(alpha)
```

In the preceding expression alpha is a real number between 0 and 360. The interesting point is that the product of two numbers on the complex unit circle involves a rotation. For example, suppose that we have two complex numbers z1 and z2 that lie on this circle:

```
z1 = cos(alpha1) + i*sin(alpha1)
z2 = cos(alpha2) + i*sin(alpha2)
```

Then `z1*z2` reduces to the following expression:

```
z1*z2 = cos(alpha1+alpha2) + sin(alpha1+alpha2)*i
```

For example, if `alpha = 30`, and `z = cos(30) + sin(30)*i`, then powers of z are calculated in a simple manner:

```
z^2 = cos(2*30) + sin(2*30)*i
z^3 = cos(3*30) + sin(3*30)*i
. . .
z^n = cos(n*30) + sin(n*30)*i
```

The preceding complex points have an interesting property: Each point is a rotation of the complex number `z1`. Moreover, the complex number `z1` is called a *generator* because the 30 points on the unit circle are powers of the complex number `z1`.

Complex Conjugate Root Theorem

According to the complex conjugate root theorem, if `P(x)` is a polynomial with real coefficients and `a+b*i` is a root (solution) of `P(x)`, then `a-b*i` is also a root (solution) of `P(x)`. Here are some examples:

If `P(x) = x^2+1`, then `P(x) = 0` for `x = +i` and -i (i = square root of -1).

If `P(x) = x^2+17`, then `P(x) = 0` for `x = 4+i` and `4-i` (i = square root of -1).

Hermitian Matrices

If the 2D matrix A has real entries and A transpose equals A, then A is a symmetric matrix. Earlier we discussed the notion of the conjugate of a complex number. If the matrix A has complex values, and the conjugate transpose of A equals A, then A is called a *Hermitian matrix*.

Recall that the complex conjugate of a complex number of the form `a+b*i` is a complex number of the form `a-b*i`. Here is an example of a Hermitian matrix:

$$A = \begin{bmatrix} 2 & 0 & (1+i) \\ 0 & 3 & -1 \\ (1-i) & -1 & 3 \end{bmatrix}$$

Notice that `a(3,1) != a(1,3)`, so the matrix is not symmetric (otherwise A would be symmetric). However, `a(3,1)` equals the conjugate of `a(1,3)`, which means that A is a Hermitian matrix.

SUMMARY

This chapter started with a brief description of linear algebra, followed by a discussion of concepts such as vectors, inner products of vectors, and orthogonal vectors. Other topics include the magnitude ("norm") of vectors, unit vectors, orthogonal vectors, spanning sets of vectors, and a basis.

Next you learned about matrices, and how you can add, subtract, or multiply matrices. You also saw how to compute the inverse of an invertible nxn matrix.

In addition, you saw how to create a covariance matrix and a correlation matrix, and also how to calculate its eigenvalues and eigenvectors. Furthermore, you learned about PCA, and how to construct a matrix of principal components from a set of eigenvectors.

Next, you got an overview of other dimensionality reduction techniques (PCA is one such technique), as well as the differences between linear and non-linear reduction techniques. Finally, you learned about complex numbers, the complex conjugate root theorem, and Hermitian matrices.

## CHAPTER 4

INTRODUCTION TO PYTHON

This chapter contains an introduction to Python, with information about useful tools for installing its modules, working with its basic constructs, and managing some data types.

The first part of this chapter covers a Python installation, some environment variables, and usage of the interpreter. We include code samples and how to save code in text files that you can launch from the command line. The second part of this chapter shows you how to work with simple data types, such as numbers, fractions, and strings. The third part of this chapter discusses exceptions and how to use them in scripts.

The fourth part of this chapter introduces you to ways to perform conditional logic, as well as control structures and user-defined functions. Virtually every Python program that performs useful calculations requires some type of conditional logic or control structure (or both). Although the syntax for these features is slightly different from other languages, the functionality will be familiar to you.

The fifth part of this chapter contains examples that involve nested loops and user-defined functions. We discuss recursion and how to calculate factorial values and Fibonacci numbers. The remaining portion of the chapter discusses tuples, sets, and dictionaries.

NOTE *The scripts in this book are for Python 3.x.*

TOOLS FOR PYTHON

The Anaconda Python distribution available for Windows, Linux, and Mac, and is downloadable: *http://continuum.io/downloads.*

Anaconda is well-suited for modules such as `NumPy` and `scipy`, and if you are a Windows user, Anaconda appears to be a better alternative.

easy_install and pip

Both `easy_install` and `pip` are easy to use when you need to install Python modules. Whenever you need to install a Python module, use either `easy_install` or `pip` with the following syntax:

```
easy_install <module-name>
pip install <module-name>
```

NOTE *Python-based modules are easier to install, whereas modules with code written in C are usually faster, but more difficult in terms of installation.*

virtualenv

The virtualenv tool enables you to create isolated Python environments, and its home page is available online:

http://www.virtualenv.org/en/latest/virtualenv.html

virtualenv addresses the problem of preserving the correct dependencies and versions (and indirectly permissions) for different applications. (If you are a Python novice, you might not need virtualenv right now). The next section shows you how to check whether Python is installed on your machine, and also where you can download Python.

PYTHON INSTALLATION

Before you download anything, check if you have Python already installed on your machine (which is likely if you have a Macbook or a Linux machine) by typing the following command in a command shell:

```
python -V
```

The output for the Macbook used in this book is

```
Python 3.9.1
```

NOTE *Install Python 3.9.1 (or as close as possible to this version) on your machine so that you will have the same version of Python that was used to test the scripts in this book.*

If you need to install Python on your machine, navigate to the Python home page and select the downloads link or navigate directly to this Website:

http://www.python.org/download/

In addition, PythonWin is available for Windows, and its home page is online:

http://www.cgl.ucsf.edu/Outreach/pc204/pythonwin.html

Use any text editor that can create, edit, and save Python scripts and save them as plain text files (don't use Microsoft Word).

After you have Python installed and configured on your machine, you are ready to work with the Python scripts in this book.

SETTING THE PATH ENVIRONMENT VARIABLE (WINDOWS ONLY)

The PATH environment variable specifies a list of directories that are searched whenever you specify an executable program from the command line. A very good guide to setting up your environment so that the executable is always available in every command shell is to follow the instructions found online:

http://www.blog.pythonlibrary.org/2011/11/24/python-101-setting-up-python-on-windows/

LAUNCHING PYTHON ON YOUR MACHINE

There are three different ways to launch Python:

Use the Python Interactive Interpreter.
Launch Python scripts from the command line.
Use an IDE.

The next section shows you how to launch the interpreter from the command line. Later in this chapter, we show how to launch scripts from the command line and discuss IDEs.

NOTE *The emphasis in this book is to launch scripts from the command line or to enter code in the interpreter.*

The Python Interactive Interpreter

Launch the interactive interpreter from the command line by opening a command shell and typing the following command:

```
Python
```

You will see the following prompt (or something similar):

```
Python 3.9.1 (v3.9.1:1e5d33e9b9, Dec  7 2020, 12:44:01)
[Clang 12.0.0 (clang-1200.0.32.27)] on darwin
Type "help", "copyright", "credits" or "license" for more
information.
>>>
```

Now type the expression 2 + 7 at the prompt:

```
>>> 2 + 7
```

Python displays the following result:

```
9
>>>
```

Press `ctrl-d` to exit the Python shell.

You can launch any Python script from the command line by preceding it with the word "python." For example, if you have the script `myscript.py` that contains Python commands, launch the script as follows:

```
python myscript.py
```

As a simple illustration, suppose that the script `myscript.py` contains the following code:

```
print('Hello World from Python')
print('2 + 7 = ', 2+7)
```

When you launch the preceding script, you will see the following output:

```
Hello World from Python
2 + 7 =  9
```

PYTHON IDENTIFIERS

A Python identifier is the name of a variable, function, class, module, or other object, and a valid identifier conforms to the following rules:

starts with a letter A to Z, or a to z, or an underscore (_)
zero or more letters, underscores, and digits (0 to 9)

NOTE *Python identifiers cannot contain characters such as @, $, and %.*

Python is a case-sensitive language, so "Abc" and "abc" are different identifiers. In addition, Python has the following naming conventions:

Class names start with an uppercase letter and all other identifiers with a lowercase letter.
An initial underscore is used for private identifiers.
Two initial underscores are used for strongly private identifiers.

An identifier with two initial underscores and two trailing underscores indicates a language-defined special name.

LINES, INDENTATIONS, AND MULTI-LINES

Unlike other programming languages (such as Java or Objective-C), Python uses indentations instead of curly braces for code blocks. Indentation must be consistent in a code block, as shown here:

```
if True:
    print("ABC")
    print("DEF")
else:
    print("ABC")
    print("DEF")
```

Multi-line statements can terminate with a new line or the backslash ("\") character, as shown here:

```
total = x1 + \
        x2 + \
        x3
```

You can place x1, x2, and x3 on the same line, so there is no reason to use three separate lines; however, this functionality is available in case you need to add a set of variables that do not fit on a single line.

You can specify multiple statements in one line by using a semicolon (";") to separate each statement, as shown here:

```
a=10; b=5; print(a); print(a+b)
```

The output of the preceding code snippet is as follows:

```
10
15
```

NOTE *The use of semi-colons and the continuation character are discouraged in Python.*

QUOTATION AND COMMENTS IN PYTHON

Python allows single (‘), double (“) and triple (‘” or “”””) quotes for string literals, provided that they match at the beginning and the end of the string. You can use triple quotes for strings that span multiple lines. The following examples are legal Python strings:

```
word = 'word'
line = "This is a sentence."
para = """This is a paragraph. This paragraph contains more
than one sentence."""
```

A string literal that begins with the letter "r" (for "raw") treats everything as a literal character and "escapes" the meaning of meta characters:

```
a1 = r'\n'
a2 = r'\r'
a3 = r'\t'
print('a1:',a1,'a2:',a2,'a3:',a3)
```

The output of the preceding code block is as follows:

```
a1: \n a2: \r a3: \t
```

You can embed a single quote in a pair of double quotes (and vice versa) in order to display a single quote or a double quote. Another way to accomplish the same result is to precede a single or double quote with a backslash ("\") character. The following code block illustrates these techniques:

```
b1 = "'"
b2 = '"'
b3 = '\''
b4 = "\""
print('b1:',b1,'b2:',b2)
print('b3:',b3,'b4:',b4)
```

The output of the preceding code block is as follows:

```
b1:  '  b2:  "
b3:  '  b4:  "
```

A hash sign (#) that is not inside a string literal is the character that indicates the beginning of a comment. Moreover, all characters after the # and up to the physical line end are part of the comment (and ignored by the interpreter). Consider the following code block:

```
#!/usr/bin/python
# First comment
print("Hello, Python!")   # second comment
```

This code produces the following result:

```
Hello, Python!
```

A comment may be on the same line after a statement or expression:

```
name = "Tom Jones" # This is also a comment
```

You can comment multiple lines as follows:

```
# This is comment one
# This is comment two
# This is comment three
```

A blank line in Python is a line containing only whitespace, a comment, or both.

SAVING YOUR CODE IN A MODULE

Earlier you saw how to launch the interpreter from the command line and then enter commands. However, everything you type into the interpreter is only valid for the current session. If you exit the interpreter and then launch the interpreter again, your previous definitions are no longer valid. Fortunately, Python enables you to store code in a text file.

A *module* is a text file that contains Python statements. In the previous section, you saw how the interpreter enables you to test code snippets whose definitions are valid for the current session. If you want to retain the code snippets and other definitions, place them in a text file so that you can execute that code outside of the interpreter.

The outermost statements are executed from top to bottom when the module is imported for the first time, which will then set up its variables and functions.

A module can be run directly from the command line, as shown here:

```
python First.py
```

As an illustration, place the following two statements in a text file called First.py:

```
x = 3
print(x)
```

Now type the following command:

```
python First.py
```

The output from the preceding command is 3, which is the same as executing the preceding code from the interpreter.

When a module is run directly, the special variable __name__ is set to __main__. You will often see the following type of code in a module:

```
if __name__ == '__main__':
    # do something here
    print('Running directly')
```

The preceding code snippet enables Python to determine if a module was launched from the command line or imported into another module.

SOME STANDARD MODULES IN PYTHON

The Python Standard Library provides many modules that can simplify your own scripts. A list of the Standard Library modules is available online:

http://www.python.org/doc/

Some of the most important modules include cgi, math, os, pickle, random, re, socket, sys, time, and urllib.

The code samples in this book use the modules math, os, random, and re. You need to import these modules in order to use them in your code. For example, the following code block shows you how to import standard modules:

```
import re
import sys
import time
```

The code samples in this book import one or more of the preceding modules, as well as other Python modules.

THE `HELP()` AND `DIR()` FUNCTIONS

An Internet search for Python-related topics usually returns a number of links with useful information. Alternatively, you can check the official documentation site: *docs.python.org.*

In addition, the `help()` and `dir()` functions are accessible from the interpreter. The `help()` function displays documentation strings, whereas the `dir()` function displays defined symbols. For example, if you type `help(sys,)` you see documentation for the `sys` module, whereas `dir(sys)` displays a list of the defined symbols.

Type the following command in the interpreter to display the string-related methods:

```
>>> dir(str)
```

The preceding command generates the following output:

```
['__add__', '__class__', '__contains__', '__delattr__',
'__doc__', '__eq__', '__format__', '__ge__', '__getattrib-
ute__', '__getitem__', '__getnewargs__', '__getslice__', '__
gt__', '__hash__', '__init__', '__le__', '__len__', '__lt__',
'__mod__', '__mul__', '__ne__', '__new__', '__reduce__',
'__reduce_ex__', '__repr__', '__rmod__', '__rmul__', '__
setattr__', '__sizeof__', '__str__', '__subclasshook__',
'_formatter_field_name_split', '_formatter_parser', 'capi-
talize', 'center', 'count', 'decode', 'encode', 'endswith',
'expandtabs', 'find', 'format', 'index', 'isalnum', 'isal-
pha', 'isdigit', 'islower', 'isspace', 'istitle', 'isupper',
'join', 'ljust', 'lower', 'lstrip', 'partition', 'replace',
'rfind', 'rindex', 'rjust', 'rpartition', 'rsplit', 'rstrip',
'split', 'splitlines', 'startswith', 'strip', 'swapcase',
'title', 'translate', 'upper', 'zfill']
```

The preceding list gives you a consolidated list of built-in functions. Although it is clear that the `max()` function returns the maximum value of its arguments, the purpose of other functions, such as `filter()` or `map()`, is not immediately apparent (unless you have used them in other programming languages). The preceding list provides a starting point for finding out more about various built-in functions that are not discussed in this chapter.

Note that while `dir()` does not list the names of built-in functions and variables, you can obtain this information from the standard module `__builtin__` that is automatically imported under the name `__builtins__`:

```
>>> dir(__builtins__)
```

The following command shows you how to get more information about a function:

```
help(str.lower)
```

The output from the preceding command is

```
Help on method_descriptor:
lower(...)
    S.lower() -> string

    Return a copy of the string S converted to lowercase.
(END)
```

Check the online documentation and also experiment with `help()` and `dir()` when you need additional information about a particular function or module.

COMPILE TIME AND RUNTIME CODE CHECKING

Python performs some compile-time checking, but most checks (including type and name) are deferred until code execution. Consequently, if your code references a user-defined function that that does not exist, the code will compile successfully. In fact, the code will fail with an exception only when the code execution path references the non-existent function.

As a simple example, consider the following function `myFunc` that references the non-existent function called `DoesNotExist`:

```
def myFunc(x):
    if x == 3:
        print(DoesNotExist(x))
    else:
        print('x: ',x)
```

The preceding code only fails when the `myFunc` function is passed the value 3, after which Python raises an error. Later, we discuss how to define and invoke user-defined functions, along with an explanation of the difference between local versus global variables.

Now that you understand some basic concepts and how to launch your custom modules, the next section discusses primitive data types.

SIMPLE DATA TYPES IN PYTHON

Python supports primitive data types, such as numbers (integers, floating point numbers, and exponential numbers), strings, and dates. It also supports more complex data types, such as lists (or arrays), tuples, and dictionaries, all of which are discussed later in this chapter. The next several sections discuss some of the primitive data types, along with code snippets that show you how to perform operations on those data types.

WORKING WITH NUMBERS

Python provides arithmetic operations for manipulating numbers in a manner similar to other programming languages. The following examples involve arithmetic operations on integers:

```
>>> 2+2
4
>>> 4/3
1
>>> 3*8
24
```

The following example assigns numbers to two variables and computes their product:

```
>>> x = 4
>>> y = 7
>>> x * y
28
```

The following examples demonstrate arithmetic operations involving integers:

```
>>> 2+2
4
>>> 4/3
1
>>> 3*8
24
```

Notice that division ("/") of two integers is actually truncation in which only the integer result is retained. The following example converts a floating point number into exponential form:

```
>>> fnum = 0.00012345689000007
>>> "%.14e"%fnum
'1.23456890000070e-04'
```

You can use the `int()` function and the `float()` function to convert strings to numbers:

```
word1 = "123"
word2 = "456.78"
var1 = int(word1)
var2 = float(word2)
print("var1: ",var1," var2: ",var2)
```

The output from the preceding code block is here:

```
var1:   123   var2:   456.78
```

Alternatively, you can use the `eval()` function:

```
word1 = "123"
word2 = "456.78"
var1 = eval(word1)
var2 = eval(word2)
print("var1: ",var1," var2: ",var2)
```

Attempting to convert a string that is not a valid integer or a floating point number raises an exception, so it's advisable to place your code in a `try/except` block.

Working with Other Bases

Numbers in Python are in base 10 (the default), but you can easily convert numbers to other bases. For example, the following code block initializes the variable x with the value 1234, and then displays that number in base 2, 8, and 16:

```
>>> x = 1234
>>> bin(x) '0b10011010010'
>>> oct(x) '0o2322'
>>> hex(x) '0x4d2' >>>
```

Use the `format()` function to suppress the 0b, 0o, or 0x prefixes:

```
>>> format(x, 'b') '10011010010'
>>> format(x, 'o') '2322'
>>> format(x, 'x') '4d2'
```

Negative integers are displayed with a negative sign:

```
>>> x = -1234
>>> format(x, 'b') '-10011010010'
>>> format(x, 'x') '-4d2'
```

The `chr()` Function

The `chr()` function takes a positive integer as a parameter and converts it to its corresponding alphabetic value (if one exists). The letters A through Z have decimal representation of 65 through 91 (which corresponds to hexadecimal 41 through 5b), and the lowercase letters a through z have decimal representation 97 through 122 (hexadecimal 61 through 7b).

Here is an example of using the `chr()` function to print an uppercase A:

```
>>> x=chr(65)
>>> x
'A'
```

The following code block prints the ASCII values for a range of integers:

```
result = ""
for x in range(65,91):
  print(x, chr(x))
  result = result+chr(x)+' '
print("result: ",result)
```

NOTE *Python 2 uses ASCII strings whereas Python 3 uses UTF-8.*

You can represent a range of characters with the following line:

```
for x in range(65,91):
```

However, the following equivalent code snippet is more intuitive:

```
for x in range(ord('A'), ord('Z')):
```

If you want to display the result for lowercase letters, change the preceding range from (65,91) to either of the following statements:

```
for x in range(65,91):
for x in range(ord('a'), ord('z')):
```

The round() Function in Python

The round() function enables you to round decimal values:

```
>>> round(1.23, 1)
1.2
>>> round(-3.42,1)
-3.4
```

Formatting Numbers in Python

You can specify the number of decimal places of precision to use when printing decimal numbers:

```
>>> x = 1.23456
>>> format(x, '0.2f')
'1.23'
>>> format(x, '0.3f')
'1.235'
>>> 'value is {:0.3f}'.format(x) 'value is 1.235'
>>> from decimal import Decimal
>>> a = Decimal('4.2')
>>> b = Decimal('2.1')
>>> a + b
Decimal('6.3')
>>> print(a + b)
6.3
>>> (a + b) == Decimal('6.3')
True
>>> x = 1234.56789
>>> # Two decimal places of accuracy
>>> format(x, '0.2f')
'1234.57'
>>> # Right justified in 10 chars, one-digit accuracy
>>> format(x, '>10.1f')
' 1234.6'
>>> # Left justified
>>> format(x, '<10.1f') '1234.6 '
>>> # Centered
>>> format(x, '^10.1f') ' 1234.6 '
>>> # Inclusion of thousands separator
>>> format(x, ',')
'1,234.56789'
>>> format(x, '0,.1f')
'1,234.6'
```

Before delving into code samples that work with strings, the next section briefly discusses Unicode and UTF-8, both of which are character encodings.

UNICODE AND UTF-8

A Unicode string consists of a sequence of numbers that are between 0 and 0×10ffff, where each number represents a group of bytes. An encoding is the manner in which a Unicode string is translated into a sequence of bytes. Among the various encodings, UTF-8 (Unicode Transformation Format) is perhaps the most common, and it's also the default encoding for many systems. The digit 8 in UTF-8 indicates that the encoding uses 8-bit numbers, whereas UTF-16 uses 16-bit numbers (but this encoding is less common).

The ASCII character set is a subset of UTF-8, so a valid ASCII string can be read as a UTF-8 string without any re-encoding required. In addition, a Unicode string can be converted into a UTF-8 string.

WORKING WITH UNICODE

Python supports Unicode, which means that you can render characters in different languages. Unicode data can be stored and manipulated in the same way as strings. Create a Unicode string by prepending the letter "u," as shown here:

```
>>> u'Hello from Python!'
u'Hello from Python!'
```

Special characters can be included in a string by specifying their Unicode value. For example, the following Unicode string embeds a space (which has the Unicode value 0×0020) in a string:

```
>>> u'Hello\u0020from Python!'
u'Hello from Python!'
```

Listing 4.1 displays the content of Unicode1.py, which illustrates how to display a string of characters in Japanese and another string of characters in Chinese (Mandarin).

LISTING 4.1: Unicode1.py

```
chinese1 = u'\u5c07\u63a2\u8a0e HTML5 \u53ca\u5176\u4ed6'
hiragana = u'D3 \u306f \u304b\u3063\u3053\u3043\u3043 \
u3067\u3059!'

print('Chinese:',chinese1)
print('Hiragana:',hiragana)
```

The output of Listing 4.1 is

```
Chinese: 将探討 HTML5 及其他
Hiragana: D3 は かっこいい です!
```

The next portion of this chapter shows you how to "slice and dice" text strings with built-in functions.

WORKING WITH STRINGS

Literal strings in Python 3 are Unicode by default. You can concatenate two strings using the "+" operator. The following example prints a string and then concatenates two single-letter strings:

```
>>> 'abc'
'abc'
>>> 'a' + 'b'
'ab'
```

You can use + or * to concatenate identical strings, as shown here:

```
>>> 'a' + 'a' + 'a'
'aaa'
>>> 'a' * 3
'aaa'
```

You can assign strings to variables and print them using the `print` command:

```
>>> print('abc')
abc
>>> x = 'abc'
>>> print(x)
abc
>>> y = 'def'
>>> print(x + y)
Abcdef
```

You can "unpack" the letters of a string and assign them to variables, as shown here:

```
>>> str = "World"
>>> x1,x2,x3,x4,x5 = str
>>> x1
'W'
>>> x2
'o'
>>> x3
'r'
>>> x4
'l'
>>> x5
'd'
```

The preceding code snippets shows you how easy it is to extract the letters in a text string. You can also extract substrings of a string as shown in the following examples:

```
>>> x = "abcdef"
```

```
>>> x[0]
'a'
>>> x[-1]
'f'
>>> x[1:3]
'bc'
>>> x[0:2] + x[5:]
'abf'
```

However, you will cause an error if you attempt to subtract two strings, as you probably expect:

```
>>> 'a' - 'b'
Traceback (most recent call last):
  File "<stdin>", line 1, in <module>
TypeError: unsupported operand type(s) for -: 'str' and 'str'
```

The try/except construct enables you to handle the preceding type of exception.

Comparing Strings

You can use the methods lower() and upper() to convert a string to lowercase and uppercase, respectively:

```
>>> 'Python'.lower()
'python'
>>> 'Python'.upper()
'PYTHON'
>>>
```

The methods lower() and upper() are useful for performing a case insensitive comparison of two ASCII strings. Listing 4.2 shows the content of Compare.py that uses the lower() function to compare two ASCII strings.

LISTING 4.2: Compare.py

```
x = 'Abc'
y = 'abc'

if(x == y):
  print('x and y: identical')
elif (x.lower() == y.lower()):
  print('x and y: case insensitive match')
else:
print('x and y: different')
```

Since x contains mixed case letters and y contains lowercase letters, Listing 4.2 gives the following output:

```
x and y: different
```

Formatting Strings in Python

Python provides the functions `string.lstring()`, `string.rstring()`, and `string.center()` for positioning a text string so that it is left-justified, right-justified, and centered, respectively. As you saw in a previous section, the `format()` method exists for advanced interpolation features.

Now enter the following commands in the interpreter:

```
import string

str1 = 'this is a string'
print(string.ljust(str1, 10))
print(string.rjust(str1, 40))
print(string.center(str1,40))
```

The output is as follows:

```
this is a string
                        this is a string
            this is a string
```

UNINITIALIZED VARIABLES AND THE VALUE NONE IN PYTHON

Python distinguishes between an uninitialized variable and the value None. The former is a variable that has not been assigned a value, whereas the value None is a value that indicates "no value." Collections and methods often return the value None, and you can test for the value None in conditional logic.

The next portion of this chapter shows you how to manipulate text strings with built-in functions.

SLICING AND SPLICING STRINGS

Python enables you to extract substrings of a string (called *slicing*) using array notation. Slice notation is `start:stop:step`, where the start, stop, and step values are integers that specify the start value, end value, and the increment value. The interesting part about slicing is that you can use the value -1, which operates from the right side instead of the left side of a string. Some examples of slicing a string are here:

```
text1 = "this is a string"
print('First 7 characters:',text1[0:7])
print('Characters 2-4:',text1[2:4])
print('Right-most character:',text1[-1])
print('Right-most 2 characters:',text1[-3:-1])
```

The output from the preceding code block is as follows:

```
First 7 characters: this is
Characters 2-4: is
Right-most character: g
Right-most 2 characters: in
```

Later in this chapter, we show how to insert a string in the middle of another string.

Testing for Digits and Alphabetic Characters

Python enables you to examine each character in a string and then test whether that character is a digit or an alphabetic character. This section provides a precursor to regular expressions that are discussed in Chapter 8.

Listing 4.3 shows the content of CharTypes.py, which illustrates how to determine if a string contains digits or characters. In case you are unfamiliar with the conditional "if" statement in Listing 4.3, more detailed information is available later in this chapter.

LISTING 4.3: CharTypes.py

```
str1 = "4"
str2 = "4234"
str3 = "b"
str4 = "abc"
str5 = "a1b2c3"

if(str1.isdigit()):
  print("this is a digit:",str1)

if(str2.isdigit()):
  print("this is a digit:",str2)

if(str3.isalpha()):
  print("this is alphabetic:",str3)

if(str4.isalpha()):
  print("this is alphabetic:",str4)

if(not str5.isalpha()):
  print("this is not pure alphabetic:",str5)

print("capitalized first letter:",str5.title())
```

Listing 4.3 initializes some variables, followed by two conditional tests that check whether str1 and str2 are digits using the isdigit() function. The next portion of Listing 4.3 checks if str3, str4, and str5 are alphabetic strings using the isalpha() function. The output of Listing 4.3 is as follows:

```
this is a digit: 4
this is a digit: 4234
this is alphabetic: b
this is alphabetic: abc
this is not pure alphabetic: a1b2c3
capitalized first letter: A1B2C3
```

SEARCH AND REPLACE A STRING IN OTHER STRINGS

Python provides methods for searching and also for replacing a string in a second text string. Listing 4.4 shows the content of `FindPos1.py`, which shows how to use the `find()` function to search for the occurrence of one string in another string.

LISTING 4.4: FindPos1.py

```
item1 = 'abc'
item2 = 'Abc'
text = 'This is a text string with abc'

pos1 = text.find(item1)
pos2 = text.find(item2)

print('pos1=',pos1)
print('pos2=',pos2)
```

Listing 4.4 initializes the variables `item1`, `item2`, and `text`, and then searches for the index of the contents of `item1` and `item2` in the string text. The `find()` function returns the column number where the first successful match occurs; otherwise, the `find()` function returns a −1 if a match is unsuccessful. The output from launching Listing 4.4 is here:

```
pos1= 27
pos2= -1
```

In addition to the `find()` method, you can use the `in` operator when you want to test for the presence of an element:

```
>>> lst = [1,2,3]
>>> 1 in lst
True
```

Listing 4.5 displays the content of `Replace1.py`, which shows how to replace one string with another string.

LISTING 4.5: Replace1.py

```
text = 'This is a text string with abc'
print('text:',text)
text = text.replace('is a', 'was a')
print('text:',text)
```

Listing 4.5 starts by initializing the variable text and then printing its contents. The next portion of Listing 4.5 replaces the occurrence of "is a" with "was a" in the string text, and then prints the modified string. The output from launching Listing 4.5 is as follows:

```
text: This is a text string with abc
text: This was a text string with abc
```

REMOVE LEADING AND TRAILING CHARACTERS

Python provides the functions `strip()`, `lstrip()`, and `rstrip()` to remove characters in a text string. Listing 4.6 shows the content of `Remove1.py`, which gives the code for how to search for a string.

LISTING 4.6: Remove1.py

```
text = '   leading and trailing white space   '
print('text1:','x',text,'y')

text = text.lstrip()
print('text2:','x',text,'y')

text = text.rstrip()
print('text3:','x',text,'y')
```

Listing 4.6 starts by concatenating the letter x and the contents of the variable `text`, and then printing the result. The second part of Listing 4.6 removes the leading white spaces in the string `text` and then appends the result to the letter x. The third part of Listing 4.6 removes the trailing white spaces in the string `text` (note that the leading white spaces have already been removed) and then appends the result to the letter x.

The output from launching Listing 4.6 is here:

```
text1: x    leading and trailing white space    y
text2: x leading and trailing white space    y
text3: x leading and trailing white space y
```

If you want to remove extra white spaces inside a text string, use the `replace()` function as discussed in the previous section. The following example illustrates how this can be accomplished, which also contains the `re` module as a "preview" for what you will learn in Chapter 8:

```
import re
text = 'a    b'
a = text.replace(' ', '')
b = re.sub('\s+', ' ', text)

print(a)
print(b)
```

The result is

```
ab
a b
```

Later you will see how to use the `join()` function to remove extra white spaces in a text string.

PRINTING TEXT WITHOUT NEWLINE CHARACTERS

If you need to suppress white space and a newline between objects output with multiple print statements, you can use concatenation or the `write()` function.

The first technique is to concatenate the string representations of each object using the `str()` function prior to printing the result. For example, run the following statement:

```
x = str(9)+str(0xff)+str(-3.1)
print('x: ',x)
```

The output is shown here:

```
x:  9255-3.1
```

The preceding line contains the concatenation of the numbers 9 and 255 (which is the decimal value of the hexadecimal number 0xff) and -3.1.

Incidentally, you can use the `str()` function with modules and user-defined classes. An example involving the built-in module sys is as follows:

```
>>> import sys
>>> print(str(sys))
<module 'sys' (built-in)>
```

The following code snippet illustrates how to use the `write()` function to display a string:

```
import sys
write = sys.stdout.write
write('123')
write('123456789')
```

The output is here:

```
1233
1234567899
```

TEXT ALIGNMENT

Python provides the methods `ljust()`, `rjust()`, and `center()` for aligning text. The `ljust()` and `rjust()` functions left justify and right justify a text string, respectively, whereas the `center()` function will center a string. An example is shown in the following code block:

```
text = 'Hello World'
text.ljust(20)
'Hello World '
>>> text.rjust(20)
' Hello World'
>>> text.center(20)
' Hello World '
```

You can use the `format()` function to align text. Use the <, >, or ^ characters, along with a desired width, in order to right justify, left justify, and center the text, respectively. The following examples illustrate how you can specify text justification:

```
>>> format(text, '>20')
'         Hello World'
>>>
>>> format(text, '<20')
'Hello World         '
>>>
>>> format(text, '^20')
'     Hello World     '
>>>
```

WORKING WITH DATES

Python provides a rich set of date-related functions, and this section provides one such example. Listing 4.7 shows the content of the script Datetime2.py, which displays various date-related values, such as the current date and time; the day of the week, month, and year; and the time in seconds since the beginning of the epoch.

LISTING 4.7: Datetime2.py

```
import time
import datetime

print("Time in seconds since the epoch: %s" %time.time())
print("Current date and time: " , datetime.datetime.now())
print("Or like this: " ,datetime.datetime.now().
strftime("%y-%m-%d-%H-%M"))

print("Current year: ", datetime.date.today().strftime("%Y"))
print("Month of year: ", datetime.date.today().
strftime("%B"))
print("Week number of the year: ", datetime.date.today().
strftime("%W"))
print("Weekday of the week: ", datetime.date.today().
strftime("%w"))
print("Day of year: ", datetime.date.today().strftime("%j"))
print("Day of the month : ", datetime.date.today().
strftime("%d"))
print("Day of week: ", datetime.date.today().strftime("%A"))
```

Listing 4.8 displays the output generated by running the code in Listing 4.7.

LISTING 4.8: datetime2.out

```
Time in seconds since the epoch: 1375144195.66
Current date and time:  2013-07-29 17:29:55.664164
Or like this:  13-07-29-17-29
Current year:  2013
```

```
Month of year:   July
Week number of the year:   30
Weekday of the week:   1
Day of year:   210
Day of the month :   29
Day of week:   Monday
```

Python also enables you to perform arithmetic calculates with date-related values, as shown in the following code block:

```
>>> from datetime import timedelta
>>> a = timedelta(days=2, hours=6)
>>> b = timedelta(hours=4.5)
>>> c = a + b
>>> c.days
2
>>> c.seconds
37800
>>> c.seconds / 3600
10.5
>>> c.total_seconds() / 3600
58.5
```

Converting Strings to Dates

Listing 4.9 shows the content of String2Date.py, which illustrates how to convert a string to a date and how to calculate the difference between two dates.

LISTING 4.9: String2Date.py

```
from datetime import datetime

text = '2014-08-13'
y = datetime.strptime(text, '%Y-%m-%d')
z = datetime.now()
diff = z - y
print('Date difference:',diff)
```

The output from Listing 4.9 is shown here:

```
Date difference: -210 days, 18:58:40.197130
```

EXCEPTION HANDLING IN PYTHON

Unlike JavaScript, you cannot add a number and a string in Python. However, you can detect an illegal operation using the try/except construct, which is similar to the try/catch construct in languages such as JavaScript and Java.

An example of a try/except block is here:

```
try:
    x = 4
```

```
    y = 'abc'
    z = x + y
except:
print 'cannot add incompatible types:', x, y
```

When you run the preceding code in Python, the print statement in the except code block is executed because the variables x and y have incompatible
types.

Earlier in the chapter, you also saw that subtracting two strings throws an
exception:

```
>>> 'a' - 'b'
Traceback (most recent call last):
  File "<stdin>", line 1, in <module>
TypeError: unsupported operand type(s) for -: 'str' and 'str'
```

A simple way to handle this situation is to use a try/except block:

```
>>> try:
... print('a' - 'b')
... except TypeError:
... print('TypeError exception while trying to subtract two
          strings')
... except:
... print('Exception while trying to subtract two strings')
...
```

The output from the preceding code block is as follows:

```
TypeError exception while trying to subtract two strings
```

The preceding code block specifies the finer-grained exception called TypeEr-
ror, followed by a "generic" except code block to handle all other exceptions
that might occur during the execution of your Python code. This style is similar to the exception handling in Java code.

Listing 4.10 shows the content of Exception1.py, which illustrates how
to handle various types of exceptions.

LISTING 4.10: Exception1.py

```
import sys

try:
    f = open('myfile.txt')
    s = f.readline()
    i = int(s.strip())
except IOError as err:
    print("I/O error: {0}".format(err))
except ValueError:
    print("Could not convert data to an integer.")
except:
    print("Unexpected error:", sys.exc_info()[0])
    raise
```

Listing 4.10 contains a `try` block followed by three `except` statements. If an error occurs in the `try` block, the first `except` statement is compared with the type of exception that occurred. If there is a match, then the subsequent print statement is executed, and the program terminates. If not, a similar test is performed with the second `except` statement. If neither `except` statement matches the exception, the third `except` statement handles the exception, which involves printing a message and then "raising" an exception.

Note that you can also specify multiple exception types in a single statement, as shown here:

```
except (NameError, RuntimeError, TypeError):
    print('One of three error types occurred')
```

The preceding code block is more compact, but you do not know which of the three error types occurred. Python allows you to define custom exceptions, but this topic is beyond the scope of this book.

HANDLING USER INPUT

Python enables you to read user input from the command line via the `input()` function or the `raw_input()` function. Typically, you assign user input to a variable that contains all the characters that users enter from the keyboard. User input terminates when users press the `<return>` key (which is included with the input characters). Listing 4.11 displays the contents of `UserInput1.py` that prompts users for their name and then uses interpolation to display a response.

LISTING 4.11: UserInput1.py

```
userInput = input("Enter your name: ")
print ("Hello %s, my name is Python" % userInput)
```

The output of Listing 4.11 is as follows (assume that the user entered the word "`Dave`"):

```
Hello Dave, my name is Python
```

The `print` statement in Listing 4.11 uses string interpolation via `%s`, which substitutes the value of the variable after the `%` symbol. This functionality is obviously useful when you want to specify something that is determined at run-time.

User input can cause exceptions (depending on the operations that your code performs), so it's important to include exception-handling code.

Listing 4.12 shows the content of `UserInput2.py`, which prompts users for a string and attempts to convert the string to a number in a `try/except` block.

LISTING 4.12 UserInput2.py

```
userInput = input("Enter something: ")

try:
   x = 0 + eval(userInput)
   print('you entered the number:',userInput)
except:
print(userInput,'is a string')
```

Listing 4.12 adds the number 0 to the result of converting a user's input to a number. If the conversion was successful, a message with the user's input is displayed. If the conversion failed, the except code block consists of a print statement that displays a message.

NOTE *This code sample uses the* eval() *function, which should be avoided so that your code does not evaluate arbitrary (and possibly destructive) commands.*

Listing 4.13 shows the content of UserInput3.py, which prompts users for two numbers and attempts to compute their sum in a pair of try/except blocks.

LISTING 4.13: UserInput3.py

```
sum = 0

msg = 'Enter a number:'
val1 = input(msg)

try:
   sum = sum + eval(val1)
except:
   print(val1,'is a string')

msg = 'Enter a number:'
val2 = input(msg)

try:
   sum = sum + eval(val2)
except:
   print(val2,'is a string')

print('The sum of',val1,'and',val2,'is',sum)
```

Listing 4.13 contains two try blocks, each of which is followed by an except statement. The first try block attempts to add the first user-supplied number to the variable sum, and the second try block attempts to add the second user-supplied number to the previously entered number. An error message occurs if either input string is not a valid number; if both are valid numbers, a message is displayed containing the input numbers and their sum. Be sure to read the caveat regarding the eval() function that is mentioned earlier in this Chapter.

COMMAND-LINE ARGUMENTS

Python provides a `getopt` module to parse command-line options and arguments, and the `sys` module provides access to any command-line arguments via the `sys.argv`. This serves two purposes:

`sys.argv` is the list of command-line arguments
`len(sys.argv)` is the number of command-line arguments

Here `sys.argv[0]` is the program name, so if the program is called `test.py`, it matches the value of `sys.argv[0]`.

Now you can provide input values for a program on the command line instead of providing input values by prompting users for their input.

As an example, consider the script `test.py` shown here:

```
#!/usr/bin/python
import sys
print('Number of arguments:',len(sys.argv),'arguments')
print('Argument List:', str(sys.argv))
```

Now run above script as follows:

```
python test.py arg1 arg2 arg3
```

This will produce following result:

```
Number of arguments: 4 arguments.
Argument List: ['test.py', 'arg1', 'arg2', 'arg3']
```

The ability to specify input values from the command line provides useful functionality. For example, suppose that you have a custom class that contains the methods `add` and `subtract` to add and subtract a pair of numbers.

You can use command-line arguments to specify which method to execute on a pair of numbers:

```
python MyClass add 3 5
python MyClass subtract 3 5
```

This functionality is very useful because you can programmatically execute different methods in a class, which means that you can write unit tests for your code as well.

Listing 4.14 shows the content of `Hello.py`, which illustrates how to use `sys.argv` to check the number of command line parameters.

LISTING 4.14: Hello.py

```
import sys

def main():
  if len(sys.argv) >= 2:
    name = sys.argv[1]
```

```
    else:
      name = 'World'
    print('Hello', name)

# Standard boilerplate to invoke the main() function
if __name__ == '__main__':
main()
```

Listing 4.14 defines the `main()` function that checks the number of command-line parameters. If this value is at least 2, then the variable `name` is assigned the value of the second parameter (the first parameter is `Hello.py`), otherwise `name` is assigned the value `Hello`. The `print()` statement then prints the value of the variable `name`.

The final portion of Listing 4.14 uses conditional logic to determine whether to execute the `main()` function.

PRECEDENCE OF OPERATORS IN PYTHON

When you have an expression involving numbers, you might remember that multiplication (*) and division (/) have higher precedence than addition (+) or subtraction (-). Exponentiation has even higher precedence than these four arithmetic operators.

However, instead of relying on precedence rules, it's simpler (as well as safer) to use parentheses. For example, $(x/y)+10$ is clearer than $x/y+10$, even though they are equivalent expressions.

As another example, the following two arithmetic expressions are the equivalent, but the second is less error prone than the first:

```
x/y+3*z/8+x*y/z-3*x
(x/y)+(3*z)/8+(x*y)/z-(3*x)
```

In any case, the following Website contains precedence rules for operators in Python:

http://www.mathcs.emory.edu/~valerie/courses/fall10/155/resources/op_precedence.html

PYTHON RESERVED WORDS

Every programming language has a set of reserved words, which is a set of words that cannot be used as identifiers, and Python is no exception. Python's reserved words are: and, exec, not, assert, finally, or, break, for, pass, class, from, print, continue, global, raise, def, if, return, del, import, try, elif, in, while, else, is, with, except, lambda, and yield.

If you inadvertently use a reserved word as a variable, you will see an "invalid syntax" error message instead of a "reserved word" error message. For example, suppose you create a script `test1.py` with the following code:

```
break = 2
print('break =', break)
```

If you run the preceding code, you will see the following output:

```
File "test1.py", line 2
    break = 2
          ^
SyntaxError: invalid syntax
```

However, a quick inspection of the code reveals that you are attempting to use the reserved word `break` as a variable.

WORKING WITH LOOPS IN PYTHON

Python supports `for` loops, `while` loops, and `range()` statements. The following subsections illustrate how you can use each of these constructs.

Python For Loops

Python supports the `for` loop whose syntax is slightly different from other languages (such as JavaScript and Java). The following code block shows you how to use a `for` loop to iterate through the elements in a list:

```
>>> x = ['a', 'b', 'c']
>>> for w in x:
...     print(w)
...
a
b
c
```

The preceding code snippet prints three letters on three separate lines. You can force the output to be displayed on the same line (which will "wrap" if you specify a large enough number of characters) by appending a comma (,) in the `print()` statement, as shown here:

```
>>> x = ['a', 'b', 'c']
>>> for w in x:
...     print(w, end=' ')
...
a b c
```

You can use this type of code when you want to display the contents of a text file in a single line instead of multiple lines.

Python also provides the built-in `reversed()` function that reverses the direction of the loop, as shown here:

```
>>> a = [1, 2, 3, 4, 5]
>>> for x in reversed(a):
... print(x)
5
```

```
4
3
2
1
```

Note that reversed iteration only works if the size of the current object can be determined or if the object implements a __reversed__() special method.

A For Loop with `try/except` in Python

Listing 4.15 shows the content of StringToNums.py, which illustrates how to calculate the sum of a set of integers that have been converted from strings.

LISTING 4.15: StringToNums.py

```
line = '1 2 3 4 10e abc'
sum  = 0
invalidStr = ""

print('String of numbers:',line)

for str in line.split(" "):
  try:
    sum = sum + eval(str)
  except:
    invalidStr = invalidStr + str + ' '

print('sum:', sum)
if(invalidStr != ""):
  print('Invalid strings:',invalidStr)
else:
  print('All substrings are valid numbers')
```

Listing 4.15 initializes the variables line, sum, and invalidStr, and then displays the contents of line. The next portion of Listing 4.15 splits the contents of line into words, and then uses a try block in order to add the numeric value of each word to the variable sum. If an exception occurs, the contents of the current str are appended to the variable invalidStr.

When the loop has finished execution, Listing 4.15 displays the sum of the numeric words, followed by the list of words that are not numbers. The output from Listing 4.15 is here:

```
String of numbers: 1 2 3 4 10e abc
sum: 10
Invalid strings: 10e abc
```

Numeric Exponents in Python

Listing 4.16 shows the content of Nth_exponent.py, which illustrates how to calculate intermediate powers of a set of integers.

LISTING 4.16: Nth_exponent.py

```
maxPower = 4
maxCount = 4

def pwr(num):
  prod = 1
  for n in range(1,maxPower+1):
    prod = prod*num
    print(num,'to the power',n, 'equals',prod)
  print('-----------')

for num in range(1,maxCount+1):
  pwr(num)
```

Listing 4.16 contains a function called `pwr()` that accepts a numeric value. This function contains a loop that prints the value of that number raised to the power n, where n ranges between 1 and `maxPower+1`.

The second part of Listing 4.16 contains a `for` loop that invokes the function `pwr()` with the numbers between 1 and `maxPower+1`. The output from Listing 4.16 is as follows:

```
1 to the power 1 equals 1
1 to the power 2 equals 1
1 to the power 3 equals 1
1 to the power 4 equals 1
-----------
2 to the power 1 equals 2
2 to the power 2 equals 4
2 to the power 3 equals 8
2 to the power 4 equals 16
-----------
3 to the power 1 equals 3
3 to the power 2 equals 9
3 to the power 3 equals 27
3 to the power 4 equals 81
-----------
4 to the power 1 equals 4
4 to the power 2 equals 16
4 to the power 3 equals 64
4 to the power 4 equals 256
-----------
```

NESTED LOOPS

Listing 4.17 shows the content of `Triangular1.py`, which illustrates how to print a row of consecutive integers (starting from 1), where the length of each row is one greater than the previous row.

LISTING 4.17: Triangular1.py

```
max = 8
for x in range(1,max+1):
```

```
    for y in range(1,x+1):
        print(y, '', end='')
print()
```

Listing 4.17 initializes the variable max with the value 8, followed by an outer for loop whose loop variable x ranges from 1 to max+1. The inner loop has a loop variable y that ranges from 1 to x+1, and the inner loop prints the value of y. The output of Listing 4.17 is as follows:

```
1
1 2
1 2 3
1 2 3 4
1 2 3 4 5
1 2 3 4 5 6
1 2 3 4 5 6 7
1 2 3 4 5 6 7 8
```

THE SPLIT() FUNCTION WITH FOR LOOPS

Python supports various useful string-related functions, including the split() function and the join() function. The split() function is useful when you want to tokenize ("split") a line of text into words and then use a for loop to iterate through those words and process them accordingly.

The join() function does the opposite of split(): It "joins" two or more words into a single line. You can easily remove extra spaces in a sentence by using the split() function and then invoking the join() function, thereby creating a line of text with one white space between any two words.

USING THE SPLIT() FUNCTION TO COMPARE WORDS

Listing 4.18 shows the content of Compare2.py, which illustrates how to use the split function to compare each word in a text string with another word.

LISTING 4.18: Compare2.py

```
x = 'This is a string that contains abc and Abc'
y = 'abc'
identical = 0
casematch = 0

for w in x.split():
  if(w == y):
    identical = identical + 1
  elif (w.lower() == y.lower()):
    casematch = casematch + 1

if(identical > 0):
 print('found identical matches:', identical)

if(casematch > 0):
```

```
   print('found case matches:', casematch)

if(casematch == 0 and identical == 0):
   print('no matches found')
```

Listing 4.18 uses the `split()` function to compare each word in the string x with the word abc. If there is an exact match, the variable `identical` is incremented. If a match does not occur, a case-insensitive match of the current word is performed with the string abc, and the variable `casematch` is incremented if the match is successful.

The output from Listing 4.18 is here:

```
found identical matches: 1
found case matches: 1
```

USING THE `SPLIT()` FUNCTION TO PRINT JUSTIFIED TEXT

Listing 4.19 shows the content of `FixedColumnCount.py`, which illustrates how to print a set of words from a text string as justified text using a fixed number of columns.

LISTING 4.19: FixedColumnCount1.py

```python
import string

wordCount = 0
str1 = 'this is a string with a set of words in it'

print('Left-justified strings:')
print('------------------------')
for w in str1.split():
    print('%-10s' % w)
    wordCount = wordCount + 1
    if(wordCount % 2 == 0):
        print("")
print("\n")

print('Right-justified strings:')
print('------------------------')

wordCount = 0
for w in str1.split():
    print('%10s' % w)
    wordCount = wordCount + 1
    if(wordCount % 2 == 0):
        print()
```

Listing 4.19 initializes the variables `wordCount` and `str1`, followed by two `for` loops. The first `for` loop prints the words in `str1` in left-justified format, and the second `for` loop prints the words in `str1` in right-justified format. In both loops, a linefeed is printed after a pair of consecutive words is printed, which occurs whenever the variable `wordCount` is even. The output from Listing 4.19 is as follows:

```
Left-justified strings:
-----------------------
this        is
a           string
with        a
set         of
words       in
it

Right-justified strings:
-----------------------
        this        is
           a    string
        with         a
         set        of
       words        in
          it
```

USING THE `SPLIT()` FUNCTION TO PRINT FIXED WIDTH TEXT

Listing 4.20 shows the content of `FixedColumnWidth1.py`, which illustrates how to print a text string in a column of fixed width.

LISTING 4.20: FixedColumnWidth1.py

```
import string

left = 0
right = 0
columnWidth = 8

str1 = 'this is a string with a set of words in it and it
will be split into a fixed column width'
strLen = len(str1)

print('Left-justified column:')
print('-----------------------')
rowCount = int(strLen/columnWidth)

for i in range(0,rowCount):
    left  = i*columnWidth
    right = (i+1)*columnWidth-1
    word  = str1[left:right]
    print("%-10s" % word)

# check for a 'partial row'
if(rowCount*columnWidth < strLen):
    left  = rowCount*columnWidth-1;
    right = strLen
    word  = str1[left:right]
    print("%-10s" % word)
```

Listing 4.20 initializes the integer variable `columnWidth` and the string variable `str1`. The variable `strLen` is the length of `str1`, and `rowCount` is `strLen` divided by `columnWidth`.

The next part of Listing 4.20 contains a loop that prints `rowCount` rows of characters, where each row contains `columnWidth` characters. The final portion of Listing 4.20 prints any "leftover" characters that comprise a partial row.

The newspaper-style output (but without any partial whitespace formatting) from Listing 4.20 is here:

```
Left-justified column:
----------------------
this is
a strin
 with a
set of
ords in
it and
t will
e split
into a
ixed co
umn wid
th
```

USING THE `SPLIT()` FUNCTION TO COMPARE TEXT STRINGS

Listing 4.21 shows the content of `CompareStrings1.py`, which illustrates how to determine whether the words in one text string are also words in a second text string.

LISTING 4.21: CompareStrings1.py

```
text1 = 'a b c d'
text2 = 'a b c e d'

if(text2.find(text1) >= 0):
  print('text1 is a substring of text2')
else:
  print('text1 is not a substring of text2')

subStr = True
for w in text1.split():
  if(text2.find(w) == -1):
    subStr = False
    break

if(subStr == True):
  print('Every word in text1 is a word in text2')
else:
print('Not every word in text1 is a word in text2')
```

Listing 4.21 initializes the string variables `text1` and `text2`, and uses conditional logic to determine whether `text1` is a substring of `text2` (and then prints a suitable message).

The next part of Listing 4.21 is a loop that iterates through the words in the string `text1` and checks if each of those words is also a word in the string `text2`. If a non-match occurs, the variable `subStr` is set to "False," followed by the break statement that causes an early exit from the loop. The final portion of Listing 4.21 prints the appropriate message based on the value of `subStr`. The output from Listing 4.21 is as follows:

```
text1 is not a substring of text2
Every word in text1 is a word in text2
```

USING THE `SPLIT()` FUNCTION TO DISPLAY CHARACTERS IN A STRING

Listing 4.22 shows the content of `StringChars1.py`, which illustrates how to print the characters in a text string.

LISTING 4.22: StringChars1.py

```
text = 'abcdef'
for ch in text:
    print('char:',ch,'ord value:',ord(ch))
print
```

Listing 4.22 is straightforward: a `for` loop iterates through the characters in the string `text` and then prints the character and its `ord` value. The output from Listing 4.22 is here:

```
('char:', 'a', 'ord value:', 97)
('char:', 'b', 'ord value:', 98)
('char:', 'c', 'ord value:', 99)
('char:', 'd', 'ord value:', 100)
('char:', 'e', 'ord value:', 101)
('char:', 'f', 'ord value:', 102)
```

THE `JOIN()` FUNCTION

Another way to remove extraneous spaces is to use the `join()` function:

```
text1 = '   there are     extra    spaces    '
print('text1:',text1)

text2 = ' '.join(text1.split())
print('text2:',text2)

text2 = 'XYZ'.join(text1.split())
print('text2:',text2)
```

The split() function "splits" a text string into a set of words, and also removes the extraneous white spaces. Next, the join() function "joins" together the words in the string text1, using a single white space as the delimiter. The last code portion of the preceding code block uses the string XYZ as the delimiter instead of a single white space.

The output of the preceding code block is as follows:

```
text1:    there are    extra    spaces
text2: there are extra spaces
text2: thereXYZareXYZextraXYZspaces
```

PYTHON WHILE LOOPS

You can define a while loop to iterate through a set of numbers, as shown in the following examples:

```
>>> x = 0
>>> while x < 5:
...    print(x)
...    x = x + 1
...
0
1
2
3
4
5
```

Python uses indentations instead of the curly braces that are used in other languages such as JavaScript and Java. Although the list data structure is not discussed until later in this chapter, the following simple code block contains a variant of the preceding while loop that you can use when working with lists:

```
lst  = [1,2,3,4]

while lst:
  print('list:',lst)
print('item:',lst.pop())
```

The preceding while loop terminates when the lst variable is empty, and there is no need to explicitly test for an empty list. The output from the preceding code is here:

```
list: [1, 2, 3, 4]
item: 4
list: [1, 2, 3]
item: 3
list: [1, 2]
item: 2
list: [1]
item: 1
```

This concludes the examples that use the split() function to process words and characters in a text string. The next part of this chapter shows examples of using conditional logic.

CONDITIONAL LOGIC IN PYTHON

If you have written code in other programming languages, you have undoubtedly seen if/then/else (or if-elseif-else) conditional statements. Although the syntax varies between languages, the logic is essentially the same. The following example shows you how to use if/elif statements:

```
>>> x = 25
>>> if x < 0:
...     print('negative')
... elif x < 25:
...     print('under 25')
... elif x == 25:
...     print('exactly 25')
... else:
...     print('over 25')
...
exactly 25
```

The preceding code block illustrates how to use multiple conditional statements, and the output is exactly what you expected.

THE BREAK/CONTINUE/PASS STATEMENTS

The break statement enables you to perform an "early exit" from a loop, whereas the continue statement essentially returns to the top of the loop and continues with the next value of the loop variable. The pass statement is essentially a "do nothing" statement.

Listing 4.23 shows the content of BreakContinuePass.py, which illustrates the use of these three statements.

LISTING 4.23: BreakContinuePass.py

```
print('first loop')
for x in range(1,4):
  if(x == 2):
    break
  print(x)

print('second loop')
for x in range(1,4):
  if(x == 2):
    continue
  print(x)

print('third loop')
```

```
for x in range(1,4):
  if(x == 2):
     pass
print(x)
```

The output of Listing 4.23 is as follows:

```
first loop
1
second loop
1
3
third loop
1
2
3
```

COMPARISON AND BOOLEAN OPERATORS

Python supports a variety of Boolean operators, such as `in, not in, is, is not, and, or,` and `not`. The next several sections discuss these operators and provide some examples of how to use them.

The `in/not in/is/is not` Comparison Operators

The `in` and `not in` operators are used with sequences to check whether a value occurs or does not occur in a sequence. The operators `is` and `is not` determine whether two objects are the same object, which is important for mutable objects such as lists. All comparison operators have the same priority, which is lower than that of all numerical operators. Comparisons can also be chained. For example, `a < b == c` tests whether `a` is less than `b` and moreover `b` equals `c`.

The `and`, `or`, and `not` Boolean Operators

The Boolean operators `and`, `or`, and `not` have lower priority than comparison operators. The Boolean `and` and `or` are binary operators whereas the Boolean `or` operator is a unary operator. Here are some examples:

`A and B` can only be true if both A and B are true
`A or B` is true if either A or B is true
`not(A)` is true if and only if A is false

You can also assign the result of a comparison or other `Boolean` expression to a variable, as shown here:

```
>>> string1, string2, string3 = '', 'b', 'cd'
>>> str4 = string1 or string2 or string3
>>> str4
'b'
```

The preceding code block initializes the variables `string1`, `string2`, and `string3`, where `string1` is an empty string. Next, `str4` is initialized via the `or` operator, and since the first non-null value is `string2`, the value of `str4` is equal to `string2`.

LOCAL AND GLOBAL VARIABLES

Python variables can be local or global. A variable is local to a function if the following are true:

a parameter of the function
on the left-side of a statement in the function
bound to a control structure (such as `for`, `with`, and `except`)

A variable that is referenced in a function but is not local (according to the previous list) is a non-local variable. You can specify a variable as non-local with this snippet:

```
nonlocal z
```

A variable can be explicitly declared as global with this statement:

```
global z
```

The following code block illustrates the behavior of a global versus a local variable:

```
global z
z = 3

def changeVar(z):
  z = 4
  print('z in function:',z)

print('first global z:',z)

if __name__ == '__main__':
  changeVar(z)
print('second global z:',z)
```

The output from the preceding code block is here:

```
first global z: 3
z in function: 4
second global z: 3
```

SCOPE OF VARIABLES

The accessibility or scope of a variable depends on where that variable has been defined. Python provides two scopes: global and local, with the added "twist" that global is actually module-level scope (i.e., the current file), and therefore you can have a variable with the same name in different files and they will be treated differently.

Local variables are straightforward: they are defined inside a function, and they can only be accessed inside the function where they are defined. Any variables that are not local variables have a global scope, which means that those variables are "global" *only* with respect to the file where it has been defined, and they can be accessed anywhere in a file.

There are two scenarios to consider regarding variables. First, suppose two files (aka modules) `file1.py` and `file2.py` have a variable called x, and `file1.py` also imports `file2.py`. The question now is how to disambiguate between the x in the two different modules. As an example, suppose that `file2.py` contains the following two lines of code:

```
x = 3
print('unscoped x in file2:',x)
```

Suppose that `file1.py` contains the following code:

```
import file2 as file2

x = 5
print('unscoped x in file1:',x)
print('scoped x from file2:',file2.x)
```

Launch `file1.py` from the command line, and you will see the following output:

```
unscoped x in file2: 3
unscoped x in file1: 5
scoped x from file2: 3
```

The second scenario involves a program contains a local variable and a global variable with the same name. According to the earlier rule, the local variable is used in the function where it is defined, and the global variable is used outside of that function.

The following code block illustrates the use of a global and local variable with the same name:

```
#!/usr/bin/python
# a global variable:
total = 0;

def sum(x1, x2):
    # this total is local:
    total = x1+x2;

    print("Local total : ", total)
    return total

# invoke the sum function
sum(2,3);
print("Global total : ", total)
```

When the above code is executed, it produces following result:

```
Local total :   5
Global total :  0
```

What about un-scoped variables, such as specifying the variable x without a module prefix? The answer consists of the following sequence of steps that Python will perform:

1. Check the local scope for the name.
2. Ascend the enclosing scopes and check for the name.
3. Perform Step #2 until you reach the global scope (i.e., the module level).
4. If x still hasn't been found, Python checks__builtins_

```
Python 3.9.1 (v3.9.1:1e5d33e9b9, Dec 7 2020, 12:44:01)
[Clang 12.0.0 (clang-1200.0.32.27)] on darwin
Type "help", "copyright", "credits" or "license" for more
information.
>>> x = 1
>>> g = globals()
>>> g
{'g': {...}, '__builtins__': <module '__builtin__' (built-
in)>, '__package__': None, 'x': 1, '__name__': '__main__',
'__doc__': None}
>>> g.pop('x')
1
>>> x
Traceback (most recent call last):
  File "<stdin>", line 1, in <module>
NameError: name 'x' is not defined
```

NOTE *You can access the* dicts *that Python uses to track local and global scope by invoking* locals() *and* globals(), *respectively.*

PASS BY REFERENCE VERSUS VALUE

All parameters (arguments) in the Python language are passed by reference. Thus, if you change what a parameter refers to within a function, the change is reflected in the calling function. For example:

```
def changeme(mylist):
    #This changes a passed list into this function
    mylist.append([1,2,3,4])
    print("Values inside the function: ", mylist)
    return

# Now you can call changeme function
mylist = [10,20,30]
changeme(mylist)
print("Values outside the function: ", mylist)
```

Here we are maintaining reference of the passed object and appending values in the same object, and the result is shown here:

```
Values inside the function:   [10, 20, 30, [1, 2, 3, 4]]
Values outside the function:   [10, 20, 30, [1, 2, 3, 4]]
```

The fact that values are passed by reference gives rise to the notion of mutability versus immutability that is discussed in Chapter 3.

ARGUMENTS AND PARAMETERS

Python differentiates between arguments to functions and parameter declarations in functions: a positional (mandatory) and keyword (optional/default value). This concept is important because Python has operators for packing and unpacking these kinds of arguments.

Python unpacks positional arguments from an iterable, as shown here:

```
>>> def foo(x, y):
...     return x - y
...
>>> data = 4,5
>>> foo(data) # only passed one arg
Traceback (most recent call last):
  File "<stdin>", line 1, in <module>
TypeError: foo() takes exactly 2 arguments (1 given)
>>> foo(*data) # passed however many args are in tuple
-1
```

USING A WHILE LOOP TO FIND THE DIVISORS OF A NUMBER

Listing 4.24 contains a `while` loop, conditional logic, and the `%` (modulus) operator in order to find the factors of any integer greater than 1.

LISTING 4.24: Divisors.py

```
def divisors(num):
  div = 2

  while(num > 1):
    if(num % div == 0):
      print("divisor: ", div)
      num = num / div
    else:
      div = div + 1
  print("** finished **")

divisors(12)
```

Listing 4.24 defines a function `divisors()` that takes an integer value `num` and then initializes the variable `div` with the value 2. The `while` loop divides `num` by `div` and if the remainder is 0, it prints the value of `div` and then it divides num by div; if the value is not 0, then div is incremented by 1. This while loop continues as long as the value of num is greater than 1.

The output from Listing 4.24 passing in the value 12 to the function divisors() is as follows:

```
divisor:   2
divisor:   2
divisor:   3
** finished **
```

Listing 4.25 shows the content of Divisors2.py, which contains a while loop, conditional logic, and the % (modulus) operator in order to find the factors of any integer greater than 1.

LISTING 4.25: Divisors2.py

```
def divisors(num):
  primes = ""
  div = 2

  while(num > 1):
    if(num % div == 0):
       divList = divList + str(div) + ' '
       num = num / div
    else:
       div = div + 1
  return divList

result = divisors(12)
print('The divisors of',12,'are:',result)
```

Listing 4.25 is very similar to Listing 4.24. The main difference is that Listing 4.25 constructs the variable divList (which is a concatenated list of the divisors of a number) in the while loop, and then returns the value of divList when the while loop has completed. The output from Listing 4.25 is as follows:

```
The divisors of 12 are: 2 2 3
```

Using a While Loop to Find Prime Numbers

Listing 4.26 shows the content of Divisors3.py, which contains a while loop, conditional logic, and the % (modulus) operator to count the number of prime factors of any integer greater than 1. If there is only one divisor for a number, then that number is a prime number.

LISTING 4.26: Divisors3.py

```
def divisors(num):
  count = 1
  div = 2
  while(div < num):
    if(num % div == 0):
```

```
        count = count + 1
      div = div + 1
    return count

result = divisors(12)

if(result == 1):
  print('12 is prime')
else:
print('12 is not prime')
```

USER-DEFINED FUNCTIONS IN PYTHON

Python provides built-in functions and also enables you to define your own functions. You can define functions to provide the required functionality. Here are simple rules to define a function:

Function blocks begin with the keyword `def` followed by the function name and parentheses.

Any input arguments should be placed within these parentheses.

The first statement of a function can be an optional statement – the documentation string of the function or `docstring`.

The code block within every function starts with a colon (:) and is indented.

The statement `return [expression]` exits a function, optionally passing back an expression to the caller. A return statement with no arguments is the same as `return None`.

If a function does not specify return statement, the function automatically returns None, which is a special type of value.

A very simple custom `Python` function is here:

```
>>> def func():
...    print 3
...
>>> func()
3
```

The preceding function is trivial, but it does illustrate the syntax for defining custom functions. The following example is slightly more useful:

```
>>> def func(x):
...    for i in range(0,x):
...        print(i)
...
>>> func(5)
0
1
2
3
4
```

SPECIFYING DEFAULT VALUES IN A FUNCTION

Listing 4.27 shows the content of `DefaultValues.py`, which illustrates how to specify default values in a function.

LISTING 4.27: DefaultValues.py

```
def numberFunc(a, b=10):
  print (a,b)

def stringFunc(a, b='xyz'):
  print (a,b)

def collectionFunc(a, b=None):
  if(b is None):
    print('No value assigned to b')

numberFunc(3)
stringFunc('one')
collectionFunc([1,2,3])
```

Listing 4.27 defines three functions, followed by an invocation of each of those functions. The functions `numberFunc()` and `stringFunc()` print a list contain the values of their two parameters, and `collectionFunc()` displays a message if the second parameter is `None`. The output from Listing 4.27 is here:

```
(3, 10)
('one', 'xyz')
No value assigned to b
```

Returning Multiple Values from a Function

This task is accomplished by the code in Listing 4.28, which shows the content of `MultipleValues.py`.

LISTING 4.28: MultipleValues.py

```
def MultipleValues():
    return 'a', 'b', 'c'

x, y, z = MultipleValues()

print('x:',x)
print('y:',y)
print('z:',z)
```

The output from Listing 4.28 is as follows:

```
x: a
y: b
z: c
```

FUNCTIONS WITH A VARIABLE NUMBER OF ARGUMENTS

Python enables you to define functions with a variable number of arguments. This functionality is useful in many situations, such as computing the sum, average, or product of a set of numbers. For example, the following code block computes the sum of two numbers:

```
def sum(a, b):
    return a + b

values = (1, 2)
s1 = sum(*values)
print('s1 = ', s1)
```

The output of the preceding code block is as follows:

```
s1 =   3
```

However, the sum() function in the preceding code block can only be used for two numeric values.

Listing 4.29 shows the content of VariableSum1.py, which illustrates how to compute the sum of a variable number of numbers.

LISTING 4.29: VariableSum1.py

```
def sum(*values):
  sum = 0
  for x in values:
    sum = sum + x
  return sum

values1 = (1, 2)
s1 = sum(*values1)
print('s1 = ',s1)

values2 = (1, 2, 3, 4)
s2 = sum(*values2)
print('s2 = ',s2)
```

Listing 4.29 defines the function sum() whose parameter values can be an arbitrary list of numbers. The next portion of this function initializes the variable sum to 0, and then a for loop iterates through values and adds each of its elements to the variable sum. The last line in the function sum() returns the value of the variable sum. The output from Listing 4.29 is here:

```
s1 =   3
s2 =   10
```

LAMBDA EXPRESSIONS

Listing 4.30 shows the content of Lambda1.py, which illustrates how to create a simple lambda function.

LISTING 4.30: Lambda1.py

```
add = lambda x, y: x + y

x1 = add(5,7)
x2 = add('Hello', 'Python')

print(x1)
print(x2)
```

Listing 4.30 defines the lambda expression add that accepts two input parameters and then returns their sum (for numbers) or their concatenation (for strings).

The output from Listing 4.30 is as follows:

```
12
HelloPython
```

RECURSION

Recursion is a powerful technique that can provide an elegant solution to various problems. The following subsections contain examples of using recursion to calculate some well-known numbers.

Calculating Factorial Values

The factorial value of a positive integer n is the product of all the integers between 1 and n. The symbol for factorial is the exclamation point ("!") and some sample factorial values are as follows:

```
1! = 1
2! = 2
3! = 6
4! = 20
5! = 120
```

The formula for the factorial value of a number is succinctly defined as

```
Factorial(n) = n*Factorial(n-1) for n > 1 and Factorial(1) = 1
```

Listing 4.31 shows the content of Factorial.py, which illustrates how to use recursion in order to calculate the factorial value of a positive integer.

LISTING 4.31: Factorial.py

```
def factorial(num):
  if (num > 1):
    return num * factorial(num-1)
  else:
    return 1

result = factorial(5)
print('The factorial of 5 =', result)
```

Listing 4.31 contains the function `factorial` that implements the recursive definition of the factorial value of a number. The output from Listing 4.31 is here:

```
The factorial of 5 = 120
```

In addition to a recursive solution, there is also an iterative solution for calculating the factorial value of a number. Listing 4.32 shows the contents of `Factorial2.py` that illustrate how to use the `range()` function to calculate the factorial value of a positive integer.

LISTING 4.32: Factorial2.py

```
def factorial2(num):
  prod = 1
  for x in range(1,num+1):
    prod = prod * x
  return prod

result = factorial2(5)
print 'The factorial of 5 =', result
```

Listing 4.32 defines the function `factorial2()` with a parameter `num`, followed by the variable `prod` that has an initial value of 1. The next part of `factorial2()` is a loop whose loop variable x ranges between 1 and `num+1`, and each iteration through that loop multiples the value of `prod` with the value of x, thereby computing the factorial value of `num`. The output from Listing 4.32 is here:

```
The factorial of 5 = 120
```

Calculating Fibonacci Numbers

The set of Fibonacci numbers represent some interesting patterns (such as the pattern of a sunflower) in nature, and its recursive definition is as follows:

```
Fib(0) = 0
Fib(1) = 1
Fib(n) = Fib(n-1) + Fib(n-2) for n >= 2
```

Listing 4.33 shows the content of `fib.py` that illustrates how to calculate Fibonacci numbers.

LISTING 4.33: fib.py

```
def fib(num):
  if (num == 0):
    return 1
  elif (num == 1):
    return 1
  else:
    return fib(num-1) + fib(num-2)
```

```
result = fib(10)
print('Fibonacci value of 5 =', result)
```

Listing 4.33 defines the fib() function with the parameter num. If num equals 0 or 1 then fib() returns num; otherwise, fib() returns the result of adding fib(num-1) and fib(num-2). The output from Listing 4.33 is as follows:

```
Fibonacci value of 10 = 89
```

The next portion of this chapter discusses Python collections, such as lists (or arrays), sets, tuples, and dictionaries. We provide many short code blocks that will help to work with these data structures. After you have finished reading this chapter, you will be in a better position to create more complex Python modules using one or more of these data structures.

WORKING WITH LISTS

Python supports a list data type, along with a rich set of list-related functions. Since lists are not typed, you can create a list of different data types, as well as multidimensional lists. The next several sections show you how to manipulate list structures.

Lists and Basic Operations

A list consists of comma-separated values enclosed in a pair of square brackets. The following examples illustrate the syntax for defining a list, and also how to perform various operations on a list:

```
>>> list = [1, 2, 3, 4, 5]
>>> list
[1, 2, 3, 4, 5]
>>> list[2]
3
>>> list2 = list + [1, 2, 3, 4, 5]
>>> list2
[1, 2, 3, 4, 5, 1, 2, 3, 4, 5]
>>> list2.append(6)
>>> list2
[1, 2, 3, 4, 5, 1, 2, 3, 4, 5, 6]
>>> len(list)
5
>>> x = ['a', 'b', 'c']
>>> y = [1, 2, 3]
>>> z = [x, y]
>>> z[0]
['a', 'b', 'c']
>>> len(x)
3
```

You can assign multiple variables to a list, provided that the number and type of the variables match the structure. Here is an example:

```
>>> point = [7,8]
```

```
>>> x,y = point
>>> x
7
>>> y
8
```

The following example shows you how to assign values to variables from a more complex data structure:

```
>>> line = ['a', 10, 20, (2014,01,31)]
>>> x1,x2,x3,date1 = line
>>> x1
'a'
>>> x2
10
>>> x3
20
>>> date1
(2014, 1, 31)
```

If you want to access the year/month/date components of the `date1` element in the preceding code block, you can do so with the following code block:

```
>>> line = ['a', 10, 20, (2014,01,31)]
>>> x1,x2,x3,(year,month,day) = line
>>> x1
'a'
>>> x2
10
>>> x3
20
>>> year
2014
>>> month
1
>>> day
31
```

If the number and/or structure of the variables do not match the data, an error message is displayed, as shown here:

```
>>> point = (1,2)
>>> x,y,z = point
Traceback (most recent call last):
  File "<stdin>", line 1, in <module>
ValueError: need more than 2 values to unpack
```

If the number of variables that you specify is less than the number of data items, you will see an error message, as shown here:

```
>>> line = ['a', 10, 20, (2014,01,31)]
>>> x1,x2 = line
Traceback (most recent call last):
  File "<stdin>", line 1, in <module>
ValueError: too many values to unpack
```

Reversing and Sorting a List

The `reverse()` method reverses the contents of a list:

```
>>> a = [4, 1, 2, 3]
>>> a.reverse()
[3, 2, 1, 4]
```

The `sort()` method sorts a list:

```
>>> a = [4, 1, 2, 3]
>>> a.sort()
[1, 2, 3, 4]
```

You can sort a list and then reverse its contents:

```
>>> a = [4, 1, 2, 3]
>>> a.reverse(a.sort())
[4, 3, 2, 1]
```

Another way to reverse a list:

```
>>> L = [0,10,20,40]
>>> L[::-1]
[40, 20, 10, 0]
```

Keep in mind is that `reversed(array)` is an iterable and not a list. However, you can convert the reversed array to a list with this code snippet:

```
list(reversed(array)) or L[::-1]
```

Listing 4.34 contains a `while` loop whose logic is the opposite of the listing in the previous section: If num is divisible by multiple numbers (each of which is strictly less than num), then num is not prime.

LISTING 4.34: Uppercase1.py

```
list1 = ['a', 'list', 'of', 'words']
list2 = [s.upper() for s in list1]
list3 = [s for s in list1 if len(s) <=2 ]
list4 = [s for s in list1 if 'w' in s ]

print('list1:',list1)
print('list2:',list2)
print('list3:',list3)
print('list4:',list4)
```

The output from launching the code in Listing 4.34 is as follows:

```
list1: ['a', 'list', 'of', 'words']
list2: ['A', 'LIST', 'OF', 'WORDS']
list3: ['a', 'of']
list4: ['words']
```

Lists and Arithmetic Operations

The minimum value of a list of numbers is the first number in the sorted list of numbers. If you reverse the sorted list, the first number is the maximum value. There are several ways to reverse a list, starting with the technique shown in the following code:

```
x = [3,1,2,4]
maxList = x.sort()
minList = x.sort(x.reverse())

min1 = min(x)
max1 = max(x)
print min1
print max1
```

The output of the preceding code block is here:

```
1
4
```

A second (and better) way to sort a list is as follows:

```
minList = x.sort(reverse=True)
```

A third way to sort a list involves the built-in functional version of the `sort()` method, as shown here:

```
sorted(x, reverse=True)
```

The preceding code snippet is useful when you do not want to modify the original order of the list or you want to compose multiple list operations on a single line.

Lists and Filter-related Operations

Python enables you to filter a list (also called list comprehension) as shown here:

```
mylist = [1, -2, 3, -5, 6, -7, 8]
pos = [n for n in mylist if n > 0]
neg = [n for n in mylist if n < 0]

print pos
print neg
```

You can also specify `if/else` logic in a filter, as follows:

```
mylist = [1, -2, 3, -5, 6, -7, 8]
negativeList = [n if n < 0 else 0 for n in mylist]
positiveList = [n if n > 0 else 0 for n in mylist]

print positiveList
print negativeList
```

The output of the preceding code block is here:

```
[1, 3, 6, 8]
[-2, -5, -7]
[1, 0, 3, 0, 6, 0, 8]
[0, -2, 0, -5, 0, -7, 0]
```

SORTING LISTS OF NUMBERS AND STRINGS

Listing 4.35 shows the content of the script `Sorted1.py` that determines whether two lists are sorted.

LISTING 4.35: Sorted1.py

```
list1 = [1,2,3,4,5]
list2 = [2,1,3,4,5]

sort1 = sorted(list1)
sort2 = sorted(list2)

if(list1 == sort1):
  print(list1,'is sorted')
else:
  print(list1,'is not sorted')

if(list2 == sort2):
  print(list2,'is sorted')
else:
print(list2,'is not sorted')
```

Listing 4.35 initializes the lists `list1` and `list2`, and the sorted lists `sort1` and `sort2` based on the lists `list1` and `list2`, respectively. If `list1` equals `sort1` then `list1` is already sorted; similarly, if `list2` equals `sort2` then `list2` is already sorted.

The output from Listing 4.35 is as follows:

```
[1, 2, 3, 4, 5] is sorted
[2, 1, 3, 4, 5] is not sorted
```

Note that if you sort a list of character strings, the output is case sensitive, and that uppercase letters appear before lowercase letters. This is due to the fact that the collating sequence for ASCII places uppercase letters (decimal 65 through decimal 91) before lowercase letters (decimal 97 through decimal 127). The following example provides an illustration:

```
>>> list1 = ['a', 'A', 'b', 'B', 'Z']
>>> print sorted(list1)
['A', 'B', 'Z', 'a', 'b']
```

You can also specify the reverse option so that the list is sorted in reverse order:

```
>>> list1 = ['a', 'A', 'b', 'B', 'Z']
```

```
>>> print sorted(list1, reverse=True)
['b', 'a', 'Z', 'B', 'A']
```

You can even sort a list based on the length of the items in the list:

```
>>> list1 = ['a', 'AA', 'bbb', 'BBBBB', 'ZZZZZZZ']
>>> print sorted(list1, key=len)
['a', 'AA', 'bbb', 'BBBBB', 'ZZZZZZZ']
>>> print sorted(list1, key=len, reverse=True)
['ZZZZZZZ', 'BBBBB', 'bbb', 'AA', 'a']
```

You can specify str.lower if you want treat uppercase letters as though they are lowercase letters during the sorting operation, as shown here:

```
>>> print sorted(list1, key=str.lower)
['a', 'AA', 'bbb', 'BBBBB', 'ZZZZZZZ']
```

EXPRESSIONS IN LISTS

The following construct is similar to a for loop but without the colon (:) character that appears at the end of a loop construct. Consider the following example:

```
nums = [1, 2, 3, 4]
cubes = [ n*n*n for n in nums ]

print 'nums: ',nums
print 'cubes:',cubes
```

The output from the preceding code block is here:

```
nums:  [1, 2, 3, 4]
cubes: [1, 8, 27, 64]
```

CONCATENATING A LIST OF WORDS

Python provides the join() method for concatenating text strings:

```
>>> parts = ['Is', 'SF', 'In', 'California?']
>>> ' '.join(parts)
'Is SF In California?'
>>> ','.join(parts)
'Is,SF,In,California?'
>>> ''.join(parts) 'IsSFInCalifornia?'
```

There are several ways to concatenate a set of strings and then print the result. The following is the most inefficient way to do so:

```
print "This" + " is" + " a" + " sentence"
Either of the following is preferred:
print "%s %s %s %s" % ("This", "is", "a", "sentence")
print " ".join(["This","is","a","sentence"])
```

THE PYTHON RANGE() FUNCTION

In this section, we discuss the range() function that you can use to iterate through a list, as shown here:

```
>>> for i in range(0,5):
...     print i
...
0
1
2
3
4
```

You can use a for loop to iterate through a list of strings, as shown here:

```
>>> x
['a', 'b', 'c']
>>> for w in x:
...     print w
...
a
b
c
```

You can use a for loop to iterate through a list of strings and provide additional details, as shown here:

```
>>> x
['a', 'b', 'c']
>>> for w in x:
...     print len(w), w
...
1 a
1 b
1 c
```

The preceding output displays the length of each word in the list x, followed by the word itself.

Counting Digits, Uppercase, and Lowercase Letters

Listing 4.36 shows the content of the script CountCharTypes.py that counts the occurrences of digits and letters in a string.

LISTING 4.36: Counter1.py

```
str1 = "abc4234AFde"
digitCount = 0
alphaCount = 0
upperCount = 0
lowerCount = 0

for i in range(0,len(str1)):
```

```
  char = str1[i]
  if(char.isdigit()):
   #print("this is a digit:",char)
    digitCount += 1
  elif(char.isalpha()):
   #print("this is alphabetic:",char)
    alphaCount  += 1
    if(char.upper() == char):
      upperCount  += 1
    else:
      lowerCount  += 1

print('Original String:    ',str1)
print('Number of digits:   ',digitCount)
print('Total alphanumeric:',alphaCount)
print('Upper Case Count:   ',upperCount)
print('Lower Case Count:   ',lowerCount)
```

Listing 4.36 initializes counter-related variables, followed by a loop (with loop variable i) that iterates from 0 to the length of the string str1. The string variable char is initialized with the letter at index i of the string str1. The next portion of the loop uses conditional logic to determine whether char is a digit or an alphabetic character; in the latter case, the code checks whether the character is uppercase or lowercase. In all cases, the values of the appropriate counter-related variables are incremented.

The output of Listing 4.36 is here:

```
Original String:    abc4234AFde
Number of digits:   4
Total alphanumeric: 7
Upper Case Count:   2
Lower Case Count:   5
```

ARRAYS AND THE APPEND() FUNCTION

Although Python does have an array type (import array), which is essentially a heterogeneous list, the array type has no advantages over the list type other than a slight saving in memory use. You can also define heterogeneous arrays:

```
a = [10, 'hello', [5, '77']]
```

You can append a new element to an element inside a list:

```
>>> a = [10, 'hello', [5, '77']]
>>> a[2].append('abc')
>>> a
[10, 'hello', [5, '77', 'abc']]
```

You can assign simple variables to the elements of a list, as shown here:

```
myList = [ 'a', 'b', 91.1, (2014, 01, 31) ]
```

```
x1, x2, x3, x4 = myList
print 'x1:',x1
print 'x2:',x2
print 'x3:',x3
print 'x4:',x4
```

The output of the preceding code block is here:

```
x1: a
x2: b
x3: 91.1
x4: (2014, 1, 31)
```

The `split()` function is more convenient (especially when the number of elements is unknown or variable) than the preceding sample, and you will see examples of the `split()` function in the next section.

WORKING WITH LISTS AND THE SPLIT() FUNCTION

You can use the `split()` function to split the words in a text string and populate a list with those words. An example is here:

```
>>> x = "this is a string"
>>> list = x.split()
>>> list
['this', 'is', 'a', 'string']
```

A simple way to print the list of words in a text string is as follows:

```
>>> x = "this is a string"
>>> for w in x.split():
...     print w
...
this
is
a
string
```

You can also search for a word in a string:

```
>>> x = "this is a string"
>>> for w in x.split():
...     if(w == 'this'):
...         print "x contains this"
...
x contains this
...
```

COUNTING WORDS IN A LIST

Python provides the `Counter` class that enables you to count the words in a list. Listing 4.37 shows the content of `CountWord2.py` that displays the top three words with the greatest frequency.

LISTING 4.37: CountWord2.py

```
from collections import Counter

mywords = ['a', 'b', 'a', 'b', 'c', 'a', 'd', 'e', 'f', 'b']

word_counts = Counter(mywords)
topThree = word_counts.most_common(3)
print(topThree)
```

Listing 4.37 initializes the variable `mywords` with a set of characters and then initializes the variable `word_counts` by passing `mywords` as an argument to `Counter`. The variable `topThree` is an array containing the three most common characters (and their frequency) that appear in `mywords`. The output from Listing 4.37 is here:

```
[('a', 3), ('b', 3), ('c', 1)]
```

ITERATING THROUGH PAIRS OF LISTS

Python supports operations on pairs of lists, which means that you can perform vector-like operations. The following snippet multiplies every list element by 3:

```
>>> list1 = [1, 2, 3]
>>> [3*x for x in list1]
[3, 6, 9]
```

Create a new list with pairs of elements consisting of the original element and the original element multiplied by 3:

```
>>> list1 = [1, 2, 3]
>>> [[x, 3*x] for x in list1]
[[1, 3], [2, 6], [3, 9]]
```

Compute the product of every pair of numbers from two lists:

```
>>> list1 = [1, 2, 3]
>>> list2 = [5, 6, 7]
>>> [a*b for a in list1 for b in list2]
[5, 6, 7, 10, 12, 14, 15, 18, 21]
```

Calculate the sum of every pair of numbers from two lists:

```
>>> list1 = [1, 2, 3]
>>> list2 = [5, 6, 7]
>>> [a+b for a in list1 for b in list2]
[6, 7, 8, 7, 8, 9, 8, 9, 10]
```

Calculate the pair-wise product of two lists:

```
>>> [list1[i]*list2[i] for i in range(len(list1))]
[8, 12, -54]
```

OTHER LIST-RELATED FUNCTIONS

Python provides additional functions that you can use with lists, such as ap-pend(), insert(), delete(), pop(), and extend(). It also supports the functions index(), count(), sort(), and reverse(). Examples of these functions are illustrated in the following code block.

Define a list (notice that duplicates are allowed):

```
>>> a = [1, 2, 3, 2, 4, 2, 5]
```

Display the number of occurrences of 1 and 2:

```
>>> print a.count(1), a.count(2)
1 3
```

Insert -8 in position 3:

```
>>> a.insert(3,-8)
>>> a
[1, 2, 3, -8, 2, 4, 2, 5]
```

Remove occurrences of 3:

```
>>> a.remove(3)
>>> a
[1, 2, -8, 2, 4, 2, 5]
```

Remove occurrences of 1:

```
>>> a.remove(1)
>>> a
[2, -8, 2, 4, 2, 5]
```

Append 19 to the list:

```
>>> a.append(19)
>>> a
[2, -8, 2, 4, 2, 5, 19]
```

Print the index of 19 in the list:
```
>>> a.index(19)
6
```

Reverse the list:

```
>>> a.reverse()
>>> a
[19, 5, 2, 4, 2, -8, 2]
```

Sort the list:
```
>>> a.sort()
>>> a
[-8, 2, 2, 2, 4, 5, 19]
```

Extend list a with list b:

```
>>> b = [100,200,300]
>>> a.extend(b)
>>> a
[-8, 2, 2, 2, 4, 5, 19, 100, 200, 300]
```

Remove the first occurrence of 2:

```
>>> a.pop(2)
2
>>> a
[-8, 2, 2, 4, 5, 19, 100, 200, 300]
```

Remove the last item of the list:

```
>>> a.pop()
300
>>> a
[-8, 2, 2, 4, 5, 19, 100, 200]
```

Now that you understand how to use list-related operations, the next section shows you how to work with vectors.

WORKING WITH VECTORS

A vector is a one-dimensional array of values, and you can perform vector-based operations, such as addition, subtraction, and the inner product. Listing 4.38 shows the content of MyVectors.py that illustrates how to perform vector-based operations.

LISTING 4.38: MyVectors.py

```
v1 = [1,2,3]
v2 = [1,2,3]
v3 = [5,5,5]

s1 = [0,0,0]
d1 = [0,0,0]
p1 = 0

print("Initial Vectors"
print('v1:',v1)
print('v2:',v2)
print('v3:',v3)

for i in range(len(v1)):
    d1[i] = v3[i] - v2[i]
    s1[i] = v3[i] + v2[i]
    p1    = v3[i] * v2[i] + p1

print("After operations")
print('d1:',d1)
```

```
print('s1:',s1)
print('p1:',p1)
```

Listing 4.38 starts with the definition of three lists, each of which represents a vector. The lists d1 and s1 represent the difference of v2 and the sum v2, respectively. The number p1 represents the inner product (also called the "dot product") of v3 and v2. The output from Listing 4.38 is here:

```
Initial Vectors
v1: [1, 2, 3]
v2: [1, 2, 3]
v3: [5, 5, 5]

After operations
d1: [4, 3, 2]
s1: [6, 7, 8]
p1: 30
```

WORKING WITH MATRICES

A two-dimensional matrix is a two-dimensional array of values. The following code block illustrates how to access different elements in a 2D matrix:

```
mm = [["a","b","c"],["d","e","f"],["g","h","i"]];
print 'mm:        ',mm
print 'mm[0]:     ',mm[0]
print 'mm[0][1]:',mm[0][1]
```

The output from the preceding code block is as follows:

```
mm:        [['a', 'b', 'c'], ['d', 'e', 'f'], ['g', 'h', 'i']]
mm[0]:     ['a', 'b', 'c']
mm[0][1]: b
```

Listing 4.39 shows the content of My2DMatrix.py that illustrates how to create and populate 2 two-dimensional matrices.

LISTING 4.39: My2DMatrix.py

```
rows = 3
cols = 3

my2DMatrix = [[0 for i in range(rows)] for j in
range(rows)]
print('Before:',my2DMatrix)

for row in range(rows):
  for col in range(cols):
    my2DMatrix[row][col] = row*row+col*col
print('After: ',my2DMatrix)
```

Listing 4.39 initializes the variables rows and columns and then uses them to create the rows x cols matrix my2DMatrix whose values are initially 0.

The next part of Listing 4.39 contains a nested loop that initializes the element of my2DMatrix whose position is (row,col) with the value row*row+col*col. The last line of code in Listing 4.39 prints the contents of my2DArray. The output from Listing 4.39 is here:

```
Before:  [[0, 0, 0], [0, 0, 0], [0, 0, 0]]
After:   [[0, 1, 4], [1, 2, 5], [4, 5, 8]]
```

QUEUES

A queue is a FIFO ("First In, First Out") data structure. Thus, the oldest item in a queue is removed when a new item is added to a queue that is already full.

Earlier in the chapter you learned how to use a list to emulate a queue. However, there is also a queue object in Python. The following code snippets illustrate how to use a queue.

```
>>> from collections import deque
>>> q = deque('',maxlen=10)
>>> for i in range(10,20):
...     q.append(i)
...
>>> print q
deque([10, 11, 12, 13, 14, 15, 16, 17, 18, 19], maxlen=10)
```

TUPLES (IMMUTABLE LISTS)

Python supports a data type called a *tuple* that consists of comma-separated values without brackets (square brackets are for lists, round brackets are for arrays, and curly braces are for dictionaries). Various examples of tuples can be found online:

https://docs.python.org/3.6/tutorial/datastructures.html#tuples-and-sequences

The following code block illustrates how to create a tuple and create new tuples from an existing type.

Define a tuple t as follows:

```
>>> t = 1,'a', 2,'hello',3
>>> t
(1, 'a', 2, 'hello', 3)
```

Display the first element of t:

```
>>> t[0]
1
```

Create a tuple v containing 10, 11, and t:

```
>>> v = 10,11,t
>>> v
(10, 11, (1, 'a', 2, 'hello', 3))
```

Try modifying an element of t (which is immutable):

```
>>> t[0] = 1000
Traceback (most recent call last):
  File "<stdin>", line 1, in <module>
TypeError: 'tuple' object does not support item assignment
```

Python's *deduplication* is useful because you can remove duplicates from a set and obtain a list:

```
>>> lst = list(set(lst))
```

NOTE *The* in *operator on a list to search is* O(n) *whereas the* in *operator on set is* O(1).

SETS

A set is an unordered collection that does not contain duplicate elements. Use curly braces or the set() function to create sets. Set objects support set-theoretic operations such as union, intersection, and difference.

NOTE set() *is required in order to create an empty set because* {} *creates an empty dictionary.*

The following code block illustrates how to work with a set.
Create a list of elements:

```
>>> l = ['a', 'b', 'a', 'c']
```

Create a set from the preceding list:

```
>>> s = set(l)
>>> s
set(['a', 'c', 'b'])
```

Test if an element is in the set:

```
>>> 'a' in s
True
>>> 'd' in s
False
>>>
```

Create a set from a string:

```
>>> n = set('abacad')
>>> n
set(['a', 'c', 'b', 'd'])
>>>
```

Subtract n from s:

```
>>> s - n
set([])
```

Subtract s from n:

```
>>> n - s
set(['d'])
>>>
```

The union of s and n:

```
>>> s | n
set(['a', 'c', 'b', 'd'])
```

The intersection of s and n:

```
>>> s & n
set(['a', 'c', 'b'])
```

The exclusive-or of s and n:

```
>>> s ^ n
  set(['d'])
```

DICTIONARIES

Python has a key/value structure called a dictionary (`dict`) that is a hash table. A dictionary (and hash tables in general) can retrieve the value of a key in constant time, regardless of the number of entries in the dictionary (and the same is true for sets). You can think of a set as essentially just the keys (not the values) of a `dict` implementation.

The contents of `dict` can be written as a series of `key:value` pairs, as shown here:

```
dict1 = {key1:value1, key2:value2, ... }
```

The "empty `dict`" is just an empty pair of curly braces `{}`.

Creating a Dictionary

A dictionary (or hash table) contains of colon-separated key/value bindings inside a pair of curly braces:

```
dict1 = {}
dict1 = {'x' : 1, 'y' : 2}
```

The preceding code snippet defines `dict1` as an empty dictionary, and then adds two key/value bindings.

Displaying the Contents of a Dictionary

You can display the contents of `dict1` with the following code:

```
>>> dict1 = {'x':1,'y':2}
>>> dict1
```

```
{'y': 2, 'x': 1}
>>> dict1['x']
1
>>> dict1['y']
2
>>> dict1['z']
Traceback (most recent call last):
  File "<stdin>", line 1, in <module>
KeyError: 'z'
```

NOTE   *The key/value bindings for* dict *and a set are not necessarily stored in
        the same order that you defined them.*

Dictionaries also use the get method to retrieve key values:

```
>>> dict1.get('x')
1
>>> dict1.get('y')
2
>>> dict1.get('z')
```

The get method returns None (which is displayed as an empty string) instead
of an error when referencing a key that is not defined in a dictionary.

You can also use dict comprehensions to create dictionaries from expressions, as shown here:

```
>>> {x: x**3 for x in (1, 2, 3)}
{1: 1, 2: 8, 3: 37}
```

Checking for Keys in a Dictionary

You can check for the presence of a key in a dictionary:

```
>>> 'x' in dict1
True
>>> 'z' in dict1
False
```

Use square brackets for finding or setting a value in a dictionary. For example, dict['abc'] finds the value associated with the key 'abc'. You can use
strings, numbers, and tuples work as key values, and you can use any type as
the value.

If you access a value that is not in the dict, Python throws a KeyError.
Consequently, use the in operator to check if the key is in the dictionary.
Alternatively, use dict.get(key), which returns the value or None if the
key is not present. You can even use the expression get(key, not-found-
string) to specify the value to return if a key is not found.

Deleting Keys from a Dictionary

Launch the interpreter and enter the following commands:

```
>>> MyDict = {'x' : 5,  'y' : 7}
```

```
>>> MyDict['z'] = 13
>>> MyDict
{'y': 7, 'x': 5, 'z': 13}
>>> del MyDict['x']
>>> MyDict
{'y': 7, 'z': 13}
>>> MyDict.keys()
['y', 'z']
>>> MyDict.values()
[13, 7]
>>> 'z' in MyDict
True
```

Iterating Through a Dictionary

The following code snippet shows you how to iterate through a dictionary:

```
MyDict = {'x' : 5,  'y' : 7, 'z' : 13}

for key, value in MyDict.iteritems():
    print key, value
```

The output from the preceding code block is as follows:

```
y 7
x 5
z 13
```

Interpolating Data from a Dictionary

The % operator substitutes values from a dictionary into a string by name. Listing 4.40 contains an example of doing so.

LISTING 4.40: InterpolateDict1.py

```
hash = {}
hash['beverage'] = 'coffee'
hash['count'] = 3

# %d for int, %s for string
s = 'Today I drank %(count)d cups of %(beverage)s' % hash
print('s:', s)
```

The output from the preceding code block is here:

```
Today I drank 3 cups of coffee
```

DICTIONARY FUNCTIONS AND METHODS

Python provides various functions and methods, such as cmp(), len(), and str(), that compare two dictionaries, return the length of a dictionary, and display a string representation of a dictionary, respectively.

You can also manipulate the contents of a dictionary using the functions clear() to remove all elements, copy() to return a copy, get() to retrieve the value of a key, items() to display the (key, value) pairs of a dictionary, keys() to display the keys of a dictionary, and values() to return the list of values of a dictionary.

DICTIONARY FORMATTING

The % operator works conveniently to substitute values from a dictionary into a string by name:

```
#create a dictionary
>>> h = {}
#add a key/value pair
>>> h['item'] = 'beer'
>>> h['count'] = 4
#interpolate using %d for int, %s for string
>>> s = 'I want %(count)d bottles of %(item)s' % h
>>> s
'I want 4 bottles of beer'
```

ORDERED DICTIONARIES

Regular dictionaries iterate over key/value pairs in arbitrary order. Python 2.7 introduced a new OrderedDict class in the collections module. The OrderedDict API provides the same interface as regular dictionaries but iterates over keys and values in a guaranteed order depending on when a key was first inserted:

```
>>> from collections import OrderedDict
>>> d = OrderedDict([('first', 1),
...                  ('second', 2),
...                  ('third', 3)])
>>> d.items()
[('first', 1), ('second', 2), ('third', 3)]
```

If a new entry overwrites an existing entry, the original insertion position is left unchanged:

```
>>> d['second'] = 4
>>> d.items()
[('first', 1), ('second', 4), ('third', 3)]
```

Deleting an entry and reinserting it will move it to the end:

```
>>> del d['second']
>>> d['second'] = 5
>>> d.items()
[('first', 1), ('third', 3), ('second', 5)]
```

Sorting Dictionaries

Python enables you to support the entries in a dictionary. For example, you can modify the code in the preceding section to display the alphabetically sorted words and their associated word count.

Python Multi Dictionaries

You can define entries in a dictionary so that they reference lists or other types of structures. Listing 4.41 shows the content of `MultiDictionary1.py` that illustrates how to define more complex dictionaries.

LISTING 4.41: MultiDictionary1.py

```
from collections import defaultdict

d = {'a' : [1, 2, 3], 'b' : [4, 5]}
print 'firsts:',d

d = defaultdict(list)
d['a'].append(1)
d['a'].append(2)
d['b'].append(4)
print 'second:',d

d = defaultdict(set)
d['a'].add(1)
d['a'].add(2)
d['b'].add(4)
print 'third:',d
```

Listing 4.41 starts by defining the dictionary d and printing its contents. The next portion of Listing 4.41 specifies a list-oriented dictionary, and then modifies the values for the keys a and b. The final portion of Listing 4.41 specifies a set-oriented dictionary, and then modifies the values for the keys a and b as well. The output from Listing 4.41 is here:

```
first: {'a': [1, 2, 3], 'b': [4, 5]}
second: defaultdict(<type 'list'>, {'a': [1, 2], 'b': [4]})
third: defaultdict(<type 'set'>, {'a': set([1, 2]), 'b': set([4])})
```

OTHER SEQUENCE TYPES IN PYTHON

Python supports seven sequence types: `str`, `unicode`, `list`, `tuple`, `bytearray`, `buffer`, and `xrange`.

You can iterate through a sequence and retrieve the position index and corresponding value at the same time using the `enumerate()` function.

```
>>> for i, v in enumerate(['x', 'y', 'z']):
...     print i, v
...
...
0 x
1 y
2 z
```

`Bytearray` objects are created with the built-in function `bytearray()`. Although buffer objects are not directly supported by Python syntax, you can create them via the built-in `buffer()` function.

Objects of type xrange are created with the xrange() function. An xrange object is similar to a buffer in the sense that there is no specific syntax to create them. Moreover, xrange objects do not support operations such as slicing, concatenation, or repetition.

At this point, you have seen all the Python types that you will encounter in the remaining chapters of this book, so it makes sense to discuss mutable and immutable types, which is the topic of the next section.

MUTABLE AND IMMUTABLE TYPES IN PYTHON

Python represents its data as objects. Some of these objects (such as lists and dictionaries) are mutable, which means you can change their content without changing their identity. Objects such as integers, floats, strings, and tuples are objects that cannot be changed. There is a difference between changing the value versus assigning a new value to an object; you cannot change a string, but you can assign it a different value. This detail can be verified by checking the id value of an object, as shown in Listing 4.42.

LISTING 4.42: Mutability.py

```
s = "abc"
print('id #1:', id(s))
print('first char:', s[0])

try:
  s[0] = "o"
except:
  print('Cannot perform reassignment')

s = "xyz"
print('id #2:',id(s))
s += "uvw"
print('id #3:',id(s))
```

The output of Listing 4.42 is here:

```
id #1: 4297972672
first char: a
Cannot perform reassignment
id #2: 4299809336
id #3: 4299777872
```

Thus, a type is immutable if its value cannot be changed (even though it's possible to assign a new value to such a type), otherwise a type is mutable. The immutable objects are of type bytes, complex, float, int, str, or tuple. Dictionaries, lists, and sets are mutable. The key in a hash table must be an immutable type.

Since strings are immutable in Python, you cannot insert a string in the "middle" of a given text string unless you construct a second string using concatenation. For example, suppose you have the string

```
"this is a string"
```

and you want to create the following string:

```
"this is a longer string"
```

The following code block illustrates how to perform this task:

```
text1 = "this is a string"
text2 = text1[0:10] + "longer" + text1[9:]
print 'text1:',text1
print 'text2:',text2
```

The output of the preceding code block is as follows:

```
text1: this is a string
text2: this is a longer string
```

THE TYPE () FUNCTION

The type() primitive returns the type of any object, including primitives, functions, and user-defined objects. The following code sample displays the type of an integer and a string:

```
var1 = 123
var2 = 456.78
print "type var1: ",type(var1)
print "type var2: ",type(var2)
```

The output of the preceding code block is here:

```
type var1:  <type 'int'>
type var2:  <type 'float'>
```

SUMMARY

This chapter showed you how to work with numbers and perform arithmetic operations on numbers, and then you learned how to work with strings and use string operations. The next chapter shows you how to work with conditional statements, loops, and user-defined functions.

Next, you learned about condition logic, such as if/elif statements. You also learned how to work with loops, including for loops and while loops. In addition, you saw how to compute various values, such as the factorial value of a positive integer and a set of Fibonacci values.

In addition, you saw how to work with various data types. In particular, you learned about tuples, sets, and dictionaries. Then you learned how to work with lists and how to use list-related operations to extract sub-lists.

## CHAPTER 5

INTRODUCTION TO NUMPY

This chapter provides a quick introduction to the Python NumPy library, which provides useful functionality, not only for "regular" Python scripts, but also for Python-based scripts with TensorFlow. For instance, this chapter contains NumPy code samples containing loops, arrays, and lists. We also discuss dot products, the `reshape()` method, how to plot with Matplotlib (discussed in more detail in Chapter 4), and examples of linear regression.

The first part of this chapter briefly discusses NumPy and some of its useful features. The second part contains examples of working arrays in NumPy, and contrasts some of the APIs for lists with the same APIs for arrays. In addition, we show how to compute the exponent-related values (such as the square or cube) of elements in an array.

The second part of the chapter introduces sub-ranges, which are very useful (and frequently used) for extracting portions of datasets in machine learning tasks. Some of the code samples handle negative (-1) sub-ranges for vectors as well as for arrays because they are interpreted one way for vectors and a different way for arrays.

The third part of this chapter delves into other NumPy methods, including the `reshape()` method, which useful when working with image files: some TensorFlow APIs require converting a 2D array of (R,G,B) values into a corresponding one-dimensional vector.

The fourth part of this chapter encompasses linear regression, the mean squared error (MSE), and how to calculate MSE with the `linspace()` API.

WHAT IS NUMPY?

NumPy is a Python library that contains many convenient methods and aids with program performance. NumPy provides a core library for scientific computing in Python, with performant multi-dimensional arrays and good vectorized math functions, along with support for linear algebra and random numbers.

NumPy is modeled after MATLAB, with support for lists, arrays, and so forth. NumPy is easier to use than MATLAB, and it's very common in Tensor-Flow code as well as Python code.

Useful NumPy Features

The NumPy package provides the `ndarray` object that encapsulates multidimensional arrays of homogeneous data types. Many `ndarray` operations are performed in compiled code to improve performance.

There are important differences between NumPy arrays and the standard Python sequences. First, NumPy arrays have a fixed size, whereas Python lists can expand dynamically. Second, NumPy arrays are homogeneous, which means that the elements in a NumPy array must have the same data type. Third, NumPy arrays support more efficient execution (and require less code) of various types of operations on large numbers of data

WHAT ARE NUMPY ARRAYS?

An *array* is a set of consecutive memory locations used to store data. Each item in the array is called an *element*. The number of elements in an array is called the *dimension* of the array. A typical array declaration is as follows:

```
arr1 = np.array([1,2,3,4,5])
```

The preceding code snippet declares `arr1` as an array of five elements, which you can access via `arr1[0]` through `arr1[4]`. Notice that the first element has an index value of 0, and the second element has an index value of 1. Thus, if you declare an array of 100 elements, then the 100th element has index value of 99.

NOTE *The first position in a NumPy array has index 0.*

NumPy treats arrays as vectors. Math operations are performed element-by-element. Remember the following difference: "doubling" an array multiplies each element by 2, whereas "doubling" a list appends a list to itself.

Listing 5.1 shows the contents of `nparray1.py` that illustrate some operations on a NumPy array.

LISTING 5.1: nparray1.py

```
import numpy as np

list1 = [1,2,3,4,5]
print(list1)

arr1  = np.array([1,2,3,4,5])
```

```
print(arr1)

list2 = [(1,2,3),(4,5,6)]
print(list2)

arr2  = np.array([(1,2,3),(4,5,6)])
print(arr2)
```

Listing 5.1 defines the variables `list1` and `list2` (which are Python lists), as well as the variables `arr1` and `arr2` (which are arrays), and prints their values. The output from launching Listing 5.1 is

```
[1, 2, 3, 4, 5]
[1 2 3 4 5]
[(1, 2, 3), (4, 5, 6)]
[[1 2 3]
 [4 5 6]]
```

WORKING WITH LOOPS

Listing 5.2 shows the content of `loop1.py`, which illustrates how to iterate through the elements of a NumPy array and a Python list.

LISTING 5.2: loop1.py

```
import numpy as np

list = [1,2,3]
arr1 = np.array([1,2,3])

for e in list:
  print(e)

for e in arr1:
  print(e)

list1 = [1,2,3,4,5]
```

Listing 5.2 initializes the variable `list`, which is a list, and also the variable `arr1`, which is an array. The next portion of Listing 5.2 contains two loops, each of which iterates through the elements in `list` and `arr1`. The syntax is identical in both loops. The output from launching Listing 5.2 is here:

```
1
2
3
1
2
3
```

APPENDING ELEMENTS TO ARRAYS (1)

Listing 5.3 shows the contents of `append1.py` that illustrate how to append elements to a NumPy array and a Python list.

LISTING 5.3: append1.py

```
import numpy as np

arr1 = np.array([1,2,3])

# these do not work:
#arr1.append(4)
#arr1 = arr1 + [5]

arr1 = np.append(arr1,4)
arr1 = np.append(arr1,[5])

for e in arr1:
  print(e)

arr2 = arr1 + arr1

for e in arr2:
print(e)
```

Listing 5.3 initializes the variable `list`, which is a Python list, and also the variable `arr1`, which is a NumPy array. The output from launching Listing 5.3 is as follows:

```
1
2
3
4
5
2
4
6
8
10
```

APPENDING ELEMENTS TO ARRAYS (2)

Listing 5.4 shows the content of `append2.py`, which illustrates how to append elements to a NumPy array and a Python list.

LISTING 5.4: append2.py

```
import numpy as np

arr1 = np.array([1,2,3])
arr1 = np.append(arr1,4)
```

```
for e in arr1:
  print(e)

arr1 = np.array([1,2,3])
arr1 = np.append(arr1,4)

arr2 = arr1 + arr1

for e in arr2:
print(e)
```

Listing 5.4 initializes the variable arr1, which is a NumPy array. Notice that NumPy arrays do not have an "append" method: this method is available through NumPy itself. Another important difference between Python lists and NumPy arrays is that the "+" operator concatenates Python lists, whereas this operator doubles the elements in a NumPy array. The output from launching Listing 5.4 is as follows:

```
1
2
3
4
2
4
6
8
```

MULTIPLYING LISTS AND ARRAYS

Listing 5.5 shows the content of multiply1.py that illustrates how to replicate a Python list and double elements in a NumPy array.

LISTING 5.5: multiply1.py

```
import numpy as np

list1 = [1,2,3]
arr1  = np.array([1,2,3])
print('list:  ',list1)
print('arr1:  ',arr1)
print('2*list:',2*list)
print('2*arr1:',2*arr1)
```

Listing 5.5 contains a Python list called list and a NumPy array called arr1. The print() statements display the contents of list and arr1, as well as the result of doubling list1 and arr1. Recall that "doubling" a Python list is different from doubling a Python array, which you can see in the output from launching Listing 5.5:

```
('list:  ', [1, 2, 3])
('arr1:  ', array([1, 2, 3]))
('2*list:', [1, 2, 3, 1, 2, 3])
('2*arr1:', array([2, 4, 6]))
```

DOUBLING THE ELEMENTS IN A LIST

Listing 5.6 shows the contents of `double_list1.py`, which illustrate how to double the elements in a Python list.

LISTING 5.6: double_list1.py

```
import numpy as np

list1 = [1,2,3]
list2 = []

for e in list1:
  list2.append(2*e)

print('list1:',list1)
print('list2:',list2)
```

Listing 5.6 contains a Python list called `list1` and an empty NumPy list called `list2`. The next code snippet iterates through the elements of `list1` and appends them to the variable `list2`. The pair of `print()` statements display the contents of `list1` and `list2` to show you that they are the same. The output from launching Listing 5.6 is here:

```
('list: ', [1, 2, 3])
('list2:', [2, 4, 6])
```

LISTS AND EXPONENTS

Listing 5.7 shows the content of `exponent_list1.py`, which illustrates how to compute exponents of the elements in a Python list.

LISTING 5.7: exponent_list1.py

```
import numpy as np

list1 = [1,2,3]
list2 = []

for e in list1:
  list2.append(e*e) # e*e = squared

print('list1:',list1)
print('list2:',list2)
```

Listing 5.7 contains a Python list called `list1` and an empty NumPy list called `list2`. The next code snippet iterates through the elements of `list1` and appends the square of each element to the variable `list2`. The pair of `print()` statements display the contents of `list1` and `list2`. The output from launching Listing 5.7 is here:

```
('list1:', [1, 2, 3])
('list2:', [1, 4, 9])
```

ARRAYS AND EXPONENTS

Listing 5.8 shows the content of `exponent_array1.py`, which illustrates how to compute exponents of the elements in a NumPy array.

LISTING 5.8: exponent_array1.py

```python
import numpy as np

arr1 = np.array([1,2,3])
arr2 = arr1**2
arr3 = arr1**3

print('arr1:',arr1)
print('arr2:',arr2)
print('arr3:',arr3)
```

Listing 5.8 contains a NumPy array called arr1 followed by two NumPy arrays called arr2 and arr3. Notice the compact manner in which arr2 is initialized with the square of the elements in arr1, followed by the initialization of arr3 with the cube of the elements in arr1. The three print() statements display the contents of arr1, arr2, and arr3. The output from launching Listing 5.8 is here:

```
('arr1:', array([1, 2, 3]))
('arr2:', array([1, 4, 9]))
('arr3:', array([ 1,  8, 27]))
```

MATH OPERATIONS AND ARRAYS

Listing 5.9 shows the contents of `mathops_array1.py` that illustrate how to perform math operations on the elements in a NumPy array.

LISTING 5.9: mathops_array1.py

```python
import numpy as np
arr1 = np.array([1,2,3])
sqrt = np.sqrt(arr1)
log1 = np.log(arr1)
exp1 = np.exp(arr1)

print('sqrt:',sqrt)
print('log1:',log1)
print('exp1:',exp1)
```

Listing 5.9 contains a NumPy array called arr1 followed by three arrays called sqrt, log1, and exp1 that are initialized with the square root, the log, and the exponential value of the elements in arr1, respectively. The three print()

statements display the contents of sqrt, log1, and exp1. The output from launching Listing 5.9 is here:

```
('sqrt:', array([1.       , 1.41421356, 1.73205081]))
('log1:', array([0.       , 0.69314718, 1.09861229]))
('exp1:', array([2.71828183, 7.3890561, 20.08553692]))
```

WORKING WITH "-1" SUB-RANGES WITH VECTORS

Listing 5.10 shows the content of npsubarray2.py, which illustrates how to select subranges of the elements in a NumPy array.

LISTING 5.10: npsubarray2.py

```
import numpy as np

# -1 => "all except the last element in …" (row or col)

arr1  = np.array([1,2,3,4,5])
print('arr1:',arr1)
print('arr1[0:-1]:',arr1[0:-1])
print('arr1[1:-1]:',arr1[1:-1])
print('arr1[::-1]:', arr1[::-1]) # reverse!
```

Listing 5.10 contains a NumPy array called arr1 followed by four print statements, each of which displays a different sub-range of values in arr1. The output from launching Listing 5.10 is as follows:

```
('arr1:',        array([1, 2, 3, 4, 5]))
('arr1[0:-1]:', array([1, 2, 3, 4]))
('arr1[1:-1]:', array([2, 3, 4]))
('arr1[::-1]:', array([5, 4, 3, 2, 1]))
```

WORKING WITH "-1" SUB-RANGES WITH ARRAYS

Listing 5.11 shows the content of np2darray2.py, which illustrates how to select matrix subranges of the elements in a NumPy array.

LISTING 5.11: np2darray2.py

```
import numpy as np

# -1 => "the last element in …" (row or col)

arr1  = np.array([(1,2,3),(4,5,6),(7,8,9),(10,11,12)])
print('arr1:',        arr1)
print('arr1[-1,:]:',  arr1[-1,:])
print('arr1[:,-1]:',  arr1[:,-1])
print('arr1[-1:,-1]:',arr1[-1:,-1])
```

Listing 5.11 contains a NumPy array called `arr1` followed by four `print` statements, each of which displays a different sub-range of values in `arr1`. The output from launching Listing 5.11 is

```
(arr1:', array([[1,   2,   3],
                [4,   5,   6],
                [7,   8,   9],
                [10, 11, 12]]))
(arr1[-1,:]]',   array([10, 11, 12]))
(arr1[:,-1]:',   array([3,   6,   9, 12]))
(arr1[-1:,-1]]', array([12]))
```

OTHER USEFUL NUMPY METHODS

The following methods are very useful.

The method np.zeros() initializes an array with 0 values.
The method np.ones() initializes an array with 1 values.
The method np.empty()initializes an array with 0 values.
The method np.arange() provides a range of numbers.
The method np.shape() displays the shape of an object.
The method np.reshape() *(Very useful!)*
The method np.linspace() *(Useful in regression!)*
The method np.mean() computes the mean of a set of numbers.
The method np.std() computes the standard deviation of a set of numbers.

Although the `np.zeros()` and `np.empty()` both initialize a 2D array with 0, `np.zeros()` requires less execution time. You could also use `np.full(size, 0)`, but this method is the slowest of all three methods.

The `reshape()` method and the `linspace()` method are useful for changing the dimensions of an array and generating a list of numeric values, respectively. The `reshape()` method often appears in TensorFlow code, and the `linspace()` method is useful for generating a set of numbers in linear regression (discussed in Chapter 4). The `mean()` and `std()` methods are useful for calculating the mean and the standard deviation of a set of numbers. For example, you can use these two methods to resize the values in a Gaussian distribution so that their mean is 0 and the standard deviation is 1. This process is called *standardizing* a Gaussian distribution.

ARRAYS AND VECTOR OPERATIONS

Listing 5.12 shows the content of `array_vector.py` that illustrates how to perform vector operations on the elements in a NumPy array.

LISTING 5.12: *array_vector.py*

```
import numpy as np
```

```
a = np.array([[1,2], [3, 4]])
b = np.array([[5,6], [7,8]])

print('a:         ', a)
print('b:         ', b)
print('a + b:     ', a+b)
print('a - b:     ', a-b)
print('a * b:     ', a*b)
print('a / b:     ', a/b)
print('b / a:     ', b/a)
print('a.dot(b):',a.dot(b))
```

Listing 5.12 contains two NumPy arrays called a and b followed by eight `print` statements, each of which displays the result of applying a different arithmetic operation to the arrays a and b. The output from launching Listing 5.12 is here:

```
('a      :   ', array([[1, 2], [3, 4]]))
('b      :   ', array([[5, 6], [7, 8]]))
('a + b:     ', array([[ 6,  8], [10, 12]]))
('a - b:     ', array([[-4, -4], [-4, -4]]))
('a * b:     ', array([[ 5, 12], [21, 32]]))
('a / b:     ', array([[0, 0], [0, 0]]))
('b / a:     ', array([[5, 3], [2, 2]]))
('a.dot(b):', array([[19, 22], [43, 50]]))
```

NUMPY AND DOT PRODUCTS (1)

Listing 5.13 shows the contents of `dotproduct1.py`, which illustrate how to perform the dot product on the elements in a NumPy array.

LISTING 5.13: dotproduct1.py

```
import numpy as np

a = np.array([1,2])
b = np.array([2,3])

dot2 = 0
for e,f in zip(a,b):
  dot2 += e*f

print('a:    ',a)
print('b:    ',b)
print('a*b: ',a*b)
print('dot1:',a.dot(b))
print('dot2:',dot2)
```

Listing 5.13 contains two NumPy arrays called a and b followed by a simple loop that computes the dot product of a and b. The next section contains five `print` statements that display the contents of a and b, their inner product that's calculated in three different ways. The output from launching Listing 5.13 is as follows:

```
('a:     ', array([1, 2]))
('b:     ', array([2, 3]))
('a*b:   ', array([2, 6]))
('dot1:', 8)
('dot2:', 8)
```

NUMPY AND DOT PRODUCTS (2)

NumPy arrays support a "dot" method for calculating the inner product of an array of numbers, which uses the same formula that you use for calculating the inner product of a pair of vectors. Listing 5.14 shows the contents of dot-product2.py that illustrate how to calculate the dot product of two NumPy arrays.

LISTING 5.14: dotproduct2.py

```
import numpy as np

a = np.array([1,2])
b = np.array([2,3])

print('a:          ',a)
print('b:          ',b)
print('a.dot(b):   ',a.dot(b))
print('b.dot(a):   ',b.dot(a))
print('np.dot(a,b):',np.dot(a,b))
print('np.dot(b,a):',np.dot(b,a))
```

Listing 5.14 contains two NumPy arrays called a and b followed by six print statements that display the contents of a and b, and also their inner product that is calculated in three different ways. The output from launching Listing 5.14 is as follows:

```
('a:          ', array([1, 2]))
('b:          ', array([2, 3]))
('a.dot(b):   ', 8)
('b.dot(a):   ', 8)
('np.dot(a,b):', 8)
('np.dot(b,a):', 8)
```

NUMPY AND THE LENGTH OF VECTORS

The *norm* of a vector (or an array of numbers) is the length a vector, which is the square root of the dot product of a vector with itself. NumPy also provides the sum and square functions that you can use to calculate the norm of a vector.

Listing 5.15 shows the content of array_norm.py, which illustrates how to calculate the magnitude ("norm") of a NumPy array of numbers.

LISTING 5.15: array_norm.py

```
import numpy as np

a       = np.array([2,3])
asquare = np.square(a)
asqsum  = np.sum(np.square(a))
anorm1  = np.sqrt(np.sum(a*a))
anorm2  = np.sqrt(np.sum(np.square(a)))
anorm3  = np.linalg.norm(a)

print('a:        ',a)
print('asquare:',asquare)
print('asqsum: ',asqsum)
print('anorm1: ',anorm1)
print('anorm2: ',anorm2)
print('anorm3: ',anorm3)
```

Listing 5.15 contains an initial NumPy array called a, followed by the array asquare and the numeric values asqsum, anorm1, anorm2, and anorm3. The array asquare contains the square of the elements in the array a, and the numeric value asqsum contains the sum of the elements in the array asquare. Next, the numeric value anorm1 equals the square root of the sum of the square of the elements in a. The numeric value anorm2 is the same as anorm1, computed in a slightly different fashion. Finally, the numeric value anorm3 is equal to anorm2, but as you can see, anorm3 is calculated via a single method, whereas anorm2 requires a succession of methods.

The last portion of Listing 5.15 consists of six print statements, each of which displays the computed values. The output from launching Listing 5.15 is shown here:

```
('a:        ', array([2, 3]))
('asquare:', array([4, 9]))
('asqsum: ', 13)
('anorm1: ', 3.605551275463989)
('anorm2: ', 3.605551275463989)
('anorm3: ', 3.605551275463989)
```

NUMPY AND OTHER OPERATIONS

NumPy provides the * operator to multiply the components of two vectors to produce a third vector whose components are the products of the corresponding components of the initial pair of vectors. This operation is called a *Hadamard product*, named after a famous mathematician. If you then add the components of the third vector, the sum is equal to the inner product of the initial pair of vectors.

Listing 5.16 shows the content of otherops.py, which illustrates how to perform other operations on a NumPy array.

LISTING 5.16: otherops.py

```
import numpy as np

a = np.array([1,2])
b = np.array([3,4])

print('a:              ',a)
print('b:              ',b)
print('a*b:            ',a*b)
print('np.sum(a*b): ',np.sum(a*b))
print('(a*b.sum()): ',(a*b).sum())
```

Listing 5.16 contains two NumPy arrays called a and b followed five print statements that display the contents of a and b, their Hadamard product, and also their inner product that's calculated in two different ways. The output from launching Listing 5.16 is as follows:

```
('a:              ', array([1, 2]))
('b:              ', array([3, 4]))
('a*b:            ', array([3, 8]))
('np.sum(a*b): ', 11)
('(a*b.sum()): ', 11)
```

NUMPY AND THE RESHAPE () METHOD

NumPy arrays support the reshape method that enables you to restructure the dimensions of an array of numbers. In general, if an array contains m elements, where m is a positive integer, then that array can be restructured as an m1 × m2 array, where m1 and m2 are positive integers such that m1*m2 = m.

Listing 5.17 shows the contents of numpy_reshape.py that illustrate how to use the reshape() method on a NumPy array.

LISTING 5.17: numpy_reshape.py

```
import numpy as np

x = np.array([[2, 3], [4, 5], [6, 7]])
print(x.shape) # (3, 2)

x = x.reshape((2, 3))
print(x.shape) # (2, 3)
print('x1:',x)

x = x.reshape((-1))
print(x.shape) # (6,)
print('x2:',x)

x = x.reshape((6, -1))
print(x.shape) # (6, 1)
print('x3:',x)
```

```
x = x.reshape((-1, 6))
print(x.shape) # (1, 6)
print('x4:',x)
```

Listing 5.17 contains a NumPy array called x whose dimensions are 3×2, followed by a set of invocations of the `reshape()` method that reshape the contents of x. The first invocation of the `reshape()` method changes the shape of x from 3×2 to 2×3. The second invocation changes the shape of x from 2×3 to 6×1. The third invocation changes the shape of x from 1×6 to 6×1. The final invocation changes the shape of x from 6×1 to 1×6 again.

Each invocation of the `reshape()` method is followed by a `print()` statement so that you can see the effect of the invocation. The output from launching Listing 5.17 is as follows:

```
(3, 2)
(2, 3)
('x1:', array([[2, 3, 4],
       [5, 6, 7]]))
(6,)
('x2:', array([2, 3, 4, 5, 6, 7]))
(6, 1)
('x3:', array([[2],
       [3],
       [4],
       [5],
       [6],
       [7]]))
(1, 6)
```

CALCULATING THE MEAN AND STANDARD DEVIATION

If you need to review these concepts from statistics (and perhaps also the median and mode, as well), please read the appropriate on-line tutorials.

NumPy provides various built-in functions that perform statistical calculations, such as the following:

```
np.linspace() <= useful for regression
np.mean()
np.std()
```

The `np.linspace()` method generates a set of equally spaced numbers between a lower bound and an upper bound. The `np.mean()` and `np.std()` methods calculate the mean and standard deviation, respectively, of a set of numbers. Listing 5.18 shows the content of `sample_mean_std.py`, which illustrates how to calculate statistical values from a NumPy array.

LISTING 5.18: sample_mean_std.py

```
import numpy as np
```

```
x2 = np.arange(8)
print('mean = ',x2.mean())
print('std  = ',x2.std())

x3 = (x2 - x2.mean())/x2.std()
print('x3 mean = ',x3.mean())
print('x3 std  = ',x3.std())
```

Listing 5.18 contains a NumPy array x2 that consists of the first eight integers. Next, the mean() and std() that are associated with x2 are invoked to calculate the mean and standard deviation, respectively, of the elements of x2. The output from launching Listing 5.18 is here:

```
('a:            ', array([1, 2]))
('b:            ', array([3, 4]))
```

CODE SAMPLE WITH MEAN AND STANDARD DEVIATION

The code sample in this section extends the code sample in the previous section with additional statistical values, and the code in Listing 5.19 can be used for any data distribution. The code sample uses random numbers simply for the purposes of illustration. After you have launched the code sample, replace those numbers with values from a CSV file or some other dataset containing meaningful values.

This section does not provide details regarding the meaning of quartiles, but you can learn about quartiles online:

https://en.wikipedia.org/wiki/Quartile

Listing 5.19 shows the contents of stat_values.py that illustrate how to display various statistical values from a NumPy array of random numbers.

LISTING 5.19: stat_values.py

```
import numpy as np

from numpy import percentile
from numpy.random import rand

# generate data sample
data = np.random.rand(1000)

# calculate quartiles, min, and max
quartiles = percentile(data, [25, 50, 75])
data_min, data_max = data.min(), data.max()

# print summary information
print('Minimum:  %.3f' % data_min)
print('Q1 value: %.3f' % quartiles[0])
print('Median:   %.3f' % quartiles[1])
print('Mean Val: %.3f' % data.mean())
print('Std Dev:  %.3f' % data.std())
```

```
print('Q3 value: %.3f' % quartiles[2])
print('Maximum:  %.3f' % data_max)
```

The data sample (shown in bold) in Listing 5.19 is from a uniform distribution between 0 and 1. The `percentile()` function calculates a linear interpolation (average) between observations, which is needed to calculate the median of a sample with an even number of values. The functions `min()` and `max()` calculate the smallest and largest values in the data sample. The output from launching Listing 5.19 is here:

```
Minimum:    0.000
Q1 value:  0.237
Median:    0.500
Mean Val:  0.495
Std Dev:   0.295
Q3 value:  0.747
Maximum:   0.999
```

Trimmed Mean and Weighted Mean

In addition to the arithmetic mean, there are variants that are known as the weighted mean and a trimmed mean (also called a truncated mean).

A *trimmed mean* is a robust estimate (i.e., a metric that is not sensitive to outliers). As a simple example of a trimmed mean, suppose that you have five scores for the evaluation of a product. Exclude the highest and lowest scores and then compute the average of the remaining three scores. If you have multiple sets of five scores, repeat the preceding process and then compute the average of the set of trimmed mean values.

A *weighted mean* is better suited when your sample represents different groups in a dataset. Assigning a larger weight to groups that are under-represented yields a weighted mean that more accurate represents the various groups in the dataset. However, keep in mind that outliers can affect the mean as well as the weighted mean.

The weighted mean is the same as the expected value. In case you are unfamiliar with the notion of an expected value, suppose that the set P = {p1,p2,...,pn} is a probability distribution, which means that the numeric values in the set P must be non-negative and have a sum equal to 1. In addition, suppose that V = {v1,v2,...,vn} is a set of numeric scores that are assigned to n features of a product M. The values in the set V are probably positive integers in some range (e.g., between 1 and 10).

Then the *expected value* E for that product is computed as follows:

```
E = p1*v1 + p2*v2 + ... + pn*vn
```

The final chapter contains more detailed information about Matplotlib in order to plot various charts and graphs. However, the code samples in the next several sections contain some rudimentary APIs from Matplotlib. The code samples start with simple examples of line segments, followed by an introduction to linear regression.

WORKING WITH LINES IN THE PLANE (OPTIONAL)

This section contains a short review of lines in the Euclidean plane, so you can skip this section if you are comfortable with this topic. A minor point that's often overlooked is that lines in the Euclidean plane have infinite length. If you select two distinct points of a line, then all the points between those two selected points is a *line segment*. A *ray* is a "half infinite" line: When you select one point as an endpoint, then all the points on one side of the line constitute a ray.

For example, the points in the plane whose y-coordinate is 0 is the same line as the x-axis, whereas the points between (0,0) and (1,0) on the x-axis form a line segment. In addition, the points on the x-axis that are to the right of (0,0) form a ray, and the points on the x-axis that are to the left of (0,0) also form a ray.

For simplicity and convenience, in this book we'll use the terms "line" and "line segment" interchangeably, and now let's delve into the details of lines in the Euclidean plane. Here is the equation of a (non-vertical) line in the Euclidean plane:

```
y = m*x + b
```

The value of m is the slope of the line and the value of b is the y-intercept (i.e., the place where the non-vertical line intersects the y-axis). The following form for a line in the plane is a more general equation that includes vertical lines:

```
a*x + b*y + c = 0
```

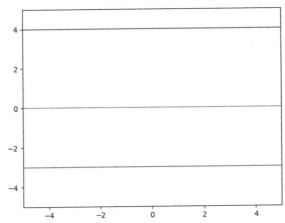

FIGURE 5.1 A graph of three horizontal lines whose equations (from top to bottom) are $y = 3$, $y = 0$, and $y = -3$

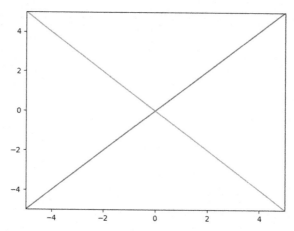

FIGURE 5.2 A graph of two slanted lines whose equations are y = x and y = -x

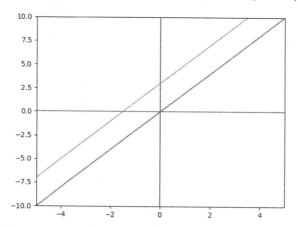

FIGURE 5.3 A graph of two slanted parallel lines whose equations are $y = 2*x$ and $y = 2*x+3$

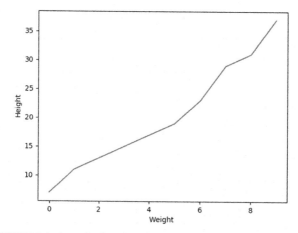

FIGURE 5.4 A piece-wise linear graph consisting of connected line segments

PLOTTING RANDOMIZED POINTS WITH NUMPY AND MATPLOTLIB

The previous section contains simple examples of line segments, but the code is deferred until Chapter 10. This section and the next section contain code samples with Matplotlib APIs that are not discussed; however, the code is straightforward, so you can infer its purpose. In addition, you can learn more about Matplotlib in Chapter 10 (which focuses on data visualization) or read a short online tutorial for more details.

Listing 5.20 shows the contents of np_plot.py, which illustrate how to plot multiple points on a line in the plane.

LISTING 5.20: np_plot.py

```
import numpy as np
import matplotlib.pyplot as plt

x = np.random.randn(15,1)
y = 2.5*x + 5 + 0.2*np.random.randn(15,1)

plt.scatter(x,y)
plt.show()
```

Listing 5.20 starts with two import statements, followed by the initialization of x as a set of random values via the NumPy randn() API. Next, y is assigned a range of values that consist of two parts: a linear equation with input values from the x values, which is combined with a randomization factor.

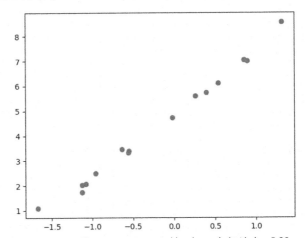

FIGURE 5.5: The output generated by the code in Listing 5.20.

PLOTTING A QUADRATIC WITH NUMPY AND MATPLOTLIB

Listing 5.21 shows the content of np_plot_quadratic.py that illustrates how to plot a quadratic function in the plane.

LISTING 5.21: *np_plot_quadratic.py*

```
import numpy as np
import matplotlib.pyplot as plt

x = np.linspace(-5,5,num=100)[:,None]
y = -0.5 + 2.2*x +0.3*x**3+ 2*np.random.randn(100,1)

plt.plot(x,y)
plt.show()
```

Listing 5.21 starts with two `import` statements, followed by the initialization of x as a range of values via the `NumPy linspace()` API. Next, y is assigned a range of values that fit a quadratic equation, which are based on the values for the variable x.

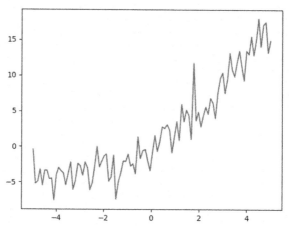

FIGURE 5.6 The output generated by the code in Listing 5.21

WHAT IS LINEAR REGRESSION?

Linear regression was created in 1805 (more than two hundred years ago), and it's an important algorithm in statistical analysis and in machine learning. Any decent statistical package supports linear regression and invariably supports polynomial regression. Linear regression involves lines, which are polynomials of degree one, whereas polynomial regression involves fitting higher degree polynomials to a dataset.

In general terms, linear regression finds the equation of the best fitting hyperplane that approximates a dataset, where a hyperplane has a degree one less than the dimensionality of the dataset. In particular, if the dataset is in the Euclidean plane, the hyperplane is simply a line; if the dataset is in 3D, the hyperplane is a "regular" plane.

Linear regression is suitable when the points in a dataset are distributed in such a way that they can reasonably be approximated by a hyperplane. If not, you can try to fit other types of multi-variable polynomial surfaces to the points in the dataset.

Keep in mind two other details. First, the best fitting hyperplane does not necessarily intersect all (or even most of) the points in the dataset. In fact, the best fitting hyperplane might not intersect any points in the dataset. The purpose of a best fitting hyperplane is to approximate the points in dataset as closely as possible. Second, linear regression is not the same as curve fitting, which attempts to find a polynomial that passes through a set of points.

Here are some details about curve fitting. Given n points in the plane (no two of which have the same x value), there is a polynomial of a degree less than or equal to n-1 that passes through those points. Thus, a line (which has degree one) passes through any pair of non-vertical points in the plane. For any triple of points in the plane, there is a quadratic equation or a line that passes through those points.

In some cases, a lower degree polynomial is available. For instance, consider the set of 100 points in which the x value equals the y value. The line y = x (a polynomial of degree one) passes through all of those points.

However, the extent to which a line "represents" a set of points in the plane depends on how closely those points can be approximated by a line.

What is Multivariate Analysis?

Multivariate analysis generalizes the equation of a line in the Euclidean plane, and it has the following form:

```
y = w1*x1 + w2*x2 + . . . + wn*xn + b
```

As you can see, the preceding equation contains a linear combination of the variables x1, x2, ..., xn. In this book, we usually work with datasets that involve lines in the Euclidean plane.

What about Non-Linear Datasets?

Simple linear regression finds the best fitting line that fits a dataset, but what happens if the dataset does not fit a line in the plane? This is an excellent question! In such a scenario, we look for other curves to approximate the dataset, such a quadratic, cubic, or higher-degree polynomials. However, these alternatives involve trade-offs, as we'll discuss later.

Another possibility is to use a continuous piece-wise linear function, which is a function that comprises a set of line segments, where the adjacent line segments are connected. If one or more pairs of adjacent line segments are not connected, then it's a piece-wise linear function (i.e., the function is discontinuous). In either case, line segments have degree one, which involves a lower computational complexity than higher-order polynomials.

Thus, given a set of points in the plane, try to find the best fitting line that fits those points, after addressing the following questions:

1. How do we know that a line fits the data?
2. What if a different type of curve is a better fit?
3. What does best fit mean?

One way to check if a line fits the data well is through a simple visual check: display the data in a graph and if the data conforms to the shape of a line reasonably well, then a line might be a good fit. However, this is a subjective decision, and a sample dataset that does not fit a line is shown in Figure 5.7.

Figure 5.7 shows a dataset containing many points that are not on a line.

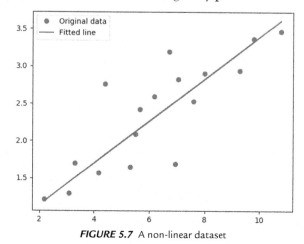

FIGURE 5.7 A non-linear dataset

If a line does not appear to be a good fit for the data, then perhaps a quadratic or cubic (or even higher degree) polynomial has the potential of being a better fit. Let's defer the non-linear scenario and make the assumption that a line would be a good fit for the data. There is a well-known technique for finding the best fitting line for such a dataset, and it's called Mean Squared Error (MSE).

THE MSE (MEAN SQUARED ERROR) FORMULA

Figure 5.8 shows the formula for the MSE (Mean Squared Error). The MSE is the sum of the squares of the difference between an *actual* y value and the *predicted* y value, divided by the number of points. Note that the predicted y value is the y value that each data point would have if that data point were actually on the best-fitting line.

In general, the goal is to minimize the error, which determines the best fitting line in the case of linear regression. However, you might be satisfied with a "good enough" value when the time and/or cost for any additional reduction in the error is deemed prohibitive, which means that this decision is not a purely programmatic decision.

Figure 5.8 shows the formula for MSE for calculating the best-fitting line for a set of points in the plane.

$$MSE = \frac{1}{n}\sum_{i=1}^{n}(Y_i - \hat{Y}_i)^2$$

FIGURE 5.8 The MSE formula

Other Error Types

Although we only discuss the MSE for linear regression in this book, there are other types of formulas for errors that you can use for linear regression, some of which are listed here:

MSE
RMSE
RMSPROP
MAE

The MSE is the basis for the preceding error types. For example, RMSE is the Root Mean Squared Error, which is the square root of the MSE.

The MAE is the *Mean Absolute Error*, which is the sum of the absolute value of the differences of the y terms (not the square of the differences of the y terms).

The RMSProp optimizer utilizes the magnitude of recent gradients to normalize the gradients. Maintain a moving average over the *Root Mean Squared* (RMS, which is the square root of the MSE) gradients, and then divide that term by the current gradient.

Although it's easier to compute the derivative of MSE (because it's a differentiable function), it's also true that MSE is more susceptible to outliers, more so than MAE. The reason is simple. A squared term can be significantly larger than adding the absolute value of a term. For example, if a difference term is 10, then the squared term 100 is added to MSE, whereas only 10 is added to MAE. Similarly, if a difference term is -20, then the squared term 400 is added to MSE, whereas only 20 (which is the absolute value of -20) is added to MAE.

Non-Linear Least Squares

When predicting housing prices, where the dataset contains a wide range of values, techniques such as linear regression or random forests can cause the model to overfit the samples with the highest values to reduce quantities such as the mean absolute error.

In this scenario, you probably want an error metric, such as the relative error, that reduces the importance of fitting the samples with the largest values. This technique is called *non-linear least squares*, which may use a log-based transformation of labels and predicted values.

CALCULATING THE MSE MANUALLY

Let's look at two simple graphs, each of which contains a line that approximates a set of points in a scatter plot. Notice that the line segment is the same for both sets of points, but the datasets are slightly different. We manually calculate the MSE for both datasets and determine which value of MSE is smaller.

Figure 5.9 shows a set of points and a line that is a potential candidate for best-fitting line for the data.

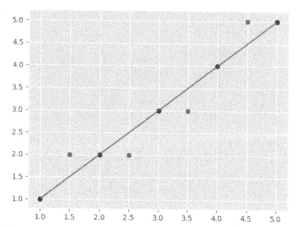

FIGURE 5.9 A line graph that approximates the points of a scatter plot

The MSE for the line in Figure 5.9 is computed as follows:

```
MSE = [1*1+(-1)*(-1)+(-1)*(-1)+1*1]/9 = 4/9
```

Figure 5.10 also shows a set of points and a line that is a potential candidate for best-fitting line for the data.

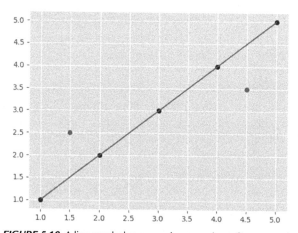

FIGURE 5.10 A line graph that approximates points of a scatter plot

The MSE for the line in Figure 5.10 is computed as follows:

```
MSE = [(-2)*(-2) + 2*2]/9 = 8/9
```

Thus, the line in Figure 5.9 has a smaller MSE than the line in Figure 5.10.

In these two figures, we calculated the MSE easily and quickly, but in general, it's significantly more difficult. For instance, if we plot 10 points in the Euclidean plane that do not closely fit a line, with individual terms that involve non-integer values, we would probably need a calculator. A better solution involves NumPy functions, as discussed in the next section.

FIND THE BEST-FITTING LINE IN NUMPY

Earlier in this chapter, you saw examples of lines in the plane, including horizontal, slanted, and parallel lines. Most of those lines have a positive slope and a non-zero value for their y-intercept. Although there are scatterplots of data points in the plane where the best-fitting line has a negative slope, the examples in this book involve scatterplots whose best-fitting line has a positive slope.

Listing 5.22 shows the content of find_best_fit.py, which illustrates how to determine the best fitting line for a set of points in the Euclidean plane. The solution is based on closed form formulas (from statistics).

LISTING 5.22: find_best_fit.py

```
import numpy as np

xs = np.array([1,2,3,4,5], dtype=np.float64)
ys = np.array([1,2,3,4,5], dtype=np.float64)

def best_fit_slope(xs,ys):
    m = (((np.mean(xs)*np.mean(ys))-np.mean(xs*ys)) /
         ((np.mean(xs)**2) - np.mean(xs**2)))
    b = np.mean(ys) - m * np.mean(xs)

    return m, b

m,b = best_fit_slope(xs,ys)
print('m:',m, 'b:',b)
```

Listing 5.22 starts with two arrays xs and ys that are initialized with the first five positive integers. The Python function best_fit_slope() calculates the optimal values of m (the slope) and b (the y-intercept) of a set of numbers. The output from Listing 5.22 is as follows:

```
m: 1.0 b: 0.0
```

Notice that the arrays xs and ys are identical, which means that these points lie on the identity function whose slope is 1. By simple extrapolation, the point (0,0) is also a point on the same line. Hence, the y-intercept of this line must equal 0.

If you are interested, you can search online to find the derivation for the values of m and b. In this chapter, we're going to skip the derivation, and proceed with examples of calculating the MSE. The first example involves calculating the MSE manually, followed by an example that uses NumPy formulas to perform the calculations.

CALCULATING MSE BY SUCCESSIVE APPROXIMATION (1)

This section contains a code sample that uses a simple technique for successively determining better approximations for the slope and y-intercept of a best-fitting line. Recall that an approximation of a derivative is the ratio of "delta y" divided by "delta x." The "delta" values calculate the difference of the y values and the difference of the x values, respectively, of two nearby points (x1,y1) and (x2,y2) on a function. Hence, the delta-based approximation ratio is (y2-y1)/(x2-x1).

The technique in this section involves a simplified approximation for the delta values: We assume that the denominators are equal to 1. As a result, we need only calculate the numerators of the delta values: in this code sample, those numerators are the variables dw and db.

Listing 5.23 shows the content of plain_linreg1.py, which illustrates how to compute the MSE with simulated data.

LISTING 5.23: plain_linreg1.py

```
import numpy as np
import matplotlib.pyplot as plt

X = [0,0.12,0.25,0.27,0.38,0.42,0.44,0.55,0.92,1.0]
Y = [0,0.15,0.54,0.51,0.34,0.1, 0.19,0.53,1.0,0.58]

costs = []
#Step 1: Parameter initialization
W = 0.45 # the initial slope
b = 0.75 # the initial y-intercept

for i in range(1, 100):
  #Step 2: Calculate Cost
  Y_pred = np.multiply(W, X) + b
  loss_error = 0.5 * (Y_pred - Y)**2
  cost = np.sum(loss_error)/10

  #Step 3: Calculate dw and db
  db = np.sum((Y_pred - Y))
  dw = np.dot((Y_pred - Y), X)
  costs.append(cost)

  #Step 4: Update parameters:
  W = W - 0.01*dw
  b = b - 0.01*db

  if i%10 == 0:
    print("Cost at", i,"iteration = ", cost)

#Step 5: Repeat via a for loop with 1000 iterations

#Plot cost versus # of iterations
print("W = ", W,"& b = ",  b)
plt.plot(costs)
```

```
plt.ylabel('cost')
plt.xlabel('iterations (per tens)')
plt.show()
```

Listing 5.23 defines the variables X and Y that are simple arrays of numbers (this is our dataset). Next, the costs array is initialized as an empty array, and we append successive cost approximations to this array. The variables W and b correspond to the slope and y-intercept, and they are initialized with the values 0.45 and 0.75, respectively (feel free to experiment with these values).

The next portion of Listing 5.23 is a for loop that executes 100 times. During each iteration, the variables Y_pred, loss_error, and cost are computed, and they correspond to the predicted value, the error, and the cost, respectively (remember that we are performing linear regression). The value of cost (which is the error for the current iteration) is then appended to the costs array.

Next, the variables dw and db are calculated. These correspond to "delta w" and "delta b" that we'll use to update the values of W and b, respectively. The code is reproduced here:

```
#Step 4: Update parameters:
W = W - 0.01*dw
b = b - 0.01*db
```

Notice that dw and db are both multiplied by the value 0.01, which is the value of our "learning rate" (experiment with this value as well).

The next code snippet displays the current cost, which is performed every tenth iteration through the loop. When the loop finishes execution, the values of W and b are displayed, and a plot is displayed that shows the cost values on the vertical axis and the loop iterations on the horizontal axis. The output from Listing 5.23 is as follows:

```
Cost at 10 iteration =   0.04114630674619491
Cost at 20 iteration =   0.026706242729839395
Cost at 30 iteration =   0.024738889446900423
Cost at 40 iteration =   0.023850565034634254
Cost at 50 iteration =   0.0231499048706651
Cost at 60 iteration =   0.02255361434242207
Cost at 70 iteration =   0.0220425055291673
Cost at 80 iteration =   0.021604128492245713
Cost at 90 iteration =   0.021228111750568435
W =   0.47256473531193927 & b =   0.19578262688662174
```

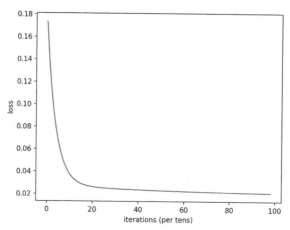

FIGURE 5.11 A plot of the cost-versus-iterations for Listing 5.23

CALCULATING MSE BY SUCCESSIVE APPROXIMATION (2)

In the previous section, you saw how to calculate the delta approximations to determine the equation of a best-fitting line for a set of points in a 2D plane. The example in this section generalizes the code in the previous section by adding an outer loop that represents the number of epochs. The number of epochs specifies the number of times that an inner loop is executed.

Listing 5.24 shows the contents of plain_linreg2.py, which illustrate how to compute the MSE with simulated data.

LISTING 5.24: plain_linreg2.py

```
import numpy as np
import matplotlib.pyplot as plt

# %matplotlib inline
X = [0,0.12,0.25,0.27,0.38,0.42,0.44,0.55,0.92,1.0]
Y = [0,0.15,0.54,0.51, 0.34,0.1,0.19,0.53,1.0,0.58]

#uncomment to see a plot of X versus Y values
#plt.plot(X,Y)
#plt.show()

costs = []
#Step 1: Parameter initialization
W = 0.45
b = 0.75

epochs = 100
lr = 0.001

for j in range(1, epochs):
    for i in range(1, 100):
        #Step 2: Calculate Cost
```

```
Y_pred = np.multiply(W, X) + b
Loss_error = 0.5 * (Y_pred - Y)**2
cost = np.sum(Loss_error)/10

#Step 3: Calculate dW and db
db = np.sum((Y_pred - Y))
dw = np.dot((Y_pred - Y), X)
costs.append(cost)

#Step 4: Update parameters:
W = W - lr*dw
b = b - lr*db

if i%50 == 0:
   print("Cost at epoch", j,"= ", cost)

#Plot cost versus # of iterations
print("W = ", W,"& b = ",  b)
plt.plot(costs)
plt.ylabel('cost')
plt.xlabel('iterations (per tens)')
plt.show()
```

Compare the new contents of Listing 5.24 (shown in bold) with the contents of Listing 5.23: The changes are minimal, and the main difference is to execute the inner loop 100 times for each iteration of the outer loop, which also executes 100 times. The output from Listing 5.24 is here:

```
('Cost at epoch', 1, '= ', 0.07161762489862147)
('Cost at epoch', 2, '= ', 0.030073922512586938)
('Cost at epoch', 3, '= ', 0.025415528992988472)
('Cost at epoch', 4, '= ', 0.024227826373677794)
('Cost at epoch', 5, '= ', 0.02346241967071181)
('Cost at epoch', 6, '= ', 0.022827707922883803)
('Cost at epoch', 7, '= ', 0.022284262669854064)
('Cost at epoch', 8, '= ', 0.02181735173716673)
('Cost at epoch', 9, '= ', 0.021416050179776294)
('Cost at epoch', 10, '= ', 0.02107112540934384)
// details omitted for brevity
('Cost at epoch', 90, '= ', 0.018960749188638278)
('Cost at epoch', 91, '= ', 0.01896074755776306)
('Cost at epoch', 92, '= ', 0.018960746155994725)
('Cost at epoch', 93, '= ', 0.018960744951148113)
('Cost at epoch', 94, '= ', 0.018960743915559485)
('Cost at epoch', 95, '= ', 0.018960743025451313)
('Cost at epoch', 96, '= ', 0.018960742260386375)
('Cost at epoch', 97, '= ', 0.018960741602798474)
('Cost at epoch', 98, '= ', 0.018960741037589136)
('Cost at epoch', 99, '= ', 0.018960740551780944)
('W = ', 0.6764145874436108, '& b = ', 0.09976839618922698)
```

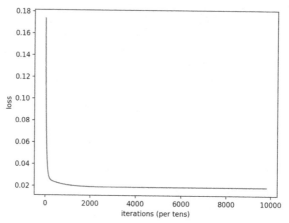

FIGURE 5.12 The plot of cost-versus-iterations for Listing 5.24.

Notice that Figure 5.12 has 10,000 iterations on the horizontal axis, whereas Figure 5.11 has only 100 iterations on the horizontal axis.

GOOGLE COLABORATORY

Depending on the hardware, GPU-based TF 2 code is typically at least 15 times faster than CPU-based TF 2 code. However, the cost of a good GPU can be a significant factor. Although NVIDIA provides GPUs, those consumer-based GPUs are not optimized for multi-GPU support (which *is* supported by TF 2).

Fortunately, Google Colaboratory is an affordable alternative that provides free GPU support, and also runs as a Jupyter notebook environment. In addition, Google Colaboratory executes your code in the cloud and involves zero configuration, and it's available online:

https://colab.research.google.com/notebooks/welcome.ipynb

The Jupyter notebook is suitable for training simple models and testing ideas quickly. Google Colaboratory makes it easy to upload local files, install software in Jupyter notebooks, and even connect Google Colaboratory to a Jupyter runtime on your local machine.

Some of the supported features of Colaboratory include TF 2 execution with GPUs, visualization using Matplotlib, and the ability to save a copy of your Google Colaboratory notebook to Github by using `File > Save a copy to GitHub`.

Moreover, you can load any `.ipynb` on GitHub by just adding the path to the URL *colab.research.google.com/github/* (see the Colaboratory website for details).

Google Colaboratory has support for other technologies such as HTML and SVG, enabling you o render SVG-based graphics in notebooks that are in Google Colaboratory. One point to keep in mind: any software that you install in a Google Colaboratory notebook is only available on a per-session basis. If you log out and log in again, you need to perform the same installation steps that you performed during your earlier Google Colaboratory session.

As mentioned earlier, there is one other nice feature of Google Colaboratory: You can execute code on a GPU for up to twelve hours per day for free. This free GPU support is extremely useful for people who don't have a suitable GPU on their local machine (which is probably the majority of users)., You can launch TF 2 code to train neural networks in less than 20 or 30 minutes that would otherwise require multiple hours of CPU-based execution time.

You can also launch Tensorboard inside a Google Colaboratory notebook with the following command (replace the specified directory with your own location):

```
%tensorboard --logdir /logs/images
```

Keep in mind the following details about Google Colaboratory. First, whenever you connect to a server in Google Colaboratory, you start what's known as a *session*. You can execute the code in a session with a CPU (the default), a GPU, or a TPU (which is available for free), and you can execute your code without any time limit for your session. However, if you select the GPU option for your session, *only the first 12 hours of GPU execution time are free*. Any additional GPU time during that same session incurs a small charge (see the website for those details).

Any software that you install in a Jupyter notebook during a given session will *not* be saved when you exit that session. For example, the following code snippet installs TFLearn in a Jupyter notebook:

```
!pip install tflearn
```

When you exit the current session and later start a new session, you need to install TFLearn again, as well as any other software (such as Github repositories) that you also installed in any previous session.

Incidentally, you can also run TF 2 code and TensorBoard in Google Colaboratory. Navigate to this link for more information:

https://www.tensorflow.org/tensorboard/r2/tensorboard_in_notebooks

Uploading CSV Files in Google Colaboratory

Listing 5.25 shows the content of `upload_csv_file.ipynb`, which illustrates how to upload a CSV file in a Google Colaboratory notebook.

LISTING 5.25: upload_csv_file.ipynb

```
import pandas as pd

from google.colab import files
uploaded = files.upload()

df = pd.read_csv("weather_data.csv")
```

```
print("dataframe df:")
df
```

Listing 5.25 uploads the CSV file `weather_data.csv`, whose contents are not shown because they are not important for this example. The code shown in bold is the Colaboratory-specific code that is required to upload the CSV file. When you launch this code, you will see a small button labeled "Browse," which you must click and then select the CSV file that is listed in the code snippet. After doing so, the rest of the code is executed and you will see the contents of the CSV file displayed in your browser session.

NOTE *You must supply the CSV file* `weather_data.csv` *if you want to launch this Jupyter notebook successfully in Google Colaboratory.*

SUMMARY

This chapter introduced you to the NumPy library for Python. You learned how to write Python scripts containing loops, arrays, and lists. You also saw how to work with dot products, the `reshape()` method, plotting with Matplotlib (discussed in more detail in Chapter 7), and examples of linear regression.

Then you learned how to work with sub-ranges of arrays, and also negative sub-ranges of vectors and arrays, both of which are useful for extracting portions of datasets in machine learning tasks. You also saw other NumPy operations, such as the `reshape()` method that is extremely useful (and very common) when working with images files.

Next, you learned how to use NumPy for linear regression, the mean squared error (MSE), and how to calculate MSE with the `linspace()` method. Finally, you got an introduction Google Colaboratory where you can take advantage of the free GPU time when you launch Jupyter notebooks.

## CHAPTER 6

INTRODUCTION TO PANDAS

This chapter introduces you to Pandas and provides code samples that illustrate some of its useful features. If you are familiar with these topics, skim through the material and peruse the code samples, just in case they contain some new information.

The first part of this chapter contains a brief introduction to Pandas. This section contains code samples that illustrate some features of data frames and a brief discussion of series, which are two of the main features of Pandas.

The second part of this chapter discusses various types of data frames that you can create, such as numeric and Boolean data frames. In addition, we discuss examples of creating data frames with NumPy functions and random numbers. We also examine examples of converting between Python dictionaries and JSON-based data, and how to create a Pandas data frame from JSON-based data.

WHAT IS PANDAS?

Pandas is a Python package that is compatible with other Python packages, such as NumPy and Matplotlib. Install Pandas by opening a command shell and invoking this command for Python 3.x:

```
pip3 install pandas
```

In many ways, the semantics of the APIs in the Pandas library are similar to a spreadsheet, along with support for xsl, xml, html, and csv file types. Pandas provides a data type called a data frame (similar to a Python dictionary) with an extremely powerful functionality.

Pandas data frames support a variety of input types, such as ndarray, list, dict, or series.

The data type `series` is another mechanism for managing data. In addition to performing an online search for more details regarding `Series`, the following article contains a good introduction:

https://towardsdatascience.com/20-examples-to-master-pandas-series-bc4c68200324

Pandas Options and Settings

You can change the default values of environment variables:

```
import pandas as pd

display_settings = {
    'max_columns': 8,
    'expand_frame_repr': True,  # Wrap to multiple pages
    'max_rows': 20,
    'precision': 3,
    'show_dimensions': True
}

for op, value in display_settings.items():
pd.set_option("display.{}".format(op), value)
```

Include the preceding code block in your own code if you want Pandas to display a maximum of 20 rows and 8 columns, and floating point numbers displayed with 3 decimal places. Set `expand_frame_rep` to True if you want the output to "wrap around" to multiple pages. The preceding `for` loop iterates through `display_settings` and sets the options equal to their corresponding values.

In addition, the following code snippet displays all Pandas options and their current values in your code:

```
print(pd.describe_option())
```

There are various other operations that you can perform with options and their values (such as the `pd.reset()` method for resetting values), as described in the Pandas user guide:

https://pandas.pydata.org/pandas-docs/stable/user_guide/options.html

Pandas Data Frames

In simplified terms, a Pandas data frame is a two-dimensional data structure, and it's convenient to think of the data structure in terms of rows and columns. Data frames can be labeled (rows as well as columns), and the columns can contain different data types. The source of the dataset for a Pandas data frame can be a data file, a database table, and a Web service. The data frame features include

Data frame methods
Data frame statistics

Grouping, pivoting, and reshaping
Handle missing data
Join data frames

The code samples in this chapter show you almost all the features in the preceding list.

Data Frames and Data Cleaning Tasks

The specific tasks that you need to perform depend on the structure and contents of a dataset. In general, you will perform a workflow with the following steps, not necessarily always in this order (and some might be optional). All of the following steps can be performed with a Pandas data frame:

- Read data into a data frame
- Display top of data frame
- Display column data types
- Display non_missing values
- Replace NA with a value
- Iterate through the columns
- Statistics for each column
- Find missing values
- Total missing values
- Percentage of missing values
- Sort table values
- Print summary information
- Columns with > 50% missing
- Rename columns

This chapter contains sections that illustrate how to perform many of the steps in the preceding list.

Alternatives to Pandas

Before delving into the code samples, there are alternatives to Pandas that offer very useful features, some of which are in the following list:

PySpark (for large datasets)
Dask (for distributed processing)
Modin (faster performance)
Datatable (R data.table for Python)

The inclusion of these alternatives is not intended to diminish Pandas. Indeed, you might not need any of the functionality in the preceding list. However, you might need such functionality in the future, so it's worthwhile for you to know about these alternatives now (and there may be even more powerful alternatives at some point in the future).

A PANDAS DATA FRAME WITH A NUMPY EXAMPLE

Listing 6.1 shows the content of `pandas_df.py` that illustrates how to define several data frames and display their contents.

LISTING 6.1: pandas_df.py

```
import pandas as pd
import numpy as np

myvector1 = np.array([1,2,3,4,5])
print("myvector1:")
print(myvector1)
print()

mydf1 = pd.DataFrame(myvector1)
print("mydf1:")
print(mydf1)
print()

myvector2 = np.array([i for i in range(1,6)])
print("myvector2:")
print(myvector2)
print()

mydf2 = pd.DataFrame(myvector2)
print("mydf2:")
print(mydf2)
print()

myarray = np.array([[10,30,20],
[50,40,60],[1000,2000,3000]])
print("myarray:")
print(myarray)
print()

mydf3 = pd.DataFrame(myarray)
print("mydf3:")
print(mydf3)
print()
```

Listing 6.1 starts with standard `import` statements for Pandas and NumPy, followed by the definition of two one-dimensional NumPy arrays and a two-dimensional NumPy array. Each NumPy variable is followed by a corresponding Pandas data frame (`mydf1`, `mydf2`, and `mydf3`). Now launch the code in Listing 6.1 to see the following output, and you can compare the NumPy arrays with the Pandas data frames:

```
myvector1:
[1 2 3 4 5]

mydf1:
   0
```

```
0  1
1  2
2  3
3  4
4  5

myvector2:
[1 2 3 4 5]

mydf2:
   0
0  1
1  2
2  3
3  4
4  5

myarray:
[[   10    30    20]
 [   50    40    60]
 [1000 2000 3000]]

mydf3:
      0     1     2
0    10    30    20
1    50    40    60
2  1000  2000  3000
```

By contrast, the following code block illustrates how to define a Pandas Series:

```
names = pd.Series(['SF', 'San Jose', 'Sacramento'])
sizes = pd.Series([852469, 1015785, 485199])
df = pd.DataFrame({ 'Cities': names, 'Size': sizes })
print(df)
```

Create a Python file with the preceding code (along with the required import statement), and when you launch that code, you will see the following output:

```
   City name     sizes
0         SF    852469
1   San Jose   1015785
2 Sacramento    485199
```

DESCRIBING A PANDAS DATA FRAME

Listing 6.2 shows the content of pandas_df_describe.py, which illustrates how to define a Pandas data frame that contains a 3×3 NumPy array of integer values, where the rows and columns of the data frame are labeled. Other aspects of the data frame are also displayed.

LISTING 6.2: pandas_df_describe.py

```
import numpy as np
import pandas as pd
```

```
myarray = np.array([[10,30,20],
[50,40,60],[1000,2000,3000]])

rownames = ['apples', 'oranges', 'beer']
colnames = ['January', 'February', 'March']

mydf = pd.DataFrame(myarray, index=rownames,
columns=colnames)
print("contents of df:")
print(mydf)
print()

print("contents of January:")
print(mydf['January'])
print()

print("Number of Rows:")
print(mydf.shape[0])
print()

print("Number of Columns:")
print(mydf.shape[1])
print()

print("Number of Rows and Columns:")
print(mydf.shape)
print()

print("Column Names:")
print(mydf.columns)
print()

print("Column types:")
print(mydf.dtypes)
print()

print("Description:")
print(mydf.describe())
print()
```

Listing 6.2 starts with two standard import statements followed by the variable myarray, which is a 3×3 NumPy array of numbers. The variables rownames and colnames provide names for the rows and columns, respectively, of the Pandas data frame mydf, which is initialized as a Pandas data frame with the specified data source (i.e., myarray).

The first portion of the output below requires a single print statement (which simply displays the contents of mydf). The second portion of the output is generated by invoking the describe() method that is available for any Pandas data frame. The describe() method is useful: you will see various statistical quantities, such as the mean, standard deviation minimum, and maximum performed by *columns* (not rows), along with values for the 25th, 50th, and 75th percentiles. The output of Listing 6.2 is here:

```
contents of df:
         January  February  March
apples        10        30     20
oranges       50        40     60
beer        1000      2000   3000

contents of January:
apples        10
oranges       50
beer        1000
Name: January, dtype: int64

Number of Rows:
3

Number of Columns:
3

Number of Rows and Columns:
(3, 3)

Column Names:
Index(['January', 'February', 'March'], dtype='object')

Column types:
January      int64
February     int64
March        int64
dtype: object

Description:
          January     February       March
count    3.000000     3.000000     3.000000
mean   353.333333   690.000000  1026.666667
std    560.386771  1134.504297  1709.073823
min     10.000000    30.000000    20.000000
25%     30.000000    35.000000    40.000000
50%     50.000000    40.000000    60.000000
75%    525.000000  1020.000000  1530.000000
max   1000.000000  2000.000000  3000.000000
```

PANDAS BOOLEAN DATA FRAMES

Pandas supports Boolean operations on data frames, such as the logical OR, the logical AND of a pair of data frames, and also logical negation. Listing 6.3 shows the content of pandas_boolean_df.py that illustrates how to define a Pandas data frame whose rows and columns are Boolean values.

LISTING 6.3: pandas_boolean_df.py

```
import pandas as pd

df1 = pd.DataFrame({'a': [1, 0, 1], 'b': [0, 1, 1] },
dtype=bool)
```

```
df2 = pd.DataFrame({'a': [0, 1, 1], 'b': [1, 1, 0] },
                   dtype=bool)

print("df1 & df2:")
print(df1 & df2)

print("df1 | df2:")
print(df1 | df2)

print("df1 ^ df2:")
print(df1 ^ df2)
```

Listing 6.3 initializes the data frames df1 and df2, and then computes df1 & df2, df1 | df2, and df1 ^ df2, which represent the logical AND, the logical OR, and the logical negation, respectively, of df1 and df2. The output from launching the code in Listing 6.3 is as follows:

```
df1 & df2:
       a      b
0  False  False
1  False   True
2   True  False
df1 | df2:
      a     b
0  True  True
1  True  True
2  True  True
df1 ^ df2:
       a      b
0   True   True
1   True  False
2  False   True
```

Transposing a Pandas Data Frame

The T attribute (as well as the transpose function) enables you to generate the transpose of a Pandas data frame, similar to the NumPy ndarray. The transpose operation switches rows to columns and columns to rows. For example, the following code snippet defines a Pandas data frame df1 and then displays the transpose of df1:

```
df1 = pd.DataFrame({'a': [1, 0, 1], 'b': [0, 1, 1] },
dtype=int)

print("df1.T:")
print(df1.T)
```

The output is here:

```
df1.T:
   0  1  2
a  1  0  1
b  0  1  1
```

The following code snippet defines Pandas data frames `df1` and `df2` and then displays their sum:

```
df1 = pd.DataFrame({'a' : [1, 0, 1], 'b' : [0, 1, 1] },
                   dtype=int)
df2 = pd.DataFrame({'a' : [3, 3, 3], 'b' : [5, 5, 5] },
                   dtype=int)
print("df1 + df2:")
print(df1 + df2)
```

The output is here:

```
df1 + df2:
   a  b
0  4  5
1  3  6
2  4  6
```

PANDAS DATA FRAMES AND RANDOM NUMBERS

Listing 6.4 shows the content of `pandas_random_df.py` that illustrates how to create a Pandas data frame with random numbers.

LISTING 6.4: pandas_random_df.py

```
import pandas as pd
import numpy as np

df = pd.DataFrame(np.random.randint(1, 5, size=(5, 2)),
columns=['a','b'])
df = df.append(df.agg(['sum', 'mean']))

print("Contents of data frame:")
print(df)
```

Listing 6.4 defines the Pandas data frame `df` that consists of 5 rows and 2 columns of random integers between 1 and 5. Notice that the columns of `df` are labeled "a" and "b." In addition, the next code snippet appends two rows consisting of the sum and the mean of the numbers in both columns. The output of Listing 6.4 is here:

```
      a     b
0     1.0   2.0
1     1.0   1.0
2     4.0   3.0
3     3.0   1.0
4     1.0   2.0
sum   10.0  9.0
mean  2.0   1.8
```

Listing 6.5 shows the content of `pandas_combine_df.py` that illustrates how to combine Pandas data frames.

LISTING 6.5: pandas_combine_df.py

```
import pandas as pd
import numpy as np

df = pd.DataFrame({'foo1' : np.random.randn(5),
                   'foo2' : np.random.randn(5)})

print("contents of df:")
print(df)

print("contents of foo1:")
print(df.foo1)

print("contents of foo2:")
print(df.foo2)
```

Listing 6.5 defines the Pandas data frame df that consists of 5 rows and 2 columns (labeled "foo1" and "foo2") of random real numbers between 0 and 5. The next portion of Listing 6.5 shows the content of df and foo1. The output of Listing 6.5 is as follows:

```
contents of df:
        foo1        foo2
0   0.274680  _0.848669
1  _0.399771  _0.814679
2   0.454443  _0.363392
3   0.473753   0.550849
4  _0.211783  _0.015014
contents of foo1:
0      0.256773
1      1.204322
2      1.040515
3     _0.518414
4      0.634141
Name: foo1, dtype: float64
contents of foo2:
0     _2.506550
1     _0.896516
2     _0.222923
3      0.934574
4      0.527033
Name: foo2, dtype: float64
```

READING CSV FILES IN PANDAS

Pandas provides the read_csv() method for reading the contents of CSV files. For example, Listing 6.6 shows the contents of sometext.txt that contain labeled data (spam or ham), and Listing 6.7 shows the contents of read_csv_file.py that illustrate how to read the contents of a CSV file.

LISTING 6.6: sometext.txt

```
type    text
```

```
ham      Available only for today
ham      I'm joking with you
spam     Free entry in 2 a wkly comp
ham      U dun say so early hor
ham      I don't think he goes to usf
spam     FreeMsg Hey there
ham      my brother is not sick
ham      As per your request Melle
spam     WINNER!! As a valued customer
```

LISTING 6.7: read_csv_file.py

```
import pandas as pd
import numpy as np

df = pd.read_csv('sometext.csv', delimiter='\t')

print("=> First five rows:")
print(df.head(5))
```

Listing 6.7 reads the contents of sometext.csv, whose columns are separated by a tab ("\t") delimiter. Launch the code in Listing 6.7 to see the following output:

```
=> First five rows:
    type                              text
0   ham       Available only for today
1   ham               I'm joking with you
2   spam    Free entry in 2 a wkly comp
3   ham             U dun say so early hor
4   ham     I don't think he goes to usf
```

The default value for the head() method is 5, but you can display the first n rows of a data frame df with the code snippet df.head(n).

You can also use the sep parameter specifies a different separator, and the names parameter specifies the column names in the data that you want to read, an example of which is here:

```
df2 = pd.read_csv("data.csv",sep="|",
            names=["Name","Surname","Height","Weight"])
```

Pandas also provides the read_table() method for reading the contents of CSV files, which uses the same syntax as the read_csv() method.

THE LOC() AND ILOC() METHODS IN PANDAS

If you want to display the contents of a record in a data frame, specify the index of the row in the loc() method. For example, the following code snippet displays the data by feature name in a data frame df:

```
df.loc[feature_name]
```

Select the first row of the "height" column in the data frame:

```
df.loc([0], ['height'])
```

The following code snippet uses the `iloc()` function to display the first 8 records of the name column with this code snippet:

```
df.iloc[0:8]['name']
```

CONVERTING CATEGORICAL DATA TO NUMERIC DATA

One common task in machine learning involves converting a feature containing character data into a feature that contains numeric data. Listing 6.8 shows the contents of `cat2numeric.py` that illustrate how to replace a text field with a corresponding numeric field.

LISTING 6.8: cat2numeric.py

```
import pandas as pd
import numpy as np

df = pd.read_csv('sometext.csv', delimiter='\t')

print("=> First five rows (before):")
print(df.head(5))
print("------------------------")
print()

# map ham/spam to 0/1 values:
df['type'] = df['type'].map( {'ham':0 , 'spam':1} )

print("=> First five rows (after):")
print(df.head(5))
print("------------------------")
```

Listing 6.8 initializes the data frame `df` with the contents of the CSV file `sometext.csv`, and then displays the contents of the first five rows by invoking `df.head(5)`, which is also the default number of rows to display.

The next code snippet in Listing 6.8 invokes the `map()` method to replace occurrences of `ham` with 0 and replace occurrences of `spam` with 1 in the column labeled `type`, as shown here:

```
df['type'] = df['type'].map( {'ham':0 , 'spam':1} )
```

The last portion of Listing 6.8 invokes the `head()` method again to display the first five rows of the dataset after having renamed the contents of the column type. Launch the code in Listing 6.8 to see the following output:

```
=> First five rows (before):
    type                      text
0   ham        Available only for today
1   ham            I'm joking with you
```

```
2   spam   Free entry in 2 a wkly comp
3   ham           U dun say so early hor
4   ham   I don't think he goes to usf
------------------------------

=> First five rows (after):
    type                         text
0      0      Available only for today
1      0             I'm joking with you
2      1   Free entry in 2 a wkly comp
3      0           U dun say so early hor
4      0   I don't think he goes to usf


------------------------------
```

As another example, Listing 6.9 shows the contents of `shirts.csv` and Listing 6.10 shows the contents of `shirts.py`; these examples illustrate four techniques for converting categorical data into numeric data.

LISTING 6.9: shirts.csv

```
type,ssize
shirt,xxlarge
shirt,xxlarge
shirt,xlarge
shirt,xlarge
shirt,xlarge
shirt,large
shirt,medium
shirt,small
shirt,small
shirt,xsmall
shirt,xsmall
shirt,xsmall
```

LISTING 6.10: shirts.py

```python
import pandas as pd

shirts = pd.read_csv("shirts.csv")
print("shirts before:")
print(shirts)
print()

# TECHNIQUE #1:
#shirts.loc[shirts['ssize']=='xxlarge','size'] = 4
#shirts.loc[shirts['ssize']=='xlarge', 'size'] = 4
#shirts.loc[shirts['ssize']=='large',  'size'] = 3
#shirts.loc[shirts['ssize']=='medium', 'size'] = 2
#shirts.loc[shirts['ssize']=='small',  'size'] = 1
#shirts.loc[shirts['ssize']=='xsmall', 'size'] = 1

# TECHNIQUE #2:
#shirts['ssize'].replace('xxlarge', 4, inplace=True)
```

```
#shirts['ssize'].replace('xlarge',  4, inplace=True)
#shirts['ssize'].replace('large',   3, inplace=True)
#shirts['ssize'].replace('medium',  2, inplace=True)
#shirts['ssize'].replace('small',   1, inplace=True)
#shirts['ssize'].replace('xsmall',  1, inplace=True)

# TECHNIQUE #3:
#shirts['ssize'] = shirts['ssize'].apply({'xxlarge':4,
'xlarge':4, 'large':3, 'medium':2, 'small':1, 'xsmall':1}.
get)

# TECHNIQUE #4:
shirts['ssize'] = shirts['ssize'].replace(regex='xlarge',
                                           value=4)
shirts['ssize'] = shirts['ssize'].replace(regex='large',
                                           value=3)
shirts['ssize'] = shirts['ssize'].replace(regex='medium',
                                           value=2)
shirts['ssize'] = shirts['ssize'].replace(regex='small',
                                           value=1)

print("shirts after:")
print(shirts)
```

Listing 6.10 starts with a code block of six statements that uses direct comparison with strings to make numeric replacements. For example, the following code snippet replaces all occurrences of the string xxlarge with the value 4:

```
shirts.loc[shirts['ssize']=='xxlarge','size'] = 4
```

The second code block consists of six statements that use the replace() method to perform the same updates, an example of which is shown here:

```
shirts['ssize'].replace('xxlarge', 4, inplace=True)
```

The third code block consists of a single statement that uses the apply() method to perform the same updates, as shown here:

```
shirts['ssize'] = shirts['ssize'].apply({'xxlarge':4,
'xlarge':4, 'large':3, 'medium':2, 'small':1, 'xsmall':1}.
get)
```

The fourth code block consists of four statements that use regular expressions to perform the same updates, an example of which is shown here:

```
shirts['ssize'] = shirts['ssize'].replace(regex='xlarge',
                                           value=4)
```

Since the preceding code snippet matches xxlarge as well as xlarge, we only need four statements instead of six statements. (If you are unfamiliar with regular expressions, you can read examples in Chapter 8.) Now launch the code in Listing 6.10 to see the following output:

```
shirts before
```

```
        type      size
0      shirt   xxlarge
1      shirt   xxlarge
2      shirt    xlarge
3      shirt    xlarge
4      shirt    xlarge
5      shirt     large
6      shirt    medium
7      shirt     small
8      shirt     small
9      shirt    xsmall
10     shirt    xsmall
11     shirt    xsmall

shirts after:
        type   size
0      shirt      4
1      shirt      4
2      shirt      4
3      shirt      4
4      shirt      4
5      shirt      3
6      shirt      2
7      shirt      1
8      shirt      1
9      shirt      1
10     shirt      1
11     shirt      1
```

MATCHING AND SPLITTING STRINGS IN PANDAS

Listing 6.11 shows the content of shirts_str.py, which illustrates how to match a column value with an initial string and how to split a column value based on a letter.

LISTING 6.11: shirts_str.py

```
import pandas as pd

shirts = pd.read_csv("shirts.csv")
print("shirts:")
print(shirts)
print()

print("shirts starting with xl:")
print(shirts[shirts.ssize.str.startswith('xl')])
print()

print("Exclude 'xlarge' shirts:")
print(shirts[shirts['ssize'] != 'xlarge'])
print()

print("first three letters:")
shirts['sub1'] = shirts['ssize'].str[:3]
```

```
print(shirts)
print()

print("split ssize on letter 'a':")
shirts['sub2'] = shirts['ssize'].str.split('a')
print(shirts)
print()

print("Rows 3 through 5 and column 2:")
print(shirts.iloc[2:5, 2])
print()
```

Listing 6.11 initializes the data frame df with the contents of the CSV file shirts.csv, and then displays the contents of df. The next code snippet in Listing 6.11 uses the startswith() method to match the shirt types that start with the letters xl, followed by a code snippet that displays the shorts whose size does not equal the string xlarge.

The next code snippet uses the construct str[:3] to display the first three letters of the shirt types, followed by a code snippet that uses the split() method to split the shirt types based on the letter "a."

The final code snippet invokes iloc[2:5,2] to display the contents of rows 3 through 5 inclusive, and only the second column. The output of Listing 6.11 is as follows:

```
shirts:
      type    ssize
0    shirt  xxlarge
1    shirt  xxlarge
2    shirt   xlarge
3    shirt   xlarge
4    shirt   xlarge
5    shirt    large
6    shirt   medium
7    shirt    small
8    shirt    small
9    shirt   xsmall
10   shirt   xsmall
11   shirt   xsmall

shirts starting with xl:
     type   ssize
2   shirt  xlarge
3   shirt  xlarge
4   shirt  xlarge

Exclude 'xlarge' shirts:
      type    ssize
0    shirt  xxlarge
1    shirt  xxlarge
5    shirt    large
6    shirt   medium
7    shirt    small
8    shirt    small
```

```
9    shirt   xsmall
10   shirt   xsmall
11   shirt   xsmall

first three letters:
     type     ssize  sub1
0    shirt  xxlarge   xxl
1    shirt  xxlarge   xxl
2    shirt   xlarge   xla
3    shirt   xlarge   xla
4    shirt   xlarge   xla
5    shirt    large   lar
6    shirt   medium   med
7    shirt    small   sma
8    shirt    small   sma
9    shirt   xsmall   xsm
10   shirt   xsmall   xsm
11   shirt   xsmall   xsm

split ssize on letter 'a':
     type     ssize  sub1        sub2
0    shirt  xxlarge   xxl  [xxl, rge]
1    shirt  xxlarge   xxl  [xxl, rge]
2    shirt   xlarge   xla   [xl, rge]
3    shirt   xlarge   xla   [xl, rge]
4    shirt   xlarge   xla   [xl, rge]
5    shirt    large   lar    [l, rge]
6    shirt   medium   med    [medium]
7    shirt    small   sma    [sm, ll]
8    shirt    small   sma    [sm, ll]
9    shirt   xsmall   xsm   [xsm, ll]
10   shirt   xsmall   xsm   [xsm, ll]
11   shirt   xsmall   xsm   [xsm, ll]

Rows 3 through 5 and column 2:
2    xlarge
3    xlarge
4    xlarge
Name: ssize, dtype: object
```

CONVERTING STRINGS TO DATES IN PANDAS

Listing 6.12 shows the content of `string2date.py`, which illustrates how to convert strings to date formats.

LISTING 6.12: string2date.py

```
import pandas as pd

bdates1 = {'strdates':  ['20210413','20210813','20211225'],
           'people': ['Sally','Steve','Sarah']
          }

df1 = pd.DataFrame(bdates1, columns =
['strdates','people'])
```

```
df1['dates'] = pd.to_datetime(df1['strdates'],
format='%Y%m%d')
print("=> Contents of data frame df1:")
print(df1)
print()
print(df1.dtypes)
print()

bdates2 = {'strdates':   ['13Apr2021','08Aug2021','25D
          ec2021'], 'people': ['Sally','Steve','Sarah']
          }

df2 = pd.DataFrame(bdates2, columns =
['strdates','people'])
df2['dates'] = pd.to_datetime(df2['strdates'],
format='%d%b%Y')
print("=> Contents of data frame df2:")
print(df2)
print()

print(df2.dtypes)
print()
```

Listing 6.12 initializes the data frame df1 with the contents of bdates1, and then converts the strdates column to dates using the %Y%m%d format. The next portion of Listing 6.12 initializes the data frame df2 with the contents of bdates2, and then converts the strdates column to dates using the %d%b%Y format. Now launch the code in Listing 6.12 to see the following output:

```
=> Contents of data frame df1:
    strdates people        dates
0   20210413  Sally 2021-04-13
1   20210813  Steve 2021-08-13
2   20211225  Sarah 2021-12-25

strdates                 object
people                   object
dates          datetime64[ns]
dtype: object

=> Contents of data frame df2:
     strdates people        dates
0   13Apr2021  Sally 2021-04-13
1   08Aug2021  Steve 2021-08-08
2   25Dec2021  Sarah 2021-12-25

strdates                 object
people                   object
dates          datetime64[ns]
dtype: object
```

MERGING AND SPLITTING COLUMNS IN PANDAS

Listing 6.13 shows the contents of `employees.csv` and Listing 6.14 shows the contents of `emp_merge_split.py`; these examples illustrate how to merge columns and split columns of a CSV file.

LISTING 6.13: employees.csv

```
name,year,month
Jane-Smith,2015,Aug
Dave-Smith,2020,Jan
Jane-Jones,2018,Dec
Jane-Stone,2017,Feb
Dave-Stone,2014,Apr
Mark-Aster,,Oct
Jane-Jones,NaN,Jun
```

LISTING 6.14: emp_merge_split.py

```python
import pandas as pd

emps = pd.read_csv("employees.csv")
print("emps:")
print(emps)
print()

emps['year']  = emps['year'].astype(str)
emps['month'] = emps['month'].astype(str)

# separate column for first name and for last name:
emps['fname'],emps['lname'] = emps['name'].str.
split("-",1).str

# concatenate year and month with a "#" symbol:
emps['hdate1'] = emps['year'].
astype(str)+"#"+emps['month'].astype(str)

# concatenate year and month with a "-" symbol:
emps['hdate2'] = emps[['year','month']].agg('-'.join,
axis=1)

print(emps)
print()
```

Listing 6.14 initializes the data frame `df` with the contents of the CSV file `employees.csv`, and then displays the contents of `df`. The next pair of code snippets invoke the `astype()` method to convert the contents of the `year` and `month` columns to strings.

The next code snippet in Listing 6.14 uses the `split()` method to split the name column into the columns `fname` and `lname` that contain the first name and last name, respectively, of each employee's name:

```python
emps['fname'],emps['lname'] = emps['name'].str.split
                              ("-",1).str
```

The next code snippet concatenates the contents of the year and month string with a "#" character to create a new column called hdate1:

```
emps['hdate1'] = emps['year'].
astype(str)+"#"+emps['month'].astype(str)
```

The final code snippet concatenates the contents of the year and month string with a "-" to create a new column called hdate2, as shown here:

```
emps['hdate2'] = emps[['year','month']].
agg('-'.join, axis=1)
```

Now launch the code in Listing 6.14 to see the following output:

```
emps:
        name     year month
0   Jane-Smith   2015.0   Aug
1   Dave-Smith   2020.0   Jan
2   Jane-Jones   2018.0   Dec
3   Jane-Stone   2017.0   Feb
4   Dave-Stone   2014.0   Apr
5   Mark-Aster      NaN   Oct
6   Jane-Jones      NaN   Jun

        name     year month fname  lname      hdate1       hdate2
0   Jane-Smith   2015.0   Aug  Jane  Smith  2015.0#Aug  2015.0-Aug
1   Dave-Smith   2020.0   Jan  Dave  Smith  2020.0#Jan  2020.0-Jan
2   Jane-Jones   2018.0   Dec  Jane  Jones  2018.0#Dec  2018.0-Dec
3   Jane-Stone   2017.0   Feb  Jane  Stone  2017.0#Feb  2017.0-Feb
4   Dave-Stone   2014.0   Apr  Dave  Stone  2014.0#Apr  2014.0-Apr
5   Mark-Aster      nan   Oct  Mark  Aster     nan#Oct     nan-Oct
6   Jane-Jones      nan   Jun  Jane  Jones     nan#Jun     nan-Jun
```

There is one other detail regarding the following commented out code snippet:

```
#emps['fname'],emps['lname'] = emps['name'].str.
                              split("-",1).str
```

The following deprecation message is displayed if you uncomment the preceding code snippet:

```
#FutureWarning: Columnar iteration over characters
#will be deprecated in future releases.
```

COMBINING PANDAS DATA FRAMES

Pandas supports the concat() method to concatenate data frames. Listing 6.15 shows the contents of concat_frames.py that illustrate how to combine two data frames.

LISTING 6.15: concat_frames.py
```
import pandas as pd

can_weather = pd.DataFrame({
```

```
        "city": ["Vancouver","Toronto","Montreal"],
        "temperature": [72,65,50],
        "humidity": [40, 20, 25]
})

us_weather = pd.DataFrame({
        "city": ["SF","Chicago","LA"],
        "temperature": [60,40,85],
        "humidity": [30, 15, 55]
})

df = pd.concat([can_weather, us_weather])
print(df)
```

The first line in Listing 6.15 is an `import` statement, followed by the definition of the data frames `can_weather` and `us_weather` that contain weather-related information for cities in Canada and the USA, respectively. The data frame `df` is the vertical concatenation of `can_weather` and `us_weather`. The output from Listing 6.15 is here:

```
0   Vancouver      40            72
1     Toronto      20            65
2    Montreal      25            50
0          SF      30            60
1     Chicago      15            40
2          LA      55            85
```

DATA MANIPULATION WITH PANDAS DATA FRAMES (1)

As an example, suppose that we have a two-person company that keeps track of income and expenses on a quarterly basis, and we want to calculate the profit/loss for each quarter, as well as the overall profit/loss.

Listing 6.16 shows the content of `pandas_quarterly_df1.py`, which illustrates how to define a Pandas data frame consisting of income-related values.

LISTING 6.16: pandas_quarterly_df1.py

```
import pandas as pd

summary = {
        'Quarter': ['Q1', 'Q2', 'Q3', 'Q4'],
        'Cost':    [23500, 34000, 57000, 32000],
        'Revenue': [40000, 40000, 40000, 40000]
}

df = pd.DataFrame(summary)

print("Entire Dataset:\n",df)
print("Quarter:\n",df.Quarter)
print("Cost:\n",df.Cost)
print("Revenue:\n",df.Revenue)
```

Listing 6.16 defines the variable `summary` that contains hard-coded quarterly information about cost and revenue for our two-person company. In general, these hard-coded values would be replaced by data from another source (such as a CSV file), so think of this code sample as a simple way to illustrate some of the functionality that is available in Pandas data frames.

The variable df is a data frame based on the data in the summary variable. The three print statements display the quarters, the cost per quarter, and the revenue per quarter. The output from Listing 6.16 is as follows:

```
Entire Dataset:
     Cost Quarter  Revenue
0    23500      Q1    40000
1    34000      Q2    60000
2    57000      Q3    50000
3    32000      Q4    30000

Quarter:
0      Q1
1      Q2
2      Q3
3      Q4
Name: Quarter, dtype: object

Cost:
0      23500
1      34000
2      57000
3      32000
Name: Cost, dtype: int64

Revenue:
0      40000
1      60000
2      50000
3      30000
Name: Revenue, dtype: int64
```

DATA MANIPULATION WITH PANDAS DATA FRAMES (2)

Let's suppose that we have a two-person company that keeps track of income and expenses on a quarterly basis, and we want to calculate the profit/loss for each quarter, and also the overall profit/loss.

Listing 6.17 shows the content of pandas_quarterly_df2.py, which illustrates how to define a Pandas data frame consisting of income-related values.

LISTING 6.17: pandas_quarterly_df2.py
```
import pandas as pd

summary = {
    'Quarter': ['Q1', 'Q2', 'Q3', 'Q4'],
    'Cost':    [-23500, -34000, -57000, -32000],
    'Revenue': [40000, 40000, 40000, 40000]
}
```

```
df = pd.DataFrame(summary)
print("First Dataset:\n",df)

df['Total'] = df.sum(axis=1)
print("Second Dataset:\n",df)
```

Listing 6.17 defines the variable summary that contains quarterly information about cost and revenue for our two-person company. The variable df is a data frame based on the data in the summary variable. The three print() statements display the quarters, the cost per quarter, and the revenue per quarter. The output from Listing 6.17 is as follows:

```
First Dataset:
      Cost Quarter  Revenue
0 -23500      Q1     40000
1 -34000      Q2     60000
2 -57000      Q3     50000
3 -32000      Q4     30000

Second Dataset:
      Cost Quarter  Revenue   Total
0 -23500      Q1     40000   16500
1 -34000      Q2     60000   26000
2 -57000      Q3     50000   -7000
3 -32000      Q4     30000   -2000
```

DATA MANIPULATION WITH PANDAS DATA FRAMES (3)

Let's start with the same assumption as the previous section. We have a two-person company that keeps track of income and expenses on a quarterly basis, and we want to calculate the profit/loss for each quarter, and also the overall profit/loss. In addition, we want to compute column totals and row totals.

Listing 6.18 shows the content of pandas_quarterly_df3.py that illustrates how to define a Pandas data frame consisting of income-related values.

LISTING 6.18: pandas_quarterly_df3.py

```
import pandas as pd

summary = {
    'Quarter': ['Q1', 'Q2', 'Q3', 'Q4'],
    'Cost':    [_23500,  _34000,  _57000,  _32000],
    'Revenue': [40000, 40000, 40000, 40000]
}

df = pd.DataFrame(summary)
print("First Dataset:\n",df)

df['Total'] = df.sum(axis=1)
df.loc['Sum'] = df.sum()
print("Second Dataset:\n",df)
```

```
# or df.loc['avg'] / 3
#df.loc['avg'] = df[:3].mean()
#print("Third Dataset:\n",df)
```

Listing 6.18 defines the variable `summary` that contains quarterly information about cost and revenue for our two-person company. The variable `df` is a data frame based on the data in the `summary` variable. The three `print()` statements display the quarters, the cost per quarter, and the revenue per quarter. The output from Listing 6.18 is shown here:

```
First Dataset:
      Cost   Quarter   Revenue
0  -23500      Q1       40000
1  -34000      Q2       60000
2  -57000      Q3       50000
3  -32000      Q4       30000

Second Dataset:
       Cost    Quarter   Revenue   Total
0    -23500       Q1       40000   16500
1    -34000       Q2       60000   26000
2    -57000       Q3       50000   -7000
3    -32000       Q4       30000   -2000
Sum -146500   Q1Q2Q3Q4   180000   33500
```

PANDAS DATA FRAMES AND CSV FILES

The code samples in several earlier sections contain hard-coded data inside the Python scripts. However, it's also common to read data from a CSV file. You can use the Python `csv.reader()` function, the NumPy `loadtxt()` function, or the Pandas function `read_csv()` function (shown in this section) to read the contents of CSV files.

Listing 6.19 shows the content of `weather_data.py`, which illustrates how to read a CSV file, initialize a Pandas data frame with the contents of that CSV file, and display various subsets of the data in the data frames.

LISTING 6.19: weather_data.py

```
import pandas as pd

df = pd.read_csv("weather_data.csv")

print(df)
print(df.shape)   # rows, columns
print(df.head())  # df.head(3)
print(df.tail())
print(df[1:3])
print(df.columns)
print(type(df['day']))
print(df[['day','temperature']])
print(df['temperature'].max())
```

Listing 6.19 invokes the `read_csv()` function to read the contents of the CSV file `weather_data.csv`, followed by a set of `print()` statements that displays various portions of the CSV file. The output from Listing 6.19 is as follows:

```
day,temperature,windspeed,event
7/1/2018,42,16,Rain
7/2/2018,45,3,Sunny
7/3/2018,78,12,Snow
7/4/2018,74,9,Snow
7/5/2018,42,24,Rain
7/6/2018,51,32,Sunny
```

In some situations, you might need to apply Boolean conditional logic to filter out some rows of data, based on a condition that's applied to a column value.

Listing 6.20 shows the content of the CSV file `people.csv` and Listing 6.21 shows the content of `people_pandas.py`; these code snippets illustrate how to define a Pandas data frame that reads the CSV file and manipulates the data.

LISTING 6.20: people.csv

```
fname,lname,age,gender,country
john,smith,30,m,usa
jane,smith,31,f,france
jack,jones,32,m,france
dave,stone,33,m,italy
sara,stein,34,f,germany
eddy,bower,35,m,spain
```

LISTING 6.21: people_pandas.py

```
import pandas as pd

df = pd.read_csv('people.csv')
df.info()
print('fname:')
print(df['fname'])
print('_____')
print('age over 33:')
print(df['age'] > 33)
print('_____')
print('age over 33:')
myfilter = df['age'] >  33
print(df[myfilter])
```

Listing 6.21 populates the data frame `df` with the contents of the CSV file `people.csv`. The next portion of Listing 6.21 displays the structure of `df`, followed by the first names of all the people.

Next, Listing 6.21 displays a tabular list of six rows containing either True or False, depending on whether a person is over 33 or at most 33, respectively.

The final portion of Listing 6.21 displays a tabular list of two rows containing all the details of the people who are over 33. The output from Listing 6.21 is shown here:

```
myfilter = df['age'] >  33
<class 'pandas.core.frame.Data frame'>
RangeIndex: 6 entries, 0 to 5
Data columns (total 5 columns):
fname       6 non_null object
lname       6 non_null object
age         6 non_null int64
gender      6 non_null object
country     6 non_null object
dtypes: int64(1), object(4)
memory usage: 320.0+ bytes

fname:
0     john
1     jane
2     jack
3     dave
4     sara
5     eddy
Name: fname, dtype: object


age over 33:
0     False
1     False
2     False
3     False
4      True
5      True
Name: age, dtype: bool


age over 33:
   fname   lname  age gender country
4   sara   stein   34      f  france
5   eddy   bower   35      m  France
```

MANAGING COLUMNS IN DATA FRAMES

This section contains various subsections with short code blocks that illustrate how to perform column-based operations on a data frame, which resemble the operations in a Python dictionary.

For example, the following code snippet illustrates how to define a Pandas data frame whose data values are from a Python dictionary:

```
df = pd.DataFrame.from_dict(dict([('A',[1,2,3]),
('B',[4,5,6])]), orient='index', columns=['one', 'two',
'three'])
print(df)
```

The output from the preceding code snippet is here:

```
     one  two  three
A     1    2      3
B     4    5      6
```

Switching Columns

The following code snippet defines a Pandas data frame and then switches the order of the columns:

```
df = pd.DataFrame.from_dict(dict([('A',[1,2,3]),(
'B',[4,5,6])]), orient='index', columns=['one', 'two',
'three'])

print("initial data frame:")
print(df)
print()

switched = ['three','one','two']
df=df.reindex(columns=switched)
print("switched columns:")
print(df)
print()
```

The output from the preceding code block is shown here:

```
initial data frame:
     one  two  three
A     1    2      3
B     4    5      6

switched columns:
     three  one  two
A        3    1    2
B        6    4    5
```

Appending Columns

The following code snippet computes the product of two columns and appends the result as a new column to the contents of the data frame df:

```
df['four'] = df['one'] * df['two']
print(df)
```

The output from the preceding code block is as follows:

```
     one  two  three  four
A     1    2      3     2
B     4    5      6    20
```

The following operation squares the contents of a column in the data frame df:

```
df['three'] = df['two'] * df['two']
print(df)
```

The output from the preceding code block is here (notice the numbers shown in bold):

```
    one   two   three   four
A    1     2      4       2
B    4     5     25      20
```

The following operation appends a new column called flag that contains True or False, based on whether the numeric value in the "one" column is greater than 2:

```
import numpy as np
rand = np.random.randn(2)
df.insert(1, 'random', rand)
print(df)
```

The output from the preceding code block is here:

```
    one     random    two   three   four    flag
A    1   -1.703111     2      4       2    False
B    4    1.139189     5     25      20    True
```

Deleting Columns

Columns can be deleted, as shown in following code snippet that deletes the "two" column:

```
del df['two']
print(df)
```

The output from the preceding code block is shown here:

```
one     random   three   four    flag
A    1  -0.460401     4      2   False
B    4   1.211468    25     20   True
```

Columns can be removed, as shown in following code snippet that deletes the "three" column:

```
three = df.pop('three')
print(df)
```

```
    one     random   four    flag
A    1   -0.544829     2   False
B    4    0.581476    20   True
```

Inserting Columns

When inserting a scalar value, it will be propagated to fill the column:

```
df['foo'] = 'bar'
print(df)
```

The output from the preceding code snippet is shown here:

```
     one    random  four   flag   foo
A      1 -0.187331     2  False   bar
B      4 -0.169672    20   True   bar
```

When inserting a `series` that does not have the same index as the data frame, it will be "conformed" to the index of the data frame:

```
df['one_trunc'] = df['one'][:1]
print(df)
```

The output from the preceding code snippet is here:

```
     one    random  four   flag   foo  one_trunc
A      1  0.616572     2  False   bar        1.0
B      4 -0.802656    20   True   bar        NaN
```

You can insert raw `ndarrays`, but their length must match the length of the index of the data frame.

The following operation inserts a column of random numbers in index position 1 (which is the second column) in the data frame `df`:

```
import numpy as np
rand = np.random.randn(2)
df.insert(1, 'random', rand)
print(df)
```

The output from the preceding code block is shown here:

```
     one    random  two  three  four
A      1 -1.703111    2      4     2
B      4  1.139189    5     25    20
```

Scaling Numeric Columns

Pandas makes it easy to scale the values in numeric columns. The value in every numeric column of the first row is assigned the value of 1, and the remaining column values are scaled accordingly. Note that values are scaled on a column-by-column basis, which is to say, the columns are treated independently of each other.

Listing 6.22 shows the content of `numbers.csv` and Listing 6.23 shows the content of `scale_columns.py`; these examples illustrate how to scale the values in numeric columns.

LISTING 6.22: numbers.csv

```
qtr1,qtr2,qtr3,qtr4
100,330,445,8000
200,530,145,3000
2000,1530,4145,5200
900,100,280,2000
```

LISTING 6.23: scale_columns.py

```python
import pandas as pd

filename="numbers.csv"

# read CSV file and display its contents:
df = pd.read_table(filename,delimiter=',')
print("=> contents of df:")
print(df)
print()

print("=> df.iloc[0]:")
print(df.iloc[0])
print()

df2 = df # save the data frame

# df/df.iloc[0] scales the columns:
df = df/df.iloc[0]
print("=> contents of df:")
print(df)
print()

# df2/df2['qtr1'].iloc[0] scales column qtr1:
df2['qtr1'] = df2['qtr1']/(df2['qtr1']).iloc[0]
print("=> contents of df2:")
print(df2)
print()
```

Listing 6.23 initializes the variable df as a data frame with the contents of the CSV file numbers.csv. Next, a print() statement displays the contents of df, followed by the contents of the column whose index is 0.

Next, the data frame df2 is initialized as a copy of df, followed by a division operation in df whereby the elements of every row are divided by their counterparts in df.iloc[0]. The final code block in Listing 6.23 updates the first column of df2 (which is a copy of the original contents of df) by an operation that effectively involves division by 100. Now launch the code in Listing 6.23 to see the following output:

```
=> contents of df:
    qtr1  qtr2  qtr3  qtr4
0    100   330   445  8000
1    200   530   145  3000
2   2000  1530  4145  5200
3    900   100   280  2000

=> df.iloc[0]:
qtr1      100
qtr2      330
qtr3      445
qtr4     8000
Name: 0, dtype: int64
```

```
=> contents of df:
    qtr1        qtr2        qtr3      qtr4
0   1.0    1.000000    1.000000    1.000
1   2.0    1.606061    0.325843    0.375
2  20.0    4.636364    9.314607    0.650
3   9.0    0.303030    0.629213    0.250

=> contents of df2:
    qtr1   qtr2   qtr3   qtr4
0   1.0    330    445   8000
1   2.0    530    145   3000
2  20.0   1530   4145   5200
3   9.0    100    280   2000
```

The preceding code will result in an error if the CSV file contains any non-numeric columns. However, in the latter case, you can specify the list of numeric columns whose values are to be scaled, an example of which is shown in the final code block in Listing 6.23.

MANAGING ROWS IN PANDAS

Pandas supports various row-related operations, such as finding duplicate rows, selecting a range of rows, deleting rows, and inserting new rows. The following subsections contain code sample that illustrate how to perform these operations.

Selecting a Range of Rows in Pandas

Listing 6.24 shows the contents of `duplicates.csv` and Listing 6.25 shows the contents of `row_range.py`; these examples illustrate how to select a range of rows in a Pandas data frame.

LISTING 6.24: duplicates.csv

```
fname,lname,level,dept,state
Jane,Smith,Senior,Sales,California
Dave,Smith,Senior,Devel,California
Jane,Jones,Year1,Mrktg,Illinois
Jane,Jones,Year1,Mrktg,Illinois
Jane,Stone,Senior,Mrktg,Arizona
Dave,Stone,Year2,Devel,Arizona
Mark,Aster,Year3,BizDev,Florida
Jane,Jones,Year1,Mrktg,Illinois
```

LISTING 6.25: row_range.py

```
import pandas as pd

df = pd.read_csv("duplicates.csv")

print("=> contents of CSV file:")
print(df)
```

```
print()

print("=> Rows 4 through 7 (loc):")
print(df.loc[4:7,:])
print()

print("=> Rows 4 through 6 (iloc):")
print(df.iloc[4:7,:])
print()
```

Listing 6.25 initializes the data frame df with the contents of the CSV file duplicates.csv, and then displays the contents of df. The next portion of Listing 6.25 displays the contents of rows 4 through 7, followed by the contents of rows 4 through 6. Launch the code in Listing 6.25 to see the following output:

```
=> contents of CSV file:
    fname  lname   level    dept       state
0   Jane   Smith   Senior   Sales    California
1   Dave   Smith   Senior   Devel    California
2   Jane   Jones   Year1    Mrktg     Illinois
3   Jane   Jones   Year1    Mrktg     Illinois
4   Jane   Stone   Senior   Mrktg     Arizona
5   Dave   Stone   Year2    Devel     Arizona
6   Mark   Aster   Year3    BizDev    Florida
7   Jane   Jones   Year1    Mrktg     Illinois

=> Rows 4 through 7 (loc):
    fname  lname   level    dept      state
4   Jane   Stone   Senior   Mrktg    Arizona
5   Dave   Stone   Year2    Devel    Arizona
6   Mark   Aster   Year3    BizDev   Florida
7   Jane   Jones   Year1    Mrktg    Illinois

=> Rows 4 through 6 (iloc):
    fname  lname   level    dept      state
4   Jane   Stone   Senior   Mrktg    Arizona
5   Dave   Stone   Year2    Devel    Arizona
6   Mark   Aster   Year3    BizDev   Florida
```

Finding Duplicate Rows in Pandas

Listing 6.26 shows the contents of duplicates.py that illustrate how to find duplicate rows in a Pandas data frame.

LISTING 6.26: duplicates.py

```
import pandas as pd

df = pd.read_csv("duplicates.csv")
print("Contents of data frame:")
print(df)
print()
```

```
print("Duplicate rows:")
#df2 = df.duplicated(subset=None)
df2 = df.duplicated(subset=None, keep='first')
print(df2)
print()

print("Duplicate first names:")
df3 = df[df.duplicated(['fname'])]
print(df3)
print()

print("Duplicate first name and level:")
df3 = df[df.duplicated(['fname','level'])]
print(df3)
print()
```

Listing 6.26 initializes the data frame df with the contents of the CSV file du-plicates.csv, and then displays the contents of df. The next portion of List-ing 6.26 displays the duplicate rows by invoking the duplicated() method, whereas the next portion of Listing 6.26 displays only the first name fname of the duplicate rows.

The final portion of Listing 6.26 displays the first name fname as well as the level of the duplicate rows. Launch the code in Listing 6.26 to see the fol-lowing output:

```
Contents of data frame:
    fname   lname   level    dept      state
0   Jane    Smith   Senior   Sales   California
1   Dave    Smith   Senior   Devel   California
2   Jane    Jones   Year1    Mrktg    Illinois
3   Jane    Jones   Year1    Mrktg    Illinois
4   Jane    Stone   Senior   Mrktg     Arizona
5   Dave    Stone   Year2    Devel     Arizona
6   Mark    Aster   Year3   BizDev     Florida
7   Jane    Jones   Year1    Mrktg    Illinois

Duplicate rows:
0      False
1      False
2      False
3       True
4      False
5      False
6      False
7       True
dtype: bool

Duplicate first names:
    fname   lname   level    dept     state
2   Jane    Jones   Year1    Mrktg   Illinois
3   Jane    Jones   Year1    Mrktg   Illinois
4   Jane    Stone   Senior   Mrktg    Arizona
5   Dave    Stone   Year2    Devel    Arizona
7   Jane    Jones   Year1    Mrktg   Illinois
```

```
Duplicate first name and level:
    fname  lname    level    dept     state
3   Jane   Jones    Year1    Mrktg    Illinois
4   Jane   Stone    Senior   Mrktg    Arizona
7   Jane   Jones    Year1    Mrktg    Illinois
```

Listing 6.27 shows the content of drop_duplicates.py, which illustrates how to remove duplicate rows in a Pandas data frame.

LISTING 6.27: drop_duplicates.py

```
import pandas as pd

df = pd.read_csv("duplicates.csv")
print("Contents of data frame:")
print(df)
print()

print("=> number of duplicate rows:", df.duplicated().
sum())
print()

print("=> row number(s) of duplicate rows:")
print(np.where(df.duplicated() == True)[0])
print()

fname_filtered = df.drop_duplicates(['fname'])
print("Drop duplicate first names:")
print(fname_filtered)
print()

fname_lname_filtered = df.drop_duplicates(['fname','lname'])
print("Drop duplicate first and last names:")
print(fname_lname_filtered)
print()
```

Listing 6.27 initializes the data frame df with the contents of the CSV file duplicates.csv, and then displays the contents of df. The next portion of Listing 6.27 deletes the rows that have duplicate fname values, followed by a code block that eliminates rows with duplicate fname and lname values. Launch the code in Listing 6.27 to see the following output:

```
Contents of data frame:
    fname  lname    level    dept     state
0   Jane   Smith    Senior   Sales    California
1   Dave   Smith    Senior   Devel    California
2   Jane   Jones    Year1    Mrktg    Illinois
3   Jane   Jones    Year1    Mrktg    Illinois
4   Jane   Stone    Senior   Mrktg    Arizona
5   Dave   Stone    Year2    Devel    Arizona
6   Mark   Aster    Year3    BizDev   Florida
7   Jane   Jones    Year1    Mrktg    Illinois

=> number of duplicate rows: 2
```

```
=> row number(s) of duplicate rows:
[3 7]

Drop duplicate first names:
   fname  lname  level    dept      state
0  Jane   Smith  Senior   Sales   California
1  Dave   Smith  Senior   Devel   California
6  Mark   Aster  Year3    BizDev    Florida

Drop duplicate first and last names:
   fname  lname  level    dept      state
0  Jane   Smith  Senior   Sales   California
1  Dave   Smith  Senior   Devel   California
2  Jane   Jones  Year1    Mrktg    Illinois
4  Jane   Stone  Senior   Mrktg     Arizona
5  Dave   Stone  Year2    Devel     Arizona
6  Mark   Aster  Year3    BizDev    Florida
```

Inserting New Rows in Pandas

Listing 6.28 shows the contents of emp_ages.csv and Listing 6.29 shows the contents of insert_row.py; these examples illustrate how to insert a new row in a Pandas data frame.

LISTING 6.28: emp_ages.csv

```
fname,lname,age
Jane,Smith,32
Dave,Smith,10
Jane,Jones,65
Jane,Jones,65
Jane,Stone,25
Dave,Stone,45
Mark,Aster,53
Jane,Jones,58
```

LISTING 6.29: insert_row.py

```
import pandas as pd

filename="emp_ages.csv"
df = pd.read_table(filename,delimiter=',')

new_row = pd.DataFrame({'fname':'New','lname':'Person',
                        'age':777},index=[0])
df = pd.concat([new_row, df]).reset_index(drop = True)

print("insert new first row in df:")
print(df.head(3))
print()
```

Listing 6.29 contains an import statement and then initializes the variable df with the contents of the CSV file emp_ages.csv. The next code snippet defines the variable new_row, whose contents are compatible with the structure of df, and then appends the contents of new_row to the data frame df. Launch the code in Listing 6.29 to see the following output:

```
     fname    lname   age
0    New      Person   777
1    Jane     Smith    32
2    Dave     Smith    10
```

HANDLING MISSING DATA IN PANDAS

Listing 6.30 shows the contents of employees2.csv and Listing 6.31 shows the contents of dup_missing.py; these code samples illustrate how to find duplicate rows and missing values in a Pandas data frame.

LISTING 6.30: employees2.csv

```
name,year,month
Jane-Smith,2015,Aug
Jane-Smith,2015,Aug
Dave-Smith,2020,
Dave-Stone,,Apr
Jane-Jones,2018,Dec
Jane-Stone,2017,Feb
Jane-Stone,2017,Feb
Mark-Aster,,Oct
Jane-Jones,NaN,Jun
```

LISTING 6.31: missing_values.py

```
import pandas as pd
import matplotlib.pyplot as plt
import numpy as np
import seaborn as sns

# the meaning of two strings:
#NA:  Not Available (Pandas)
#NaN: Not a Number (Pandas)
#NB:  NumPy uses np.nan() to check for NaN values

df = pd.read_csv("employees2.csv")

print("=> contents of CSV file:")
print(df)
print()

print("=> any NULL values per column?")
print(df.isnull().any())
print()

print("=> count of NAN/MISSING values in each column:")
print(df.isnull().sum())
print()
```

```
print("=> count of NAN/MISSING values in each column:")
print(pd.isna(df).sum())
print()

print("=> count of NAN/MISSING values in each column
(sorted):")
print(df.isnull().sum().sort_values(ascending=False))
print()

nan_null = df.isnull().sum().sum()
miss_values = df.isnull().any().sum()

print("=> count of NaN/MISSING values:",nan_null)
print("=> count of MISSING values:",miss_values)
print("=> count of NaN values:",nan_null-miss_values)
```

Listing 6.31 initializes the data frame df with the contents of the CSV file employees2.csv, and then displays the contents of df. The next portion of Listing 6.31 displays the number of null values that appear in any row or column. The next portion of Listing 6.31 displays the fields and the names of the fields that have null values, which are the year and month columns of the CSV file.

The next two code blocks of Listing 6.31 display the number of NaN values in the data frame using the method df.isnull().sum() and pd.isna(df). sum(), respectively (the result is the same).

The final portion of Listing 6.31 initializes the variables nan_null and miss_values that are 4 and 2, respectively, and then displays their values as well as the differences of their values. Launch the code in Listing 6.31 to see the following output:

```
=> contents of CSV file:
            name      year month
0    Jane-Smith    2015.0   Aug
1    Jane-Smith    2015.0   Aug
2    Dave-Smith    2020.0   NaN
3    Dave-Stone       NaN   Apr
4    Jane-Jones    2018.0   Dec
5    Jane-Stone    2017.0   Feb
6    Jane-Stone    2017.0   Feb
7    Mark-Aster       NaN   Oct
8    Jane-Jones       NaN   Jun

=> any NULL values per column?
name       False
year        True
month       True
dtype: bool

=> count of NAN/MISSING values in each column:
name       0
year       3
month      1
dtype: int64
```

```
=> count of NAN/MISSING values in each column:
name      0
year      3
month     1
dtype: int64

=> count of NAN/MISSING values in each column (sorted):
year      3
month     1
name      0
dtype: int64

=> count of NaN/MISSING values: 4
=> count of MISSING values: 2
=> count of NaN values: 2
```

Multiple Types of Missing Values

Listing 6.32 shows the content of `employees3.csv` that contains multiple types of missing values. Listing 6.33 shows the contents of the Python file `missing_multiple_types.py` that illustrates how to specify multiple missing value types when reading `employees3.csv` into a Pandas data frame.

LISTING 6.32: employees3.csv

```
name,year,month
Jane-Smith,2015,Aug
Dave-Smith,2020,NaN
Dave-Stone,?,Apr
Jane-Jones,2018,Dec
Jane-Stone,2017,Feb
Jane-Stone,2017,Feb
Mark-Aster,na,Oct
Jane-Jones,!,Jun
```

LISTING 6.33: missing_multiple_types.py

```
import pandas as pd

missing_values = ["na", "?", "!", "NaN"]
df = pd.read_csv("employees3.csv", na_values = missing_values)

print("=> contents of CSV file:")
print(df)
print()
```

Listing 6.33 is almost the same as previous examples. The only difference is shown in the pair of code snippets (in bold) that illustrates how to specify multiple missing value types.

Test for Numeric Values in a Column

Listing 6.34 displays the content of test_for_numeric.py, which illustrates how to check if a value in a row is numeric.

LISTING 6.34: test_for_numeric.py

```
import pandas as pd
import numpy as np

missing_values = ["na", "?", "!", "NaN"]
df = pd.read_csv("employees3.csv",
                 na_values = missing_values)

print("=> contents of CSV file:")
print(df)
print()

count = 0
for row in df['year']:
  try:
    int(row)
    df.loc[count," "] = np.nan
  except ValueError:
    count += 1

print("non-numeric count:",count)
```

Launch the code in Listing 6.34 to see the following output:

```
=> contents of CSV file:
          name     year month
0  Jane-Smith   2015.0   Aug
1  Jane-Smith   2015.0   Aug
2  Dave-Smith   2020.0   NaN
3  Dave-Stone      NaN   Apr
4  Jane-Jones   2018.0   Dec
5  Jane-Stone   2017.0   Feb
6  Jane-Stone   2017.0   Feb
7  Mark-Aster      NaN   Oct
8  Jane-Jones      NaN   Jun

non-numeric count: 3
```

Replacing NaN Values in Pandas

Listing 6.35 shows the content of missing_fill_drop.py, which illustrates how to replace missing values in a Pandas data frame.

LISTING 6.35: missing_fill_drop.py

```
import pandas as pd

df = pd.read_csv("employees2.csv")
```

```
print("=> contents of CSV file:")
print(df)
print()

print("Check for NANs:")
print(pd.isna(df))
print()

print("Drop missing data:")
df2 = df.dropna(axis=0, how='any')
print(df2)
print()

print("Replace missing data:")
print(df.fillna(7777))
print()
```

Listing 6.35 initializes the data frame df with the contents of the CSV file employees2.csv, and then displays the contents of df. The next portion of Listing 6.35 checks for NaN values and displays a tabular result in which each cell is either False or True, depending on whether the respective entry is NaN or not NaN, respectively.

The next code snippet initializes the data frame df2 with the contents of df, and then drops all rows in df2 that contain a NaN value. The final code snippet in Listing 6.35 replaces all occurrences of NaN with the value 7777 (there is nothing special about this value: It's simply for the purpose of demonstration).

Launch the code in Listing 6.35 to see the following output:

```
=> contents of CSV file:
          name      year month
0   Jane-Smith   2015.0   Aug
1   Jane-Smith   2015.0   Aug
2   Dave-Smith   2020.0   NaN
3   Dave-Stone      NaN   Apr
4   Jane-Jones   2018.0   Dec
5   Jane-Stone   2017.0   Feb
6   Jane-Stone   2017.0   Feb
7   Mark-Aster      NaN   Oct
8   Jane-Jones      NaN   Jun

=> Check for NANs:
    name     year   month
0  False    False   False
1  False    False   False
2  False    False    True
3  False     True   False
4  False    False   False
5  False    False   False
6  False    False   False
7  False     True   False
8  False     True   False
```

```
=> Drop missing data:
           name     year month
0    Jane-Smith   2015.0   Aug
1    Jane-Smith   2015.0   Aug
4    Jane-Jones   2018.0   Dec
5    Jane-Stone   2017.0   Feb
6    Jane-Stone   2017.0   Feb

=> Replace missing data:
           name     year month
0    Jane-Smith   2015.0   Aug
1    Jane-Smith   2015.0   Aug
2    Dave-Smith   2020.0   7777
3    Dave-Stone   7777.0   Apr
4    Jane-Jones   2018.0   Dec
5    Jane-Stone   2017.0   Feb
6    Jane-Stone   2017.0   Feb
7    Mark-Aster   7777.0   Oct
8    Jane-Jones   7777.0   Jun
```

SORTING DATA FRAMES IN PANDAS

Listing 6.36 shows the contents of sort_df.py that illustrate how to sort the rows in a Pandas data frame.

LISTING 6.36: sort_df.py

```python
import pandas as pd

df = pd.read_csv("duplicates.csv")
print("Contents of data frame:")
print(df)
print()

df.sort_values(by=['fname'], inplace=True)
print("Sorted (ascending) by first name:")
print(df)
print()

df.sort_values(by=['fname'], inplace=True,ascending=False)
print("Sorted (descending) by first name:")
print(df)
print()

df.sort_values(by=['fname','lname'], inplace=True)
print("Sorted (ascending) by first name and last name:")
print(df)
print()
```

Listing 6.36 initializes the data frame df with the contents of the CSV file du-plicates.csv, and then displays the contents of df. The next portion of Listing 6.36 displays the rows in ascending order based on the first name, and the next code block displays the rows in descending order based on the first name.

The final code block in Listing 6.36 displays the rows in ascending order based on the first name as well as the last name. Launch the code in Listing 6.36 to see the following output:

```
Contents of data frame:
   fname  lname   level    dept      state
0  Jane   Smith   Senior   Sales   California
1  Dave   Smith   Senior   Devel   California
2  Jane   Jones   Year1    Mrktg    Illinois
3  Jane   Jones   Year1    Mrktg    Illinois
4  Jane   Stone   Senior   Mrktg    Arizona
5  Dave   Stone   Year2    Devel    Arizona
6  Mark   Aster   Year3   BizDev    Florida
7  Jane   Jones   Year1    Mrktg    Illinois

Sorted (ascending) by first name:
   fname  lname   level    dept      state
1  Dave   Smith   Senior   Devel   California
5  Dave   Stone   Year2    Devel    Arizona
0  Jane   Smith   Senior   Sales   California
2  Jane   Jones   Year1    Mrktg    Illinois
3  Jane   Jones   Year1    Mrktg    Illinois
4  Jane   Stone   Senior   Mrktg    Arizona
7  Jane   Jones   Year1    Mrktg    Illinois
6  Mark   Aster   Year3   BizDev    Florida

Sorted (descending) by first name:
   fname  lname   level    dept      state
6  Mark   Aster   Year3   BizDev    Florida
0  Jane   Smith   Senior   Sales   California
2  Jane   Jones   Year1    Mrktg    Illinois
3  Jane   Jones   Year1    Mrktg    Illinois
4  Jane   Stone   Senior   Mrktg    Arizona
7  Jane   Jones   Year1    Mrktg    Illinois
1  Dave   Smith   Senior   Devel   California
5  Dave   Stone   Year2    Devel    Arizona

Sorted (ascending) by first name and last name:
   fname  lname   level    dept      state
1  Dave   Smith   Senior   Devel   California
5  Dave   Stone   Year2    Devel    Arizona
2  Jane   Jones   Year1    Mrktg    Illinois
3  Jane   Jones   Year1    Mrktg    Illinois
7  Jane   Jones   Year1    Mrktg    Illinois
0  Jane   Smith   Senior   Sales   California
4  Jane   Stone   Senior   Mrktg    Arizona
6  Mark   Aster   Year3   BizDev    Florida
```

WORKING WITH GROUPBY() IN PANDAS

Listing 6.37 shows the contents of groupby1.py that illustrate how to invoke the groupby() method to compute the subtotals of the feature values.

LISTING 6.37: groupby1.py

```python
import pandas as pd

# colors and weights of balls:
data = {'color':['red','blue','blue','red','blue'],
        'weight':[40,50,20,30,90]}
df1 = pd.DataFrame(data)
print("df1:")
print(df1)
print()
print(df1.groupby('color').mean())
print()

red_filter = df1['color']=='red'
print(df1[red_filter])
print()
blue_filter = df1['color']=='blue'
print(df1[blue_filter])
print()

red_avg = df1[red_filter]['weight'].mean()
blue_avg = df1[blue_filter]['weight'].mean()
print("red_avg,blue_avg:")
print(red_avg,blue_avg)
print()

df2 = pd.DataFrame({'color':['blue','red'],'weight':
                    [red_avg,blue_avg]})
print("df2:")
print(df2)
print()
```

Listing 6.37 defines the variable data containing the color and weight values, and then initializes the data frame df with the contents of the variable data. The next two code blocks define red_filter and blue_filter that match the rows whose colors are red and blue, respectively, and then prints the matching rows.

The next portion of Listing 6.37 defines the two filters red_avg and blue_ avg that calculate the average weight of the red value and the blue values, respectively. The last code block in Listing 6.37 defines the data frame df2 with a color color and a weight column, where the latter contains the average weight of the red values and the blue values. Launch the code in Listing 6.37 to see the following output:

```
initial data frame:
df1:
   color  weight
0    red      40
1   blue      50
2   blue      20
3    red      30
4   blue      90
```

```
        weight
color
blue    53.333333
red     35.000000

    color  weight
0     red      40
3     red      30

    color  weight
1    blue      50
2    blue      20
4    blue      90

red_avg,blue_avg:
35.0 53.333333333333336

df2:
   color     weight
0   blue   35.000000
red    53.333333
```

WORKING WITH APPLY() AND MAPAPPLY() IN PANDAS

Earlier in this chapter you saw an example of the `apply()` method for modifying the categorical values of a feature in the CSV file `shirts.csv`. This section contains more examples of the `apply()` method.

Listing 6.38 shows the content of `apply1.py`, which illustrates how to invoke the Pandas `apply()` method to compute the cube of a column of numbers.

LISTING 6.38: apply1.py

```
import pandas as pd

df = pd.DataFrame({'X1': [1,2,3], 'X2': [10,20,30]})

def cube(x):
  return x * x * x

df1 = df.apply(cube)
# same result:
# df1 = df.apply(lambda x: x * x * x)

print("initial data frame:")
print(df)
print("cubed values:")
print(df1)
```

Listing 6.38 initializes the data frame `df` with columns `X1` and `X2`, where the values for `X2` are 10 times the corresponding values in `X1`. Next, the Python function `cube()` returns the cube of its argument. Listing 6.38 then defines the variable `df1` by invoking the `apply()` function, which specifies the user-defined Python function cube(), and then prints the values of df as well as df1. Launch the code in Listing 6.38 to see the following output:

```
initial data frame:
   X1  X2
0   1  10
1   2  20
2   3  30
cubed values:
   X1      X2
0   1    1000
1   8    8000
2  27   27000
```

Apply a function to a data frame that multiplies all values in the "height" column of the data frame by 3:

```
df["height"].apply(lambda height: 3 * height)
```

OR:

```
def multiply(x):
    return x * 3
df["height"].apply(multiply)
```

Listing 6.39 shows the contents of apply2.py that illustrate how to invoke the apply() method to compute the sum of a set of values.

LISTING 6.39: apply2.py

```
import pandas as pd
import numpy as np

df = pd.DataFrame({'X1': [10,20,30], 'X2': [50,60,70]})

df1 = df.apply(np.sum, axis=0)
df2 = df.apply(np.sum, axis=1)

print("initial data frame:")
print(df)
print("add values (axis=0):")
print(df1)
print("add values (axis=1):")
print(df2)
```

Listing 6.39 is a variation of Listing 6.38. The variables df1 and df2 contain the column-wise sum and the row-wise sum, respectively, of the data frame df. Launch the code in Listing 6.39 to see the following output:

```
   X1  X2
0  10  50
1  20  60
2  30  70
```

```
add values (axis=0):
X1      60
X2     180
dtype: int64

add values (axis=1):
0       60
1       80
2      100
dtype: int64
```

Listing 6.40 shows the contents of mapapply1.py that illustrate how to invoke the mapapply() method to compute the square of a column of numbers.

LISTING 6.40: mapapply1.py

```
import pandas as pd
import math

df = pd.DataFrame({'X1': [1,2,3], 'X2': [10,20,30]})
df1 = df.applymap(math.sqrt)

print("initial data frame:")
print(df)
print("square root values:")
print(df1)
```

Listing 6.40 is another variant of Listing 6.38. In this case, the variable df1 is defined by invoking the mapapply() function on the variable df, which in turn references (but does not execute) the math.sqrt() function.

Next, a print() statement displays the contents of df, followed by a print() statement that displays the contents of df1. It is at this point that the built-in math.sqrt() function is invoked to calculate the square root of the numeric values in df. Launch the code in Listing 6.40 to see the following output:

```
initial data frame:
   X1  X2
0   1  10
1   2  20
2   3  30

square root values:
          X1        X2
0  1.000000  3.162278
1  1.414214  4.472136
3  1.732051  5.477226
```

Listing 6.41 shows the content of mapapply2.py, which illustrates how to invoke the applymap() method to convert strings to lowercase and upper-case.

LISTING 6.41: mapapply2.py

```python
import pandas as pd

df = pd.DataFrame({'fname': ['Jane'], 'lname': ['Smith']},
                  {'fname': ['Dave'], 'lname': ['Jones']})

df1 = df.applymap(str.lower)
df2 = df.applymap(str.upper)

print("initial data frame:")
print(df)
print()
print("lowercase:")
print(df1)
print()
print("uppercase:")
print(df2)
print()
```

Listing 6.41 initializes the variable df with two first and last name pairs, and then defines the variables df1 and df2 by invoking the applymap() method to the strings in the data frame df. The data frame df1 converts its input values to lowercase, whereas the data frame df2 converts its input values to uppercase. Launch the code in Listing 6.41 to see the following output:

```
initial data frame:
        fname  lname
fname   Jane   Smith
lname   Jane   Smith

lowercase:
        fname  lname
fname   jane   smith
lname   jane   smith

uppercase:
        fname  lname
fname   JANE   SMITH
lname   JANE   SMITH
```

HANDLING OUTLIERS IN PANDAS

If you are unfamiliar with outliers and anomalies, please read the sections "Missing Data, Anomalies, and Outliers" in Chapter 1 section to grasp Pandas code to find outliers in a dataset. The key idea involves finding the "z score" of the values in the dataset, which involves calculating the mean value and standard deviation std, and then mapping each value x in the dataset to the value (x-mean)/std.

Next, specify a value of z (such as 3) and find the rows whose z score is greater than 3. These are the rows that contain values that are considered outliers. *Note that a suitable value for the z score is your decision (not some other external factor).*

Listing 6.42 shows the contents of `outliers_zscores.py` that illustrate how to find rows of a dataset whose z-score greater than (or less than) a specified value.

LISTING 6.42: outliers_zscores.py

```
import numpy as np
import pandas as pd
from scipy import stats
from sklearn import datasets

df = datasets.load_iris()
columns = df.feature_names
iris_df = pd.DataFrame(df.data)
iris_df.columns = columns

print("=> iris_df.shape:",iris_df.shape)
print(iris_df.head())
print()

z = np.abs(stats.zscore(iris_df))
print("z scores for iris:")
print("z.shape:",z.shape)

upper = 2.5
lower = 0.01
print("=> upper outliers:")
print(z[np.where(z > upper)])
print()

outliers = iris_df[z < lower]
print("=> lower outliers:")
print(outliers)
print()
```

Listing 6.42 initializes the variable `df` with the contents of the built-in `Iris` dataset (see the section in Chapter 1 for an introduction to Sklearn). Next, the variable `columns` is initialized with the column names, and the data frame `iris_df` is initialized from the content of `df.data` that contains the actual data for the `Iris` dataset. In addition, `iris_df.columns` is initialized with the contents of the variable `columns`.

The next portion of Listing 6.42 displays the shape of the data frame `iris_df`, followed by the `zscore` of the `iris_df` data frame, which is computed by subtracting the mean and then dividing by the standard deviation (performed for each row).

The last two portions of Listing 6.42 display the outliers (if any) whose `zscore` is outside the interval [0.01, 2.5]. Launch the code in Listing 6.42 to see the following output:

```
=> iris_df.shape: (150, 4)
     sepal length (cm)  sepal width (cm)  petal length (cm)  petal width (cm)
0                  5.1               3.5                1.4               0.2
1                  4.9               3.0                1.4               0.2
2                  4.7               3.2                1.3               0.2
3                  4.6               3.1                1.5               0.2
4                  5.0               3.6                1.4               0.2


z scores for iris:
z.shape: (150, 4)


=> upper outliers:
[3.09077525 2.63038172]


=> lower outliers:
     sepal length (cm)  sepal width (cm)  petal length (cm)  petal width (cm)
73                 6.1               2.8                4.7               1.2
82                 5.8               2.7                3.9               1.2
90                 5.5               2.6                4.4               1.2
92                 5.8               2.6                4.0               1.2
95                 5.7               3.0                4.2               1.2
```

PANDAS DATA FRAMES AND SCATTERPLOTS

Listing 6.43 shows the content of pandas_scatter_df.py, which illustrates how to generate a scatterplot from a data frame.

LISTING 6.43: pandas_scatter_df.py

```python
import numpy as np
import pandas as pd
import matplotlib.pyplot as plt
from pandas import read_csv
from pandas.plotting import scatter_matrix

myarray = np.array([[10,30,20],
[50,40,60],[1000,2000,3000]])

rownames = ['apples', 'oranges', 'beer']
colnames = ['January', 'February', 'March']

mydf = pd.DataFrame(myarray, index=rownames,
columns=colnames)

print(mydf)
print(mydf.describe())

scatter_matrix(mydf)
plt.show()
```

Listing 6.43 starts with various import statements, followed by the definition of the NumPy array myarray. Next, the variables myarray and colnames are initialized with values for the rows and columns, respectively. The next portion of Listing 6.43 initializes the data frame `mydf` so that the rows and columns are labeled in the output, as shown here:

```
         January  February  March
apples        10        30     20
oranges       50        40     60
beer        1000      2000   3000

           January      February        March
count     3.000000      3.000000     3.000000
mean    353.333333    690.000000  1026.666667
std     560.386771   1134.504297  1709.073823
min      10.000000     30.000000    20.000000
25%      30.000000     35.000000    40.000000
50%      50.000000     40.000000    60.000000
75%     525.000000   1020.000000  1530.000000
max    1000.000000   2000.000000  3000.0000000
```

PANDAS DATA FRAMES AND SIMPLE STATISTICS

Listing 6.44 shows a portion of the CSV file `housing.csv` and Listing 6.45 shows the contents of `housing_stats.py`; these samples illustrate how to gather basic statistics from `housing.csv` in a Pandas data frame.

LISTING 6.44: housing.csv

```
price,bedrooms,bathrooms,sqft_living
221900,3,1,1180
538000,3,2.25,2570
180000,2,1,770
604000,4,3,1960
510000,3,2,1680
// details omitted for brevity
785000,4,2.5,2290
450000,3,1.75,1250
228000,3,1,1190
345000,5,2.5,3150
600000,3,1.75,1410
```

LISTING 6.45: housing_stats.py

```python
import pandas as pd

df = pd.read_csv("housing.csv")

minimum_bdrms = df["bedrooms"].min()
median_bdrms  = df["bedrooms"].median()
maximum_bdrms = df["bedrooms"].max()

print("minimum # of bedrooms:",minimum_bdrms)
print("median  # of bedrooms:",median_bdrms)
print("maximum # of bedrooms:",maximum_bdrms)
print("")
```

```
print("median values:",df.median().values)
print("")

prices = df["price"]
print("first 5 prices:")
print(prices.head())
print("")

median_price = df["price"].median()
print("median price:",median_price)
print("")

corr_matrix = df.corr()
print("correlation matrix:")
print(corr_matrix["price"].sort_values(ascending=False))
```

Listing 6.45 initializes the data frame df with the contents of the CSV file
housing.csv. The next three variables are initialized with the minimum,
median, and maximum number of bedrooms, and then these values are displayed.

The next portion of Listing 6.45 initializes the variable prices with the
contents of the prices column of the data frame df. Next, the first five rows
are printed via the prices.head() statement, followed by the median value
of the prices.

The final portion of Listing 6.45 initializes the variable corr_matrix with
the contents of the correlation matrix for the data frame df, and then displays
its contents. The output from Listing 6.45 is shown here:

```
minimum # of bedrooms: 2
median  # of bedrooms: 3.0
maximum # of bedrooms: 5

median values: [4.5900e+05 3.0000e+00 1.7500e+00 1.7125e+03]

first 5 prices:
0    221900
1    538000
2    180000
3    604000
4    510000
Name: price, dtype: int64

median price: 459000.0

correlation matrix:
price          1.000000
sqft_living    0.620634
bathrooms      0.440047
bedrooms       0.379300
Name: price, dtype: float64
```

AGGREGATE OPERATIONS IN PANDAS DATA FRAMES

The `agg()` function is an alias for *aggregate*, which performs aggregate (multiple) operations on columns (the Pandas documentations states "use the alias").

Listing 6.46 shows the content of `aggregate1.py`, which illustrates how to perform aggregate operations with the data in a data frame.

LISTING 6.46: aggregate1.py

```
import pandas as pd

df = pd.DataFrame([[4, 2, 3, 1],
                   [8, 1, 5, -4],
                   [6, 9, 8, -8]],
                  columns=['X1', 'X2', 'X3', 'X4'])

print("=> data frame:")
print(df)
print()

print("=> Aggregate sum and min over the rows:")
print(df.agg(['sum', 'min', 'max']))
print()

print("=> Aggregate mean over the columns:")
print(df.agg("mean", axis="columns"))
print()
```

Listing 6.46 initializes the data frame `df` with the contents of a 3×4 array of numeric values, and then displays the contents of `df`. The next code snippet invokes the `agg()` method in order to append the methods `sum()`, `min()`, and `max()` to `df`. The result is a new 3×4 array of values where the rows contain the sum, minimum, and maximum of the values in each column of `df`. The final code snippet displays a row of data that contains the mean of each column of `df`. Launch the code in Listing 6.46 to see the following output:

```
=> data frame:
   X1  X2  X3  X4
0   4   2   3   1
1   8   1   5  -4
2   6   9   8  -8

=> Aggregate sum and min over the rows:
     X1  X2  X3  X4
sum  18  12  16 -11
min   4   1   3  -8
max   8   9   8   1

=> Aggregate mean over the columns:
0    2.50
1    2.50
2    3.75
dtype: float64
```

AGGREGATE OPERATIONS WITH THE `TITANIC.CSV` DATASET

Listing 6.47 shows the contents of `aggregate2.py` that illustrate how to perform aggregate operations with columns in the CSV file `titanic.csv`.

LISTING 6.47: aggregate2.py

```
import pandas as pd

#Loading titanic.csv in Seaborn:
#df = sns.load_dataset('titanic')
df = pd.read_csv("titanic.csv")

# convert floating point values to integers:
df['survived'] = df['survived'].astype(int)

# specify column and aggregate functions:
aggregates1 = {'embark_town': ['count', 'nunique', 'size']}

# group by 'deck' value and apply aggregate functions:
result = df.groupby(['deck']).agg(aggregates1)
print("=> Grouped by deck:")
print(result)
print()

# some details regarding count() and nunique():
# count() excludes NaN values whereas size() includes them
# nunique() excludes NaN values in the unique counts

# group by 'age' value and apply aggregate functions:
result2 = df.groupby(['age']).agg(aggregates1)
print("=> Grouped by age (before):")
print(result2)
print()

# some "age" values are missing (so drop them):
df = df.dropna()

# convert floating point values to integers:
df['age'] = df['age'].astype(int)

# group by 'age' value and apply aggregate functions:
result3 = df.groupby(['age']).agg(aggregates1)
print("=> Grouped by age (after):")
print(result3)
print()
```

Listing 6.47 initializes the data frame `df` with the contents of the CSV file `ti-tanic.csv`. The next code snippet converts floating point values to integers, followed by defining the variable `aggregates1` that specifies the functions `count()`, `nunique()`, and `size()` that will be invoked on the `embark_town` field.

The next code snippet initializes the variable `result` after invoking the `groupby()` method on the `deck` field, followed by invoking the `agg()` method.

The next code block performs the same computation to initialize the variable `result2`, except that the `groupby()` function is invoked on the `age` field instead of the `embark_town` field. Notice the comment section regarding the `count()` and `nunique()` functions. Let's eliminate the rows with missing values via `df.dropna()` and investigate how that affects the calculations.

After removing the rows with missing values, the final code block initializes the variable `result3` in exactly the same way that `result2` was initialized. Launch the code in Listing 6.47 to see the following output:

```
=> Grouped by deck:
          embark_town
                  count nunique size
deck
A                   15        2    15
B                   45        2    47
C                   59        3    59
D                   33        2    33
E                   32        3    32
F                   13        3    13
G                    4        1     4

=> Grouped by age (before):
          age
          count nunique size
age
0.42        1        1     1
0.67        1        1     1
0.75        2        1     2
0.83        2        1     2
0.92        1        1     1
...        ...      ...   ...
70.00       2        1     2
70.50       1        1     1
71.00       2        1     2
74.00       1        1     1
80.00       1        1     1

[88 rows x 3 columns]

=> Grouped by age (after):
          age
          count nunique size
age
0           1        1     1
1           1        1     1
2           3        1     3
3           1        1     1
4           3        1     3
6           1        1     1
11          1        1     1
14          1        1     1
15          1        1     1
```

```
// details omitted for brevity
60      2       1       2
61      2       1       2
62      1       1       1
63      1       1       1
64      1       1       1
65      2       1       2
70      1       1       1
71      1       1       1
80      1       1       1
```

SAVE DATA FRAMES AS CSV FILES AND ZIP FILES

Listing 6.48 shows the contents of `save2csv.py` that illustrate how to save a Pandas data frame as a CSV file and as a zip file that contains both the CSV file and the contents of the data frame.

LISTING 6.48: save2csv.py

```python
import pandas as pd

df = pd.DataFrame({'fname':'Jane','lname':'Smith','age':25},
                  {'fname':'Dave','lname':'Jones','age':35},
                  {'fname':'Sara','lname':'Stone','age':45})

# save data frame to CSV file:
print("Saving data to save.csv:")
df.to_csv("save.csv",index=False)

# save data frame as CSV file in a zip file:
compression_opts = dict(method='zip',archive_name='save2.
                        csv')
df.to_csv('save2.zip', index=False, compression=compression_
          opts)
```

Listing 6.48 defines the data frame `df` that contains three rows of data, with values for the first name, last name, and age of three people. The next code snippet invokes the `to_csv()` method to save the contents of `df` to the CSV file `save2.csv`. The final code snippet also invokes the `to_csv()` method, this time to save the contents of `save2.csv` in the zip file `save2.zip`. Launch the code in Listing 6.48; after doing this, you will see two new files in the directory where you launched this Python script:

```
save.csv
save2.zip
```

PANDAS DATA FRAMES AND EXCEL SPREADSHEETS

Listing 6.49 shows the content of `write_people_xlsx.py`, which illustrates how to read data from a CSV file and then create an Excel spreadsheet with that data.

LISTING 6.49: write_people_xlsx.py

```
import pandas as pd

df1 = pd.read_csv("people.csv")
df1.to_excel("people.xlsx")

#optionally specify the sheet name:
#df1.to_excel("people.xlsx", sheet_name='Sheet_name_1')
```

Listing 6.49 contains the usual `import` statement, after which the variable `df1` is initialized with the contents of the CSV file `people.csv`. The final code snippet then creates the Excel spreadsheet `people.xlsx` with the contents of the data frame `df1`, which contains the contents of the CSV file `people.csv`.

Launch `write_people_xlsx.py` from the command line and then open the newly created Excel spreadsheet `people.xlsx` to confirm its contents.

Listing 6.50 shows the contents of `read_people_xslx.py` that illustrate how to read data from an Excel spreadsheet and create a Pandas data frame with that data.

LISTING 6.50: read_people_xslx.py

```
import pandas as pd

df = pd.read_excel("people.xlsx")
print("Contents of Excel spreadsheet:")
print(df)
```

Listing 6.50 shows that the Pandas data frame `df` is initialized with the contents of the spreadsheet `people.xlsx` (the contents are the same as `people.csv`) via the function `read_excel()`. The output from Listing 6.50 is shown here:

```
df1:
   Unnamed: 0 fname   lname   age gender  country
0           0 john    smith   30      m      usa
1           1 jane    smith   31      f   france
2           2 jack    jones   32      m   france
3           3 dave    stone   33      m    italy
4           4 sara    stein   34      f  germany
5           5 eddy    bower   35      m    spain
```

WORKING WITH JSON-BASED DATA

A JSON object consists of data represented as colon-separated name/value pairs, and data objects are separated by commas. An object is specified inside curly braces {}, and an array of objects is indicated by square brackets []. Note that character-valued data elements are inside quotes "" (no quotes for numeric data).

Here is a simple example of a JSON object:

```
{ "fname":"Jane", "lname":"Smith", "age":33, "city":"SF" }
```

Here is a simple example of an array of JSON objects:

```
[
{ "fname":"Jane", "lname":"Smith", "age":33, "city":"SF" },
{ "fname":"John", "lname":"Jones", "age":34, "city":"LA" },
{ "fname":"Dave", "lname":"Stone", "age":35, "city":"NY" },
]
```

Python Dictionary and JSON

The Python json library enables you to work with JSON-based data in Python.

Listing 6.51 shows the contents of dict2json.py that illustrate how to convert a Python dictionary to a JSON string.

LISTING 6.51: dict2json.py

```
import json

dict1 = {}
dict1["fname"] = "Jane"
dict1["lname"] = "Smith"
dict1["age"]   = 33
dict1["city"]  = "SF"

print("Python dictionary to JSON data:")
print("dict1:",dict1)
json1 = json.dumps(dict1, ensure_ascii=False)
print("json1:",json1)
print("")

# convert JSON string to Python dictionary:
json2 = '{"fname":"Dave", "lname":"Stone", "age":35,
"city":"NY"}'
dict2 = json.loads(json2)
print("JSON data to Python dictionary:")
print("json2:",json2)
print("dict2:",dict2)
```

Listing 6.51 invokes the json.dumps() function to perform the conversion from a Python dictionary to a JSON string. Launch the code in Listing 6.51 to see the following output:

```
Python dictionary to JSON data:
dict1: {'fname': 'Jane', 'lname': 'Smith', 'age': 33,
       'city': 'SF'}
json1: {"fname": "Jane", "lname": "Smith", "age": 33,
       "city": "SF"}

JSON data to Python dictionary:
json2: {"fname":"Dave", "lname":"Stone", "age":35,
       "city":"NY"}
dict2: {'fname': 'Dave', 'lname': 'Stone', 'age': 35,
       'city': 'NY'}
```

Python, Pandas, and JSON

Listing 6.52 shows the content of `pd_python_json.py`, which illustrates how to convert a Python dictionary to a Pandas data frame and then convert the data frame to a JSON string.

LISTING 6.52: pd_python_json.py

```
import json
import pandas as pd

dict1 = {}
dict1["fname"] = "Jane"
dict1["lname"] = "Smith"
dict1["age"]   = 33
dict1["city"]  = "SF"

df1 = pd.DataFrame.from_dict(dict1, orient='index')
print("Pandas df1:")
print(df1)
print()

json1 = json.dumps(dict1, ensure_ascii=False)
print("Serialized to JSON1:")
print(json1)
print()

print("Data frame to JSON2:")
json2 = df1.to_json(orient='split')
print(json2)
```

Listing 6.52 initializes a Python dictionary `dict1` with multiple attributes for a user (first name, last name, and so forth). Next, the data frame `df1` is created from the Python dictionary `dict2json.py`, and its contents are displayed.

The next portion of Listing 6.52 initializes the variable `json1` by serializing the contents of `dict2json.py`, and its contents are displayed. The last code block in Listing 6.52 initializes the variable `json2` to the result of converting the data frame `df1` to a JSON string. Launch the code in Listing 6.52 to see the following output:

```
dict1: {'fname': 'Jane', 'lname': 'Smith', 'age': 33,
        'city': 'SF'}
Pandas df1:
           0
fname    Jane
lname    Smith
age        33
city       SF

Serialized to JSON1:
{"fname": "Jane", "lname": "Smith", "age": 33, "city": "SF"}

Data frame to JSON2:
```

```
{"columns":[0],"index":["fname","lname","age","city"],"data
":[["Jane"],["Smith"],[33],["SF"]]}
json1: {"fname": "Jane", "lname": "Smith", "age": 33,
"city": "SF"}
```

USEFUL ONE-LINE COMMANDS IN PANDAS

This section contains an eclectic mix of one-line commands in Pandas (some of which you have already seen in this chapter) that are useful to know: Drop a feature in a data frame:

```
df.drop('feature_variable_name', axis=1)
```

Convert object type to float in a data frame:

```
pd.to_numeric(df["feature_name"], errors='coerce')
```

Convert data in a Pandas data frame to NumPy array:

```
df.as_matrix()
```

Rename the fourth column of the data frame as "height:"

```
df.rename(columns = {df.columns[3]:'height'}, inplace=True)
```

Get the unique entries of the column "first" in a data frame:

```
df["first"].unique()
```

Display the number of different values in the first column:

```
df["first"].nunique()
```

Create a data frame with columns 'first" and "last" from an existing data frame:

```
new_df = df[["name", "size"]]
```

Sort the data in a data frame:

```
df.sort_values(ascending = False)
```

Filter the data column named "size" to display only values equal to 7:

```
df[df["size"] == 7]
```

Display at most 1000 characters in each cell:

```
pd.set_option('max_colwidth', 1000)
```

Display at most 20 data frame rows:

```
pd.set_option('max_rows', 20)
```

Display at most 1000 columns:

```
pd.set_option('max_columns', 1000)
```

Display a random set of n rows:

```
df.sample(n)
```

WHAT IS METHOD CHAINING?

Method chaining refers to combining method invocations without intermediate code. Method chaining is available in many languages, including Java, Scala, and JavaScript. Code that uses method chaining tends to be more compact, more performant, and easier to understand than other types of code. However, debugging such code can be difficult, especially in long method chains.

As a general rule, start by invoking a sequence of methods, and after ensuring that the code is correct, construct method chains with at most five or six methods. However, if a method inside a method chain also invokes other functions, then split the chain into two parts to increase readability. Since there is no "best" way to determine the number of methods in a method chain, experiment with method chains of different sizes (and differing complexity) until you determine a style that works best for you.

Pandas and Method Chaining

Recently, Pandas improved its support for method chaining, which includes the methods `assign()`, `pivot_table()`, and `query()`. Moreover, the `pipe()` method supports method chaining that contains user-defined methods. The following code snippet illustrate show to use method chaining in order to invoke several Pandas methods:

```
import pandas as pd
pd.read_csv('data.csv')
   .fillna(...)
   .query('...')
   .assign(...)
   .pivot_table(...)
   .rename(...)
```

Consult the online documentation for more details regarding method chaining in Pandas.

PANDAS PROFILING

Pandas profiling is a useful Python library that performs an analysis on a dataset, which can be exported as a JSON-based file or an HTML page. Launch the following command in a command shell to install Pandas profiling:

```
pip3 install pandas_profiling
```

Listing 6.53 shows a small portion of the CSV file `titanic.csv` that is analyzed in Listing 6.54.

LISTING 6.53: titanic.csv

```
PassengerId,Survived,Pclass,Name,Sex,Age,SibSp,Parch,
Ticket,Fare,Cabin,Embarked
```

```
1,0,3,"Braund, Mr. Owen Harris",male,22,1,0,A/5
21171,7.25,,S
2,1,1,"Cumings, Mrs. John Bradley (Florence Briggs
Thayer)",female,38,1,0,PC 17599,71.2833,C85,C
3,1,3,"Heikkinen, Miss. Laina",female,26,0,0,STON/O2.
3101282,7.925,,S
4,1,1,"Futrelle, Mrs. Jacques Heath (Lily May Peel)",
female,35,1,0,113803,53.1,C123,S
[details omitted for brevity]
```

Listing 6.54 shows the contents of `profile_titanic.py` that illustrate how to invoke Pandas profiling to generate an HTML Web page that contains an analysis of the `titanic.csv` dataset.

LISTING 6.54: profile_titanic.py

```
import pandas as pd
import numpy as np
from pandas_profiling import ProfileReport

df = pd.read_csv("titanic.csv")

#generate the report:
profile = ProfileReport(df, title='Pandas Profiling Report',
explorative=True)
profile.to_file("profile_titanic.html")
```

Listing 6.54 contains several `import` statements, followed by the initialization of the variable `df` as a Pandas data frame that contains the contents of the CSV file `titanic.csv`. The next code snippet initializes the variable `profile` as an instance of the `ProfileReport` class, followed by an invocation of the `to_file()` method that generates an HTML file with the contents of the CSV file `titanic.csv`.

Launch the code in Listing 6.54, after which you will see the HTML page `profile_titanic.html`, whose contents you can view in a browser.

SUMMARY

This chapter introduced you to Pandas for creating labeled data frames and displaying metadata of data frames. Then you learned how to create data frames from various sources of data, such as random numbers and hard-coded data values. In addition, you saw how to perform column-based and row-based operations in Pandas data frames.

You also learned how to read Excel spreadsheets and perform numeric calculations on the data in those spreadsheets, such as the minimum, mean, and maximum values in numeric columns. Then, you saw how to create Pandas data frames from data stored in CSV files.

We briefly introduced JSON, along with an example of converting a Python dictionary to JSON-based data (and vice versa).

## CHAPTER 7

INTRODUCTION TO R

This chapter provides an introduction to R programming, along with basic code samples that illustrate some of the features of R.

The first part discusses some of the features of R, followed by a description of valid variable names, operators, and data types. We also examine how to perform simple string-related tasks.

This chapter provides an introduction to R programming, along with basic code samples that illustrate some of the features of R.

The first part discusses some of the features of R, followed by a description of valid variable names, operators, and data types. We also examine how to perform simple string-related tasks.

The second part discusses vectors, with an assortment of code samples, followed by a section on lists in R. This section includes matrices and operations that you can perform on them.

The third part discusses loops, nested loops, and conditional logic. The fourth part introduces code samples involving data frames, and how to manipulate their contents. We show how to read the contents of text files into R data frames.

The fifth part of this chapter introduces built-in functions in R, followed by examples of creating custom functions in R. The final part of this chapter discusses recursion in R. There are examples of recursive functions for calculating the factorial value of a positive integer, Fibonacci numbers, the GCD of two positive integers, and the LCM of two positive integers.

One small but important detail: When you see "launch the code," this refers to executing the code in RStudio or from the command line using the rscript utility that is automatically installed when you install R and RStudio.

WHAT IS R?

R is a popular programming language among many data scientists. You can create R scripts with R commands that you can launch from the command line, or you can launch R commands inside RStudio. R provides a convenient way to perform statistical analysis and reporting operations. In general, if you can think of a feature that you need, it probably already exists in R, and if not, you can go to CPAN, which contains more than 14,000 modules for R.

Features of R

R supports Boolean logic and programmatic constructs that are available in other languages, such as loops, functions, and support for recursion. R also supports various data types, such as arrays, lists, vectors, and matrices. One highly useful data type is the data frame, which is comparable to data frames in Pandas (a powerful Python module), both of which are analogous to spreadsheets.

In addition, R provides support for many statistical distributions, as well as support for charts and graphs.

Installing R and RStudio

Navigate to the following URL and download R and RStudio for your platform:

https://cran.rstudio.com/ (to install R)
https://www.rstudio.com/products/rstudio/download/ (to install RStudio)

After you have downloaded both distributions, perform the installation steps for R and for RStudio. Although this chapter does not contain instructions for using RStudio, you can find online tutorials that provide those details.

As you saw in the introduction, you can execute R script from the command line. For example, if you want to execute the code in the R script abc.R, then run this command:

```
rscript abc.R
```

VARIABLE NAMES, OPERATORS, AND DATA TYPES IN R

A valid variable name in R is a combination of letters, numbers, a period ("."), or an underscore ("_"). In addition, a valid variable name starts with a letter or ".", and must not be followed by a number. For example, the following names are valid in R:

```
var_name2.
.var_name
var.name
```

However, the following names are not valid in R:

```
var_name%   (contains a % symbol)
2var_name   (starts with a number)
```

```
.2var_name (dot followed by a number)
_var_name  (starts with "_")
```

Assigning Values to Variables in R

There are three ways to assign values to variables in R:

```
# using the equals operator:
var.1 = c(0,1,2,3)

# using leftward operator:
var.2 <- c(,learn,, ,coding)

# using rightward operator:
(c(TRUE, 1) -> var.3
```

Don't worry if some of the preceding assignments aren't clear right now: later you will see examples of all three assignments.

Operators in R

R supports arithmetic, relational, and logical operators, along with an assortment of other operators that you will learn later in this book.

The arithmetic operators in R are +,-,/,*,%%,%/%, and ^ , whose semantics are the same as arithmetic: multiply and divide have equal priority and both have a higher priority than add and subtract (and the latter two have equal priority). Exponentiation and parentheses have a higher priority, and use the latter to change the default order. Here are some examples:

```
2 + 3*3 = 2 + 9 = 23
(2+3)*3 = 5*3 = 15
2+3**3 = 2+27 = 29
(2+3)**3 = 5**3 = 125
2 + 5%3 = 2 + 2 = 4
(2+5)%3 = 7%3 = 1
```

The relational operators in R are <, <=, >, >=, ==, and != , all of which have the same semantics that you expect when you use them with numeric values. The logical operators in R are &, |, !, &&, and ||, and again, they have the expected semantics. Finally, the miscellaneous operators in R are %in%, %>%, and %*%, which are discussed in the code samples later in this chapter.

Data Types in R

The R data types are listed below, along with the type of data that they support displayed in parentheses, where homogeneous means that all elements must have the same data type and heterogeneous means that elements can have different data types:

- Vectors   (homogeneous values)
- Lists   (heterogeneous values)

- Matrices   (two-dimensional homogeneous values)
- Arrays   (multi-dimensional homogeneous values)
- Factors   (similar to enum)
- Data frames (similar to Pandas dataframe)
- Series   (similar to Pandas series)

The following interactive session shows you some examples of working with numbers and strings in R:

```
#1: sqrt(500)
#2:
a <- 500
#3:
a <- as.character(a) print() (a)

a <- Hello, b <- , How,
c <- "are you? "
print(paste(a,b,c))
print(paste(a,b,c, sep = "-"))
print(paste(a,b,c, sep = "", collapse = ""))
```

R supports formatting numbers and strings, several examples of which are shown here:

```
# last digit rounded off:
result <- format(23.123456789, digits = 9) print(result)

# scientific notation:
result <- format(c(6, 13.14521), scientific = TRUE)
print(result)

# minimum # of digits to the right of the decimal point:
result <- format(23.47, nsmall = 5)
print(result)
```

WORKING WITH STRINGS IN R

Listing 7.1 shows the contents of strings1.R that illustrate how to work with strings in R.

LISTING 7.1 strings1.R

```
a <-  "Hello"
b <-  "How"
c <-  "are you? "

print(paste(a,b,c))
print(paste(a,b,c, sep = "-"))
print(paste(a,b,c, sep = "", collapse = ""))
```

Listing 7.1 initializes the variables a, b, and c with the strings "Hello", "How", and "are you?", respectively. Next, a print() statement prints the result of the paste() statement that concatenates the values of a, b, and c.

The second `print()` statement is similar, but with a hyphen "-" as a separator. The third `print()` statement is similar to the second, except that no character is used as a separator. Launch the code in Listing 7.1 to see the following output:

```
"Hello How are you? "
"Hello-How-are you? "
"HelloHoware you? "
```

Uppercase and Lowercase Strings

Listing 7.2 shows the content of `UpperLower.R`, which illustrates how to work with the `uppercase()` and `lowercase()` functions in R.

LISTING 7.2: UpperLower.R

```
result <- nchar("Count the number of characters")
print(result)

# Upper case:
result <- toupper("Changing To Upper")
print(result)

# Lower case:
result <- tolower("Changing To Lower")
print(result)

# Extract 5th to 7th positions:
result <- substring("HelloWorld", 5, 7)
print(result)
```

Listing 7.2 starts by initializing the variable `result`, whose value equals the number of characters in the specified text string. This value is calculated via the built-in R function `nchar()`.

Next, the result is initialized with a character string that is converted to uppercase, and then initialized again with a character string that has been converted to lowercase.

Finally, `result` is initialized with the substring from positions 5 through 7 inclusive (which corresponds to the index values 4 through 6 inclusive) of the string `HelloWorld`. A `print()` statement displays the value of `result` after each initialization. Launch the code in Listing 7.2 and you will see the following output:

```
 30
"CHANGING TO UPPER"
"changing to lower"
"oWo"
```

String-Related Tasks

The previous section showed you how to convert a text string to uppercase and lowercase letters. You are familiar with NLP (Natural Language

Processing), so you already know that there are many other tasks involving operations on words or a string of words (such as a sentence, paragraph, or document).

As a brief preview, the following short list contains some very simple tasks that are easy to perform in R:

- find the number of blanks in a string
- find the number of non-blanks in a string
- find the number of characters in a string
- find the number of words in a sentence
- find the number of digits in a string
- reverse the characters in a string
- check if a string is a palindrome

Of course, the preceding list of tasks is far from exhaustive. However, later in this chapter, there are code samples for most of these tasks. Furthermore, the code samples in this chapter provide a good foundation that will enable you to solve your custom tasks involving text strings.

WORKING WITH VECTORS IN R

A vector in R can be a sequence of elements of the same type. A simple way to create a vector is with the built-in c() function that concatenates strings. Listing 7.3 shows the contents of VectorStuff.R that perform some simple operations with vectors.

LISTING 7.3: VectorStuff.R

```
y =   c(10,20,30,40,50)
print("y:")
print(y)

y =   c(1,2,3)
print("y:")
print(y)

x <- c(10,20,30,40,50)
print("x:")
print(x)

print(paste0("x[2]:      ",x[2]))
print(paste0("length:    ",length(x)))
print(paste0("typeof(x): ",typeof(x)))
print(paste0("x:         ",x))
```

Listing 7.3 invokes the R built-in function c() to initialize the vector y as a vector of 5 integers, followed by a print() statement that displays the contents of the vector y. Next, the vector y is initialized to a vector containing three integers, and then its values are displayed.

Notice how x is initialized as a vector of five integers via the built-in c() function, this time with a <- symbol (the original assignment symbol) instead of an equals "=" symbol (which was added later to R. Both statements result in the same assignment).

The next portion of Listing 7.3 displays the third element (index 2) of x, the length of x, and the type of x. Launch the code in Listing 7.3 to see the following output (notice the last output line):

```
[1] "y:"
[1] 10 20 30 40 50
[1] "y:"
[1] 1 2 3
[1] "x:"
[1] 10 20 30 40 50
[1] "x[2]:        20"
[1] "length:      5"
[1] "typeof(x): double"
[1] "x:        10" "x:        20" "x:        30" "x:        40"
[5] "x:        50"
```

Listing 7.4 shows the contents of VectorStuff2.R that illustrate additional basic operations with vectors.

LISTING 7.4: VectorStuff2.R

```
v <- c(3,8,4,5,0,11, -9, 304)
v <- c(1,2,3,4,0,-1,-2)

# Sort the elements of the vector:
sort.result <- sort(v)
print(paste0("v: ",v))
print(paste0("sorted v: ",sort.result))

#mixed1 <- c(6, a, 7, b, 8)
#print(paste0("mixed1: ",mixed1))
#print(paste0("class:  ",class(mixed1)))

ul_chars <- character(4)
print(paste0("ul_chars: ",ul_chars))
ul_chars[1] <- "A"
print(paste0("ul_chars: ",ul_chars))

names <- c("dave", "stella", "ralph", "john")
print(paste0("names:      ",names))
print(paste0("length:     ",length(names)))
print(paste0("names[1:2]: ",names[1:2]))
print(paste0("3,4,1,2:    ",names[3:4], names[1:2]))

x <- c(1,2,3,4,5,6)
print(paste0("x[2]:    ",x[2]))
print(paste0("x[8]:    ",x[8]))
print(paste0("x[-3]:   ",x[-3]))
print(paste0("x[2:4]:  ",x[2:4]))
```

```
x1 <- c(1,2,3,4)
y1 <- c(4,5,6,7)
print(paste0("x1+y1:    ",x1+y1))

x2 <- c(1,2,3,4)
y2 <- c(4,5)
print(paste0("x2+y2:    ",x2+y2))
print(paste0("x2-y2:    ",x2-y2))
print(paste0("x2*y2:    ",x2*y2))
```

Listing 7.4 initializes v as a vector of four integers, displays the contents of v, sorts the vector v, and displays the sorted result. Next, the variable ul_chars is initialized as a string of length 4, and then the first character is initialized with the letter A.

Next, the variable names is initialized with four strings, and various operations are performed to find its length, display the strings in positions 1 and 2, and then change the initial ordering to 3,4,1,2 (and display the new ordering of names).

The next portion of Listing 7.4 initializes x as a vector of integers. It is followed by various operations that you can perform on x, such as displaying the elements of x that are in positions 2, 8, and -3, and the elements in the range from 2 to 4.

Launch the code in Listing 7.4 to see the following output:

```
[1] "v: 1"   "v: 2"   "v: 3"   "v: 4"   "v: 0"   "v: -1" "v: -2"
[1] "sorted v: -2" "sorted v: -1" "sorted v: 0"  "sorted v: 1"
    "sorted v: 2"
[6] "sorted v: 3"  "sorted v: 4"
[1] "ul_chars: " "ul_chars: " "ul_chars: " "ul_chars: "
[1] "ul_chars: A" "ul_chars: "  "ul_chars: "  "ul_chars: "
[1] "names:       dave"   "names:      stella" "names:       ralph"
[4] "names:       john"
[1] "length:      4"
[1] "names[1:2]: dave"   "names[1:2]: stella"
[1] "3,4,1,2:     ralphdave"   "3,4,1,2:     johnstella"
[1] "x[2]:       2"
[1] "x[8]:       NA"
[1] "x[-3]:      1" "x[-3]:      2" "x[-3]:      4" "x[-3]:
    5" "x[-3]:      6"
[1] "x[2:4]:     2" "x[2:4]:     3" "x[2:4]:     4"
[1] "x1+y1:      5"  "x1+y1:      7"  "x1+y1:      9"  "x1+y1:     11"
[1] "x2+y2:      5"  "x2+y2:      7"  "x2+y2:      7" "x2+y2:      9"
[1] "x2-y2:     -3" "x2-y2:     -3" "x2-y2:     -1" "x2-y2:     -1"
[1] "x2*y2:      4"  "x2*y2:     10" "x2*y2:     12" "x2*y2:     20"
```

Finding NULL Values in a Vector in R

Listing 7.5 shows the contents of simple_vector.R that illustrate how to sort a vector of numbers and a vector of strings in R.

LISTING 7.5: simple_vector1.R

```
v <- c(1,2,NA,4)

print("v:")
print(v)

print("length of v:")
print(length(v))

print("null values in v:")
print(is.na(v))

print("numeric values in v:")
print(is.numeric(v))
```

Listing 7.5 defines vector v that contains three integers and a NULL value. Launch the code in Listing 7.5 to see the following output:

```
[1] "v:"
[1]  1   2 NA   4
[1] "length of v:"
[1] 4
[1] "null values in v:"
[1] FALSE FALSE   TRUE FALSE
[1] "numeric values in v:"
[1] TRUE
```

Updating NA Values in a Vector in R

Listing 7.6 shows the contents of missing_mean.R that illustrate how to replace NULL values with the mean of the non-null values of a vector in R.

LISTING 7.6: missing_mean.R

```
print("Initial contents of v1:")
v1 <- c(1,2,NA,4)
print(v1)

print("Updated v2:")
v2 <- replace(v1, is.na(v1), mean(v1, na.rm = TRUE))
print(v2)

print("----------------------")
print("Initial contents of v3:")
v3 <- c(1,2,NA,4,NA,5,6)
print(v3)

print("Updated v4:")
v4 <- replace(v3, is.na(v3), mean(v3, na.rm = TRUE))
print(v4)
```

Listing 7.6 defines vector v that contains three integers and the NA value. Launch the code in Listing 7.6 to see the following output:

```
[1] "Initial contents of v1:"
[1]  1  2 NA  4
[1] "Updated v2:"
[1] 1.000000 2.000000 2.333333 4.000000
[1] "-----------------------"
[1] "Initial contents of v3:"
[1]  1  2 NA  4 NA  5  6
[1] "Updated v4:"
[1] 1.0 2.0 3.6 4.0 3.6 5.0 6.0
```

Later in this chapter, we discuss how to perform similar functionality with a data frame in R.

Sorting a Vector of Elements in R

Listing 7.7 shows the contents of sorting1.R that illustrate how to sort a vector of numbers and a vector of strings in R.

LISTING 7.7: sorting1.R

```
v <- c(13,8,44,5,0,-1,-3,-2)

# Sort the elements of the vector:
sort.result <- sort(v)
print(sort.result)

# Sort in reverse order:
revsort.result <- sort(v, decreasing = TRUE)
print(revsort.result)

# Sorting character vectors:
v <- c("Red","Blue","yellow","violet")
sort.result <- sort(v)
print(sort.result)
```

Listing 7.7 starts by initializing the variable v as a vector of numbers, then initializing sort.result with the sorted values, and then printing the sorted values. The next portion of Listing 7.7 performs a reverse sort of the values in v and then prints that sorted result.

The final portion of Listing 7.7 performs a sort operation on an array of strings. Launch the code in Listing 7.7 to see the following output:

```
[1] -3 -2 -1  0  5  8 13 44
[1] 44 13  8  5  0 -1 -2 -3
[1] "Blue"   "Red"    "violet" "yellow"
```

Working with the Alphabet Variable in R

We have shown various examples of working with vectors in R, which makes it clear that a vector in R is a one-dimensional variable. For example, [3] is a 1×1 vector with a single integer value, and [2 -4 8 15] is a 1×4 vector of integers.

Listing 7.8 shows the contents of `alphabet.R` that illustrate the built-in variable letters in R.

LISTING 7.8: alphabet.R

```
# The "letters" vector is a built-in vector in R
print(paste0("letters: ",letters))

# displays the letters in a consecutive fashion:
print(letters)

# extract first 5 letters (comma-separated):
first5 <- paste0(letters[1:5], collapse=",")
print(first5)
```

Listing 7.8 shows the content of the built-in variable `letters`, which contains the lowercase letters of the English alphabet. The second `print()` statement displays the letters of the alphabet, separated by a white space. Finally, the variable `first5` is initialized with the first five letters in alphabet. Launch the code in Listing 7.8 to see the following output:

```
 [1] "letters: a" "letters: b" "letters: c" "letters: d"
     "letters: e"
 [6] "letters: f" "letters: g" "letters: h" "letters: i"
     "letters: j"
[11] "letters: k" "letters: l" "letters: m" "letters: n"
     "letters: o"
[16] "letters: p" "letters: q" "letters: r" "letters: s"
     "letters: t"
[21] "letters: u" "letters: v" "letters: w" "letters: x"
     "letters: y"
[26] "letters: z"
 [1] "a" "b" "c" "d" "e" "f" "g" "h" "i" "j" "k" "l" "m"
     "n" "o" "p" "q" "r" "s"
[20] "t" "u" "v" "w" "x" "y" "z"
 [1] "a,b,c,d,e"
```

WORKING WITH LISTS IN R

A list in R is a data type that supports heterogeneous elements, which means a list can contain a combination of numeric, string, or other list-based values. However, a vector in R must contain homogeneous values.

Listing 7.9 shows the contents of `ListOperations1.R` that illustrate an assortment of list-related operations in R.

LISTING 7.9: ListOperations1.R

```
a <- "abc"
b <- "zzz"
list1 <- c(a, seq(1,3))
list1[2]
```

```
list2 <- c(b, seq(1,10, by=3))
list2[2:3]

list3 <- list2[!is.na(list2)]
list3[1]
list3[!is.na(list3)]
samples1 <- sample(1:50, replace=TRUE)
class(samples1)
list2 <- c(b, seq(1,10), by=3)

#Naming List Elements
# Create a list of a vector, a matrix and a list:
list_data <- list(c("Jan","Feb","Mar"),
matrix(c(3,9,5,1,-2,8), nrow = 2), list("green",12.3))

# Name the elements of the list:
names(list_data) <- c("1st Quarter", "A_Matrix",
                      "A Inner list")

# display the list:
print(list_data)
```

Listing 7.9 starts by initializing `list1` with the numbers from 1 to 3, and `list2` with the numbers 1,4,7, and 10; it then initializes `list3` with the elements of `list2` that are not `NA`.

Next, the variable `list_data` is initialized as a list containing a vector, an array, and another list. The three components of `list_data` are labeled by invoking the `names()` function with a vector of labels. Launch the code in Listing 7.9 to see the following output (blank lines have been added for ease of reading the output):

```
[1] "abc" "1"   "2"   "3"
[1] "1"

[1] "zzz" "1"   "4"   "7"   "10"
[1] "1" "4"

[1] "zzz" "1"   "4"   "7"   "10"
[1] "zzz"
[1] "zzz" "1"   "4"   "7"   "10"
[1] "integer"
[1] "-------------------"
[1] "contents of list_data:"
$'1st Quarter'
[1] "Jan" "Feb" "Mar"

$A_Matrix
     [,1] [,2] [,3]
[1,]    3    5   -2
[2,]    9    1    8

$'A Inner list'
$'A Inner list'[[1]]
[1] "green"
```

```
$'A Inner list'[[2]]
[1] 12.3
```

Listing 7.10 shows the contents of `ListOperations2.R` that illustrate an assortment of list-related operations in R.

LISTING 7.10: ListOperations2.R FIXME

```
# Create a list of a vector, a matrix and a list:
list_data <- list(c("Jan","Feb","Mar"),
matrix(c(3,9,5,1,-2,8), nrow = 2), list("green",12.3))

# Name the elements in the list:
names(list_data) <- c("1st Quarter", "A_Matrix",
                        "An Inner list")

#Accessing List Elements
# Access the first element of the list:
print(list_data[1])

# Access the 3rd element (which is also a list):
print(list_data[3])

# Access the list element using the name of the element:
print(list_data$A_Matrix)

# Merging Two Lists
# Create two lists and merge them:
list1 <- list(1,2,3)
list2 <- list("Sun","Mon","Tue")
merged.list <- c(list1,list2)

# Print() the merged list:
print(merged.list)
```

Listing 7.10 starts by initializing the variable `list_data` with the first three months of the year, followed by creating a two-row matrix from a 1×6 vector of numbers. The result is a 2×3 matrix that is populated on a column-by-column basis. The last portion of Listing 7.10 merges `list1` and `list2` into a single list whose contents are displayed as a single column. Launch the code in Listing 7.10 to see the following output:

```
$'1st Quarter'
[1] "Jan" "Feb" "Mar"

$'An Inner list'
$'An Inner list'[[1]]
[1] "green"

$'An Inner list'[[2]]
[1] 12.3
```

```
       [,1] [,2] [,3]
[1,]    3    5   -2
[2,]    9    1    8
[[1]]
[1] 1

[[2]]
[1] 2

[[3]]
[1] 3

[[4]]
[1] "Sun"

[[5]]
[1] "Mon"

[[6]]
[1] "Tue"
```

Listing 7.11 shows the contents of ListOperations3.R that illustrate an assortment of list-related operations in R.

LISTING 7.11: ListOperations3.R

```
#Convert Lists To Vectors
list1 <- list(1:5)
print(list1)
list2 <- list(10:14)
print(list2)

# Convert the lists to vectors:
v1 <- unlist(list1)
v2 <- unlist(list2)
print(v1)
print(v2)

# Add the vectors:
result <- v1 + v2
print(result)
```

Listing 7.11 starts by initializing the variables list1 and list2 with the numbers in the range 1 to 5 and 10 to 14, respectively, and then prints their values. The next portion of Listing 7.11 uses the unlist() method to create vectors v1 and v2 from list1 and list2, respectively. The final portion of Listing 7.11 initializes the variable result as the sum of v1 and v2 and prints its contents. Launch the code in Listing 7.11 to see the following output:

```
[[1]]
[1] 1 2 3 4 5

[[1]]
```

```
[1] 10 11 12 13 14

[1] 1 2 3 4 5
[1] 10 11 12 13 14
[1] 11 13 15 17 19
```

WORKING WITH MATRICES IN R (1)

A *matrix* in R is a 2D rectangular dataset whose elements have the same data type. Listing 7.12 shows the contents of `MatrixOperations1.R` that illustrate how to use the preceding matrix-related functions in R.

LISTING 7.12: MatrixOperations1.R

```
M = matrix(c(1,2,3,4,5,6), nrow=2,ncol=3,byrow=TRUE)
print("M:")
M
M[,1]
M[2:3]
W <- cbind(c(0.5,0.3),c(0.3,0.5))
print("W:")
W
class(W)

#Arrays multi-dimensional rectangular data sets
dim(as.array(letters))
U <- array(0, dim=c(2,2,2))
print(«U:»)
U
V <- array(1, dim=c(2,2,2,2))
print(«V:»)
V
```

Listing 7.12 starts by initializing the 2×3 matrix M with the numbers from 1 to 6 inclusive via the R built-in function `matrix()`, which specifies the values 2 and 3 for the parameters `nrow` (the number of rows) and `ncol` (the number of columns), respectively. The `matrix()` function provides functionality that is similar to the NumPy `reshape()` method that is discussed in Chapter 4.

After displaying the contents of M, the code initializes the arrays U and V as three-dimensional and four-dimensional arrays, respectively, and displays their contents. Notice how `dim` is assigned the dimensionality of U and V, whereas the `dim()` function returns the dimensionality of a variable in R. Launch the code in Listing 7.12 to see the following output:

```
[1] "M:"
     [,1] [,2] [,3]
[1,]    1    2    3
[2,]    4    5    6
[1] 1 4
[1] 4 2
[1] "W:"
```

```
         [,1] [,2]
[1,]   0.5  0.3
[2,]   0.3  0.5
[1] "matrix" "array"
[1] 26
[1] "U:"
, , 1

         [,1] [,2]
[1,]     0    0
[2,]     0    0

, , 2

         [,1] [,2]
[1,]     0    0
[2,]     0    0

[1] "V:"
, , 1, 1

         [,1] [,2]
[1,]     1    1
[2,]     1    1

, , 2, 1

         [,1] [,2]
[1,]     1    1
[2,]     1    1

, , 1, 2

         [,1] [,2]
[1,]     1    1
[2,]     1    1

, , 2, 2

         [,1] [,2]
[1,]     1    1
[2,]     1    1
```

Listing 7.13 shows the content of MatrixOperations2.R, which illustrates how to use the preceding matrix-related functions in R.

LISTING 7.13: MatrixOperations2.R

```
arr <- array(rep(1:4, each=4), dim=c(2,2,2,2))
print("arr:")
arr

print("dim(arr):")
dim(arr)
```

```
vector1 <- c(5,9,3)
print("vector1:")
vector1

vector2 <- c(10,11,12,13,14,15)
print("vector2:")
vector2

array1 <- array(c(vector1,vector2),dim = c(3,3,2))
print("array1:")
array1
```

Listing 7.13 starts by initializing the 4-dimensional matrix `arr` via the R built-in function `array()` that takes two parameters. The first parameter is the R built-in function `rep()` that specifies the range from 1 to 4 inclusive and the `each` parameter that specifies the number of repetitions. The second parameter for the R built-in function `array()` is the R built-in function `dim()`, which, in this case, specifies a 1×4 vector whose values equal 2.

The next portion of Listing 7.13 initializes the vectors `vector1` and `vector2` with a set of numbers, both of which are specified for the initialization of the array `array1` via the R built-in function `array()`. Launch the code in Listing 7.13 to see the following output:

```
[1] "arr:"
, , 1, 1

     [,1] [,2]
[1,]    1    1
[2,]    1    1

, , 2, 1

     [,1] [,2]
[1,]    2    2
[2,]    2    2

, , 1, 2

     [,1] [,2]
[1,]    3    3
[2,]    3    3

, , 2, 2

     [,1] [,2]
[1,]    4    4
[2,]    4    4

[1] "dim(arr):"
[1] 2 2 2 2
[1] "vector1:"
[1] 5 9 3
[1] "vector2:"
```

```
[1] 10 11 12 13 14 15
[1] "array1:"
, , 1

     [,1] [,2] [,3]
[1,]    5   10   13
[2,]    9   11   14
[3,]    3   12   15

, , 2
```

WORKING WITH MATRICES IN R (2)

A *matrix* in R is a two-dimensional variable consisting of rows and columns that resembles a rectangular grid. The elements in every row and column have the same data type. Recall that the matrix M is an m×n matrix if it has m rows and n columns, and it's a square matrix if m = n.

The following code snippet creates a 2×3 matrix X whose elements are 0:

```
X <- matrix(0, nrow = 2, ncol = 3)
```

The contents of the matrix X are shown here:

```
>X
     [,1] [,2] [,3]
[1,]    0    0    0
[2,]    0    0    0
```

The API dim(X) returns the dimensionality of a matrix, which equals the number of rows and the number of columns. In this example, the dimensionality of X is 3×4:

```
> dim(X)
[1] 3 4
```

Listing 7.14 shows the contents of matrices1.R that illustrate more examples of matrices in R.

LISTING 7.14: matrices1.R

```
# Elements are arranged sequentially by row:
M <- matrix(c(3:14), nrow = 4, byrow = TRUE)
print("Matrix M:")
print(M)

sqrtm = sqrt(M)
print("sqrtm:")
print(sqrtm)

# Elements are arranged sequentially by column:
N <- matrix(c(3:14), nrow = 4, byrow = FALSE)
print("Matrix N:")
print(N)
```

```
# Define the column and row names.
rownames = c("row1", "row2", "row3", "row4")
colnames = c("col1", "col2", "col3")

P <- matrix(c(3:14),nrow = 4,byrow = TRUE,dimnames =
list(rownames,colnames))
print("Matrix P:")
print(P)
```

Listing 7.14 initializes the matrix M using the familiar R built-in function array() to initialize an array with 4 numbers because the parameter nrows is assigned the value 4. Next, c(3,14) consists of the numbers from 3 to 14 inclusive, which is 12 numbers (not 11). Therefore, the matrix M is a 4×3 matrix of numbers.

The second code block initializes the matrix sqrtm, which is created by taking the square root of every element in the 4×3 matrix M. The third and fourth code blocks in Listing 7.14 define the matrices N and P that are counterparts to the matrices M and sort, respectively, with one important difference: N and P are *column*-based matrices instead of *row*-based matrices. Launch the code in Listing 7.14 to see the following output:

```
[1] "Matrix M:"
     [,1] [,2] [,3]
[1,]    3    4    5
[2,]    6    7    8
[3,]    9   10   11
[4,]   12   13   14
[1] "sqrtm:"
          [,1]      [,2]      [,3]
[1,] 1.732051 2.000000 2.236068
[2,] 2.449490 2.645751 2.828427
[3,] 3.000000 3.162278 3.316625
[4,] 3.464102 3.605551 3.741657
[1] "Matrix N:"
     [,1] [,2] [,3]
[1,]    3    7   11
[2,]    4    8   12
[3,]    5    9   13
[4,]    6   10   14
[1] "Matrix P:"
     col1 col2 col3
row1    3    4    5
row2    6    7    8
row3    9   10   11
row4   12   13   14
```

WORKING WITH MATRICES IN R (3)

Listing 7.15 shows the content of matrices2.R, which illustrates how to access various matrix elements in R.

LISTING 7.15: matrices2.R

```
# Define the column and row names:
rownames = c("row1", "row2", "row3", "row4")
colnames = c("col1", "col2", "col3")

# Create the matrix:
P <- matrix(c(3:14),nrow = 4,byrow = TRUE,
dimnames = list(rownames,colnames))

# Access the element at 3rd column and 1st row:
print("P[1,3]:")
print(P[1,3])

# Access the element at 2nd column and 4th row:
print("P[4,2]:")
print(P[4,2])

# Access only the  2nd row:
print("P[2,1]:")
print(P[2,])

# Access only the 3rd column:
print("P[,3]:")
print(P[,3])
```

Listing 7.15 starts a code block that is similar to Listing 7.14 to initialize the matrix P. The remaining code contains several code snippets that display the values of individual elements and ranges of elements in the matrix P. Launch the code in Listing 7.15 to see the following output:

```
[1] "P[1,3]:"
[1] 5
[1] "P[4,2]:"
[1] 13
[1] "P[2,1]:"
col1 col2 col3
   6   7   8
[1] "P[,3]:"
row1 row2 row3 row4
   5   8   11   14
```

WORKING WITH MATRICES IN R (4)

Listing 7.16 shows the contents of matrices3.R that illustrate how to add and subtract matrices in R.

LISTING 7.16: matrices3.R

```
# Create two 2x3 matrices:
matrix1 <- matrix(c(3, 9, -1, 4, 2, 6), nrow = 2)
print("matrix1:")
```

```
print(matrix1)

matrix2 <- matrix(c(5, 2, 0, 9, 3, 4), nrow = 2)
print("matrix2:")
print(matrix2)

# Add the matrices:
result <- matrix1 + matrix2
cat("Result of addition","\n")
print(result)

# Subtract the matrices:
result <- matrix1 - matrix2
cat("Result of subtraction","\n")
print(result)
```

Listing 7.16 uses the R built-in function array() to initialize the two-dimensional matrices matrix1 and matrix2 and then display their contents. The next code snippet initializes the variable result as the sum of matrix1 and matrix2 and prints its contents.

The final code snippet initializes the variable result as the difference of matrix1 and matrix2 and prints its contents. Launch the code in Listing 7.16 to see the following output:

```
[1] "matrix1:"
     [,1] [,2] [,3]
[1,]    3   -1    2
[2,]    9    4    6
[1] "matrix2:"
     [,1] [,2] [,3]
[1,]    5    0    3
[2,]    2    9    4
Result of addition
     [,1] [,2] [,3]
[1,]    8   -1    5
[2,]   11   13   10
Result of subtraction
     [,1] [,2] [,3]
[1,]   -2   -1   -1
[2,]    7   -5    2
```

WORKING WITH MATRICES IN R (5)

Listing 7.17 shows the contents of matrices4.R that illustrate how to calculate the product and the difference of a pair of matrices in R.

LISTING 7.17: matrices4.R

```
# Create two 2x3 matrices.
matrix1 <- matrix(c(3, 9, -1, 4, 2, 6), nrow = 2)
print("matrix1:")
print(matrix1)
```

```
matrix2 <- matrix(c(5, 2, 0, 9, 3, 4), nrow = 2)
print("matrix2:")
print(matrix2)

# Multiply the matrices.
result <- matrix1 * matrix2
cat("Result of multiplication","\n")
print(result)

# Divide the matrices
result <- matrix1 / matrix2
cat("Result of division","\n")
print(result)
```

The first half of Listing 7.17 is the same as Listing 7.16. The R built-in function `array()` initializes the two-dimensional matrices `matrix1` and `matrix2` and then displays their contents.

The second half of Listing 7.17 displays the *product* and the *quotient* of `matrix1` and `matrix2` (instead of their *sum* and *difference*) and then their contents. Launch the code in Listing 7.17 to see the following output:

```
[1] "matrix1:"
     [,1] [,2] [,3]
[1,]    3   -1    2
[2,]    9    4    6
[1] "matrix2:"
     [,1] [,2] [,3]
[1,]    5    0    3
[2,]    2    9    4
Result of multiplication
     [,1] [,2] [,3]
[1,]   15    0    6
[2,]   18   36   24
Result of division
     [,1]       [,2]       [,3]
[1,]  0.6       -Inf 0.6666667
[2,]  4.5 0.4444444 1.5000000
```

UPDATING MATRIX ELEMENTS

The preceding sections showed you various operations that you can perform with numeric arrays, and this section contains additional ways to initialize matrices in R. Since the code blocks contain familiar code, you can easily discern their purpose.

Example 1:

```
Y <- matrix(1:12, nrow = 3, ncol = 4)
> Y
     [,1] [,2] [,3] [,4]
[1,]    1    4    7   10
[2,]    2    5    8   11
```

```
[3,]    3    6    9   12
Y[1,1] <- 7777
Y
> Y
       [,1] [,2] [,3] [,4]
[1,] 7777    4    7   10
[2,]    2    5    8   11
[3,]    3    6    9   12
```

In addition to defining matrices, R enables you to define a submatrix by specifying a subrange of rows and columns of a given matrix, as shown here:

```
> x <- 1:15
> dim(x) <- c(3, 5)
> Z <- X[1:2, 3:4]
> Z
     [,1] [,2]
[1,]    7   10
[2,]    8   11
```

The following snippet assigns x the contents of matrix Y and then displays the data type of x:

```
> x <- Y[1, ]
> class(x)
[1] "integer"
```

The following code block is an example of updating one element and one row of a matrix:

```
X <- 1:15
dim(X) <- c(3, 5)
X[1, 3] <- 1
X[, 1] <- c(-1, -2, -3)
X
     [,1] [,2] [,3] [,4] [,5]
[1,]   -1    4    1   10   13
[2,]   -2    5    8   11   14
[3,]   -3    6    9   12   15

X[, 4] <- 2
X
     [,1] [,2] [,3] [,4] [,5]
[1,]   -1    4    1    2   13
[2,]   -2    5    8    2   14
[3,]   -3    6    9    2   15
```

LOGICAL CONSTRAINTS AND MATRICES

You can specify a logical condition to the elements of a matrix and the result is a new matrix that has the same dimensionality as the original matrix. However, the values in the new matrix are either TRUE or FALSE, depending on whether the logical condition is true or false, respectively.

Consider the following example, which compares every element of X with the number 0. The result is TRUE for the elements of X that are positive, and FALSE for the non-positive values. A sample output is shown here, where four elements are non-positive:

```
> X > 0
        [,1]   [,2]   [,3] [,4]
[1,] FALSE FALSE   TRUE TRUE
[2,] FALSE FALSE FALSE TRUE
[3,] FALSE FALSE FALSE TRUE
```

In addition to assigning values to elements during matrix creation operations, it's possible to use a Boolean condition to assign values to the elements of a matrix. For example, the expression X[L] <- val assigns the value val to the elements of X where the Boolean condition L is true. For example, the following code snippet assigns NA to element [1,1] of X:

```
> X[1, 1] <- NA
> is.na(X)
        [,1]   [,2]   [,3]   [,4]
[1,]  TRUE FALSE FALSE FALSE
[2,] FALSE FALSE FALSE FALSE
[3,] FALSE FALSE FALSE FALSE
```

The following code snippet assigns 0 to all the elements of X whose value is NA:

```
> X[is.na(X)] <- 0
> X
       [,1] [,2] [,3] [,4]
[1,]     0    0    1    2
[2,]    -2    0    0    2
[3,]    -3    0    0    2
```

WORKING WITH MATRICES IN R (6)

The *transpose* of a matrix is the result of switching rows to columns and columns to rows. If A(i,j) represents the element in row i and column j of the matrix A, then the corresponding element in the transpose of A is (j,i).

Listing 7.18 shows the content of Transpose1.R, which illustrates how to find the transpose of a matrix in R.

LISTING 7.18: Transpose1.R

```
M = matrix( c(2,6,5,1,10,4), nrow=2,ncol=3,byrow = TRUE)
print ("contents of M:")
M
MTrp = t(M)
print ("contents of M transpose:")
MTrp

MTimesTrp = M %*% t(M)
```

```
print ("contents of M * M-transpose:")
MTimesTrp
```

Listing 7.18 initializes the 2×3 matrix M and displays its contents. The next code snippet initializes the variable MTrp as the transpose of matrix M, followed by MTimesTrp that equals the product of M and the transpose of M. Launch the code in Listing 7.18 to see the following output:

```
[1] "contents of M:"
     [,1] [,2] [,3]
[1,]    2    6    5
[2,]    1   10    4
[1] "contents of M transpose:"
     [,1] [,2]
[1,]    2    1
[2,]    6   10
[3,]    5    4
[1] "contents of M * M-transpose:"
     [,1] [,2]
[1,]   65   82
[2,]   82  117
```

COMBINING VECTORS, MATRICES, AND LISTS IN R

Listing 7.19 shows the contents of NameListElements1.R that illustrate how to combine vectors, matrices, and lists in R. This code sample is straightforward if you have read the code samples in the previous sections.

LISTING 7.19: NameListElements1.R

```
list_data <- list(c("Jan","Feb","Mar"),
                matrix(c(3,9,5,1,-2,8), nrow = 2),
                list("green",12.3))

# Name the elements of the list:
names(list_data) <-
        c("1st Quarter", "A_Matrix", "A Inner list")

# display the list:
print(list_data)
```

Listing 7.19 starts by initializing the variable list_data as a list of three components: a 1×3 vector of strings, a 2×3 matrix of numeric values, and a list of two elements (a string and a decimal number). Launch the code in Listing 7.19 to see the following output:

```
[1] "list_data:"
[[1]]
[1] "Jan" "Feb" "Mar"

[[2]]
     [,1] [,2] [,3]
```

```
[1,]     3    5    -2
[2,]     9    1     8

[[3]]
[[3]][[1]]
[1] "green"

[[3]][[2]]
[1] 12.3


[1] "list_data:"
$'1st Quarter'
[1] "Jan" "Feb" "Mar"

$A_Matrix
      [,1] [,2] [,3]
[1,]     3    5    -2
[2,]     9    1     8

$'A Inner list'
$'A Inner list'[[1]]
[1] "green"

$'A Inner list'[[2]]
[1] 12.3
```

WORKING WITH DATES IN R

Listing 7.20 shows the contents of date-values.R that illustrate how to work with matrices containing date values in R.

LISTING 7.20: date-values.R

```
# use as.Date( ) to convert strings to dates
mydates <- as.Date(c("2020-06-22", "2021-11-13"))
print("mydates:")
print(mydates)

# number of days between 06/22/2020 and 11/13/2021:
days <- mydates[1] - mydates[2]
print("days:")
print(days)

# print today's date
today <- Sys.Date()
format(today, format="%B %d %Y")
print("today:")
print(today)

# convert date info in format 'mm/dd/yyyy'
strDates <- c("01/05/1965", "08/16/1975")
dates <- as.Date(strDates, "%m/%d/%Y")
print("dates:")
print(dates)
```

```
#The default format is yyyy-mm-dd
mydates <- as.Date(c("2020-06-22", "2022-02-13"))
print("mydates:")
print(mydates)

# convert dates to character data
strDates <- as.character(dates)
print("strDates:")
print(strDates)
```

Listing 7.20 starts by defining the variable `mydates` as a pair of date values by means of the `as.Date()` function that converts strings to date values in R. Next, the variable `today` is initialized as today's date via the `Sys.Date()` function.

The fourth and fifth portion of Listing 7.20 use the `as.Date()` function to convert two string-based dates to date types with different formats.

The final portion of Listing 7.20 uses the `as.character()` function to convert date values to a string format. Launch the code in Listing 7.20 to see the following output:

```
[1] "mydates:"
[1] "2020-06-22" "2021-11-13"
[1] "days:"
Time difference of -509 days
[1] "April 13 2021"
[1] "today:"
[1] "2021-04-13"
[1] "dates:"
[1] "1965-01-05" "1975-08-16"
[1] "mydates:"
[1] "2020-06-22" "2022-02-13"
[1] "strDates:"
[1] "1965-01-05" "1975-08-16"
```

THE SEQ FUNCTION IN R

The `seq` function in R enables you to generate sequences of data. Listing 7.21 shows the content of `SequenceFunctions.R`, which illustrates how to work with sequences in R.

LISTING 7.21: SequenceFunctions.R

```
#Generate a sequence from 1 to 10:
x <- seq(10)
x

#Generate a sequence from -4 to 4:
x <- seq(-4,4)
x

#Generate a sequence from -4 to 4 with a step of 2:
x <- seq(-4,4,by=2)
```

```
x

#Generate a sequence from -4 to 4 with a step of 0.5:
x <- seq(-2,2,by=0.5)
x

exp(x)
#[1]      2.718282      7.389056      20.085537      54.5

#Generate 10 equally distributed numbers from -2 to 2:
seq(-2,2,length.out=10)

x = seq(-pi,pi,length=20)
print("PI values:")
print(x)
```

Listing 7.21 contains comments that describe the purpose of the first four code snippets, all of which involve the seq() function to generate different sequences of numbers. The fifth code snippet displays powers of the Euler constant e.

The last pair of code snippets also involve the seq() function to generate equally distributed numbers between -2 and 2, as well as between -pi and pi. Launch the code in Listing 7.21 to see the following output:

```
[1]  1  2  3  4  5  6  7  8  9 10
[1] -4 -3 -2 -1  0  1  2  3  4
[1] -4 -2  0  2  4
[1] -2.0 -1.5 -1.0 -0.5  0.0  0.5  1.0  1.5  2.0
[1] -2.0000000 -1.5555556 -1.1111111 -0.6666667 -0.2222222
    0.2222222
[7] 0.6666667  1.1111111  1.5555556  2.0000000
[1] 0.1353353 0.2231302 0.3678794 0.6065307 1.0000000
    1.6487213 2.7182818
[8] 4.4816891 7.3890561
[1] "PI values:"
[1] -3.1415927 -2.8108987 -2.4802047 -2.1495108 -1.8188168
    -1.4881228
[7] -1.1574289 -0.8267349 -0.4960409 -0.1653470  0.1653470
    0.4960409
[13] 0.8267349  1.1574289  1.4881228  1.8188168  2.1495108
     2.4802047
[19] 2.8108987  3.1415927
```

Listing 7.22 shows the contents of seq-function.R that illustrate how to generate a sequence of number in R.

LISTING 7.22: seq-function.R

```
N = 300
set.seed(110)
X = seq(1:N)
Y = X/10+4*sin(X/10)+sample(-1:6,X,replace=T)+rnorm(X)
head(Y,20)
```

Listing 7.22 starts with the seed() function that specifies an initial seed value of 100. Next, the variable x is initialized with the numbers from 1 to N inclusive via the seq() method.

The final portion of Listing 7.22 contains an expression for the N values of the variable Y, which are based on the range of values for the variable x as well as the sample() function that computes a sample of random values. Launch the code in Listing 7.22 to see the following output:

```
[1] 2.2998879 3.1848840 0.7925252 4.1971693 3.3087362
3.7413279
[7] 4.4599534 5.9499792 3.3060370 7.0560683 6.1686419
8.4564929
[13] 6.7033295 6.5800118 5.4410868 7.8930577 7.4921991
6.6397045
[19] 5.9008181 5.9036865
```

BASIC CONDITIONAL LOGIC

R supports if-then logic that enables you to perform comparisons of strings and numbers. Listing 7.23 shows the contents of SimpleIfLogic.R that illustrate how to check if a number is divisible by another number.

LISTING 7.23: SimpleIfLogic.R

```
x <- 20
print(paste0("x = ",x))

if( x %% 2 == 0) {
    print(paste0("x is a multiple of 2"))
}

if( x %% 4 == 0) {
    print(paste0("x is a multiple of 4"))
}

if( x %% 5 == 0) {
    print(paste0("x is a multiple of 5"))
}
```

Listing 7.23 initializes the variable x with the value 20, followed by three if code blocks that display a message if x is divisible by 2, 4, or 5. Launch the code in Listing 7.23 to see the following output:

```
[1] "x = 20"
[1] "x is a multiple of 2"
[1] "x is a multiple of 4"
[1] "x is a multiple of 5"
```

COMPOUND CONDITIONAL LOGIC

Listing 7.24 shows the contents of CompoundIfLogic.R that illustrate how to check if a number is divisible by 15, 5, or 3 (in this order).

LISTING 7.24: CompoundIfLogic.R

```
x <- 30
print(paste0("x = ",x))

if( (x %% 3 == 0) && (x %% 5 == 0) ) {
   print(paste0("x is a multiple of 3 and 5"))
} else if( x %% 5 == 0) {
   print(paste0("x is a multiple of 5"))
} else if( x %% 3 == 0) {
   print(paste0("x is a multiple of 3"))
} else {
   print(paste0("x is not a multiple of 3 or 5"))
}
```

Listing 7.24 initializes the variable x with the value 30 and displays its value. The main code block contains a sequence of if/else-if statements, which continue to execute until a conditional statement is true, after which a print() statement displays a message and then execution will stop.

Specifically, if the first if statement is true, then x is a multiple of 15 and a message is displayed. The remainder of the code will not be executed. However, if the first if statement is false and the first else-if is true, then x is a multiple of 5 (but not a multiple of 15), and a message is displayed: the other else-if statements are not executed.

If x is not a multiple of 15 and also not a multiple of 5 and it is a multiple of 3, then a message is displayed, and the final else statement is not executed. Finally, if x is not a multiple of 15, 3, and 5, then the else statement is executed and a message is displayed. Launch the code in Listing 7.24 to see the following output:

```
[1] "x = 30"
[2] "x is a multiple of 3 and 5"
```

Suppose you modify the code in Listing 7.24 with the following code block and retain the same value for x:

```
if( (x %% 3 == 0) && (x %% 5 == 0) ) {
   print(paste0("x is a multiple of 3 and 5"))
}
if( x %% 5 == 0) {
   print(paste0("x is a multiple of 5"))
}
if( x %% 3 == 0) {
   print(paste0("x is a multiple of 3"))
}
```

The output from the new code block is shown here (which should be no surprise):

```
[1] "x = 30"
[2] "x is a multiple of 3 and 5"
[2] "x is a multiple of 5"
[2] "x is a multiple of 3"
```

WORKING WITH USER INPUT

The built-in R function `scan()` enables you to capture user input from the command line. Press the <RETURN> key after each number, and press <RE-TURN> twice to indicate that you have finished entering data from the command line.

Listing 7.25 shows the contents of `UserInput.R` that illustrate how to prompt users for input from the command line.

LISTING 7.25: UserInput.R

```
a <- scan(x)
```

Listing 7.25 is simple. It contains a single statement that invokes the `scan()` function to assign a user's input to the variable a. Launch the code in Listing 7.25 and enter some values:

```
1: 13
2: -8
3: 123
4: 99
5: xyz
Read 5 items.
```

A TRY/CATCH BLOCK IN R

The following code block in R contains a loop to print the logarithm of the elements of a list:

```
mylist = list(1, 2, 3, 4, -5, 'abc', 0)

for(value in mylist) {
   print(paste("log of", value, "=", log(value)))
}
```

However, the logarithm of 0, negative-numbers, and non-numeric values is undefined. Hence, the preceding code will fail when you execute its contents. The solution is to "wrap" the code inside a try/catch block, as shown here:

```
for(value in mylist) {
   tryCatch(print(paste("log of", value, "=", log(value))),
      warning = function(w) {print(paste("negative
                              argument", value));
                              log(-value)},
      error = function(e) {print(paste("non-numeric
argument", value));
                           NaN})
}
```

In the preceding code block, a warning message is displayed when a negative value is encountered, and an error message is displayed when a non-numeric value is encountered.

The preceding code block is an example of a `try/catch` block, which is ideal for handling user-supplied data. Another example of `try/catch` in R that illustrates additional options is here:

```
tryCatch( { result <- log(-1); print(result) }
           , warning = function(w) { print("invalid input")
})
```

```
found_error = FALSE
tryCatch( { result <- log(-1); print(result) }
           , error = function(e) {found_error <<- TRUE}
           , warning = function(w) { print("invalid input")}})
```

The preceding code block displays the following output (same output twice):

```
[1] "invalid input"
[1] "invalid input"
```

There are situations where you need to ensure that user input is of a particular type. For instance, when you prompt users for a numeric value (such as age), you want to handle the situation where non-numeric data is entered, such as A23 or abc. Consult the online documentation for more information.

LINEAR REGRESSION IN R

Linear regression in R is easy compared to other languages. The following three lines of code are enough to find the best-fitting line for a random set of 100 pairs of x-values and y-values:

```
x <- rnorm(100)
y <- rnorm(100)
fit <- lm(y~x)

capture.output(summary(fit))
capture.output(summary(fit), file="lm.out.txt")
# Send all output to a file (not expressions)
sink("lm.sink.txt")

# Start sink
mean(x)
summary(fit)

# Stop sink
sink()
```

WORKING WITH SIMPLE LOOPS IN R

Listing 7.26 shows the content of `simpleloop1.R,` which illustrates how to work with loops in R.

LISTING 7.26: simpleloop1.R

```
x <- c(2,5,3,9,8,11,6)

count <- 0
sum <- 0
for (val in x) {
    count = count+1
    sum = sum + val
}

print(paste0("count: ",count)
print(paste0("sum:    ",sum)
```

Listing 7.26 initializes the vector x with seven positive integers and the variable count with the value 0. Next, a loop iterates through the elements in x, incrementing the value of count during each iteration. Launch the code in Listing 7.26 to see the following output:

```
[1] "count: 7"
[1] "sum:    44
```

WORKING WITH NESTED LOOPS IN R

Listing 7.27 shows the contents of nestedloop1.R that illustrate how to work with nested loops in R.

LISTING 7.27: nestedloop1.R

```
x <- c(1,2,3)
y <- c(10,20,30)

for (x1 in x) {
    for (y1 in y) {
        print(paste0("(",x1,",",y1,")"))
    }
}
```

Listing 7.27 initializes the vectors x and y with positive integers, along with a nested loop that displays pairs of numeric values. The first value is an element of x, and the second value is an element of y. Launch the code in Listing 7.27 to see the following output:

```
[1] "(1,10)"
[1] "(1,20)"
[1] "(1,30)"
[1] "(2,10)"
[1] "(2,20)"
[1] "(2,30)"
[1] "(3,10)"
[1] "(3,20)"
[1] "(3,30)"
```

WORKING WITH WHILE LOOPS IN R

Listing 7.28 shows the contents of `whileleloop1.R` that illustrate how to work with loops in R.

LISTING 7.28: whileloop1.R

```
i <- 1

while (i < 6) {
    print(paste0("i: ",i))

    i = i+1
}
```

Listing 7.28 initializes the variable i with the value i and then executes a `while` loop that prints the value of i and continues doing so as long as i is less than 6. Launch the code in Listing 7.28 to see the following output:

```
[1] "i:  1"
[1] "i:  2"
[1] "i:  3"
[1] "i:  4"
[1] "i:  5"
```

WORKING WITH CONDITIONAL LOGIC IN R

Listing 7.29 shows the contents of `ifelse1.R` that illustrate how to work with conditional logic inside a `for` loop in R.

LISTING 7.29: ifelse1.R

```
nums = c(5,7,2,9)

for (a in nums) {
    if (a %% 2 == 0) {
      print(paste0(a," is even"))
    } else {
      print(paste0(a," is odd"))
    }
}
```

Listing 7.29 initializes the variable nums with four positive integers, followed by a loop that displays one message if the current number is even, and a different message of the number is odd.

Launch the code in Listing 7.29 to see the following output:

```
[1] "5 is odd"
[1] "7 is odd"
[1] "2 is even"
[1] "9 is odd"
```

ADD A SEQUENCE OF NUMBERS IN R

Listing 7.30 shows the content of SumOfN.R, which illustrates how to compute the sum of the integers from 1 to num inclusive in R.

LISTING 7.30: SumOfN.R

```
num <- 20
sum = (num * (num + 1)) / 2;
print(paste("The sum of the first",num,"numbers =", sum))
```

Listing 7.30 initializes the variable num with the value 20 and then uses a well-known formula to compute the sum of the integers between 1 and num. Launch the code in Listing 7.30 to see the following output:

```
[1] "The sum of the first 20 numbers = 210"
```

CHECK IF A NUMBER IS PRIME IN R

Listing 7.31 shows the contents of PrimeNumber.R that illustrate how to work with conditional logic and a loop in R to determine whether a positive integer is prime. The upper bound of the loop can be reduced from num-1 to sqrt(num)+1, which is more efficient for large values of num.

LISTING 7.31: PrimeNumber.R

```
num <- 20

# prime numbers are >= 2
flag = 1
if(num > 1) {
    # check for factors
    flag = 1
    for(i in 2:(num-1)) {
        if ((num %% i) == 0) {
            print(paste(i,"is a divisor of",num))
            flag = 0
            break
        }
    }
}

if(num == 2)
    flag = 1

if(flag == 1) {
    print(paste(num,"is a prime number"))
} else {
    print(paste(num,"is not a prime number"))
}
```

Listing 7.31 initializes the value of num to 20, followed by an `if` statement to ensure that its value is greater than 1 because you can assign a negative value to num.

Next, a loop iterates through the integers from 2 to num-1 inclusive, and if any of those numbers divides num with remainder zero, a message is displayed and an early exit occurs. The remaining portion of Listing 7.31 checks the value of flag to and uses its value to display an appropriate message. Launch the code in Listing 7.31 to see the following output:

```
[1] "2 is a divisor of 20"
[1] "20 is not a prime number"
```

CHECK IF NUMBERS IN AN ARRAY ARE PRIME IN R

Listing 7.32 shows the contents of `PrimeNumbers.R` that illustrate how to check if any of the numbers in an array is prime.

LISTING 7.33: PrimeNumbers.R

```r
prime <- function(num) {
    # prime numbers are >= 2
    flag = 1
    if(num > 1) {
        # check for factors
        flag = 1
        for(i in 2:(num-1)) {
            if ((num %% i) == 0) {
                flag = 0
                break
            }
        }
    }

    if(num == 2)
        flag = 1

    if(flag == 1) {
        print(paste(num,"is a prime number"))
    } else {
        print(paste(num,"is not a prime number"))
    }
}

for (num in 10:20){
  prime(num)
}

arr <- c(7, 17, 25, 99)
for (num in arr){
  prime(num)
}
```

Listing 7.32 defines the custom function `prime()`, whose code is the same as the code in Listing 7.31, but rewritten as a custom function. The last portion of Listing 7.32 contains a loop that iterates through the numbers from 10 to 10 and invokes the `prime()` function to determine whether those numbers are prime.

The second loop is similar. It also iterates through the numbers in a list and invokes the `prime()` function to determine whether that number is prime. Launch the code in Listing 7.32 to see the following output:

```
[1] "10 is not a prime number"
[1] "11 is a prime number"
[1] "12 is not a prime number"
[1] "13 is a prime number"
[1] "14 is not a prime number"
[1] "15 is not a prime number"
[1] "16 is not a prime number"
[1] "17 is a prime number"
[1] "18 is not a prime number"
[1] "19 is a prime number"
[1] "20 is not a prime number"
[1] "7 is a prime number"
[1] "17 is a prime number"
[1] "25 is not a prime number"
[1] "99 is not a prime number"
```

CHECK FOR LEAP YEARS IN R

Listing 7.33 shows the contents of `CheckForLeapYear.R` that illustrate how to use multiple conditional logic statements to determine whether a given year is a leap year in R.

LISTING 7.33: CheckForLeapYear.R

```
###########################################
# A year is a leap year if the following:
# 1) it is a multiple of 4 AND
# 2) a century must be a multiple of 400
#
# => 2000 is a leap year but 1900 is not.
# => 6, 82, and 1910 are not leap years.
###########################################
year <- 1900

if((year %% 4) == 0) {
    if((year %% 100) == 0) {
        if((year %% 400) == 0) {
            print(paste(year,"is a leap year"))
        } else {
            print(paste(year,"is not a leap year"))
        }
    } else {
        print(paste(year,"is a leap year"))
```

```
   }
} else {
   print(paste(year,"is not a leap year"))
}
```

Listing 7.33 initializes the variable `year` with the value 1900, followed by a set of nested `if` statements that implement the logic that is described in the comment block. Launch the code in Listing 7.33 to see the following output:

```
[1] "1900 is not a leap year"
```

WELL-FORMED TRIANGLE VALUES IN R

Listing 7.34 shows the content of `SumOfAngles.R`, which illustrates how to determine whether three angles form a triangle in the Euclidean plane. The comment block contains the necessary and sufficient conditions for three angles to form a triangle.

LISTING 7.34: SumOfAngles.R

```
a1 = 40, a2 = 80, a3 = 0

a1 = 40
a2 = 80
a3 = 60

print(paste0("a1: ",a1))
print(paste0("a2: ",a2))
print(paste0("a3: ",a3))

###############################
# ensure the following are true:
# 1) a1>0 and a1 < 180
# 2) a2>0 and a2 < 180
# 3) a1+a1 < 180
###############################

if( ((a1 <= 0) || (a1 >= 180)) ||
    ((a2 <= 0) || (a2 >= 180)) )
{
   print(paste0("angles out of range: ",a1,a2))
} else {
   if( a1+a2 >= 180 ) {
      print(paste0("a1 + a2 is too large:", a1+a2))
   } else {
      a3 = 180 - (a1+a2)
      print(paste0("a1, a2, and a3 form a triangle:",
               a1," ",a2," ",a3))
   }
}
```

Listing 7.34 initializes the variables a1, a2, and a3 with three positive integer values. The next set of `if/else` statements implement the logic described in the comment block. Launch the code in Listing 7.34 to see the following output:

```
[1] "a1: 40"
[1] "a2: 80"
[1] "a3: 60"
[1] "a1, a2, and a3 form a triangle:40 80 60"
```

WHAT ARE FACTORS IN R?

Factors in R are similar to enum (enumeration) in other languages. Factors are created via the factor() function. Listing 7.35 shows the contents of factors1.R that illustrate how to define factors in R.

LISTING 7.35: factors1.R

```
a <-  "Hello"
mycolors <- c('green','green','yellow','red','red','red',
              'green')

# Create a factor object:
myfactors <- factor(mycolors)
print("contents of the myfactors vector:")
print(myfactors)

print("the number of levels in myfactors:")
print(nlevels(myfactors))
```

Listing 7.35 defines a vector of strings mycolors and then initializes the variable myfactors with the "factors" in the variable mycolors, which consists of three distinct colors. Launch the code in Listing 7.35 to see the following output:

```
[1] "contents of the myfactors vector:"
[1] green   green   yellow red    red    red    green
Levels: green red yellow
[1] "the number of levels in myfactors:"
[1] 3
```

Consult the online documentation for information regarding additional features that are available via the nlevels() function.

WHAT ARE DATA FRAMES IN R?

A data frame in R is similar to a Pandas data frame, which in turn is similar to a spreadsheet. Moreover, column-related and row-related operations on a data frame are similar to the corresponding operations on a spreadsheet: insert, delete, or move rows and columns.

In addition, you can update values based on various criteria, such as "filling in" missing values or modifying existing values. A list data type in R is compatible with data.frame if any of the following is true:

Components must be vectors (numeric, character, logical) or factors.
All vectors and factors must have the same lengths.

Matrices and other data frames can be combined with vectors to form a data frame if the dimensions are compatible.

Data frames are essentially data objects in tabular form, with heterogeneous columns of data, created via the data.frame() function. Listing 7.36 shows the contents of simple_df.R that define a data frame consisting of three 1×3 vectors consisting of three positive integers.

LISTING 7.36: simple_df.R

```
mydf <- data.frame(
   attr1 <- c(1,2,3),
   attr2 <- c(4,5,6),
   attr3 <- c(7,8,9)
)

print("contents of attr1 of mydf:")
print(mydf[,1])
print("contents of attr2 of mydf:")
print(mydf[,2])
print("contents of attr3 of mydf:")
print(mydf[,3])

# second data frame:
attr4 <- c('a','b','c')
attr5 <- c('d','e','f')

mydf2 <- data.frame(
   attr4,
   attr5
)

print("contents of mydf2:")
print(mydf2)
```

Listing 7.36 starts by initializing the variable mydf as a data frame that consists of three rows with the numbers from 1 to 9 inclusive. The next portion of Listing 7.36 creates the data frame mydf2 that consists of two columns (and three rows) of letters from a to f inclusive. Launch the code in Listing 7.36 to see the following output:

```
[1] "contents of attr1 of mydf:"
[1] 1 2 3
[1] "contents of attr2 of mydf:"
[1] 4 5 6
```

```
[1] "contents of attr3 of mydf:"
[1] 7 8 9

[1] "contents of mydf2:"
  attr4 attr5
1     a     d
2     b     e
3     c     f
```

The next several sections contain various short yet illustrative examples of performing operations on the contents of data frames in R.

WORKING WITH DATA FRAMES IN R (1)

Listing 7.37 shows the content of data frame2.R, which illustrates how to work with a data frame in R.

LISTING 7.37: data frame2.R

```
# Create the data frame:
emp.data <- data.frame(
  emp_id = c (1:5),
  emp_name = c("Rick","Dan","Michelle","Ryan","Gary"),
  salary = c(623.3,515.2,611.0,729.0,843.25),

  start_date =
    as.Date(c("2012-01-01","2013-09-23","2014-11-15",
            "2014-05-11","2015-03-27")),
    stringsAsFactors = FALSE
)

# Print the data frame:
print(emp.data)

# Get the structure of the data frame:
str(emp.data)

# Print the summary:
print(summary(emp.data))
```

Listing 7.37 starts by defining the variable emp.data that contains the id value, the name, the salary, and the start date for 5 employees. The next code snippet displays the contents of emp.data, followed by the structure of emp.data. The final code snippet displays summary information for emp.data. Launch the code in Listing 7.37 to see the following output:

```
  emp_id emp_name salary start_date
1      1     Rick 623.30 2012-01-01
2      2      Dan 515.20 2013-09-23
3      3 Michelle 611.00 2014-11-15
4      4     Ryan 729.00 2014-05-11
5      5     Gary 843.25 2015-03-27
```

```
'data.frame':   5 obs. of  4 variables:
 $ emp_id    : int  1 2 3 4 5
 $ emp_name  : chr  "Rick" "Dan" "Michelle" "Ryan" ...
 $ salary    : num  623 515 611 729 843
 $ start_date: Date, format: "2012-01-01" "2013-09-23" ...
     emp_id       emp_name              salary          start_date
 Min.   :1   Length:5           Min.   :515.2   Min.   :2012-01-01
 1st Qu.:2   Class :character   1st Qu.:611.0   1st Qu.:2013-09-23
 Median :3   Mode  :character   Median :623.3   Median :2014-05-11
 Mean   :3                      Mean   :664.4   Mean   :2014-01-14
 3rd Qu.:4                      3rd Qu.:729.0   3rd Qu.:2014-11-15
 Max.   :5                      Max.   :843.2   Max.   :2015-03-27
```

WORKING WITH DATA FRAMES IN R (2)

Listing 7.38 shows the contents of data frame3.R that illustrate how to work with a data frame in R.

LISTING 7.38: data frame3.R

```
# Create the data frame:
emp.data <- data.frame(
  emp_id = c (1:5),
  emp_name = c("Rick","Dan","Michelle","Ryan","Gary"),
  salary = c(623.3,515.2,611.0,729.0,843.25),

  start_date =
    as.Date(c("2012-01-01","2013-09-23","2014-11-15",
              "2014-05-11","2015-03-27")),
    stringsAsFactors = FALSE
)

# Print the data frame:
print(emp.data)

# Get the structure of the data frame:
str(emp.data)

# Print the summary:
print(summary(emp.data))

# Extract Specific columns:
result <- data.frame(emp.data$emp_name,emp.data$salary)
print(result)
```

Listing 7.38 contains the same code as Listing 7.37, plus an extra code block that is shown in bold in Listing 7.38. This new code block creates the variable result as a data frame that consist of the employee names and salaries in emp. data that is previously defined in Listing 7.38. Launch the code in Listing 7.38 to see the following output (and the new output is shown in bold):

```
  emp_id emp_name salary start_date
1      1     Rick 623.30 2012-01-01
2      2      Dan 515.20 2013-09-23
```

```
3        3 Michelle 611.00 2014-11-15
4        4      Ryan 729.00 2014-05-11
5        5      Gary 843.25 2015-03-27
'data.frame':   5 obs. of  4 variables:
 $ emp_id    : int  1 2 3 4 5
 $ emp_name  : chr  "Rick" "Dan" "Michelle" "Ryan" ...
 $ salary    : num  623 515 611 729 843
 $ start_date: Date, format: "2012-01-01" "2013-09-23" ...
      emp_id      emp_name        salary        start_date
 Min.   :1   Length:5        Min.   :515.2   Min.   :2012-01-01
 1st Qu.:2   Class :character 1st Qu.:611.0   1st Qu.:2013-09-23
 Median :3   Mode  :character Median :623.3   Median :2014-05-11
 Mean   :3                    Mean   :664.4   Mean   :2014-01-14
 3rd Qu.:4                    3rd Qu.:729.0   3rd Qu.:2014-11-15
 Max.   :5                    Max.   :843.2   Max.   :2015-03-27
   emp.data.emp_name emp.data.salary
1              Rick          623.30
2               Dan          515.20
3          Michelle          611.00
4              Ryan          729.00
5              Gary          843.25
```

WORKING WITH DATA FRAMES IN R (3)

Listing 7.39 shows the contents of data frame4.R that illustrate how to work with a data frame in R.

LISTING 7.39: data frame4.R

```
# Create the data frame:
emp.data <- data.frame(
  emp_id = c (1:5),
  emp_name = c("Rick","Dan","Michelle","Ryan","Gary"),
  salary = c(623.3,515.2,611.0,729.0,843.25),

  start_date =
    as.Date(c("2012-01-01","2013-09-23","2014-11-15",
              "2014-05-11","2015-03-27")),
    stringsAsFactors = FALSE
)

# Print the data frame:
print(emp.data)

# Get the structure of the data frame:
str(emp.data)

# Print the summary:
print(summary(emp.data))

# Extract specific columns:
result <- data.frame(emp.data$emp_name,emp.data$salary)
print(result)
```

```
# Extract first two rows:
result <- emp.data[1:2,]
print(result)
```

Listing 7.39 contains the same code as Listing 7.38, plus a code block that is shown in bold. The new code block initializes the variable `result` with the contents of the name and salary columns of `emp.data` and then prints the contents of `result`. Launch the code in Listing 7.39 to see the following output (and the new output is shown in bold):

```
  emp_id emp_name salary start_date
1      1     Rick 623.30 2012-01-01
2      2      Dan 515.20 2013-09-23
3      3 Michelle 611.00 2014-11-15
4      4     Ryan 729.00 2014-05-11
5      5     Gary 843.25 2015-03-27
,data.frame':   5 obs. of  4 variables:
 $ emp_id    : int  1 2 3 4 5
 $ emp_name  : chr  "Rick" "Dan" "Michelle" "Ryan" ...
 $ salary    : num  623 515 611 729 843
 $ start_date: Date, format: "2012-01-01" "2013-09-23" ...
     emp_id      emp_name           salary         start_date
 Min.   :1   Length:5          Min.   :515.2   Min.   :2012-01-01
 1st Qu.:2   Class :character  1st Qu.:611.0   1st Qu.:2013-09-23
 Median :3   Mode  :character  Median :623.3   Median :2014-05-11
 Mean   :3                     Mean   :664.4   Mean   :2014-01-14
 3rd Qu.:4                     3rd Qu.:729.0   3rd Qu.:2014-11-15
 Max.   :5                     Max.   :843.2   Max.   :2015-03-27
   emp.data.emp_name emp.data.salary
1               Rick          623.30
2                Dan          515.20
3           Michelle          611.00
4               Ryan          729.00
5               Gary          843.25
  emp_id emp_name salary start_date
1      1     Rick  623.3 2012-01-01
2      2      Dan  515.2 2013-09-23
```

SORT A DATA FRAME BY COLUMN

Often data are better viewed when sorted. The function order sorts a column and gives output that can sort the rows of a data.frame. The following sorts measures by age.

```
> measrsByAge <- measrs2[order(measrs2[,+    "age"]), ]
> measrsByAge
   gender    ht wt age
S5      F 166.0 72  22
S1      M 172.0 91  28
S4      M 170.0 68  38
S3      F 165.0 74  43
S2      M 186.5 99  55
```

rev reverses the order from increasing to decreasing.

```
> measrsByHt <- measrs2[rev(order(measrs2[,
+           "ht"])), ]
> measrsByHt
   gender   ht wt age
S2      M 186.5 99  55
S1      M 172.0 91  28
S4      M 170.0 68  38
S5      F 166.0 72  22
S3      F 165.0 74  43
```

READING EXCEL FILES IN R

Listing 7.40 shows the contents of readXSL.R that illustrate how to read the contents of an XLS spreadsheet into a data frame in R.

LISTING 7.40: readXLS.R

```
library(readxl)
dfb <- read_excel("employees.xlsx")

print("The first five rows of employees.xlsx:")
head(dfb)

print("A Summary of employees.xlsx:")
summary(dfb)
```

In Listing 7.40, after loading the readxl library, the variable dfb is initialized from the contents of the employees.xlsx spreadsheet. The first five rows are displayed, followed by a summary, as shown below:

```
[1] "The first five rows of employees.xlsx:"
# A tibble: 6 x 10
    id fname lname gender    title    q1    q2    q3    q4 country
  <dbl> <chr> <chr> <chr>    <chr> <dbl> <dbl> <dbl> <dbl>   <chr>
1 1000  john smith      m marketing 20000 12000 18000 25000     usa
2 2000  jane smith      f developer 30000 15000 11000 35000  france
3 3000  jack jones      m     sales 10000 19000 12000 15000     usa
4 4000  dave stone      m   support 15000 17000 14000 18000  france
5 5000  sara stein      f   analyst 25000 22000 18000 28000   italy
6 6000  eddy bower      m developer 14000 32000 28000 10000  france

[1] "A Summary of employees.xlsx:"
      id          fname               lname             gender
Min.   :1000   Length:6           Length:6           Length:6
1st Qu.:2250   Class :character   Class :character   Class :character
Median :3500   Mode  :character   Mode  :character   Mode  :character
Mean   :3500
3rd Qu.:4750
Max.   :6000
   title              q1                q2                q3
Length:6        Min.   :10000     Min.   :12000     Min.   :11000
Class :character 1st Qu.:14250    1st Qu.:15500     1st Qu.:12500
Mode  :character Median :17500    Median :18000     Median :16000
```

```
                        Mean    :19000   Mean    :19500   Mean    :16833
                        3rd Qu.:23750    3rd Qu.:21250    3rd Qu.:18000
                        Max.    :30000   Max.    :32000   Max.    :28000
            q4          country
  Min.    :10000    Length:6
  1st Qu.:15750     Class :character
  Median :21500     Mode  :character
  Mean    :21833
  3rd Qu.:27250
  Max.    :35000
```

READING SQLITE TABLES IN R

Listing 7.41 shows the contents of readSQLite.R that illustrate how to read the contents of a built-in RSQLite database (which is the counterpart to SQLITE) in R.

LISTING 7.41: readSQLite.R

```
library(RSQLite)
library(DBI)

print("Establishing database connection...")
db = RSQLite::datasetsDb()

# display the tables in the database
print("Reading database tables...")
dbListTables(db)

print("Reading contents of mtcars table...")
dbReadTable(db, "mtcars")

# filter the data
print("Listing rows in the mtcars table...")
dbGetQuery(db, "SELECT * FROM mtcars")

print("Disconnecting database connection...")
dbDisconnect(db)
```

Listing 7.41 starts by referencing the RSQLite and DBI libraries for managing database connections. Next, db is initialized with the list of built-in databases in R. The specific table that we want to examine is called mtcars, which we access via this code snippet:

```
dbReadTable(db, "mtcars")
```

The next portion of Listing 7.41 executes a SELECT statement that retrieves all the rows from the mtcars table and displays its contents. The final code snippet disconnects from the database. Launch the code in Listing 7.41 to see the following output:

```
[1] "Establishing database connection..."
```

```
[1] "Reading database tables..."
[1] "BOD"               "CO2"              "ChickWeight"       "DNase"
[5] "Formaldehyde"      "Indometh"         "InsectSprays"      "LifeCycleSavings"
[9] "Loblolly"          "Orange"           "OrchardSprays"     "PlantGrowth"
[13] "Puromycin"        "Theoph"           "ToothGrowth"       "USArrests"
[17] "USJudgeRatings"   "airquality"       "anscombe"          "attenu"
[21] "attitude"         "cars"             "chickwts"          "esoph"
[25] "faithful"         "freeny"           "infert"            "iris"
[29] "longley"          "morley"           "mtcars"            "npk"
[33] "pressure"         "quakes"           "randu"             "rock"
[37] "sleep"            "stackloss"        "swiss"             "trees"
[41] "warpbreaks"       "women"
```

```
[1] "Reading contents of mtcars table..."
             row_names mpg cyl  disp  hp drat    wt  qsec vs am gear carb
1             Mazda RX4 21.0   6 160.0 110 3.90 2.620 16.46  0  1    4    4
2         Mazda RX4 Wag 21.0   6 160.0 110 3.90 2.875 17.02  0  1    4    4
3            Datsun 710 22.8   4 108.0  93 3.85 2.320 18.61  1  1    4    1
4        Hornet 4 Drive 21.4   6 258.0 110 3.08 3.215 19.44  1  0    3    1
5     Hornet Sportabout 18.7   8 360.0 175 3.15 3.440 17.02  0  0    3    2
6               Valiant 18.1   6 225.0 105 2.76 3.460 20.22  1  0    3    1
7            Duster 360 14.3   8 360.0 245 3.21 3.570 15.84  0  0    3    4
8             Merc 240D 24.4   4 146.7  62 3.69 3.190 20.00  1  0    4    2
9              Merc 230 22.8   4 140.8  95 3.92 3.150 22.90  1  0    4    2
10             Merc 280 19.2   6 167.6 123 3.92 3.440 18.30  1  0    4    4
// rows omitted for brevity
22     Dodge Challenger 15.5   8 318.0 150 2.76 3.520 16.87  0  0    3    2
23           AMC Javelin 15.2   8 304.0 150 3.15 3.435 17.30  0  0    3    2
24           Camaro Z28 13.3   8 350.0 245 3.73 3.840 15.41  0  0    3    4
25     Pontiac Firebird 19.2   8 400.0 175 3.08 3.845 17.05  0  0    3    2
26            Fiat X1-9 27.3   4  79.0  66 4.08 1.935 18.90  1  1    4    1
27        Porsche 914-2 26.0   4 120.3  91 4.43 2.140 16.70  0  1    5    2
28         Lotus Europa 30.4   4  95.1 113 3.77 1.513 16.90  1  1    5    2
29       Ford Pantera L 15.8   8 351.0 264 4.22 3.170 14.50  0  1    5    4
30         Ferrari Dino 19.7   6 145.0 175 3.62 2.770 15.50  0  1    5    6
31        Maserati Bora 15.0   8 301.0 335 3.54 3.570 14.60  0  1    5    8
32           Volvo 142E 21.4   4 121.0 109 4.11 2.780 18.60  1  1    4    2
[1] "Disconnecting database connection..."
```

READING TEXT FILES IN R

Listing 7.42 and Listing 7.43 show the contents of the files people.csv and employees.txt, respectively, that are referenced in Listing 7.44.

LISTING 7.42: people.csv

```
fname,lname,age,gender,country
john,smith,30,m,usa
jane,smith,31,f,france
jack,jones,32,m,france
dave,stone,33,m,italy
sara,stein,34,f,germany
eddy,bower,35,m,spain
```

LISTING 7.43: employees.txt

```
Name:   Jane Edwards
EmpId: 12345
Address: 123 Main Street Chicago Illinois

Name:   John Smith
EmpId: 23456
Address: 432 Lombard Avenue SF California
```

Listing 7.44 shows the content of `read_table.R`, which illustrates how to use the `read_table` function to populate data frames with the contents of the files `people.csv` and `employees.txt`.

LISTING 7.44: read_table.R

```
# 1) read data and exclude header row
df <- read.table("people.csv", header = FALSE)
print("df:")
df

# 2) read comma-delimited data and include header row
df <- read.table("people.csv", header = TRUE, sep = ",")
print("df:")
df

# 3) Read a file with multi-line records
df <- read.delim("employees.txt", sep="$")
print("df:")
df
```

Listing 7.44 contains three main blocks of code. The first code block populates the data frame `df` only with data (i.e., the header information is excluded), whereas the second code block populates the data frame `df` with data *and* the header information.

The third code block populates the data frame `df` with the contents of `employees.txt` and specifies "$" as the record delimiter, which means that each line is treated as a row of data. Launch the code in Listing 7.42 to see the following output:

```
[1] "df:"
                                  V1
1 fname,lname,age,gender,country
2             john,smith,30,m,usa
3           jane,smith,31,f,france
4           jack,jones,32,m,france
5            dave,stone,33,m,italy
6          sara,stein,34,f,germany
7           eddy,bower,35,m,spain
[1] "df:"
   fname lname age gender country
1  john smith  30      m     usa
2  jane smith  31      f  france
```

```
3   jack jones   32     m  france
4   dave stone   33     m   italy
5   sara stein   34     f germany
6   eddy bower   35     m   spain
[1] "df:"
                        Name...Jane.Edwards
1                         EmpId: 12345
2 Address: 123 Main Street Chicago Illinois
3                         Name:   John Smith
4                         EmpId: 23456
5 Address: 432 Lombard Avenue SF California
```

SAVING AND RESTORING OBJECTS IN R

Listing 7.45 shows the contents of readtable2.R that illustrate how to save the contents of a variable to a text file, modify the value of a variable, and then restore the original value of the variable from the text file in R.

LISTING 7.45: save_restore.R

```
print("Saving v to file saved_vector.Rdata")
v <- c(1,2,NA,4)
save(v, file="saved_vector.Rdata")

# data frame:
mydf <- data.frame(
  attr1 <- c(1,2,3),
  attr2 <- c(4,5,6),
  attr3 <- c(7,8,9)
)
print("Saving df to file saved_data frame.Rdata")
save(mydf, file="saved_data frame.Rdata")

print("New contents of v:")
v <- c(-1234)
print(v)

print("New contents of mydf:")
mydf <- data.frame(c(-1234))
print(mydf)

print("Restoring v from file saved_vector.Rdata")
load("saved_vector.Rdata")

print("Restoring mydf from file saved_data frame.Rdata")
load("saved_data frame.Rdata")

print("Restored contents of v:")
print(v)

print("Restored contents of mydf:")
print(mydf)
```

Listing 7.45 consists of three sections of code. The first part defines and saves a vector v and also defines and saves a data frame mydf. The second part assigns different values to v an mydf to test whether they will be assigned the restored values.

The third part restores the values of v and mydf, which confirms that the code is working correctly and as expected. Launch the code in Listing 7.45 to see the following output:

```
[1] "Saving v to file saved_vector.Rdata"
[1] "Saving df to file saved_data frame.Rdata"
[1] "New contents of v:"
[1] -1234
[1] "New contents of mydf:"
  c..1234.
1    -1234
[1] "Restoring v from file saved_vector.Rdata"
[1] "Restoring mydf from file saved_data frame.Rdata"
[1] "Restored contents of v:"
[1]   1  2 NA   4
[1] "Restored contents of mydf:"
  attr1....c.1..2..3. attr2....c.4..5..6.  attr3....c.7..8..9.
1                   1                    4                    7
2                   2                    5                    8
3                   3                    6                    9
```

DATA VISUALIZATION IN R

As you might have already surmised, R supports an assortment of charts and graphs for displaying data in a graphical manner. R makes it easy to render data in graphical form and to save that graphics data as a PNG file.

Some of the built-in chart-related functions can generate the following types of output:

bar charts
line graphs
histograms
pie charts
boxplots

WORKING WITH BAR CHARTS IN R (1)

Listing 7.46 shows the contents of barchart1.R that illustrate how to display a bar chart in R.

LISTING 7.46: barchart1.R

```
# Create the data for the chart:
H <- c(7,12,28,3,41)

# Give the chart file a name:
```

```
png(file = "barchart.png")

# Plot the bar chart:
barplot(H)

# Save the file:
dev.off()
```

Listing 7.46 initializes the variable H with 5 values for a bar chart, and then specifies the name barchart.png as the filename of the binary file where the bar chart will be stored.

The next code snippet renders the bar chart via the barplot() function and then invokes dev.off() to save the bar chart as the specified filename. Launch the code in Listing 7.46 to generate the bar chart that is shown in Figure 7.1.

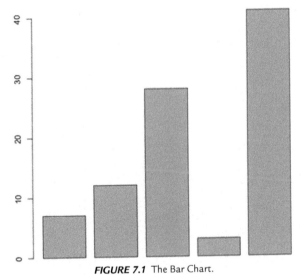

FIGURE 7.1 The Bar Chart.

WORKING WITH BAR CHARTS IN R (2)

Listing 7.47 shows the contents of barchart2.R that illustrate how to display a bar chart in R.

LISTING 7.47: barchart2.R

```
# Create the data for the chart:
H <- c(7,12,28,3,41)
M <- c("Mar","Apr","May","Jun","Jul")

# Give the chart file a name:
png(file = "barchart_months_revenue.png")

# Plot the bar chart:
```

```
barplot(H,names.arg=M,xlab="Month",ylab="Revenue",
col="blue", main="Revenue chart",border="red")

# Save the file:
dev.off()
```

Listing 7.47 initializes the variable H as a 1×5 vector of numbers and the variable M with 5 months of the year. The next code snippet specifies monthly_ revenue.png as the name of the binary file where the bar chart will be stored.

The next code snippet renders the bar chart via the barplot() function, along with various parameters, such as the labels for the horizontal and vertical axes via xlab and ylab, respectively.

The final code snippet invokes dev.off() to save the bar chart as the specified filename. Launch the code in Listing 7.47 to generate a bar chart with the monthly revenue that is shown in Figure 7.2.

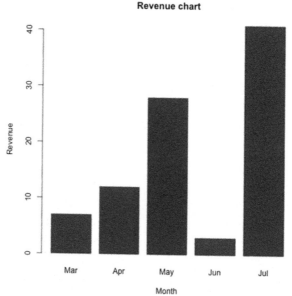

Revenue chart

FIGURE 7.2 The revenue chart generated by the code in Listing 7.47

WORKING WITH LINE GRAPHS IN R

Listing 7.48 shows the contents of linegraph1.R that illustrate how to display a bar chart in R.

LISTING 7.48: linegraph1.R
```
# Create the data for the chart:
v <- c(7,12,28,3,41)

# Give the chart file a name:
png(file = "line_chart.png")
```

```
# Plot the line graph:
plot(v,type = "o")

# Save the file:
dev.off()
```

Listing 7.48 initializes the variable v with 5 values for a line graph, and then specifies the name `line_chart.png` as the filename of the binary file where the line graph will be stored.

The next code snippet renders the line graph via the `plot()` function and then invokes `dev.off()` to save the bar chart as the specified filename.

Launch the code in Listing 7.48 to generate the bar chart shown in Figure 7.3.

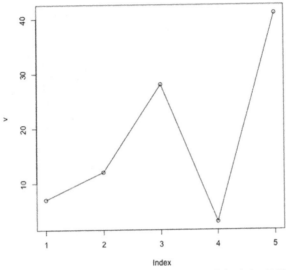

FIGURE 7.3 The line graph generated by the code in Listing 7.48

If you are interested in more examples of charts and graphs, the companion files contain code samples for generating multi-line graphs, histograms, scatterplot, box plots, and pie charts:

- `linegraphLabels1.R`
- `multilinegraph1.R`
- `histogram1.R`
- `scatterplot1.R`
- `scatterplotMatrix1.R`
- `boxplott1.R`
- `piechart1.R`
- `piechart3D1.R`

In most cases, the preceding code samples are similar to the code samples in this Chapter.

WORKING WITH FUNCTIONS IN R

R provides a vast set of built-in functions, some of which you have already seen earlier in this chapter, such as `toupper()` and `tolower()`, which convert a string to uppercase and lowercase letters, respectively.

However, sometimes the existing functions in R do not provide the functionality that you need to perform specific tasks. Fortunately, R makes it easy to define custom functions. Listing 7.49 shows the contents of `BasicFunctions.R` that illustrate how to perform various operations in R.

LISTING 7.49: BasicFunctions.R

```
x <- c(1,2,NA,3)
mean(x)
mean(x, na.rm=TRUE)

#check for missing values
is.na(x) # returns TRUE if x is missing
y <- c(1,2,3,NA)
is.na(y) # returns a vector (F F F T)

table(is.na(x))

sum(is.na(x))

sum(!is.na(x))
v <- c(NA, NA, 0.5, 1, 12, 15, 3)
summary(v)
v <- c(-1, "-nodata-", 0.5, 1, 12, 15, 3)
table(v)

summary(na.omit(x))
```

Listing 7.49 initializes the variable x as a list with four values (including NA) and then invokes the `mean()` method to calculate mean of those values. The second invocation of the `mean()` method specifies `na.rm=TRUE`, which means that N/A values are ignored during the calculation of the mean. Launch the code in Listing 7.49 to see the following output:

```
[1] NA
[1] 2
[1] FALSE FALSE  TRUE FALSE
[1] FALSE FALSE FALSE  TRUE

FALSE  TRUE
    3     1
[1] 1
[1] 3
   Min. 1st Qu.  Median    Mean 3rd Qu.    Max.   NA's
    0.5     1.0     3.0     6.3    12.0    15.0      2
v
         -1 -nodata-        0.5       1      12      15       3
          1         1         1       1       1       1       1
```

```
  Min. 1st Qu.  Median   Mean 3rd Qu.   Max.
   1.0    1.5     2.0     2.0    2.5    3.0
```

The next section contains examples of built-in trigonometric functions in R, such as `sin()`, `cos()`, and `tan()`.

MATH-RELATED FUNCTIONS IN R

R supports a variety of math-related functions and trigonometric functions, as listed below:

- `sqrt()`
- `sum()`
- `cos()`
- `sin()`
- `tan()`
- `log(x)`
- `log10()`
- `exp()`
- `sqrt()`
- `round(x)`
- `signif(x)`
- `trunc(x)` - rounding functions
- `sqrt()`

The built-in trigonometric functions in R include `sin(x)`, `cos(x)`, `sin(x)`, `tan(x)`, `acos(x)`, `asin(x)`, `atan(x)`, and `atan2(y,x)`. With the exception of the function `atan2(y,x)`, the argument for all trigonometric functions in R is specific in radians (not degrees).

Listing 7.50 shows the content of `TrigFunctions.R`, which illustrates how to use some math functions and trigonometric functions in R.

LISTING 7.50: TrigFunctions.R

```r
# sine(π/2):
print("sin(pi/2):")
sin(pi/2)

# cosine(π):
print("cos(pi):")
cos(pi)

# tangent(π/3):
print("tan(pi/3):")
tan(pi/3)

# cotangent(π/3):
print("cotangent(pi/3):")
1/tan(pi/3)
```

```
#angle x where cos(x) = -1:
print("acos(-1):")
acos(-1)

#angle x where tan(x) = 0.5:
print("atan(0.5):")
atan(0.5)

#atan2() take the y and x values as arguments:
print("atan2(1,2):")
atan2(1,2)
```

Listing 7.50 is a code sample that contains code snippets for calculating the values of various trigonometric functions, including `sin()`, `cos()`, `tan()`, and `cotangent()`.

The last two code snippets display values for `arccosine()` and `arctangent()`, which are the inverse cosine and inverse tangent functions, respectively. Launch the code in Listing 7.50 to see the following output:

```
[1] "sin(pi/2):"
[1] 1
[1] "cos(pi):"
[1] -1
[1] "tan(pi/3):"
[1] 1.732051
[1] "cotangent(pi/3):"
[1] 0.5773503
[1] "acos(-1):"
[1] 3.141593
[1] "atan(0.5):"
[1] 0.4636476
[1] "atan2(1,2):"
[1] 0.4636476
[1] 2
```

SOME OPERATORS AND SET FUNCTIONS IN R

In addition to the operators that you have seen in previous sections, R provides several built-in operators for set-related operations, as listed below:

```
union()
intersect()
setdiff()
setequal()
```

The set functions `union()`, `intersect()`, `setdiff()`, and `setequal()` discard duplicates in the arguments. Moreover, these set functions apply `as.vector()` to their arguments, which changes `factors` in R to character vectors in R.

Listing 7.51 shows the contents of `ArithSetFunctions.R` that illustrate how to use set-related functions in R.

LISTING 7.51: ArithSetFunctions.R

```
print("one:")
(one <- c(sort(sample(1:20, 8)), NA))

print("two:")
(two <- c(sort(sample(5:30, 5)), NA))

union(one, two)
intersect(one, two)
setdiff(one, two)
setdiff(two, one)
setequal(one, two)

# is.element(x, y) => identical to x %in% y.
# the elements of one that are in two (9)
is.element(one, two)

# length 6
# the elements of two that are in one (6)
is.element(two, one)
```

Listing 7.51 starts by defining the variables one and two and then computing the set operations union(), intersect(), setdiff(), and setequal() with the variables one and two. The last two code snippets invoke the is.element() function on the variables one and two. Launch the code in Listing 7.51 to see the following output:

```
[1] "one:"
[1]  1  7  9 11 12 13 17 20 NA
[1] "two:"
[1]  5 13 19 26 27 NA
[1]  1  7  9 11 12 13 17 20 NA  5 19 26 27
[1] 13 NA
[1]  1  7  9 11 12 17 20
[1]  5 19 26 27
[1] FALSE
[1] FALSE FALSE FALSE FALSE FALSE  TRUE FALSE FALSE  TRUE
[1] FALSE  TRUE FALSE FALSE FALSE  TRUE
```

R supports the built-function eigen() for determining eigenvalues and eigenvectors in linear algebra, both of which are useful when you use PCA (Principal Component Analysis) on a dataset to determine the most significant features of a dataset. R also supports the built-in function deriv() for calculating symbolic and algorithmic derivatives.

THE "APPLY FAMILY" OF BUILT-IN FUNCTIONS

The following functions are in the "apply family" of R functions, and they are similar to the map() function that is available in many other languages:

apply: apply a function (e.g., mean)

```
lapply:  operates on lists
sapply:  apply for lists or vectors
```

The purpose of `apply()` is primarily to avoid explicit uses of loop constructs. They can be used for an input list, matrix, or array to apply a function. Any function can be passed into `apply()`.

Here is a simple example of the `apply()` function that calculates the sum of the columns in an array of integers:

```
m1 <- matrix(M<-(1:8),nrow=4, ncol=4)
print("m1:")
m1
m2 <- apply(m1, 2, sum)
print("m2:")
m2
```

The output of the preceding code block is shown here:

```
[1]  "m1:"
      [,1] [,2] [,3] [,4]
[1,]    1    5    1    5
[2,]    2    6    2    6
[3,]    3    7    3    7
[4,]    4    8    4    8
[1]  "m2:"
[1] 10 26 10 26
```

The `lapply()` function operates on list objects ("l" = "list") and returns a list object whose length equals the length of the input to the `lapply()` function. If you are familiar with the `map()` function from working with other programming languages, then you know the semantics of this function. Specifically, the `lapply()` function requires data in the form of a list as well as a function that you want to "apply" to each element in that list.

The following code block initializes the variable `people` with a list of first names and then invokes the `lapply()` function with the variable people and the function `toupper` that will return a list of the uppercase form of each string in the `people` variable:

```
people <- c("sara","dave","george","peter","sally")
people_upper <-lapply(people, toupper)
str(people_upper)
```

The output of the preceding code block is here:

```
List of 5
 $ : chr "SARA"
 $ : chr "DAVE"
 $ : chr "GEORGE"
 $ : chr "PETER"
 $ : chr "SALLY"
```

The `sapply()` function supports a list, a vector or a data frame as its input data and generates a vector or matrix as output, whereas `lapply()` returns a list; however, they share the same functionality.

The following code snippet returns a vector containing the square root of the numbers from 1 to 5 inclusive:

```
sapply(1:5, sqrt)
```

The following code snippet returns three vectors involving the logarithm, the exponential value, and the trigonometric tangent of the numbers from 1 to 5 inclusive:

```
sapply(c(1, 2, 3), log)
sapply(c(1, 2, 3), exp)
sapply(c(1, 2, 3), tan)
```

The output from the preceding code block is as follows:

```
[1]  0.0000000 0.6931472 1.0986123
[1]   2.718282  7.389056 20.085537
[1]   1.5574077 -2.1850399 -0.1425465
```

THE DPLYR PACKAGE IN R

R supports the `dplyr` package, which provides powerful functionality for managing data frames in R. Some frequently used `dplyr` APIs are briefly described below.

The `select()` API selects columns from a data frame.

The `filter()` API enables you to select a subset of rows based on a Boolean expression. For example, if a column contains integer values, you can select the rows for which the integer value is even (or even and larger than 10, or even and between 20 and 40, and so forth). There is no practical limit to the Boolean expression, and you can use any combination of logical operators, such as `OR`, `AND`, and `NOT`.

The `arrange()` API changes the order of rows (do not confuse this function with the `arange()` API that is available in other languages).

The `mutate()` API creates new columns (this API performs a column insert operation).

The `summarise()` API provides a summary of the values in columns, whereas the `group_by()` API is similar to `GROUP BY` in `SQL` statements (see Chapter 9 for examples of `GROUP BY`).

Before we continue, make sure that you have installed the `dplyr` package, which can be performed by either of the following code snippets:

```
# install tidyverse:
install.packages("tidyverse")

# install only dplyr:
install.packages("dplyr")
```

Listing 7.52 shows the contents of `dplyr-mtcars.R` that illustrate how to use the some of the functionality in the `dplyr` package.

LISTING 7.52: dplyr-mtcars.R

```
library(datasets)
library(dplyr)

# select columns by name:
print("=> mpg,cyl,dps,qsec:")
select_cols = select(mtcars,mpg,cyl,disp,qsec)
head(select_cols)

# data filter
print("Filter by mpg > 20 and cyl > 5:")
f = filter(mtcars, mpg > 20 & cyl > 5)
head(f)
```

Listing 7.52 starts by referencing two required R libraries and then initializes the variable `select_cols` with the specified columns from the built-in `mtcars` dataset. The next code block applies a filter to select data from the `mtcars` dataset. As noted in the print statement, the filter selects data rows where the `mpg` variable is greater than 20 and there are more than 5 cylinders. Launch the code in Listing 7.52 to see the following output:

```
[1] "=> mpg,cyl,dps,qsec:"
                    mpg cyl disp  qsec
Mazda RX4          21.0  6  160 16.46
Mazda RX4 Wag      21.0  6  160 17.02
Datsun 710         22.8  4  108 18.61
Hornet 4 Drive     21.4  6  258 19.44
Hornet Sportabout  18.7  8  360 17.02
Valiant            18.1  6  225 20.22
[1] "Filter by mpg > 20 and cyl > 5:"
   mpg cyl disp  hp drat    wt  qsec vs am gear carb
1 21.0  6  160 110 3.90 2.620 16.46  0  1    4    4
2 21.0  6  160 110 3.90 2.875 17.02  0  1    4    4
3 21.4  6  258 110 3.08 3.215 19.44  1  0    3    1
```

The `dyplr` package in R is extremely powerful and sophisticated, with support for a wide range of functionality. Consult the online documentation for more information regarding this R package.

THE PIPE OPERATOR %>%

The `pipe` operator, `%>%`, enables you to treat the output from one function as the input of a subsequent function (that's why it's called a `pipe`). In addition, `dplyr` imports this operator from another package (`magrittr`). Instead of nesting functions (executing from the inside to the outside), the idea of piping is to execute the functions from left to right.

Listing 7.53 shows the contents of `pipe1.R` that illustrate how to sort an array of random numbers in R.

LISTING 7.53: pipe1.R

```
library(magrittr)

x <- rnorm(5)
print(paste0("First content of x:"))
print(paste0(x))

# Update value of x and assign it to x
x %<>% abs %>% sort
print(paste0("Second content of x:"))
print(paste0(x))
```

Listing 7.53 references a required R library, then initializes the variable x with 5 random values, and displays the contents of x. The next code snippet defines a pipe that performs the following operations:

pass the contents of x to the `abs()` function (for absolute values)
pass the result of step 1 to the `sort()` function

Now launch the code in Listing 7.53 to see the following output:

```
[1] "content of x:"
[1] "1.23041905548521"    "0.426501888248532"
"1.08469130060061"
[4] "-0.995749885650863" "-1.02953061190553"
[1] "content of x:"
[1] "0.426501888248532" "0.995749885650863"
"1.02953061190553"
[4] "1.08469130060061"   "1.23041905548521"
```

Listing 7.54 shows the contents of `pipe2.R` that illustrate how define a longer pipe that executes several built-in functions.

LISTING 7.54: pipe2.R

```
library(magrittr)

x <- c(1,2,3,4,5)
print(paste0("content of x:"))
print(paste0(x))

# Perform operations on x:
x %>% log() %>%
    diff() %>%
    exp() %>%
    round(1)
```

Listing 7.54 imports a required library and defines the variable x as a vector of the integers from 1 to 5 inclusive. The pipe starts with the contents of x and then computes the logarithm of those values. This is followed by the `diff()` function that calculates the difference between successive values.

The next portion of the pipe calculates the exponential value of the numbers returned from the `diff()` function. The last step rounds the resulting numbers to a single decimal place. Launch the code in Listing 7.54 to see the following output:

```
[1] "content of x:"
[1] "1" "2" "3" "4" "5"
[1] 2.0 1.5 1.3 1.2
```

WORKING WITH CSV FILES IN R

R provides built-in functions for reading the contents of a CSV file. Listing 7.55 shows the contents of `readinputcsv1.R` that illustrate how to read the contents of an XML file in R.

LISTING 7.55: readinputcsv1.R

```
# Some European countries use a ";" as the delimiter in
.csv files
# Use read.csv2() as above instead of read.csv

data <- read.csv("input.csv")

print(is.data.frame(data))
print(ncol(data))
print(nrow(data))

print(data)
```

Listing 7.55 invokes the built-in R function `read.csv()` to initialize the variable `data` with the contents of the CSV file `input.csv`. The next section in Listing 7.55 displays TRUE if `data` is a data frame (and FALSE otherwise), followed by the number of columns and the number of rows in `data`.

Listing 7.56 shows the content of the CSV file `input.csv`, which is referenced in the R code in Listing 7.56.

LISTING 7.56: input.csv:

```
id,name,salary,start_date,dept
1,Rick,623.3,2012-01-01,IT
2,Dan,515.2,2013-09-23,Operations
3,Michelle,611,2014-11-15,IT
4,Ryan,729,2014-05-11,HR
 ,Gary,843.25,2015-03-27,Finance
6,Nina,578,2013-05-21,IT
7,Simon,632.8,2013-07-30,Operations
8,Thomas,722.5,2014-06-17,Finance
```

Listing 7.56 has eight rows of comma-delimited data records, the fifth of which is missing an `id` value. Another common data format is XML, which is discussed in the next section.

WORKING WITH XML IN R

R provides built-in functions for reading the contents of XML documents (consult online tutorials if you are unfamiliar with XML). Listing 7.57 shows the contents of `readxml.R` that illustrate how to read the contents of an XML file in R and perform operations on its content.

LISTING 7.57: readxml.R

```
install.packages("XML")
library(XML)

# Load the package required to read XML files:
library("XML")

# Also load the other required package:
library("methods")

# Give the input file name to the function:
result <- xmlParse(file = "input.xml")

# Print the result:
print(result)
```

Listing 7.57 loads the XML library and the `methods` library, and then initializes the variable `result` with the result of parsing the XML file `input.xml`. The last code snippet in Listing 7.57 shows the contents of the XML file.

Listing 7.58 shows the content of the XML document `input.xml`, which is referenced in Listing 7.57.

LISTING 7.58: input.xml

```
<records>
    <employee>
        <id>1</id>
        <name>rick</name>
        <salary>623.3</salary>
        <startdate>1/1/2012</startdate>
        <dept>it</dept>
    </employee>

    <employee>
        <id>2</id>
        <name>dan</name>
        <salary>515.2</salary>
        <startdate>9/23/2013</startdate>
        <dept>operations</dept>
    </employee>
```

```
    <employee>
        <id>3</id>
        <name>michelle</name>
        <salary>611</salary>
        <startdate>11/15/2014</startdate>
        <dept>it</dept>
    </employee>

    <employee>
        <id>4</id>
        <name>ryan</name>
        <salary>729</salary>
        <startdate>5/11/2014</startdate>
        <dept>hr</dept>
    </employee>

    <employee>
        <id>5</id>
        <name>gary</name>
        <salary>843.25</salary>
        <startdate>3/27/2015</startdate>
        <dept>finance</dept>
    </employee>

    <employee>
        <id>6</id>
        <name>nina</name>
        <salary>578</salary>
        <startdate>5/21/2013</startdate>
        <dept>it</dept>
    </employee>

    <employee>
        <id>7</id>
        <name>simon</name>
        <salary>632.8</salary>
        <startdate>7/30/2013</startdate>
        <dept>operations</dept>
    </employee>

    <employee>
        <id>8</id>
        <name>guru</name>
        <salary>722.5</salary>
        <startdate>6/17/2014</startdate>
        <dept>finance</dept>
    </employee>
</records>
```

READING AN XML DOCUMENT INTO AN R DATA FRAME

R provides the ability to change XML documents into R data frames. Listing 7.59 shows the contents of readxmltodata frame.R that illustrate how to read the contents of an XML file into an R data frame.

LISTING 7.59: readxmltodata frame.R

```
# Load the packages required to read XML files:
library("XML")
library("methods")

# Convert the input xml file to a data frame:
xmldata frame <- xmlToData frame("input.xml")
print(xmldata frame)
```

Listing 7.59 loads the XML library and the methods library, and then initializes the variable xmldata frame with the result of parsing the XML file input. xml. The last code snippet in Listing 7.59 shows the content of the data frame xmldata frame, which contains the contents of the XML file input.xml.

WORKING WITH JSON IN R

R provides built-in functions for reading the contents of an XML document. Listing 7.60 shows the contents of readjson.R that illustrate how to read the contents of a JSON file in R.

LISTING 7.60: readjson.R

```
# Load the package required to read JSON files:
library("rjson")

# Give the input file name to the function:
result <- fromJSON(file = "input.json")

# Print the result:
print(result)
```

Listing 7.60 loads the rjson library and then initializes the variable result with the result of parsing the JSON file input.json. The last code snippet in Listing 7.60 shows the content of result, which contains the contents of the JSON file input.json.

Listing 7.61 shows the content of the JSON file input.json referenced in Listing 7.61.

LISTING 7.61: input.json

```
{
    "ID":["1","2","3","4","5","6","7","8" ],
    "Name":["Rick","Dan","Michelle","Ryan","Gary","Nina",
            "Simon","Guru" ],
    "Salary":  ["623.3","515.2","611","729","843.25","578",
                "632.8","722.5" ],

    "StartDate":[ "1/1/2019","9/23/2020","11/15/2021",
                  "5/11/2021","3/27/2020","5/21/2020",
```

```
        "7/30/2020","6/17/2021"],
     "Dept":[ "IT","Operations","IT","HR","Finance","IT",
             "Operations","Finance"]
}
```

In addition to reading the contents of a JSON file, you can create an R data frame that contains JSON-based data, as discussed in the next section.

READING A JSON FILE INTO AN R DATA FRAME

R also provides the ability to read JSON files into R data frames. Listing 7.62 shows the contents of jsontodata frame.R that illustrate how to read the contents of a JSON file into an R data frame.

LISTING 7.62: jsontodataframe.R

```
# Load the package required to read JSON files:
library("rjson")

# Give the input file name to the function:
result <- fromJSON(file = "input.json")

# Convert JSON file to a data frame:
json_data_frame <- as.data.frame(result)

print(json_data_frame)
```

Listing 7.62 loads the rjson library and then initializes the variable result with the result of parsing the JSON file input.json. Next, the variable json_ data_frame is populated with the result of converting the result variable to an R data frame. The last code snippet in Listing 7.62 shows the content of result, which contains the contents of the JSON file input.json.

STATISTICAL FUNCTIONS IN R

One of the strengths of R is the plethora of built-in statistical functions, such as mean(), std(), var(), and cov(). Listing 7.63 shows the contents of mean-value1.R that illustrate how to calculate the mean of a set of numbers in R.

LISTING 7.63: mean-value1.R

```
# create a vector:
x <- c(12,7,3,4.2,18,2,54,-21,8,-5)

# find the mean:
result.mean <- mean(x)
print(result.mean)
```

```
# create a vector:
x <- c(12,7,3,4.2,18,2,54,-21,8,-5,NA)

# find the mean:
result.mean <-  mean(x)
print(result.mean)

# drop NA values and find the mean:
result.mean <- mean(x,na.rm = TRUE)
print(result.mean)

# create a vector:
x <- c(12,7,3,4.2,18,2,54,-21,8,-5)

# find the mean:
result.mean <- mean(x,trim = 0.3)
print(result.mean)

# create a vector:
x <- c(12,7,3,4.2,18,2,54,-21,8,-5)

# find the mean:
median.result <- median(x)
```

Listing 7.63 contains code snippets that use the R built-in mean() function to calculate the mean of a set of numbers. The mean() function also enables you to specify na.rm=TRUE, which ignores missing values when calculating the mean of a set of numeric values.

In addition, the mean() function supports the trim parameter, which specifies the fraction between 0 to 0.5 of observations to be trimmed from before the mean is computed. Launch the code in Listing 7.68 to see the following output:

```
[1]  8.22
[1]  NA
[1]  8.22
[1]  5.55
[1]  5.6
```

SUMMARY FUNCTIONS IN R

This section contains a code sample with various additional built-in statistical functions in R. Listing 7.64 shows the contents of summary-values.R that illustrate how to calculate the mean, weighted mean, minimum, maximum, median, and standard deviation of a set of numbers in R.

LISTING 7.64: summary-values.R

```
# define a sample of 50 values:
x <- sample(1:200, size = 50, replace = TRUE)

print(paste0("mean(x):   ", mean(x)))
```

```
print(paste0("min(x):    ", min(x)))
print(paste0("max(x):    ", max(x)))
print(paste0("median(x):", median(x)))

# make a copy of x:
y <- x

# randomly set 10 values to NA:
y[sample(1:50, size=10, replace=TRUE)] <- NA
print("mean of y with NA values:")
print(mean(y, na.rm=TRUE))

# Calculate a weighted mean:
scores  <- c(250, 100, 80, 360)
weights <- c(1/2, 1/4, 1/8, 1/8)
print("scores:")
print(scores)
print("weights:")
print(weights)

wm <- weighted.mean(x=scores, w=weights)
print(paste0("weighted mean: ",wm))

print(paste0("Variance of x: ",var(x)))
print(paste0("STD of y:", sd(y, na.rm=TRUE)))
```

Listing 7.64 starts with a code block that initializes the variable x as a set of 50 random values that are between 1 and 200. The next code block in Listing 7.64 calculates various numeric quantities, including the mean(), the minimum values, the maximum value, and the median() value of the numbers in x.

The next code snippet in Listing 7.64 initializes the variable y as a copy of x, randomly sets 10 values in y equal to NA, and then prints the mean of the values in y.

The next portion of Listing 7.69 initializes the variable scores with 4 integer values, followed by the variable weights with positive numbers whose sum equals 1. The values of scores and weights are specified in the function weighted.mean that calculates the weighted mean of the numbers in the weights variable. Launch the code in Listing 7.64 to see the following output:

```
[1] "mean(x):    100.12"
[1] "min(x):    2"
[1] "max(x):    196"
[1] "median(x):104"
[1] "mean of y with NA values:"
[1] 92.53659
[1] "scores:"
[1] 250 100  80 360
[1] "weights:"
[1] 0.500 0.250 0.125 0.125
[1] "weighted mean: 205"
[1] "Variance of x: 3314.10775510204"
[1] "STD of y:56.4916354697647"
```

DEFINING A CUSTOM FUNCTION IN R

A custom function in R has the following syntax, where the ellipsis is replaced with your custom R code:

```
myfunc <- function(args) { ... }
```

Listing 7.65 shows the contents of CustomFunctions.R that illustrate how to define a simple custom function to double a number and another custom function to square a number in R.

LISTING 7.65: CustomFunctions.R

```
double <- function(a)
{
    return (2*a)
}

square <- function(a)
{
    return (a*a)
}

print(paste0("3 doubled: ", double(3)))
print(paste0("3 squared: ", square(3)))
```

Listing 7.65 defines the custom R functions double() and square() that double and square a number, respectively. Launch the code in Listing 7.65 to see the following output:

```
[1] "3 doubled: 6"
[1] "3 squared: 9"
```

Listing 7.66 shows the contents of CustomFunctionsLoop.R that define a custom function to double a number and a custom function to square a number in R.

LISTING 7.66: CustomFunctionsLoop.R

```
b <- 4

# prints squares of numbers in sequence:
new.function <- function(a)
{
    for(i in 1:a)
    {
        b <- i^2
        print(b)
    }
}
new.function(6)
```

Listing 7.66 initializes the variable b with the value 4 and then defines the function new.function() that iterates through a range of numbers and displays the squares of those number. The last code snippet in Listing 7.66 invokes the R function new.function() with the value 6, which generates the following output:

```
[1] 1
[1] 4
[1] 9
[1] 16
[1] 25R:
[1] 36
```

The next portion of this chapter introduces you to recursion, which is a very powerful and elegant way to solve certain tasks. For example, you will learn how to define recursive functions for calculating factorial values, Fibonacci numbers, GCD (Greatest Common Divisor), and LCM (Lowest Common Multiple). Note that this section also illustrates how to calculate factorial values using an iterative algorithm.

https://genomicsclass.github.io/book/pages/dplyr_tutorial.html

RECURSION IN R

Recursion is powerful and elegant, yet it can be difficult to debug recursion-based functions. Some examples recursion in R that you will see later in this chapter involve calculating factorial values and Fibonacci numbers.

Sometimes it's easier to define a recursive algorithm to solve a task than to do so with a non-recursive function. However, any recursive function has a non-recursive "counterpart." However, sometimes it can be extremely difficult to define the non-recursive function that performs the same functionality as the recursive function.

For example, you will see a recursive function as well as a non-recursive function for calculating factorial values, but it's simpler to calculate Fibonacci values using a recursive function. However, it's much more efficient to store previously calculated Fibonacci values in a data structure.

CALCULATING FACTORIAL VALUES IN R (NON-RECURSIVE)

Listing 7.67 shows the contents of Factorial1.R that illustrate how to use an iterative algorithm to calculate factorial values in R.

LISTING 7.67: Factorial1.R

```
# factorial:  fact(n) = n!
num = 10
factorial = 1

# check is the number is negative, positive or zero
```

```
if(num < 0) {
    print("Sorry, factorial does not exist for negative
numbers")
} else if(num == 0) {
    print("The factorial of 0 is 1")
} else {
    for(i in 1:num) {
        factorial = factorial * i
    }
    print(paste("The factorial of", num ,"is",factorial))
}
```

Listing 7.67 starts by initializing num and factorial with the values 10 and 1, respectively, followed by conditional logic to ensures that num is non-negative.

Whenever num is a positive integer, the else code block uses an iterative solution to calculate the value of num factorial, where num is a positive integer entered by users. Launch the code in Listing 7.67 to see the following output:

```
[1] "The factorial of 10 is 3628800"
```

CALCULATING FACTORIAL VALUES IN R (RECURSIVE)

Listing 7.68 shows the contents of Factorial2.R that illustrate how to use recursion to calculate factorial values in R.

LISTING 7.68: Factorial2.R

```
# factorial:   fact(n) = n*fact(n-1)

recur_factorial <- function(n) {
    if(n <= 1) {
        return(1)
    } else {
        return(n * recur_factorial(n-1))
    }
}

recur_factorial(5)
```

Listing 7.68 defines the function recur_factorial() that uses recursion to calculate the factorial value of a positive integer. In this code sample, the code calculates the value of 5!, which equals 120. Launch the code in Listing 7.68 to see the following output:

```
[1] 120
```

CALCULATING FIBONACCI NUMBERS IN R (NON-RECURSIVE)

Listing 7.69 shows the contents of Fibonacci1.R that illustrate how to calculate Fibonacci numbers using an iterative algorithm in R.

LISTING 7.69: Fibonacci1.R

```
# Fibonacci:   F(n)  =  F(n-1) + F(n-2)
nterms = 10

# first two terms
n1 = 0
n2 = 1
count = 2

# check if the number of terms is valid
if(nterms <= 0) {
    print("Specify a positive integer")
} else {
    if(nterms == 1) {
        print("Fibonacci sequence:")
        print(n1)
    } else {
        print("Fibonacci sequence:")
        print(n1)
        print(n2)

        while(count < nterms) {
            nth = n1 + n2
            print(nth)
            # update values
            n1 = n2
            n2 = nth
            count = count + 1
        }
    }
}
```

Listing 7.69 initializes the variable `terms` with the value 10, and then initializes `n1` and `n2` with the values 0 and 1, respectively, which are the starting values for the Fibonacci sequence for this example.

Next, the `else` portion of Listing 7.69 contains a loop that iteratively calculates Fibonacci numbers. Launch the code in Listing 7.69 to see the following output:

```
[1] "Fibonacci sequence:"
[1] 0
[1] 1
[1] 1
[1] 2
[1] 3
[1] 5
[1] 8
[1] 13
[1] 21
[1] 34
```

CALCULATING FIBONACCI NUMBERS IN R (RECURSIVE)

Listing 7.70 shows the contents of `Fibonacci2.R` that illustrate how to calculate Fibonacci numbers using recursion in R.

LISTING 7.70: Fibonacci2.R

```
# Fibonacci:  F(n) = F(n-1) + F(n-2)
recurse_fibonacci <- function(n) {
    if(n <= 1) {
        return(n)
    } else {
        return(recurse_fibonacci(n-1) +
               recurse_fibonacci(n-2))
    }
}

# take input from the user
nterms = 10

# check if the number of terms is valid
if(nterms <= 0) {
    print("Specify a positive integer")
} else {
    print("Fibonacci sequence:")
    for(i in 0:(nterms-1)) {
        print(recurse_fibonacci(i))
    }
}
```

Listing 7.70 initializes the variable `terms` with the value 10, and then uses conditional logic to ensure that `terms` is not negative. Next, the `else` portion of the code uses recursion to calculate Fibonacci numbers. Launch the code in Listing 7.70 to see the following output:

```
[1] "Fibonacci sequence:"
[1] 0
[1] 1
[1] 1
[1] 2
[1] 3
[1] 5
[1] 8
[1] 13
[1] 21
[1] 34
```

CONVERT A DECIMAL INTEGER TO A BINARY INTEGER IN R

Listing 7.71 shows the contents of `converttobinary.R` that illustrate how to convert a decimal integer into a binary integer in R.

LISTING 7.71: converttobinary.R

```
# Convert decimal num into binary num via recursive
function

convert_to_binary <- function(n) {
    if(n > 1) {
        convert_to_binary(as.integer(n/2))
    }
    cat(n %% 2)
}

convert_to_binary(52)
```

Listing 7.71 defines the function `convert_to_binary` that performs a simple conditional test. If the input number n is greater than 1, then invoke the same function recursively with n replaced with n. This recursive invocation terminates when n is equal to 1, at which point the following code snippet is executed:

```
cat (1 %% 2)
```

The preceding code snippet displays the remainder of the number n divided by 2, which is either 0 or 1. The number of times that the preceding code snippet is invoked equals the number of times that the function has been recursively invoked. There is a "backlog" of invocations of this code snippet, where each invocation is performed on half of the number of its predecessor. For example, if n is 9, the following code is executed:

```
cat (9 %% 2)
cat (4 %% 2)
cat (2 %% 2)
cat (1 %% 2)
```

Launch the code in Listing 7.71 to see the following output:

```
110100
```

CALCULATING THE GCD OF TWO INTEGERS IN R

Listing 7.72 shows the contents of GCD.R that illustrate how to calculate the greatest common divisor (GCD) of two positive integers in R.

LISTING 7.72: GCD.R

```
# find the GCD of two input numbers
gcd <- function(x, y) {
    # choose the smaller number
    if(x > y) {
        smaller = y
    } else {
        smaller = x
```

```
    }
    for(i in 1:smaller) {
        if((x %% i == 0) && (y %% i == 0)) {
            gcd = i
        }
    }
    return(gcd)
}

num1 = 36
num2 = 15

print(paste("The G.C.D. of", num1,"and", num2,"is",
gcd(num1, num2)))
```

Listing 7.72 defines the custom R gcd() function that uses the Euclidean algorithm to find the GCD of two positive integers. This custom function is invoked after users provide two positive integers as input. Launch the code in Listing 7.72 to see the following output:

```
[1] "The G.C.D. of 36 and 15 is 3"
```

CALCULATING THE LCM OF TWO INTEGERS IN R

Listing 7.73 shows the contents of LCM.R that illustrate how to calculate the LCM (lowest common multiple) of two integers in R.

LISTING 7.73: LCM.R

```
a <-  "Hello"
# find the GCD of two input numbers
gcd <- function(x, y) {
    # choose the smaller number
    if(x > y) {
        smaller = y
    } else {
        smaller = x
    }
    for(i in 1:smaller) {
        if((x %% i == 0) && (y %% i == 0)) {
            gcd = i
        }
    }
    return(gcd)
}

x = 36
y = 10

# the LCM involves a simple operation:
lcm <- x * y /gcd(x,y)

print(paste("The LCM of", x,"and", y,"is", lcm))
```

Listing 7.73 defines the custom R function gcd(x, y) that you saw in an earlier example, followed by a code snippet that calculates the LCM of two positive integers, as shown here:

```
lcm <- x * y /gcd(x,y)
```

Launch the code in Listing 7.73 to see the following output:

```
[1] "The LCM of 36 and 10 is 180"
```

SUMMARY

This chapter introduced you to R variables, and how to define variables whose type is strings, lists, vectors, and matrices in R. Then you learned ways to initialize variables during their creation, as well as how to update the values of variables.

We discussed how to update the values of a specific row in two-dimensional matrices in R. Moreover, you saw how to use conditional logic to test the values in a two-dimensional matrix, and also use conditional logic to update the elements in a two-dimensional matrix. Finally, you learned how to work with dates in R.

You learned about loops in R and with nested loops, followed by conditional logic with code samples that illustrates how to write if statements, if-then statements, and if-then-else statements in R.

In addition, you learned about data frames in R, with an assortment of code samples involving data frames. Finally, you learned how to read the contents of text files into R data frames.

Then you learned about built-in functions in R, with examples of some of the more useful functions that you will probably use in your code. You also saw how to define your own functions in R so that you can perform custom tasks for which there aren't any convenient built-in R functions.

Finally, you learned about recursion in R, and how to define recursive functions to calculate the factorial value of a positive integer, Fibonacci numbers, the GCD of two positive integers, and the LCM of two positive integers.

## CHAPTER 8

REGULAR EXPRESSIONS

This chapter introduces you to regular expressions, a powerful language feature in Python. Since regular expressions are available in other programming languages (such as JavaScript and Java), the knowledge that you gain from the material in this chapter will be useful to you outside of Python.

Why would anyone be interested in learning regular expressions in a book for Python data analytics? The answer is threefold. First, you have already seen Pandas code samples in Chapter 6 that use regular expressions, which demonstrates that regular expressions are relevant to Pandas. Second, if you plan to use Pandas extensively or perhaps also work with NLP, then regular expressions will prove useful because of the ease with which you can solve certain types of tasks (such as removing HTML tags) with regular expressions. Third, the knowledge you gain from the material in this chapter will instantly transfer to other languages that support regular expressions.

This chapter contains a mixture of code blocks and complete code samples, with varying degrees of complexity, that are suitable for beginners as well as people who have had some exposure to regular expressions. In fact, you have probably used (albeit simple) regular expressions in a command line on a laptop, whether it be Windows, UNIX, or Linux-based systems.

The first part of this chapter shows you how to define regular expressions with digits and letters (uppercase as well as lowercase), and also how to use character classes in regular expressions. We discuss character sets and character classes.

The second portion discusses the Python `re` module, which contains several useful methods, such as the `re.match()` method for matching groups of characters, the `re.search()` method to perform searches in character strings, and the `findAll()` method. We also examine character classes (and how to group them) in regular expressions.

The final portion of this chapter contains an assortment of code samples, such as modifying text strings, splitting text strings with the `re.split()` method, and substituting text strings with the `re.sub()` method.

As you read the code samples in this chapter, some concepts and facets of regular expressions might make you feel overwhelmed with the density of the material if you are a novice. However, practice and repetition will help you become comfortable with regular expressions.

WHAT ARE REGULAR EXPRESSIONS?

Regular expressions are referred to as REs, or regexes, or regex patterns, and they enable you to specify expressions that can match specific "parts" of a string. For instance, you can define a regular expression to match a single character or digit, a telephone number, a zip code, or an email address. You can use metacharacters and character classes (defined in the next section) as part of regular expressions to search text documents for specific patterns. As you become familiar with RE, you will find other ways to use them.

The `re` module (added in Python 1.5) provides Perl-style regular expression patterns. Note that earlier versions of Python provided the `regex` module that was removed in Python 2.5. The `re` module provides an assortment of methods for searching text strings or replacing text strings, which is similar to the basic search and/or replace functionality that is available in word processors (but usually without regular expression support). The `re` module also provides methods for splitting text strings based on regular expressions.

Before delving into the methods in the `re` module, you need to learn about metacharacters and character classes, which are the topic of the next section.

METACHARACTERS IN PYTHON

Python supports a set of metacharacters, most of which are the same as the metacharacters in other scripting languages such as Perl, as well as programming languages such as JavaScript and Java. The complete list of metacharacters in Python is here:

```
. ^ $ * + ? { } [ ] \ | ( )
```

The meaning of the preceding metacharacters is as follows:

- ? (matches 0 or 1): the expression `a?` matches the string `a` (but not `ab`)
- `*` (matches 0 or more): the expression `a*` matches the string `aaa` (but not `baa`)
- `+` (matches 1 or more): the expression `a+` matches `aaa` (but not `baa`)
- `^` (beginning of line): the expression `^[a]` matches the string `abc` (but not `bc`)
- `$` (end of line): `[c]$` matches the string `abc` (but not `cab`)
- . (a single dot): matches any character (except `newline`)

Sometimes you need to match the metacharacters themselves rather than their representation, which can be done in two ways. The first way involves "escaping" their symbolic meaning with the backslash ("\") character. Thus, the sequences \?, *, \+, \^, \$, and \. represent the literal characters instead of their symbolic meaning. You can also "escape" the backslash character with the sequence "\\". If you have two consecutive backslash characters, you need an additional backslash for each of them, which means that "\\\\" is the "escaped" sequence for "\\".

The second way is to list the metacharacters inside a pair of square brackets. For example, [+?] treats the two characters "+" and "?" as literal characters instead of metacharacters. The second approach is obviously more compact and less prone to error (it's easy to forget a backslash in a long sequence of metacharacters). The methods in the re module support metacharacters.

NOTE *The "^" character that is to the left (and outside) of a sequence in square brackets (such as ^[A-Z]) "anchors" the regular expression to the beginning of a line, whereas the "^" character that is the first character inside a pair of square brackets negates the regular expression (such as [^A-Z]) inside the square brackets.*

The interpretation of the "^" character in a regular expression depends on its location in a regular expression, as shown here:

"^[a-z]" means any string that starts with any lowercase letter
"[^a-z]" means any string that does *not* contain any lowercase letters
"^[^a-z]" means any string that starts with anything *except* a lowercase letter
"^[a-z]$" means a single lowercase letter
"^[^a-z]$" means a single character (including digits) that is *not* a lowercase letter

As a quick preview of the re module that is discussed later in this chapter, the re.sub() method enables you to remove characters (including metacharacters) from a text string. For example, the following code snippet removes all occurrences of a forward slash ("/") and the plus sign ("+") from the variable str:

```
>>> import re
>>> str  = "this string has a / and + in it"
>>> str2 = re.sub("[/]+","",str)
>>> print('original:',str)
original: this string has a / and + in it
>>> print('replaced:',str2)
replaced: this string has a  and + in it
```

We can easily remove occurrences of other metacharacters in a text string by listing them inside the square brackets, just as we have done in the preceding code snippet.

Listing 8.1 shows the contents of `RemoveMetaChars1.py` that illustrate how to remove other metacharacters from a line of text.

LISTING 8.1: RemoveMetaChars1.py

```
import re

text1 = "meta characters ? and / and + and ."
text2 = re.sub("[/\.*?=+]+","",text1)

print('text1:',text1)
print('text2:',text2)
```

The regular expression in Listing 8.1 might seem daunting if you are new to regular expressions, but let's examine the entire expression and then the meaning of each character. The term `[/\.*?=+]` matches a forward slash ("/"), a dot ("."), a question mark ("?"), an equals sign ("="), or a plus sign ("+"). Notice that the dot "." is preceded by a backslash character "\". Doing so "escapes" the meaning of the "." metacharacter (which matches any single non-whitespace character) and treats it as a literal character.

Thus, the term `[/\.*?=+]+` means "one or more occurrences of any of the metacharacters—treated as literal characters—inside the square brackets."

Consequently, the expression `re.sub("[/\.*?=+]+","",text1)` matches any occurrence of the previously listed metacharacters, and then replaces them with an empty string in the text string specified by the variable `text1`. The output from Listing 8.1 is shown here:

```
text1: meta characters ? and / and + and .
text2: meta characters  and  and  and
```

Later in this chapter you will learn about other functions in the `re` module that enable you to modify and split text strings.

CHARACTER SETS IN PYTHON

A single digit in base 10 is a number between 0 and 9 inclusive, which is represented by the sequence `[0-9]`. Similarly, a lowercase letter can be any letter between a and z, which is represented by the sequence `[a-z]`. An uppercase letter can be any letter between A and Z, which is represented by the sequence `[A-Z]`.

The following code snippets illustrate how to specify sequences of digits and sequences of character strings using a shorthand notation that is much simpler than specifying every matching digit:

`[0-9]` matches a single digit
`[0-9][0-9]` matches 2 consecutive digits
`[0-9]{3}` matches 3 consecutive digits
`[0-9]{2,4}` matches 2, 3, or 4 consecutive digits

[0-9]{5,} matches 5 or more consecutive digits

^[0-9]+$ matches a string consisting solely of digits

You can define similar patterns using uppercase or lowercase letters in a way that is much simpler than explicitly specifying every lowercase letter or every uppercase letter:

[a-z][A-Z] matches a single lowercase letter that is followed by one uppercase letter

[a-zA-Z] matches any upper- or lowercase letter

Working with "^" and "\"

The purpose of the "^" character depends on its context in a regular expression. For example, the following expression matches a text string that starts with a digit:

^[0-9].

However, the following expression matches a text string that does *not* start with a digit because of the "^" metacharacter that is at the beginning of an expression in square brackets as well as the "^" metacharacter that is to the left (and outside) the expression in square brackets (which you learned in a previous note):

^[^0-9]

Thus, the "^" character inside a pair of matching square brackets ("[]") negates the expression immediately to its right that is also located inside the square brackets.

The backslash ("\") allows you to "escape" the meaning of a metacharacter. Consequently, a dot "." matches a single character (except for whitespace characters), whereas the sequence "\." matches the dot "." character. Other examples involving the backslash metacharacter are here:

\.H.* matches the string .Hello

H.* matches the string Hello

H.*\. matches the string Hello.

.ell. matches the string Hello

.* matches the string Hello

\..* matches the string .Hello

CHARACTER CLASSES IN PYTHON

Character classes are convenient expressions that are shorter and simpler than their "bare" counterparts that you saw in the previous section. Some convenient character sequences that express patterns of digits and letters are as follows:

\d matches a single digit
\w matches a single character (digit or letter)
\s matches a single whitespace (space, newline, return, or tab)
\b matches a boundary between a word and a nonword
\n, \r, and \t represent a newline, a return, and a tab, respectively
\ "escapes" any character

Based on the preceding definitions, \d+ matches one or more digits and \w+ matches one or more characters, both of which are more compact expressions than using character sets. In addition, we can reformulate the expressions in the previous section:

\d is the same as [0-9] and \D is the same as [^0-9]
\s is the same as [\t\n\r\f\v] and it matches any non-whitespace character, whereas \S is the opposite (it matches [^ \t\n\r\f\v])
\w is the same as [a-zA-Z0-9_] and it matches any alphanumeric character, whereas \W is the opposite (it matches [^a-zA-Z0-9_])

Additional examples are here:

\d{2} is the same as [0-9][0-9]
\d{3} is the same as [0-9]{3}
\d{2,4} is the same as [0-9]{2,4}
\d{5,} is the same as [0-9]{5,}
^\d+$ is the same as ^[0-9]+$

The curly braces ("{ }") are called quantifiers, and they specify the number (or range) of characters in the expressions that precede them.

MATCHING CHARACTER CLASSES WITH THE RE MODULE

The re module provides the following methods for matching and searching one or more occurrences of a regular expression in a text string:

match(): Determine if the RE matches at the *beginning* of the string
search(): Scan through a string, looking for *any* location where the RE matches
findall(): Find *all* substrings where the RE matches and return them as a list
finditer(): Find all substrings where the RE matches and return them as an iterator

NOTE *The* match() *function only matches patterns to the start of string.*

The next section shows you how to use the match() function in the re module.

USING THE RE.MATCH() METHOD

The re.match() method attempts to match RE patterns in a text string (with optional flags), and it has the following syntax:

```
re.match(pattern, string, flags=0)
```

The pattern parameter is the regular expression that you want to match in the string parameter. The flags parameter allows you to specify multiple flags using the bitwise OR operator that is represented by the pipe "|" symbol.

The re.match method returns a match object on success and None on failure. Use the group(num) or groups() function of the match object to get a matched expression.

group(num=0): This method returns the entire match (or specific subgroup num).

groups(): This method returns all matching subgroups in a tuple (empty if there weren't any).

NOTE *The re.match() method only matches patterns from the start of a text string, which is different from the re.search() method discussed later in this chapter.*

The following code block illustrates how to use the group() function in regular expressions:

```
>>> import re
>>> p = re.compile('(a(b)c)de')
>>> m = p.match('abcde')
>>> m.group(0)
'abcde'
>>> m.group(1)
'abc'
>>> m.group(2)
'b'
```

Notice that the higher numbers inside the group() method match more deeply nested expressions that are specified in the initial regular expression.

Listing 8.2 shows the content of MatchGroup1.py, which illustrates how to use the group() function to match an alphanumeric text string and an alphabetic string.

LISTING 8.2: MatchGroup1.py

```
import re

line1 = 'abcd123'
line2 = 'abcdefg'
mixed = re.compile(r"^[a-z0-9]{5,7}$")
line3 = mixed.match(line1)
line4 = mixed.match(line2)
```

```
print('line1:',line1)
print('line2:',line2)
print('line3:',line3)
print('line4:',line4)
print('line5:',line4.group(0))

line6 = 'a1b2c3d4e5f6g7'
mixed2 = re.compile(r"^([a-z]+[0-9]+){5,7}$")
line7 = mixed2.match(line6)

print('line6:',line6)
print('line7:',line7.group(0))
print('line8:',line7.group(1))

line9 = 'abc123fgh4567'
mixed3 = re.compile(r"^([a-z]*[0-9]*){5,7}$")
line10 = mixed3.match(line9)
print('line9:',line9)
print('line10:',line10.group(0))
```

The output from Listing 8.2 is as follows:

```
line1: abcd123
line2: abcdefg
line3: <_sre.SRE_Match object at 0x100485440>
line4: <_sre.SRE_Match object at 0x1004854a8>
line5: abcdefg
line6: a1b2c3d4e5f6g7
line7: a1b2c3d4e5f6g7
line8: g7
line9: abc123fgh4567
line10: abc123fgh4567
```

Notice that `line3` and `line7` involve two similar but different regular expressions. The variable `mixed` specifies a sequence of lowercase letters followed by digits, where the length of the text string is also between 5 and 7. The string `abcd123` satisfies all of these conditions.

   `mixed2` specifies a pattern consisting of one or more pairs, where each pair contains one or more lowercase letters followed by one or more digits, where the length of the matching pairs is also between 5 and 7. In this case, the string `abcd123` as well as the string `a1b2c3d4e5f6g7` both satisfy these criteria.

   The third regular expression `mixed3` specifies a pair such that each pair consists of zero or more occurrences of lowercase letters and zero or more occurrences of a digit, and that the number of such pairs is between 5 and 7. As you can see from the output, the regular expression in `mixed3` matches lowercase letters and digits in any order.

   In the preceding example, the regular expression specified a range for the length of the string, which involves a lower limit of 5 and an upper limit of 7. However, you can also specify a lower limit without an upper limit (or an upper limit without a lower limit).

Listing 8.3 shows the contents of `MatchGroup2.py` that illustrate how to use a regular expression and the `group()` function to match an alphanumeric text string and an alphabetic string.

LISTING 8.3: MatchGroup2.py

```
import re

alphas = re.compile(r"^[abcde]{5,}")
line1 = alphas.match("abcde").group(0)
line2 = alphas.match("edcba").group(0)
line3 = alphas.match("acbedf").group(0)
line4 = alphas.match("abcdefghi").group(0)
line5 = alphas.match("abcdefghi abcdef")

print('line1:',line1)
print('line2:',line2)
print('line3:',line3)
print('line4:',line4)
print('line5:',line5)
```

Listing 8.3 initializes the variable `alphas` as a regular expression that matches any string that starts with one of the letters a through e, and consists of at least five characters. The next portion of Listing 8.3 initializes the four variables `line1`, `line2`, `line3`, and `line4` by means of the `alphas` RE that is applied to various text strings. These four variables are set to the first matching group by means of the expression `group(0)`.

The output from Listing 8.3 is here:

```
line1: abcde
line2: edcba
line3: acbed
line4: abcde
line5: <_sre.SRE_Match object at 0x1004854a8>
```

Listing 8.4 shows the content of `MatchGroup3.py`, which illustrates how to use a regular expression with the `group()` function to match words in a text string.

LISTING 8.4: MatchGroup3.py

```
import re

line = "Giraffes are taller than elephants";

matchObj = re.match( r'(.*) are(\.*)', line, re.M|re.I)

if matchObj:
   print("matchObj.group()   : ", matchObj.group())
   print("matchObj.group(1)  : ", matchObj.group(1))
   print("matchObj.group(2)  : ", matchObj.group(2))
else:
   print("matchObj does not match line:", line)
```

The code in Listing 8.4 produces the following output:

```
matchObj.group()   :   Giraffes are
matchObj.group(1)  :   Giraffes
matchObj.group(2)  :
```

Listing 8.4 contains a pair of delimiters separated by a pipe ("|") symbol. The first delimiter is `re.M` for "multiline" (this example contains only a single line of text), and the second delimiter `re.I` means "ignore case" during the pattern matching operation. The `re.match()` method supports additional delimiters, as discussed in the next section.

OPTIONS FOR THE RE.MATCH() METHOD

The `match()` method supports various optional modifiers that affect the type of matching that will be performed. As you saw in the previous example, you can also specify multiple modifiers separated by the OR ("|") symbol. Additional modifiers that are available for RE are shown here:

`re.I` performs case-insensitive matches (see previous section)
`re.L` interprets words according to the current locale
`re.M` makes $ match the end of a line and makes ^ match the start of any line
`re.S` makes a period (".") match any character (including a newline)
`re.U` interprets letters according to the Unicode character set

Experiment with these modifiers by writing Python code that uses them in conjunction with different text strings.

MATCHING CHARACTER CLASSES WITH THE RE.SEARCH() METHOD

As you saw earlier in this chapter, the `re.match()` method only matches from the beginning of a string, whereas the `re.search()` method can successfully match a substring anywhere in a text string.

The `re.search()` method takes two arguments, a regular expression pattern and a string, and then searches for the specified pattern in the given string. The `search()` method returns a match object (if the search was successful) or `None`.

As a simple example, the following searches for the pattern `tasty` followed by a five-letter word:

```
import re

str = 'I want a tasty pizza'
match = re.search(r'tasty \w\w\w\w\w', str)

if match:
```

```
    ## 'found tasty pizza'
    print('found', match.group())
else:
print('Nothing tasty here')
```

The output of the preceding code block is as follows:

```
found tasty pizza
```

The following code block further illustrates the difference between the `match()` method and the `search()` method:

```
>>> import re
>>> print(re.search('this', 'this is the one').span())
(0, 4)
>>>
>>> print(re.search('the', 'this is the one').span())
(8, 11)
>>> print(re.match('this', 'this is the one').span())
(0, 4)
>>> print(re.match('the', 'this is the one').span())
Traceback (most recent call last):
  File "<stdin>", line 1, in <module>
AttributeError: 'NoneType' object has no attribute 'span'
```

MATCHING CHARACTER CLASSES WITH THE **FINDALL ()** METHOD

Listing 8.5 shows the contents of the script `RegEx1.py`, which illustrates how to define simple character classes that match various text strings.

LISTING 8.5: RegEx1.py

```
import re

str1 = "123456"
matches1 = re.findall("(\d+)", str1)
print('matches1:',matches1

str1 = "123456"
matches1 = re.findall("(\d\d\d)", str1)
print('matches1:',matches1

str1 = "123456"
matches1 = re.findall("(\d\d)", str1)
print('matches1:',matches1

print
str2 = "1a2b3c456"
matches2 = re.findall("(\d)", str2)
print('matches2:',matches2

print
str2 = "1a2b3c456"
matches2 = re.findall("\d", str2)
```

```
print('matches2:',matches2

print
str3 = "1a2b3c456"
matches3 = re.findall("(\w)", str3)
print('matches3:',matches3
```

Listing 8.5 contains simple regular expressions for matching digits in the variables str1 and str2. The final code block of Listing 8.5 matches every character in the string str3, effectively "splitting" str3 into a list where each element consists of one character. The output from Listing 8.5 is here (notice the blank lines after the first three output lines):

```
matches1: ['123456']
matches1: ['123', '456']
matches1: ['12', '34', '56']

matches2: ['1', '2', '3', '4', '5', '6']

matches2: ['1', '2', '3', '4', '5', '6']

matches3: ['1', 'a', '2', 'b', '3', 'c', '4', '5', '6']
```

Finding Capitalized Words in a String

Listing 8.6 shows the content of the script FindCapitalized.py that illustrates how to define simple character classes that match various text strings.

LISTING 8.6: FindCapitalized.py

```
import re

str = "This Sentence contains Capitalized words"
caps = re.findall(r'[A-Z][\w\.-]+', str)

print('str: ',str)
print('caps:',caps)
```

Listing 8.6 initializes the string variable str and the RE caps that matches any word that starts with a capital letter because the first portion of caps is the pattern [A-Z] that matches any capital letter between A and z inclusive.

The output of Listing 8.6 is shown here:

```
str:  This Sentence contains Capitalized words
caps: ['This', 'Sentence', 'Capitalized']
```

ADDITIONAL MATCHING FUNCTION FOR REGULAR EXPRESSIONS

After invoking any of the methods match(), search(), findAll(), or finditer(), you can invoke additional methods on the "matching object." An example of this functionality using the match() method is as follows:

```
import re

p1 = re.compile('[a-z]+')
m1 = p1.match("hello")
```

In the preceding code block, the `p1` object represents the compiled regular expression for one or more lowercase letters, and the "matching object" `m1` object supports the following methods:

`group()` returns the string matched by the RE
`start()` returns the starting position of the match
`end()` returns the ending position of the match
`span()` returns a tuple containing the (start, end) positions of the match

As a further illustration, Listing 8.7 shows the content of `SearchFunction1.py` that illustrates how to use the `search()` method and the `group()` method.

LISTING 8.7: SearchFunction1.py

```
import re

line = "Giraffes are taller than elephants";

searchObj = re.search( r'(.*) are(\.*)', line, re.M|re.I)

if searchObj:
   print("searchObj.group()   : ", searchObj.group())
   print("searchObj.group(1) : ", searchObj.group(1))
   print("searchObj.group(2) : ", searchObj.group(2))
else:
   print("searchObj does not match line:", line)
```

Listing 8.7 contains the variable line that represents a text string, and the variable `searchObj` is an RE involving the `search()` method and pair of pipe-delimited modifiers (discussed in more detail in the next section). If `searchObj` is not null, the if/else conditional code in Listing 8.7 displays the contents of the three groups resulting from the successful match with the contents of the variable line. The output from Listing 8.7 is as follows:

```
searchObj.group()   :  Giraffes are
searchObj.group(1) :  Giraffes
searchObj.group(2) :
```

GROUPING WITH CHARACTER CLASSES IN REGULAR EXPRESSIONS

In addition to the character classes that you have seen earlier in this chapter, you can specify subexpressions of character classes.

Listing 8.8 shows the contents of `Grouping1.py` that illustrate how to use the `search()` method.

LISTING 8.8: Grouping1.py

```
import re

p1 = re.compile('(ab)*')

print('match1:',p1.match('abababab').group())
print('span1:  ',p1.match('abababab').span())

p2 = re.compile('(a)b')
m2 = p2.match('ab')
print('match2:',m2.group(0))
print('match3:',m2.group(1))
```

Listing 8.8 starts by defining the RE p1 that matches zero or more occurrences of the string ab. The first `print()` statement displays the result of using the `match()` function of p1 (followed by the `group()` function) against a string, and the result is a string. This illustrates the use of "method chaining", which eliminates the need for an intermediate object (as shown in the second code block). The second `print()` statement displays the result of using the `match()` function of p1, followed by applying the `span()` function against a string. In this case, the result is a numeric range.

The second part of Listing 8.8 defines the RE p2 that matches an optional letter a followed by the letter b. The variable m2 invokes the match method on p2 using the string ab. The third `print()` statement displays the result of invoking `group(0)` on m2, and the fourth `print()` statement displays the result of involving `group(1)` on m2. Both results are substrings of the input string ab. Recall that `group(0)` returns the highest level match that occurred, and `group(1)` returns a more "specific" match that occurred, such as one that involves the parentheses in the definition of p2. The higher the value of the integer in the expression `group(n)`, the more specific the match.

The output from Listing 8.8 is as follows:

```
match1:  abababab
span1:   (0, 10)
match2:  ab
match3:  a
```

USING CHARACTER CLASSES IN REGULAR EXPRESSIONS

This section contains some examples that illustrate how to use character classes to match various strings and also how to use delimiters to split a text string. For example, one common date string involves a date format of the form MM/DD/YY. Another common scenario involves records with a delimiter that separates multiple fields. Usually such records contain one delimiter, but as you will see, Python makes it very easy to split records using multiple delimiters.

Matching Strings with Multiple Consecutive Digits

Listing 8.9 shows the contents of the script `MatchPatterns1.py` that illustrate how to define simple regular expressions to split the contents of a text string based on the occurrence of one or more consecutive digits.

Although the regular expressions \d+/\d+/\d+ and \d\d/\d\d/\d\d\d\d both match the string 08/13/2014, the first regular expression matches more patterns than the second regular expression, which is an "exact match" with respect to the number of matching digits that are allowed.

LISTING 8.9: MatchPatterns1.py

```
import re

date1 = '02/28/2013'
date2 = 'February 28, 2013'

# Simple matching: \d+ means match one or more digits
if re.match(r'\d+/\d+/\d+', date1):
  print('date1 matches this pattern')
else:
  print('date1 does not match this pattern')

if re.match(r'\d+/\d+/\d+', date2):
  print('date2 matches this pattern')
else:
  print('date2 does not match this pattern')
```

The output from launching Listing 8.9 is as follows:

```
date1 matches this pattern
date2 does not match this pattern
```

Reversing Words in Strings

Listing 8.10 shows the contents of the Python script `ReverseWords1.py` that illustrate how to reverse a pair of words in a string.

LISTING 8.10: ReverseWords1.py

```
import re

str1 = 'one two'
match = re.search('([\w.-]+) ([\w.-]+)', str1)

str2 = match.group(2) + ' ' + match.group(1)

print('str1:',str1)
print('str2:',str2)
```

The output from Listing 8.10 is

```
str1: one two
str2: two one
```

Now that you understand how to define regular expressions for digits and letters, let's look at some more sophisticated regular expressions.

For example, the following expression matches a string that is any combination of digits, uppercase letters, or lowercase letters (i.e., no special characters):

```
^[a-zA-Z0-9]$
```

Here is the same expression rewritten using character classes:

```
^[\w\W\d]$
```

MODIFYING TEXT STRINGS WITH THE RE MODULE

The Python re module contains several methods for modifying strings. The split() method uses a regular expression to "split" a string into a list. The sub() method finds all substrings where the regular expression matches, and then replaces them with a different string. The subn() method performs the same functionality as sub(), and returns the new string and the number of replacements. The following subsections contain examples that illustrate how to use the functions split(), sub(), and subn() in regular expressions.

SPLITTING TEXT STRINGS WITH THE RE.SPLIT() METHOD

Listing 8.11 shows the content of the script RegEx2.py, which illustrates how to define simple regular expressions to split the contents of a text string.

LISTING 8.11: RegEx2.py

```
import re

line1 = "abc def"
result1 = re.split(r'[\s]', line1)
print('result1:',result1)

line2 = "abc1,abc2:abc3;abc4"
result2 = re.split(r'[,:;]', line2)
print('result2:',result2)

line3 = "abc1,abc2:abc3;abc4 123 456"
result3 = re.split(r'[,:;\s]', line3)

print('result3:',result3)
```

Listing 8.11 contains three blocks of code, each of which uses the split() method in the re module to tokenize three different strings. The first regular expression specifies a whitespace, the second regular expression specifies three punctuation characters, and the third regular expression specifies the combination of the first two regular expressions.

The output from launching `RegEx2.py` is as follows:

```
result1: ['abc', 'def']
result2: ['abc1', 'abc2', 'abc3', 'abc4']
result3: ['abc1', 'abc2', 'abc3', 'abc4', '123', '456']
```

SPLITTING TEXT STRINGS USING DIGITS AND DELIMITERS

Listing 8.12 shows the contents of `SplitCharClass1.py` that illustrate how to use a regular expression consisting of a character class, the "." character, and a white space to split the contents of two text strings.

LISTING 8.12: SplitCharClass1.py

```
import re

line1 = '1. Section one 2. Section two 3. Section three'
line2 = '11. Section eleven 12. Section twelve 13. Section
thirteen'

print(re.split(r'\d+\. ', line1))
print(re.split(r'\d+\. ', line2))
```

Listing 8.12 contains two text strings that can be split using the same regular expression '\d+\. '. Note that if you use the expression '\d\. ', only the first text string will split correctly. The result of launching Listing 8.12 is as follows:

```
['', 'Section one ', 'Section two ', 'Section three']
['', 'Section eleven ', 'Section twelve ', 'Section thirteen']
```

SUBSTITUTING TEXT STRINGS WITH THE RE.SUB() METHOD

Earlier in this chapter, you saw a preview of using the `sub()` method to remove all the metacharacters in a text string. The following code block illustrates how to use the `re.sub()` method to substitute alphabetic characters in a text string.

```
>>> import re
>>> p = re.compile( '(one|two|three)')
>>> p.sub( 'some', 'one book two books three books')
'some book some books some books'
>>>
>>> p.sub( 'some', 'one book two books three books', count=1)
'some book two books three books'
```

The following code block uses the `re.sub()` method to insert a line feed after each alphabetic character in a text string:

```
>>> line = 'abcde'
```

```
>>> line2 = re.sub('', '\n', line)
>>> print('line2:',line2)
line2:
a
b
c
d
e
```

MATCHING THE BEGINNING AND THE END OF TEXT STRINGS

Listing 8.13 shows the contents of the script RegEx3.py that illustrate how to find substrings using the startswith() function and endswith() function.

LISTING 8.13: RegEx3.py

```
import re

line2 = "abc1,Abc2:def3;Def4"
result2 = re.split(r'[,:;]', line2)

for w in result2:
  if(w.startswith('Abc')):
    print('Word starts with Abc:',w)
  elif(w.endswith('4')):
    print('Word ends with 4:',w)
  else:
    print('Word:',w)
```

Listing 8.13 starts by initializing the string line2 (with punctuation characters as word delimiters) and the RE result2 that uses the split() function with a comma, colon, and semicolon as "split delimiters" to tokenize the string variable line2.

The output after launching Listing 8.13 is here:

```
Word: abc1
Word starts with Abc: Abc2
Word: def3
Word ends with 4: Def4
```

Listing 8.14 shows the content of the script MatchLines1.py, which illustrates how to find substrings using character classes.

LISTING 8.14: MatchLines1.py

```
import re

line1 = "abcdef"
line2 = "123,abc1,abc2,abc3"
line3 = "abc1,abc2,123,456f"
```

```
if re.match("^[A-Za-z]*$", line1):
  print('line1 contains only letters:',line1)

# better than the preceding snippet:
line1[:-1].isalpha()
  print('line1 contains only letters:',line1)

if re.match("^[\w]*$", line1):
  print('line1 contains only letters:',line1)

if re.match(r"^[^\W\d_]+$", line1, re.LOCALE):
  print('line1 contains only letters:',line1)
print

if re.match("^[0-9][0-9][0-9]", line2):
  print('line2 starts with 3 digits:',line2)

if re.match("^\d\d\d", line2):
  print('line2 starts with 3 digits:',line2)
print

if re.match(".*[0-9][0-9][0-9][a-z]$", line3):
  print('line3 ends with 3 digits and 1 char:',line3)

if re.match(".*[a-z]$", line3):
  print('line3 ends with 1 char:',line3)
```

Listing 8.14 starts by initializing three string variables line1, line2, and line3. The first RE contains an expression that matches any line containing uppercase or lowercase letters (or both):

```
if re.match("^[A-Za-z]*$", line1):
```

The following two snippets also test for the same thing:

```
line1[:-1].isalpha()
```

The preceding snippet starts from the rightmost position of the string and checks if each character is alphabetic.

The next snippet checks if line1 can be tokenized into words (a word contains only alphabetic characters):

```
if re.match("^[\w]*$", line1):
```

The next portion of Listing 8.14 checks if a string contains three consecutive digits:

```
if re.match("^[0-9][0-9][0-9]", line2):
  print('line2 starts with 3 digits:',line2)

if re.match("^\d\d\d", line2):
```

The first snippet uses the pattern [0-9] to match a digit, whereas the second snippet uses the expression \d to match a digit.

The output from Listing 8.14 is as follows:

```
line1 contains only letters: abcdef
line1 contains only letters: abcdef
line1 contains only letters: abcdef
line1 contains only letters: abcdef

line2 starts with 3 digits: 123,abc1,abc2,abc3
line2 starts with 3 digits: 123,abc1,abc2,abc3
```

COMPILATION FLAGS

Compilation flags modify the manner in which regular expressions work. Flags are available in the re module as a long name (such as IGNORECASE) and a short, one-letter form (such as I). The short form is the same as the flags in pattern modifiers in Perl. You can specify multiple flags by using the "|" symbol. For example, re.I | re.M sets both the I and M flags.

You can check the online Python documentation regarding all the available compilation flags.

COMPOUND REGULAR EXPRESSIONS

Listing 8.15 shows the content of MatchMixedCase1.py, which illustrates how to use the pipe ("|") symbol to specify two regular expressions in the same match() function.

LISTING 8.15: MatchMixedCase1.py

```
import re

line1 = "This is a line"
line2 = "That is a line"

if re.match("^[Tt]his", line1):
  print('line1 starts with This or this:')
  print(line1)

else:
  print('no match')

if re.match("^This|That", line2):
  print('line2 starts with This or That:')
  print(line2)
else:
  print('no match')
```

Listing 8.15 starts with two string variables line1 and line2, followed by an if/else conditional code block that checks if line1 starts with the RE [Tt]his, which matches the string This as well as the string this.

The second conditional code block checks if line2 starts with the string This or the string That. Notice the "^" metacharacter, which in this context anchors the RE to the beginning of the string. The output from Listing 8.15 is here:

```
line1 starts with This or this:
This is a line
line2 starts with This or That:
That is a line
```

COUNTING CHARACTER TYPES IN A STRING

You can use a regular expression to check whether a character is a digit, a letter, or some other type of character. Listing 8.16 shows the content of CountDigitsAndChars.py that performs this task.

LISTING 8.16: CountDigitsAndChars.py

```
import re

charCount  = 0
digitCount = 0
otherCount = 0

line1 = "A line with numbers: 12 345"

for ch in line1:
   if(re.match(r'\d', ch)):
      digitCount = digitCount + 1
   elif(re.match(r'\w', ch)):
      charCount = charCount + 1
   else:
      otherCount = otherCount + 1

print('charcount:',charCount)
print('digitcount:',digitCount)
print('othercount:',otherCount)
```

Listing 8.16 initializes three numeric counter-related variables, followed by the string variable line1. The next part of Listing 8.16 contains a for loop that processes each character in the string line1. The body of the for loop contains a conditional code block that checks whether the current character is a digit, a letter, or some other non-alphanumeric character. Each time there is a successful match, the corresponding "counter" variable is incremented.

The output from Listing 8.16 is as follows:

```
charcount: 16
digitcount: 5
othercount: 6
```

REGULAR EXPRESSIONS AND GROUPING

You can also "group" subexpressions and even refer to them symbolically. For example, the following expression matches zero or 1 occurrences of 3 consecutive triples of letters or digits:

```
^([a-zA-Z0-9]{3,3})?
```

The following expression matches a telephone number (such as 650-555-1212) in the United States:

```
^\d{3,3}[-]\d{3,3}[-]\d{4,4}
```

The following expression matches a zip code (such as 67827 or 94343-04005) in the United States:

```
^\d{5,5}([-]\d{5,5})?
```

The following code block partially matches an email address:

```
str = 'john.doe@google.com'
match = re.search(r'\w+@\w+', str)
if match:
  print(match.group())  ## 'doe@google'
```

Exercise: Use the preceding code block as a starting point to define a regular expression for email addresses.

SIMPLE STRING MATCHES

Listing 8.17 shows the contents of the script RegEx4.py that illustrate how to define regular expressions that match various text strings.

LISTING 8.17: RegEx4.py

```
import re

searchString = "Testing pattern matches"

expr1 = re.compile( r"Test" )
expr2 = re.compile( r"^Test" )
expr3 = re.compile( r"Test$" )
expr4 = re.compile( r"\b\w*es\b" )
expr5 = re.compile( r"t[aeiou]", re.I )

if expr1.search( searchString ):
   print('"Test" was found.')

if expr2.match( searchString ):
   print('"Test" was found at the beginning of the line.')

if expr3.match( searchString ):
   print('"Test" was found at the end of the line.')
```

```
result = expr4.findall( searchString )

if result:
   print('There are %d words(s) ending in "es":' % \)
      ( len( result ) ),

   for item in result:
      print(" " + item,)

print

result = expr5.findall( searchString )
if result:
   print('The letter t, followed by a vowel, occurs %d
times:' % \
      ( len( result ) ),

   for item in result:
      print(" "+item,)

print
```

Listing 8.17 starts with the variable searchString that specifies a text string, followed by the REs expr1, expr2, expr3. The RE expr1 matches the string Test that occurs anywhere in searchString, whereas expr2 matches Test if it occurs at the beginning of searchString, and expr3 matches Test if it occurs at the end of searchString. The RE expr matches words that end in the letters es, and the RE expr5 matches the letter t followed by a vowel.

The output from Listing 8.17 is here:

```
"Test" was found.
"Test" was found at the beginning of the line.
There are 1 words(s) ending in "es":  matches
The letter t, followed by a vowel, occurs 3 times:  Te  ti  te
```

PANDAS AND REGULAR EXPRESSIONS

This section is marked "optional" because the code snippets require an understanding of regular expressions. If you are not ready to learn about regular expressions, you can skip this section with no loss of continuity. Alternatively, you can read the material in Chapter 8 (if necessary) regarding regular expressions and then you can return to this portion of the chapter.

Listing 8.18 shows the contents pandas_regexs.py that illustrate how to extract data from a Pandas data frame using regular expressions.

LISTING 8.18: *pandas_regexs.py*

```
import pandas as pd

schedule = ["Monday: Prepare lunch at 12:30pm for VIPs",
            "Tuesday: Yoga class from 10:00am to 11:00am",
```

```
            "Wednesday: PTA meeting at library at 3pm",
            "Thursday: Happy hour at 5:45 at Julie's house.",
            "Friday: Prepare pizza dough for lunch at 12:30pm.",
            "Saturday: Early shopping for the week at 8:30am.",
            "Sunday: Neighborhood bbq block party at 2:00pm."]

# create a Pandas dataframe:
df = pd.DataFrame(schedule, columns = ['dow_of_week'])

# convert to lowercase:
df = df.applymap(lambda s:s.lower() if type(s) == str else s)
print("df:")
print(df)
print()

# character count for each string in df['dow_of_week']:
print("string lengths:")
print(df['dow_of_week'].str.len())
print()

# the number of tokens for each string in df['dow_of_week']
print("number of tokens in each string in df['dow_of_week']:")
print(df['dow_of_week'].str.split().str.len())
print()

# the number of occurrences of digits:
print("number of digits:")
print(df['dow_of_week'].str.count(r'\d'))
print()

# display all occurrences of digits:
print("show all digits:")
print(df['dow_of_week'].str.findall(r'\d'))
print()

# display hour and minute values:
print("display (hour, minute) pairs:")
print(df['dow_of_week'].str.findall(r'(\d?\d):(\d\d)'))
print()

# create new columns from hour:minute value:
print("hour and minute columns:")
print(df['dow_of_week'].str.extract(r'(\d?\d):(\d\d)'))
print()
```

Listing 8.18 initializes the variable schedule with a set of strings, each of which specifies a daily to-do item for an entire week. The format for each to-do item is of the form day:task, where is a day of the week and task is a string that specifies what needs to be done on that particular day. Next, the data frame df1 is initialized with the contents of schedule, followed by an example of defining a lambda expression that converts string-based values to lower case, as shown here:

```
df = df.applymap(lambda s:s.lower() if type(s) == str else s)
```

The preceding code snippet is useful because you do not need to specify individual columns of a data frame: the code ignores any non-string values (such as integers and floating point values).

The next pair of code blocks involve various operations using the methods `applymap()`, `split()`, and `len()` that you have seen in previous examples. The next code block displays the number of digits in each to-do item by means of the regular expression in the following code snippet:

```
print(df['dow_of_week'].str.count(r'\d'))
```

The next code block displays the actual digits (instead of the number of digits) in each to-do item by means of the regular expression in the following code snippet:

```
print(df['dow_of_week'].str.findall(r'\d'))
```

The final code block displays the strings of the form `hour:minutes` by means of the regular expression in the following code snippet:

```
print(df['dow_of_week'].str.findall(r'(\d?\d):(\d\d)'))
```

You can learn more about regular expressions by reading material in Chapter 8 of this book. Launch the code in Listing 8.18 to see the following output:

```
=> df:
                                       dow_of_week
0        monday: prepare lunch at 12:30pm for vips
1        tuesday: yoga class from 10:00am to 11:00am
2        wednesday: pta meeting at library at 3pm
3        thursday: happy hour at 5:45 at julie's house.
4     friday: prepare pizza dough for lunch at 12:30pm.
5     saturday: early shopping for the week at 8:30am.
6        sunday: neighborhood bbq block party at 2:00pm.

=> string lengths:
0    41
1    43
2    40
3    46
4    49
5    48
6    47
Name: dow_of_week, dtype: int64

=> number of tokens in each string in df['dow_of_week']:
0    7
1    7
2    7
3    8
4    8
5    8
6    7
Name: dow_of_week, dtype: int64
```

```
=> number of digits:
0    4
1    8
2    1
3    3
4    4
5    3
6    3
Name: dow_of_week, dtype: int64

=> show all digits:
0              [1, 2, 3, 0]
1    [1, 0, 0, 0, 1, 1, 0, 0]
2                       [3]
3                 [5, 4, 5]
4              [1, 2, 3, 0]
5                 [8, 3, 0]
6                 [2, 0, 0]
Name: dow_of_week, dtype: object

=> display (hour, minute) pairs:
0              [(12, 30)]
1    [(10, 00), (11, 00)]
2                     []
3               [(5, 45)]
4              [(12, 30)]
5               [(8, 30)]
6               [(2, 00)]
Name: dow_of_week, dtype: object

=> hour and minute columns:

       0    1
0     12   30
1     10   00
2    NaN  NaN
3      5   45
4     12   30
5      8   30
6      2   00
```

SUMMARY

This chapter showed you how to create various types of regular expressions. First, you learned how to define primitive regular expressions using sequences of digits, lowercase letters, and uppercase letters. Next, you learned how to use character classes, which are more convenient and simpler expressions that can perform the same functionality. You also learned how to use the Python re library to compile regular expressions and then use them to see if they match substrings of text strings.

EXERCISES

1. Given a text string, find the list of words (if any) that start or end with a vowel, and treat upper- and lowercase vowels as distinct letters. Display this list of words in alphabetical order, and also in descending order based on their frequency.

2. Given a text string, find the list of words (if any) that contain lowercase vowels or digits or both, but no uppercase letters. Display this list of words in alphabetical order, and also in descending order based on their frequency.

3. There is a spelling rule in English specifying that "the letter i is before e, except after c," which means that "receive" is correct but "recieve" is incorrect. Write a Python script that checks for incorrectly spelled words in a text string.

4. Subject pronouns cannot follow a preposition in the English language. Thus, "between you and me" and "for you and me" are correct, whereas "between you and I" and "for you and I" are incorrect. Write a Python script that checks for incorrect grammar in a text string, and search for the prepositions "between," "for," and "with." In addition, search for the subject pronouns "I," "you," "he," and "she." Modify and display the text with the correct grammar usage.

5. Find the words in a text string whose length is at most 4 and then print all the substrings of those characters. For example, if a text string contains the word "text," then print the strings "t," "te," "tex," and "text."

## CHAPTER 9

SQL *AND* NoSQL

S QL is a vast topic that fills entire books, and so this chapter contains only a subset of fundamental SQL concepts. In many cases, the concepts are often accompanied by SQL statements that show you the correct syntax. Moreover, there are various SQL scripts for creating database tables, recreating tables, and populating tables with data.

MySQL is used for the SQL portion of this chapter, partly because it is available as a free download from the Oracle Website. Fortunately, virtually everything that you learn about MySQL in this chapter transfers to other RDBMSes, such as PostgreSQL and Oracle.

This chapter includes SQL statements for creating and populating database tables in MySQL, defining single-table SQL statements, performing multi-table joins and aggregate operations in SQL, defining indexes and views, and modeling several types of entity relationships.

The latter portion of this chapter introduces NoSQL databases. We discuss MongoDB, which is a popular MySQL database, and how to manage data in a MongoDB collection.

The first section contains a brief description of SQL, and three main types of SQL commands (DCL, DDL, and DML). There are a number of examples of SQL statements that use the SELECT keyword to select data from a MySQL table.

The second section contains basic commands for creating a database in MySQL, as well as examples of creating MySQL tables and populating them with data. We discuss the keys and indexes and why the latter are very useful.

The third section delves into other aspects of SQL, such as using GROUP BY and HAVING in a SQL statement. We show how to perform a join of two MySQL tables, as well as how to use aggregate functions such as COUNT(*), MIN, MAX, and AVG.

The fourth section shows how to define a JOIN statement on two tables, which can be extended to multiple tables. We also discuss keys and indexes for relational tables. The fourth section contains code samples that illustrate how to create tables and SQL statements for one-to-many, many-to-many, and self-referential tables.

The sixth section also shows how to populate a Pandas data frame with data from a MySQL table and then save the contents of a Pandas data frame as an Excel spreadsheet.

The final section introduces you to MongoDB, which is a NoSQL database, along with concepts such as collections and documents for storing JSON-based data. This section also shows various ways of managing data in a MongoDB database.

Before working on the examples in this chapter, please keep in mind the following points. First, this chapter is designed to provide "hands-on" SQL-related content and explanations for the related concepts. Hence, this chapter does not contain any historical information regarding RDBMSes and the evolution of SQL.

Second, this chapter contains a fictitious Website whose underlying database contains four database tables. This database demonstrates how to set up a small application involving an RDBMS, but no Web-based code is provided. In addition, the sample application shows one way to define the attributes (i.e., columns) of the four tables. However, you might decide to change the structure of some of the tables (e.g., the location of the subtotals attribute in the line_items table).

Third, if you intend to create a production-quality website and RDBMS that will have many customers, consult an experienced application DBA (Database Administrator) to validate that design of the RDBMS.

WHAT IS AN RDBMS?

An RDBMS is an acronym for Relational DataBase Management System. Relational databases store data in tabular form with labelled rows and columns. Although relational databases usually provide a decent solution for storing data, speed and scalability might be an issue in some cases.

Although an RDBMS can consist of a single table, it often comprises multiple tables that have various associations with each other. A logical schema consists of the collection of tables and their relationships (along with indexes) in an RDBMS. The schema is used for generating a physical schema, which consists of all the SQL statements that are required to create the specified tables and their relationships. After the tables have been generated, you can begin inserting data and then managing the consistency of the data.

An RDBMS involves using SQL (discussed later) for managing the data in tables, as well as the concept of normal forms that specify properties of the attributes of tables. We'll defer the discussion of normal forms.

We discuss NoSQL, which refers to non-SQL or non-relational database design. NoSQL uses an alternate approach to organizing and storing data (i.e., not tabular form), and we include code samples for MongoDB (a NoSQL database).

A FOUR-TABLE RDBMS

As a simple example, suppose that the (fictitious) website at *www.mytools.com* sells tools. Let's not worry about the contents and the actual layout of the Web page: just remember that there are various input fields, the return policy for widgets, or the details of transferring the contents of the input fields to the tables in the RDBMS. At a minimum, the RDBMS for storing details about customers, their purchase orders, and items that are for sale requires the following tables:

```
customers
po_orders
line_items
item_desc
```

The following subsections describe the contents of the preceding tables, along with the relationships among these tables.

The customers Table

Although you have leeway regarding the fields (also called *attributes*) of the customers table, you need enough information to uniquely identify the customer. By analogy, the following information (except for cust_id) is required to mail an envelope to a person:

```
cust_id
fname
lname
home_address
city
state
zip_code
```

We will create the customers table with the attributes in the preceding list. Note that the cust_id attribute is called a *key* because it uniquely identifies every customer. Although we'll defer the discussion of keys to a later chapter, it's obvious that we need a mechanism for uniquely identifying every customer.

Whenever we need to refer to the details of a particular customer, we will use the associated value of cust_id to retrieve those details from the row in the customers table that has the associated cust_id.

The preceding paragraph describes the essence of linking related tables T1 and T2 in an RDBMS: the key in T1 is stored as an attribute value in T2. If we need to access related information in table T3, then we store the key in T2 as an attribute value in T3.

Note that a customers table in a production system would contain other attributes, such as the following:

```
title (Mr., Mrs., Ms., and so forth)
shipping_address
cell_phone
```

For the sake of simplicity, we'll use the initial set of attributes to define the customers table. Later, you can add the new attributes to the four-table schema to make the system more like an actual system.

Suppose that the following information pertains to customer John Smith, who has been assigned a cust_id of 1000:

```
cust_id: 1000
fname: John
lname: Smith
home_address: 1000 Appian Way
city: Sunnyvalue
state: California
zip_code:95959
```

Whenever John Smith makes a new purchase, we use the cust_id value of 1000 to create a new row for this customer in the purchase_orders table.

The purchase_orders Table

When customers visit the website, we need to create a purchase order that will be inserted as a new row in the purchase_orders table. While you might be tempted to place all the customers' details in the new row, we will identify the customer by the associated cust_id and use this value instead. Note that we create a new row in the customers table whenever new users register at the Website, whereas repeat customers are identified by an existing cust_id that must be determined by searching the customers table with the information that the customer types into the login fields of the main Web page.

We saw that the customers table contains a key attribute; similarly, the purchase_orders table requires a key attribute that we will call po_id (you are free to use a different string) in order to associate a purchase order for a given customer.

The row with a given po_id requires a cust_id attribute to also identify the customer who is making the current purchase. Also note that the cust_id will be associated with a (possibly empty) list of rows in the table purchase_orders. Specifically, let's see what happens to the purchase_orders table when John Smith (whose cust_id is 1000) makes a purchase, with a hypothetical (and randomly chosen) number of items purchased for each purchase order that is displayed in parentheses:

```
0 purchases: 0 rows in the purchase_orders table (0 items)
1 purchase:  1 row  in the purchase_orders table (3 items)
2 purchases: 2 rows in the purchase_orders table (2 items)
3 purchases: 3 rows in the purchase_orders table (4 items)
. . .
N purchases: N rows in the purchase_orders table (7 items)
```

Each purchase order involves the specified number of items (specified in parentheses). For example, when John Smith makes his first purchase, the purchase_orders table contains a row that is identified by John Smith's cust_id (which is 1000), and a generated value for po_id, which we arbitrarily set to

12500. John Smith's purchase order is a row in the `purchase_orders` table that looks like this:

```
1000|12500|<values for other fields|
```

Moreover, the purchase order with `po_id` equal to 12500 involves three purchased items: each of those three items has a corresponding row in the `line_items` table. For example, the `line_items` table with those three items might look something like this:

```
1000|12500|5000|<values for other fields|
1000|12500|5001|<values for other fields|
1000|12500|5002|<values for other fields|
```

The `line_id` values 5001, 5002, and 5003 in the three preceding rows have been chosen for convenience. In a real system, the actual numbers will be different.

After John Smith makes a second purchase, then a second purchase order is inserted in the `purchase_orders` table. He now has the following two rows in the table `purchase_orders`:

```
1000|12500|<values for other fields|
1000|12600|<values for other fields|
```

Note that the purchase order with `po_id` equal to 12600 involves *two* purchased items: both of those items have a corresponding row in the `line_items` table. For example, the `line_items` table with those items might look something like this:

```
1000|12600|5003|<values for other fields>|
1000|12600|5004|<values for other fields>|
```

The `line_id` values 5003 and 5004 in the three preceding rows have been chosen for convenience. In a real system, the actual numbers will be different.

After John Smith makes a third purchase, then a third row is inserted in the `purchase_orders` table. Now the following three rows in the `purchase_orders` table are associated with John Smith:

```
1000|12500|<values for other fields|
1000|12600|<values for other fields|
1000|12700|<values for other fields|
```

The actual `po_id` values for the preceding three rows will most likely be different, as they depend on purchases made by other customers.

Although we have not discussed `JOIN` statements, the following `SQL` statement shows the usefulness of a `JOIN` statement to display all the purchases that John Smith has made:

```
SELECT c.cust_id, o.po_id
FROM customers c, purchase_orders o
WHERE c.cust_id = o.cust_id;
```

Now let's specify the remaining attributes in the `purchase_orders` table. Although there are multiple ways to define a set of suitable attributes, let's use the following set of attributes for the `purchase_orders` table:

```
po_id
cust_id
purchase_date
purchase_subtotal
purchase_tax
purchase_bill
```

For example, suppose that customer John Smith, whose `cust_id` is 1000, purchases some widgets on December 15, 2021. There are dozens of different date formats that are supported in RDBMSes: for simplicity, we will use the MM-DD-YYYY format (which you can change to suit your needs).

Then the new row for John Smith in the `purchase_orders` table would have values that look something like the following:

```
po_id: 12500
cust_id: 1000
purchase_date: 12-01-2021
purchase_subtotal: 60.00
purchase_tax: 6.00
purchase_bill: 66.00
```

The line_items Table

At this point, let's assume that John Smith is about to make his first purchase involving widgets. Recall that customers can purchase multiple widgets, and more than one of each widget. Hence, a row in the `line_items` table requires values for the following fields:

```
line_id
po_id
cust_id
item_id
item_quantity
item_price
item_billed
```

As a concrete example, suppose that customer John Smith has decided to purchase 1 hammer, 2 screwdrivers, and 3 wrenches, which have `item_id` values of 100, 200, and 300, respectively. These three values were chosen quasi-randomly with convenient values (i.e., multiples of 100).

In addition, each item that is purchased requires a row in the `line_items` table that is identified by the `line_id` attribute. Moreover, this row also contains values for `po_id`, `cust_id`, and `item_id`. For simplicity, let's assign the values 5000, 5001, and 5002 to the `line_id` attribute for the three new rows. The three rows in the `line_items` table would have values that look something like this:

```
Row #1:
line_id: 5000
po_id: 12500
cust_id: 1000
item_id: 100
item_quantity: 1
item_price: 20.00
item_billed: 20.00

Row #2:
line_id: 5001
po_id: 12500
cust_id: 1000
item_id: 200
item_quantity: 2
item_price: 8.00
item_billed: 16.00

Row #3:
line_id: 5002
po_id: 12500
cust_id: 1000
item_id: 300
item_quantity: 3
item_price: 10.00
item_billed: 30.00
```

The item_desc Table

The item_desc table contains information about each item that is available for purchase from the Website, with the following attributes in this table:

```
item_id
item_desc
item_price
```

Here are three rows of sample values in the item_desc table:

```
item_id: 100
item_desc: hammer
item_price: 20.00

item_id: 200
item_desc: screwdriver
item_price: 8.00

item_id: 300
item_desc: wrench
item_price: 10.00
```

Let's consider the sequence of events that occurred after John Smith's first transaction:

Step 1: Customer John Smith (with cust_id 1000) initiated a purchase.
Step 2: The associated purchase order has a po_id with the value 12500.

Step 3: John Smith purchased 1 hammer, 2 screwdrivers, and 3 wrenches.

Step 4: The cost for the three items is $20.00, $16.00, and $30.00, respectively.

Step 5: The subtotal for the purchase order is $66.00.

Step 6: The tax is $6.60 (a tax rate of 10%).

Step 7: The total cost is $72.60.

The tables `customers`, `purchase_orders`, and `line_items` have been updated with new rows as follows:

1. `customers`: a row for customer John Smith
2. `purchase_orders`: a row for customer John Smith
3. `line_items`: three new rows for the new purchase order

Notice that the `item_desc` table is unaffected by a transaction. The `item_desc` table is a read-only table, and it might be a candidate for "pinning" this table in memory to improve performance.

WHAT IS SQL?

SQL is an acronym for Structured Query Language, which is used for managing data in tables in a relational database (RDBMS). SQL commands can be classified in the following four categories:

```
DCL (Data Control Language)
DDL (Data Definition Language)
DQL (Data Query Language)
DML (Data Manipulation Language)
```

The following subsections provide additional information for each item in the preceding list.

What is DCL?

DCL is an acronym for Data Control Language, which refers to any SQL statement that contains the keywords GRANT or REVOKE. These keywords grant or revoke access permissions, respectively, from any database user.

For example, the following SQL statement gives user ABC permission to view and modify records in the `employee` table:

```
GRANT ALL ON employee
TO ABC;
[WITH GRANT OPTION]
```

The GRANT OPTION enables a user to grant privileges to other database users.

By contrast, the following SQL statement revokes UPDATE privileges on the `employee` table from user ABC:

```
REVOKE UPDATE
ON employee
FROM ABC;
```

What is DDL?

DDL is an acronym for Data Definition Language, which refers to any SQL statements that contain the following keywords:

```
CREATE
ALTER
DROP
RENAME
TRUNCATE
COMMENT
```

The preceding list of SQL keywords can appear in SQL statements that refer to tables as well as views (discussed later). Here are partial examples of the way to use the keywords in the preceding list:

```
ALTER TABLE
CREATE/DROP/TRUNCATE tables
CREATE TABLE abc as (SELECT * from def);
CREATE/DROP/TRUNCATE views
CREATE/DROP indexes
```

Delete Vs. Drop Vs. Truncate

These keywords have important differences. The DELETE keyword and the TRUNCATE keyword both delete data from a table, but there can be a significant performance difference. Consider the following SQL statements (the first two delete all the rows from the customers table):

```
DELETE * FROM customers;
TRUNCATE customers;
DROP TABLE customers;
```

The DELETE statement sequentially processes all the rows in the customers table, whereas the TRUNCATE statement performs one operation to remove all rows from the customers table. Hence, TRUNCATE can be much faster than DELETE when a table contains a large number of rows. By contrast, the DROP statement eliminates the rows *and* the customers table.

Of course, if you want to remove a subset of the rows of the customers table, then you must specify a WHERE clause, so the required SQL statement would be as follows:

```
DELETE *
FROM customers;
WHERE cust_id < 10000
```

What is DQL?

DQL is an acronym for Data Query Language, which refers to any SQL statement that contains the keyword SELECT. Note that DQL can involve selecting a subset of data as well as deleting a subset of data, as shown in the following pair of SQL statements:

```
SELECT *
FROM customers
WHERE cust_id < 10000;

DELETE *
FROM customers
WHERE cust_id IN
    (SELECT cust_id FROM customers
    WHERE cust_id < 10000);
```

In case you didn't notice, the preceding DELETE statement can be rewritten more efficiently as follows:

```
DELETE *
FROM customers
WHERE cust_id < 10000;
```

What is DML?

DML is an acronym for Data Manipulation Language, which refers to SQL statements that execute queries against one or more tables in a database. DML statements are SQL statements that contain any of the following keywords:

```
INSERT
UPDATE
DELETE
MERGE
CALL
EXPLAIN PLAN
LOCK TABLE
```

In most cases, the preceding keywords modify the existing values of data in one or more tables. For example, the following SQL statement specifies the INSERT keyword in order to insert a new row into the user table (the user table is defined later in this chapter):

```
INSERT INTO user VALUES (1000, 'Developer');
```

The following SQL statement contains an example of the UPDATE keyword in order to update an attribute of a row:

```
UPDATE user
SET TITLE = 'Team Lead'
WHERE USER_ID = 1000;
```

The following SQL query can affect multiple rows in the TAX_INFO table:

```
UPDATE tax_info
SET tax_rate = tax_rate + 0.05;
```

What is TCL?

TCL is an acronym for Transaction Control Language, which refers to SQL statements that contain any of the following keywords:

```
COMMIT
ROLLBACK
SAVEPOINT
SET TRANSACTION
```

The COMMIT keyword commits the results of a SQL statement or a transaction to the underlying database, whereas the ROLLBACK keyword serves the opposite purpose. The SAVEPOINT keyword identifies a point at which a subsequent transaction can be rolled back, which occurs when the ROLLBACK keyword appears in a SQL statement that is executed. The SET TRANSACTION statement is used to specify various characteristics of the current transaction, such as the start of a transaction. When the transaction is completed, either the COMMIT keyword or the ROLLBACK keyword is invoked.

Data Types in MySQL

MySQL supports a variety of data types that you can use in table definitions, as shown below:

```
INT
DECIMAL
BIT
BOOLEAN
CHAR
VARCHAR
TEXT
DATE
TIME
DATETIME
TIMESTAMP
JSON
XML
ENUM
```

Most of the preceding datatypes are intuitively-named types. INT is for storing integer values, whereas CHAR and VARCHAR are for storing fixed length and variable length strings, respectively.

The DATE, TIME, and DATETIME data types are for storing their respective types of data, and they also provide various functions for data conversion.

The JSON data type is for storing JSON documents and the XML datatype is for storing XML documents, whereas the ENUM data type is for storing enumeration values.

WORKING WITH `MYSQL`

Oracle provides the `MySQL` database, which you can download for your operating system:

https://dev.mysql.com/downloads/

Download the `MySQL` distribution for your machine and perform the installation procedure.

Logging into My`SQL`

You can log into `MySQL` as root with the following command, which will prompt you for the root password:

```
$ mysql -u root -p
```

If you installed `MySQL` via a `DMG` file, then when you launch the preceding command, you will be prompted for the password for the root user, which is the same as the password for logging into your laptop.

Creating a My`SQL` Database

Log into `MySQL` and invoke the following command to create the `mytools` database:

```
MySQL [mysql]> create database mytools;
Query OK, 1 row affected (0.004 sec)
```

Now select the `mytools` database with the following command:

```
MySQL [mysql]> use mytools;
Database changed
```

Display the tables in the `mytools` database with the following command:

```
MySQL [mytools]> show tables;
Empty set (0.001 sec)
```

CREATING AND DROPPING TABLES

Log into `MySQL`, select the `mytools` database as described in the previous section, and then display the tables in the `mytools` database with the following command:

```
MySQL [mytools]> show tables;
Empty set (0.001 sec)
```

The preceding output makes sense because the `mytools` database is an empty database. The next section shows you how to create four tables in `MySQL`.

There are three ways to create database tables in `MySQL` as well as other `RDBMSes`. One technique is manual (shown first); another technique (shown second) invokes a `SQL` file that contains suitable `SQL` commands; and a third technique involves redirecting a `SQL` file to the `MySQL` executable from the command line.

Manually Creating Tables for mytools.com

This section shows how to manually create the four tables for the `mytools` database in `MySQL`. Specifically, you will see how to create the following four tables:

```
customers
purchase_orders
line_items
item_desc
```

Now log into `MySQL`, and after selecting the `mytools` database, type the following commands to create the required tables:

```
MySQL [mytools]> CREATE TABLE customers (cust_id INTEGER,
fname VARCHAR(20), lname VARCHAR(20), home_address
VARCHAR(20), city VARCHAR(20), state VARCHAR(20), zip_code
VARCHAR(10));

MySQL [mytools]> CREATE TABLE purchase_orders ( po_id
INTEGER, cust_id INTEGER, purchase_date date, purchase_
subtotal DECIMAL(8,2), purchase_tax DECIMAL(8,2), purchase_
bill DECIMAL(8,2));

MySQL [mytools]> CREATE TABLE line_items (line_id INTEGER,
po_id INTEGER, cust_id INTEGER, purchase_date DATE,
purchase_subtotal DECIMAL(8,2), purchase_tax DECIMAL(8,2,
purchase_bill DECIMAL(8,2));

MySQL [mytools]> CREATE TABLE item_desc (item_id INTEGER,
item_price DECIMAL(8,2), item_desc VARCHAR(80));
```

Describe the structure of the `customers` table with the following command:

```
MySQL [mytools]> desc customers;
+----------+-------------+------+-----+---------+-------+
| Field    | Type        | Null | Key | Default | Extra |
+----------+-------------+------+-----+---------+-------+
| fname    | varchar(20) | YES  |     | NULL    |       |
| lname    | varchar(20) | YES  |     | NULL    |       |
| age      | varchar(20) | YES  |     | NULL    |       |
| gender   | char(1)     | YES  |     | NULL    |       |
| country  | varchar(20) | YES  |     | NULL    |       |
+----------+-------------+------+-----+---------+-------+
5 rows in set (0.002 sec)
```

Describe the structure of the `purchase_orders` table, the `line_items` table, and the `item_desc` table with a similar `DESC` statement.

Creating Tables via a SQL Script for mytools.com (1)

The previous section shows a manual technique for creating database tables, and this section shows how to create the required tables by launching the SQL file `mytools_create_tables2.sql`, whose contents are shown in Listing 9.1.

LISTING 9.1: mytools_create_tables2.sql

```
USE DATABASE mytools;

-- drop tables if they already exist:
DROP TABLE IF EXISTS customers;
DROP TABLE IF EXISTS purchase_orders;
DROP TABLE IF EXISTS line_items;
DROP TABLE IF EXISTS item_desc;

CREATE TABLE customers (cust_id INTEGER, fname VARCHAR(20),
lname VARCHAR(20), home_address VARCHAR(20), city
VARCHAR(20), state VARCHAR(20), zip_code VARCHAR(10));

CREATE TABLE purchase_orders ( po_id INTEGER, cust_
id INTEGER, purchase_date date, purchase_subtotal
DECIMAL(8,2), purchase_tax DECIMAL(8,2), purchase_bill
DECIMAL(8,2));

CREATE TABLE line_items (po_id INTEGER, cust_id INTEGER,
line_id INTEGER, line_count INTEGER);

CREATE TABLE item_desc (item_id INTEGER, item_price
DECIMAL(8,2), item_desc VARCHAR(80));
```

Listing 9.1 contains three sections. The first section selects the `mytools` database, and the second section removes any of the four required tables if they already exist. The third section contains the SQL commands to create the four required tables.

Creating Tables via a SQL Script for mytools.com (2)

The previous section shows a manual technique for creating database tables, and this section shows how to create the required tables by launching the SQL file `mytools_create_tables.sql`, whose contents are displayed in Listing 9.2.

LISTING 9.2: mytools_create_tables2.sql

```
USE DATABASE mytools;

-- drop tables if they already exist:
DROP TABLE IF EXISTS customers;
DROP TABLE IF EXISTS purchase_orders;
DROP TABLE IF EXISTS line_items;
DROP TABLE IF EXISTS item_desc;
```

```
CREATE TABLE customers (cust_id INTEGER, fname VARCHAR(20),
lname VARCHAR(20), home_address VARCHAR(20), city
VARCHAR(20), state VARCHAR(20), zip_code VARCHAR(10));

CREATE TABLE purchase_orders ( po_id INTEGER, cust_
id INTEGER, purchase_date date, purchase_subtotal
DECIMAL(8,2), purchase_tax DECIMAL(8,2), purchase_bill
DECIMAL(8,2));

CREATE TABLE line_items (po_id INTEGER, cust_id INTEGER,
line_id INTEGER, line_count INTEGER);

CREATE TABLE item_desc (item_id INTEGER, item_price
DECIMAL(8,2), item_desc VARCHAR(80));
-- add data rows as needed
INSERT INTO item_desc VALUES (100,'hammer', 20.00);
INSERT INTO item_desc VALUES (200,'screwdriver', 8.00);
INSERT INTO item_desc VALUES (100,'wrench', 10.00);
```

Listing 9.2 is straightforward and contains three sections. The first section selects the `mytools` database, and the second section drops any of the four required tables if they already exist. The third section contains the SQL commands to create the four required tables.

Creating Tables from the Command Line

The third technique for invoking a SQL file is from the command line. First make sure that the specified database already exists (such as `mytools`). Next, invoke the following command from the command line to execute the contents of `user.sql` in MySQL:

```
mysql --password=<your-password>
--user=root mytools < user.sql
```

Listing 9.3 shows the contents of `user.sql` that illustrate how to create a database table and populate that table with data.

LISTING 9.3: user.sql

```
USE mytools;

DROP TABLE IF EXISTS user;
CREATE TABLE user (user_id INTEGER(8), user_title
VARCHAR(20));

—INSERT INTO user VALUES (1000, 'Developer');
—INSERT INTO user VALUES (2000, 'Project Lead');
—INSERT INTO user VALUES (3000, 'Dev Manager');
—INSERT INTO user VALUES (4000, 'Senior Dev Manager');
```

Log into MySQL with the following command from the command line:

```
mysql --password=<your-password> —user=root
```

Enter the following two commands (shown in bold):

```
MySQL [(none)]> use mytools;
Reading table information for completion of table and
column names
You can turn off this feature to get a quicker startup with -A

Database changed
MySQL [mytools]> desc user;
+------------+-------------+------+-----+---------+-------+
| Field      | Type        | Null | Key | Default | Extra |
+------------+-------------+------+-----+---------+-------+
| user_id    | int         | YES  |     | NULL    |       |
| user_class | int         | YES  |     | NULL    |       |
| user_title | varchar(20) | YES  |     | NULL    |       |
+------------+-------------+------+-----+---------+-------+
3 rows in set (0.002 sec)
```

Dropping Tables via a SQL Script for mytools.com

Sometimes you might want to simply drop database tables without recreating them. Listing 9.4 shows the contents of `mytools_drop_tables.sql` that illustrate how to drop database tables without recreating them.

LISTING 9.4: mytools_drop_tables.sql

```
USE DATABASE mytools;

-- drop tables if they already exist:
DROP TABLE IF EXISTS customers;
DROP TABLE IF EXISTS purchase_orders;
DROP TABLE IF EXISTS line_items;
DROP TABLE IF EXISTS item_desc;
```

Listing 9.4 is straightforward: its contents are the same as those in section 1 and section 2 of the SQL file given in Listing 9.3. However, it's useful to have a separate SQL file to simplify the process of dropping multiple tables (especially when you need to drop many tables).

POPULATING TABLES WITH SEED DATA

This section shows you the contents of four SQL files that contain "seed" data for the required tables in the `mytools` database. This data is useful for testing purposes, and you would delete this data from a production system. In fact, you can create a test database so that you can test schema changes and bug fixes before you apply those updates to a production system.

Listing 9.5 shows the contents of `customers.sql` that illustrate how to populate the `customers` table with data. Recall that the `customers` table consists of the following attributes:

```
cust_id
fname
lname
```

```
home_address
city
state
zip_code
```

LISTING 9.5: customers.sql

```
USE DATABASE mytools;
DELETE * FROM customers;

INSERT INTO customers
VALUES (1000,'John','Smith','123 Main
St','Fremont','CA','94123');
```

Listing 9.6 shows the contents of purchase_orders.sql that illustrate how to populate the purchase_orders table with data.

LISTING 9.6: purchase_orders.sql

```
USE DATABASE mytools;
DELETE * FROM purchase_orders;

INTO purchase_orders
VALUES (12500,1000,'12-01-2021',60.00,6.00,66.00);
INSERT INTO purchase_orders
VALUES (12600,1000,'02-03-2022',30.00,3.00,33.00);
INSERT INTO purchase_orders
INSERT VALUES (12700,1000,'05-07-2022',80.00,8.00,88.00);
```

Listing 9.7 shows the contents of line_items.sql that illustrate how to populate the line_items table with data.

LISTING 9.7: line_items.sql

```
USE DATABASE mytools;
DELETE * FROM line_items;

INSERT INTO line_items
VALUES (12500,1000,'12-01-2021',60.00,6.00,66.00);
```

Listing 9.8 shows the contents of item_desc.sql that illustrate how to populate the item_desc table with data. Recall that the item_desc table has the following attributes:

```
item_id
item_desc
item_price
```

Here are three rows that insert sample values in the item_desc table:

LISTING 9.8: item_desc.sql

```
USE DATABASE mytools;
DELETE * FROM item_desc;
```

```
INSERT INTO item_desc
VALUES (100,'hammer', 20.00);

INSERT INTO item_desc
VALUES (200,'screwdriver', 8.00);

INSERT INTO item_desc
VALUES (100,'wrench', 10.00);
```

Display the tables in the mytools database with the following command:

```
MySQL [mytools]> show tables;
+------------------+
| Tables_in_mytools |
+------------------+
| customers        |
| item_desc        |
| line_items       |
| purchase_orders  |
+------------------+
4 rows in set (0.002 sec)
```

The tables in this chapter contain a limited number of rows whose contents are based on simulated data, and so far, there has been no mention about best practices. However, if you reach the point where you have real customer-related data, consider the following points before you modify table structures, delete table rows, or drop tables (in other words, DDL or DML):

• make sure that you have a database backup
• create a test database
• execute SQL files in a test environment

POPULATING TABLES FROM TEXT FILES

Log into MySQL, select the mytools database, and invoke the following command to create the people table:

```
MySQL [mysql]> CREATE TABLE people (fname VARCHAR(20),
lname VARCHAR(20), age VARCHAR(20), gender CHAR(1),
country VARCHAR(20));
```

Describe the structure of the people table with the following command:

```
MySQL [mytools]> desc people;
+---------+-------------+------+-----+---------+-------+
| Field   | Type        | Null | Key | Default | Extra |
+---------+-------------+------+-----+---------+-------+
| fname   | varchar(20) | YES  |     | NULL    |       |
| lname   | varchar(20) | YES  |     | NULL    |       |
| age     | varchar(20) | YES  |     | NULL    |       |
| gender  | char(1)     | YES  |     | NULL    |       |
| country | varchar(20) | YES  |     | NULL    |       |
+---------+-------------+------+-----+---------+-------+
5 rows in set (0.002 sec)
```

Listing 9.9 shows the content of `people.csv` that contains CSV data that is intended for the `people` table.

LISTING 9.9: people.csv

```
fname,lname,age,gender,country
john,smith,30,m,usa
jane,smith,31,f,france
jack,jones,32,m,france
dave,stone,33,m,italy
sara,stein,34,f,germany
```

Listing 9.10 shows the contents of `people_data.sql` that contain several SQL statements for inserting data from `people.csv` into the `people` table.

LISTING 9.10: people_data.sql

```
INSERT INTO people VALUES ('john','smith','30','m','usa');
INSERT INTO people VALUES ('jane','smith','31','f','france');
INSERT INTO people VALUES ('jack','jones','32','m','france');
INSERT INTO people VALUES ('dave','stone','33','m','italy');
INSERT INTO people VALUES ('sara','stein','34','f','germany');
INSERT INTO people VALUES ('eddy','bower','35','m','spain');
```

As you can see, the INSERT statements in Listing 9.10 contain data that is located in `people.csv`. Now log into MySQL, select the `mytools` database (or create a new database for this table), and invoke the following command to populate the `people` table:

```
MySQL [mytools]> source people.sql
Query OK, 1 row affected (0.004 sec)
Query OK, 1 row affected (0.001 sec)
Query OK, 1 row affected (0.001 sec)
Query OK, 1 row affected (0.001 sec)
Query OK, 1 row affected (0.001 sec)
Query OK, 1 row affected (0.001 sec)
```

Execute the following SQL statement to display the contents of the `people` table:

```
MySQL [mytools]> select * from people;
+-------+-------+------+--------+---------+
| fname | lname | age  | gender | country |
+-------+-------+------+--------+---------+
| john  | smith | 30   | m      | usa     |
| jane  | smith | 31   | f      | france  |
| jack  | jones | 32   | m      | france  |
| dave  | stone | 33   | m      | italy   |
| sara  | stein | 34   | f      | germany |
| eddy  | bower | 35   | m      | spain   |
+-------+-------+------+--------+---------+
6 rows in set (0.000 sec)
```

Listing 9.10 involves manually executing each SQL statement sequentially, one SQL statement at a time; unfortunately this approach is inefficient for a large number of rows. The third option involves loading data from a CSV file into a table, as shown below:

```
MySQL [mytools]> LOAD DATA LOCAL INFILE 'people.csv' INTO
TABLE people;
```

However, you might encounter the following error (depending on the configuration of MySQL on your machine):

```
ERROR 3948 (42000): Loading local data is disabled; this must
be enabled on both the client and server sides
```

In general, a SQL script is preferred because it's easy to execute multiple times, and you can schedule SQL scripts to run as UNIX cron jobs.

SIMPLE SELECT STATEMENTS

This section contains some basic SQL statements that illustrate how to select various subsets of data from a table. For example, the following SQL statement illustrates how to select all rows from the people table:

```
MySQL [mytools]> select * from people;
+-------+-------+------+--------+---------+
| fname | lname | age  | gender | country |
+-------+-------+------+--------+---------+
| john  | smith | 30   | m      | usa     |
| jane  | smith | 31   | f      | france  |
| jack  | jones | 32   | m      | france  |
| dave  | stone | 33   | m      | italy   |
| sara  | stein | 34   | f      | germany |
| eddy  | bower | 35   | m      | spain   |
+-------+-------+------+--------+---------+
6 rows in set (0.000 sec)
```

Select Statements with a WERE Clause

The following SQL statement illustrates how to specify the WHERE keyword in a SQL statement to select a subset of rows from the people table:

```
MySQL [mytools]> select * from people where lname = 'smith';
+-------+-------+------+--------+---------+
| fname | lname | age  | gender | country |
+-------+-------+------+--------+---------+
| john  | smith | 30   | m      | usa     |
+-------+-------+------+--------+---------+
1 row in set (0.000 sec)
```

Select Statements with GROUP BY Clause

The following SQL statement illustrates how to specify GROUP BY in a SQL statement to display the number of purchase orders that were created on a daily basis:

```
SELECT purchase_date, COUNT(*)
```

```
FROM purchase_orders
GROUP BY purchase_date;
```

Select Statements with a HAVING Clause

The following SQL statement illustrates how to specify GROUP BY in a SQL statement to display the number of purchase orders that were created on a daily basis, and only those days where at least 4 purchase orders were created:

```
SELECT purchase_date, COUNT(*)
FROM purchase_orders
GROUP BY purchase_date;
HAVING COUNT(purchase_date) > 3;
```

WORKING WITH INDEXES IN SQL

SQL enables you to define one or more indexes for a table, which can greatly reduce the amount of time that is required to select a single row or a subset of rows from a table.

A SQL index on a table consists of one or more attributes in a table. SQL updates in a table that has one or more indexes requires more time than updates without the existence of indexes on that table because both the table and the index (or indexes) must be updated. Therefore, it's better to create indexes on tables that involve table columns that are frequently searched.

Here are two examples of creating indexes on the customers table:

```
CREATE INDEX idx_cust_lname
ON customers (lname);

CREATE INDEX idx_cust_lname_fname
ON customers (lname,fname);
```

WHAT ARE KEYS IN AN RDBMS?

A *key* is a value used to identify a record in a table uniquely. A key could be a single column or combination of multiple columns.

A *primary key* is a single column value used to identify a database record uniquely, and it has the following properties:

- A primary key cannot be NULL.
- A primary key value must be unique.
- The primary key values should rarely be changed.
- The primary key must be given a value when a new record is inserted.
- A table can have only one primary key

A *composite key* is a primary key composed of multiple columns used to identify a record uniquely.

A *foreign key* references the primary key of another table. A foreign key exists when a pair of tables have a master/detail relationship, such as a purchase order and its line items, or a student and the list of enrolled courses. A foreign key has the following properties:

A foreign key can have a different name from its primary key.

It ensures rows in one table have corresponding rows in another.

Unlike the primary key, they do not have to be unique (and often they aren't).

Foreign keys can be null, even though primary keys cannot be.

NOTE *Columns in a table that are not used to identify a record uniquely are called non-key columns.*

If a table contains the first name and last name of customers, you might be tempted to define a key consisting of the first name and last name attributes. However, this key does not guarantee that each row can be uniquely identified. It's possible to have more than one JOHN SMITH in a table of customers. You could include a middle initial as an attribute and also in the index, but it's still possible to have more than one JOHN B SMITH in a customer table.

Fortunately, there is a simple solution. Define an integer-valued attribute that auto increments whenever a new customer is inserted into a customers table (or whichever table where you want to insert new data). An index on this attribute guarantees uniqueness because each row has a unique value for this attribute. Moreover, an integer-based index requires less storage than a character-based index.

AGGREGATE AND BOOLEAN OPERATIONS IN SQL

SQL supports various operations that perform aggregate operations, such as COUNT(*), MIN, MAX, and AVG, all of which are intuitively named operations. In addition, MySQL provides functions to convert text to either uppercase or lowercase letters.

For example, the following SQL statement returns the number of rows in a customers table:

```
SELECT COUNT(*)
FROM CUSTOMERS;
```

The following SQL statement returns the minimum value in the AGE attribute of a customers table:

```
SELECT MIN(AGE)
FROM CUSTOMERS;
```

The following SQL statement returns the maximum value in the AGE attribute of a customers table:

```
SELECT MAX(AGE)
FROM CUSTOMERS;
```

The following SQL statement returns the average value in the AGE attribute of a customers table:

```
SELECT AVG(AGE)
FROM CUSTOMERS;
```

The following SQL statement returns the uppercase letters of all the first names in the FNAME attribute of a customers table:

```
SELECT UPPERCASE(FNAME)
FROM CUSTOMERS;
```

The following SQL statement returns the lowercase letters of all the first names in the FNAME attribute of a customers table:

```
SELECT LOWERCASE(FNAME)
FROM CUSTOMERS;
```

The following SQL statement returns the set of distinct first names in the FNAME attribute of a customers table, thereby eliminating duplicate names in the output:

```
SELECT DISTINCT(FNAME)
FROM CUSTOMERS;
```

MySQL also provides the following logical operators that can be used to form more complex filtering conditions:

```
AND
OR
NOT
```

For example, the following SQL statement returns the lowercase letters of the fname attribute for rows in which the first name starts with T *and* whose last name starts with S in the customers table:

```
SELECT LOWERCASE(FNAME)
FROM CUSTOMERS
WHERE FNAME LIKE 'T%' AND LNAME LIKE 'S%'
```

The following SQL statement returns the lowercase letters of the fname attribute for rows in which the first name starts with T *or* whose last name starts with S in the customers table:

```
SELECT LOWERCASE(FNAME)
FROM CUSTOMERS
WHERE FNAME LIKE 'T%' OR LNAME LIKE 'S%'
```

The following SQL statement returns the lowercase letters of the fname attribute for rows in which the first name starts with T and whose last name starts with S in the customers table:

```
SELECT LOWERCASE(FNAME)
```

```
FROM CUSTOMERS
WHERE FNAME LIKE 'T%' OR LNAME LIKE 'S%'
```

The following SQL statement returns the lowercase letters of the fname attribute for rows in which the first name does not start with T in the customers table:

```
SELECT LOWERCASE(FNAME)
FROM CUSTOMERS
WHERE FNAME NOT LIKE 'T%'
```

SQL also supports the IN operator, which involves specifying a set of values. For example, the following SQL statement returns the lowercase letters of the fname attribute for rows in which the first name starts with T and whose cust_id is in the list of specified values:

```
SELECT LOWERCASE(FNAME)
FROM CUSTOMERS
WHERE FNAME LIKE 'T%' AND CUST_ID IN (1000,2000,3000);
```

In addition, SQL provides the BETWEEN keyword that is useful for specifying a range of dates. For example, the following SQL statement returns the PO_ID from the purchase_orders table where the purchase date is between 12-01-2021 and 12-01-2022:

```
SELECT PO_ID
FROM PURCHASE_ORDERS
WHERE PURCHASE_DATE BETWEEN '12-01-2021' and '12-01-2022'
```

The following SQL statement returns the PO_ID from the purchase_orders table and no more than 1000 such rows:

```
SELECT PO_ID
FROM PURCHASE_ORDERS
WHERE PURCHASE_DATE BETWEEN '12-01-2021' and '12-01-2022'
LIMIT 1000
```

The following SQL statement returns last names of the customers in the customers table whose FNAME is NULL:

```
SELECT FNAME,LNAME
FROM CUSTOMERS
WHERE FNAME IS NULL
```

The following SQL statement returns the first names and last names of the customers in the customers table whose LNAME starts with S:

```
SELECT FNAME,LNAME
FROM CUSTOMERS
WHERE LNAME LIKE 'S%'
```

In addition to the keywords in this section, the following link contains a list of many useful SQL keywords:

https://www.kdnuggets.com/2018/07/sql-cheat-sheet.html

JOINING TABLES IN SQL

The JOIN keyword enables you to retrieve logically information that resides in multiple tables, which you can perform in several ways:

```
INNER JOIN
LEFT OUTER JOIN
RIGHT OUTER JOIN
CROSS JOIN
```

An INNER JOIN returns rows from a table that has matching rows in another table, which means that data must exist in *both* tables.

A LEFT JOIN also involves two tables, and returns rows from the left and either 1) matching rows from the right table, or 2) NULL if no matching rows exist in the right table.

Similarly, a RIGHT JOIN returns all rows from the right table and either 1) matching rows from the left table or 2) NULL if no matching rows are found in the left table.

A CROSS JOIN returns a Cartesian product of rows from multiple tables. By contrast, a self-join joins a table to itself (using a table alias) and then connects rows within the same table using inner join and left join.

DEFINING VIEWS IN MYSQL

A casual meaning of the word "view" typically refers to a partial or complete perspective of something physical. For instance, an apartment with a limited view of the beach suggests that only a partial view is possible from that apartment.

For spreadsheets, the data that is visible is typically a subset of the complete set of data values (particularly for large spreadsheets). The visible data is the view of a subset of the spreadsheet.

For a database, the definition of a view is based on a SELECT statement that returns data from various combinations of tables and other views in the database. After defining a view, you can grant access to the view (but not the underlying tables in the SELECT statement) to various users' views stored in the database, and they can be referenced in SQL statements in the same way that you reference tables.

The simplest view that you can define is a view that is based on all the columns of a single table:

```
CREATE VIEW V_CUST AS
SELECT * FROM CUSTOMERS
```

The preceding view does not provide you with information that is directly accessible from the underlying table. However, if you change the definition of the `customers` table, the definition of the view `V_CUST` remains the same.

In general, a view provides access to a subset of the data (either a subset of the columns, a subset of rows, or both) that is available in a table, such as the following example:

```
CREATE VIEW V_CUST2 AS
SELECT * FROM CUSTOMERS
WHERE CUST.LNAME LIKE 'S%'
```

The view `V_CUST2` is limited to a subset of the rows in the `customers` table. Specifically, only the customers whose last name is like `S%` (i.e., a last name that starts with the letter `S`).

Views do not store any data. The data that is retrieved via the `SELECT` statement involving a view is based on the underlying `SQL` query that was specified during the creation of the view. Consequently, you can also think of a view as a "virtual table."

Hence, if the `customers` table contains customers with last names that start with the letter `S` and some other letter, then the following queries return the same set of rows:

```
SELECT * FROM CUSTOMERS
SELECT * FROM V_CUST
```

However, the following queries return a different set of rows:

```
SELECT * FROM V_CUST2
SELECT * FROM V_CUST
```

Here are examples of a view that is defined over a single table:

```
MySQL [mytools]> CREATE VIEW VIEW1 AS (SELECT * FROM people);
1 row in set (0.002 sec)
```

Note that `VIEW1` accesses all attributes in all rows in the `people` table; however, you can define a view that contains a subset of the attributes of an underlying table, such as the view `VIEW2` that is defined here:

```
MySQL [mytools]> CREATE VIEW VIEW2 AS (SELECT fname,lname
FROM people);
1 row in set (0.002 sec)
```

There are several advantages of `RDBMS` views, as listed below (in no particular order):

- Reduce the complexity of SQL statements
- Increase the number of security layers
- Enable consistency of business logic
- Provide backward compatibility

SQL queries can involve literally dozens of tables and views whose SELECT statement can require several pages for its definition. In such cases, it's much simpler to define a view "on top of" the complex SQL query. The latter approach is simpler (i.e., knowledge of the underlying tables and views) and less error prone because of the simplicity of the definition of the view.

Moreover, the definition of a view can omit attributes that contain confidential information, after which access to the view is granted to users and access to the underlying tables is not granted.

For situations involving multiple queries that contain the same set of formulas, a view definition can effectively mask the underlying details (which are often of no interest to users).

As mentioned earlier in this section, you can define a view over multiple tables via a JOIN statement, which you will see later in this chapter.

ENTITY RELATIONSHIPS

An entity in this section refers to a table in an RDBMS, and there are several possible relationships between a pair of tables, as listed here:

- one-to-many
- many-to-one
- many-to-many
- self-referential

A *one-to-many* relationship is a parent/child relationship. For example, a one-to-many relationship is a purchase_orders table and a line_items table, where each row in the purchase_orders table has one or more rows in the line_items table. Each row in the latter contains item_id, item_price, and item_count (number of items purchased). The bill for each customer is based on the rows in the line_items table that belongs to a given customer. The total equals the sum of (item price) * (items ordered), plus taxes and other fees.

An example of a *many-to-many* relationship is a students table and a courses table. Each student can enroll in one or more courses, and each course contains one or more students. This relationship is modeled by creating a so-called "join" table whose primary key is the union of the primary key for the students table and the primary key for the courses table. Thus, the students table and the courses table both have a one-to-many relationship with the join table.

An example of a *self-referential* table is an employees table that contains employee-related information, including the manager of each employee. However, if you exclude information about each employee's manager, the table is most likely not a self-referential table.

Code samples for each of the preceding entity relationships are discussed in the following sections.

ONE-TO-MANY ENTITY RELATIONSHIPS

Listing 9.11 shows the contents of `purchase_orders.sql` that illustrate how to create a `purchase_orders` table and then populate the table with some simulated data.

LISTING 9.11: purchase_orders.sql

```
DROP TABLE IF EXISTS purchase_orders;

CREATE TABLE purchase_orders ( po_id INTEGER, cust_
id INTEGER, purchase_date date, purchase_subtotal
DECIMAL(8,2), purchase_tax DECIMAL(8,2), purchase_bill
DECIMAL(8,2));

INSERT INTO purchase_orders
VALUES (12500,1000,'12-01-2021',60.00,6.00,66.00);
INSERT INTO purchase_orders
VALUES (12600,1000,'02-03-2022',30.00,3.00,33.00);
INSERT INTO purchase_orders
VALUES (12700,1000,'05-07-2022',80.00,8.00,88.00);
```

Listing 9.12 shows the contents of `line_items.sql` that illustrate how to create a `line_items` table and then populate the table with some simulated data.

LISTING 9.12: line_items.sql

```
-- line_id, po_id, cust_id, purchase_date, purchase_
subtotal, purchase_tax, purchase_bill
DROP TABLE IF EXISTS line_items;

CREATE TABLE line_items (line_id INTEGER, po_id INTEGER,
cust_id INTEGER, purchase_date DATE, purchase_subtotal
DECIMAL(8,2), purchase_tax DECIMAL(8,2, purchase_bill
DECIMAL(8,2));

INSERT INTO line_items
VALUES (12500,1000,'12-01-2021',60.00,6.00,66.00);
```

MANY-TO-MANY ENTITY RELATIONSHIPS

Although our four-table database contains only one-to-many relationships, there are various scenarios that involve many-to-many relationships, and this section contains one of those scenarios.

Listing 9.13 shows the contents of `students.sql` that illustrate how to create a `students` table and then populate the table with some simulated data.

LISTING 9.13: students.sql

```
DROP TABLE IF EXISTS students;
```

```
CREATE TABLE students (student_id VARCHAR(20), fname
VARCHAR(20), lname VARCHAR(20), age INT(2), gender
CHAR(1));

INSERT INTO students VALUES ('1010','john','smith','30','m');
INSERT INTO students VALUES ('1020','jane','smith','31','f');
INSERT INTO students VALUES ('1030','jack','jones','32','m');
INSERT INTO students VALUES ('1040','dave','stone','33','m');
INSERT INTO students VALUES ('1050','sara','stein','34','f');
INSERT INTO students VALUES ('1060','eddy','bower','35','m');
```

Listing 9.14 shows the contents of `students.sql` that illustrate how to create a `students` table and then populate the table with some simulated data.

LISTING 9.14: courses.sql

```
DROP TABLE IF EXISTS courses;

CREATE TABLE courses (course_id VARCHAR(20), cname
VARCHAR(20), cdept VARCHAR(20), credits INT(2));

INSERT INTO courses VALUES ('5010','Calculus
                            1','Mathematics',4);
INSERT INTO courses VALUES ('5020','Calculus
                            2','Mathematics',4);
INSERT INTO courses VALUES ('5030','Calculus
                            3','Mathematics',4);
INSERT INTO courses VALUES ('5040','Topology',
                            'Mathematics',5);
INSERT INTO courses VALUES ('5050','Statistics',
                            'Mathematics',3);
INSERT INTO courses VALUES ('6000','Economics',
                            'Economics',  4);
INSERT INTO courses VALUES ('7000','Chemistry',
                            'Chemistry',  4);
INSERT INTO courses VALUES ('8000','Physics',
                            'Physics',    4);
```

Listing 9.15 shows the contents of `schedule.sql` that illustrate how to create a table for students and their enrolled courses, and then populate the table with some simulated data.

LISTING 9.15: schedule.sql

```
DROP TABLE IF EXISTS schedule;

CREATE TABLE schedule (year VARCHAR(4), term VARCHAR(10),
student_id VARCHAR(20), course_id VARCHAR(20));

INSERT INTO schedule VALUES ('2020','SPRING','1010','5010');
INSERT INTO schedule VALUES ('2020','SPRING','1020','5010');
INSERT INTO schedule VALUES ('2020','SUMMER','1020','5020');
INSERT INTO schedule VALUES ('2020','SUMMER','1020','5030');
INSERT INTO schedule VALUES ('2020','FALL',  '1030','5040');
```

```
INSERT INTO schedule VALUES ('2020','FALL',  '1030','5050');
INSERT INTO schedule VALUES ('2020','FALL',  '1040','6000');
INSERT INTO schedule VALUES ('2020','FALL',  '1040','7000');
INSERT INTO schedule VALUES ('2020','FALL',  '1050','6000');
INSERT INTO schedule VALUES ('2020','FALL',  '1050','7000');
INSERT INTO schedule VALUES ('2020','FALL',  '1060','6000');
INSERT INTO schedule VALUES ('2020','FALL',  '1060','7000');
```

SELF-REFERENTIAL ENTITY RELATIONSHIPS

Listing 9.16 shows the contents of `employees_data.sql` that illustrate how to create an `employees` table and then populate the table with some simulated data.

LISTING 9.16: employees_data.sql
```
—emp_id, mgr_id, title
DROP TABLE IF EXISTS employees;

CREATE TABLE employees (INT(8),INT(8),VARCHAR(20));

INSERT INTO employees VALUES (1000, 2000, 'Developer');
INSERT INTO employees VALUES (2000, 3000, 'Project Lead');
INSERT INTO employees VALUES (3000, 4000, 'Dev Manager');
INSERT INTO employees VALUES (4000, 4000, 'Senior Dev
Manager');
```

WORKING WITH SUBQUERIES IN SQL

SQL enables you to define a *correlated subquery*, which is a query nested inside another query. The nested query returns one or more values that are then used by the surrounding or "outer" SQL query. In general, SQL queries without subqueries are preferred for two reasons. First, SQL queries with subqueries can be difficult to debug (or to understand). The second reason pertains to performance: It's possible that a subquery will be evaluated once for *every* row processed by the outer query, which can reduce the query's performance.

For example, the following correlated query determines the employees whose salary is above the average salary for their department, and the subquery is part of the WHERE clause:

```
SELECT employee_number, name
FROM employees emp
WHERE salary > (
  SELECT AVG(salary)
  FROM employees
  WHERE department = emp.department);
```

As another example, the following correlated subquery appears in the SELECT clause (instead of the WHERE clause), to print the entire list of employees alongside the average salary for each employee's department:

```
SELECT employee_number,name,
   (SELECT AVG(salary)
      FROM employees
      WHERE department = emp.department) AS department_
average
FROM employees emp
```

OTHER TASKS IN SQL

SQL enables you to define queries to solve tasks of varying complexity, and in this section you will learn how to solve several SQL tasks. Suppose that we have a table consisting of the following names and salaries:

```
Name      Salary
---------------
BoB       100000
Sara      150000
Fred       80000
Dave      200000
```

The following SQL query finds the employee with the highest salary (which is clearly Dave):

```
SELECT name, MAX(salary) as salary FROM employee
```

We can nest the preceding SQL query to define the following correlated subquery to find the employee with the second largest salary:

```
SELECT name, MAX(salary) AS salary
FROM employee
WHERE salary < (SELECT MAX(salary)
               FROM employee);
```

Correlated subqueries are not necessarily unique. In fact, the following SQL query returns the same result as the previous correlated subquery:

```
SELECT name, MAX(salary) AS salary
FROM employee
WHERE salary IN
(SELECT salary FROM employee MINUS SELECT MAX(salary)
FROM employee);
```

Yet another correlated subquery that returns the same result as the previous correlated subquery is shown here:

```
SELECT name, MAX(salary) AS salary
FROM employee
WHERE salary  (SELECT MAX(salary)
FROM employee);
```

Given multiple SQL statements that accomplish the same task, test (i.e., execute) them to determine which one has the best performance. If the performance of two SQL queries is essential the same, then favor the SQL query that is simpler and more intuitive to understand (and perhaps will be easier to debug or modify).

The next task involves finding the average price of items in several stores and displaying the results in decreasing order of the average price.

```
+----------+---------------+-------+----------+
| item_id  | description   | price | store_id |
+----------+---------------+-------+----------+
|        1 | apple         | 2.45  |        1 |
|        2 | banana        | 3.45  |        1 |
|        3 | cereal        | 4.20  |        2 |
|        4 | milk          | 3.80  |        1 |
|        5 | lettuce       | 1.80  |        1 |
+----------+---------------+-------+----------+
```

We can solve the preceding task by performing following steps:

- apply the `avg()` function to the `price` column
- group the values by `store id`
- sort via the `ORDER` clause

Here is the resultant SQL query after performing the preceding three steps:

```
SELECT avg(price), store_id
FROM items
GROUP by store_id
ORDER BY avg(price);
```

The output from executing the preceding SQL query is as follows:

```
+------------+----------+
| avg(price) | store_id |
+------------+----------+
|   1.833333 |        1 |
|   3.650000 |        3 |
|   3.820000 |        2 |
+------------+----------+
```

READING MYSQL DATA FROM PANDAS

The preceding sections in this chapter showed you how to invoke SQL statements from the MySQL prompt, either via individual SQL statements or via files that contain SQL statements. This section (and subsequent sections) shows you how use Python to invoke SQL statements.

Listing 9.17 shows the contents of `read_sql_table.py`, which reads the contents of the `people` table in a Pandas data frame.

LISTING 9.17: read_sql_table.py

```
from sqlalchemy import create_engine
import pymysql
import pandas as pd
```

```
engine = create_engine('mysql+pymysql://root:your-root-id-
here@127.0.0.1',pool_recycle=3600)
dbConn = engine.connect()
frame   = pd.read_sql("select * from pandas.people", dbConn);

pd.set_option('display.expand_frame_repr', False)
print(frame)
dbConn.close()
```

Listing 9.17 starts with two `import` statements that provide an interface to a `MySQL` database (make sure that it's been started), followed by an `import` statement that enables us to populate a `Pandas` data frame with the rows that are selected by a `SQL` statement.

The next code block in Listing 9.17 instantiates the variable `engine` via the function `create_engine` (which is available from the first `import` statement). Next, the variable `dbConn` is a connection to our `MySQL` database. At this point, we can instantiate the variable `frame`, which is a `Pandas` data frame that contains the result of retrieving all the rows from the `people` database.

The third code block in Listing 9.17 shows the contents of the data frame `frame` and then closes the database connection `dbConn`. Launch the following command in a command shell:

```
python3 read_sql_table.py
You will see the following output:
   fname  lname age gender  country
0  john   smith 30     m        usa
1  jane   smith 31     f     france
2  jack   jones 32     m     france
3  dave   stone 33     m      italy
4  sara   stein 34     f    germany
5  eddy   bower 35     m      spain
```

Listing 9.18 shows the content of `sql_query.py`, which reads the contents of the `people` table in a `Pandas` data frame.

LISTING 9.18: sql_query.py

```
from sqlalchemy import create_engine
import pymysql
import pandas as pd

engine = create_engine('mysql+pymysql://
root:<your-password-here>@127.0.0.1',pool_recycle=3600)

query_1 = '''
select * from pandas.people
'''

print("create dataframe from table:")
df_2 = pd.read_sql_query(query_1, engine)

print("dataframe:")
print(df_2)
```

The first two code blocks in Listing 9.18 are the same as those in Listing 9.17, and are required for the same reason. The third code block defines the variable `query_1` as a string that contains a SQL statement for selecting all the rows in the `people` table.

The fourth code block initializes the variable `df_2` with the results of executing the SQL query that is defined in the variable `df_1`. The final portion of Listing 9.18 shows the contents of the data frame. Launch the following command in a command shell:

```
python3 sql_query.py
```

You will see the following output:

```
   fname  lname age gender  country
0  john   smith  30    m       usa
1  jane   smith  31    f     france
2  jack   jones  32    m     france
3  dave   stone  33    m      italy
4  sara   stein  34    f    germany
5  eddy   bower  35    m      spain
```

Launch the following command in a command shell:

```
python3 sql_query.py
```

After the preceding command has executed, you will see the following output:

```
   fname  lname age gender  country
0  john   smith  30    m       usa
1  jane   smith  31    f     france
2  jack   jones  32    m     france
3  dave   stone  33    m      italy
4  sara   stein  34    f    germany
5  eddy   bower  35    m      spain
```

EXPORT SQL DATA TO EXCEL

Listing 9.19 shows the content of `sql_query_excel.py`, which reads the contents of the `people` table into a `Pandas` data frame and then exports the contents of the data frame to an `Excel` spreadsheet.

LISTING 9.19: sql_query_excel.py

```
from sqlalchemy import create_engine
import pymysql
import pandas as pd

engine = create_engine('mysql+pymysql://root:your-root-
password@127.0.0.1',pool_recycle=3600)

query_1 = '''
select * from pandas.people
'''
```

```
print("create dataframe from table:")
df_2 = pd.read_sql_query(query_1, engine)

print("Contents of Pandas dataframe:")
print(df_2)

import openpyxl
print("saving dataframe to people.xlsx")
df_2.to_excel('people.xlsx', index=False)
```

Listing 9.19 contains the same code as Listing 9.18, along with a new code block, as shown here:

```
import openpyxl
print("saving dataframe to people.xlsx")
df_2.to_excel('people.xlsx', index=False)
```

The `import` statement in the preceding code block provides an interface between `Pandas` and `XLS` spreadsheets. Install `openpyxl` via the following statement (in case you have not already done so):

```
pip3 install openpyxl
```

The remaining two code snippets display the contents of the data frame `df_2` and then save its contents to the `XLS` spreadsheet `people.xlsx`. Launch the following command in a command shell:

```
python3 sql_query_excel.py
```

WHAT IS NORMALIZATION?

`RDBMS` normalization reduces data inconsistency and data redundancy. For example, if the `managers` table and the `employees` table contain a row with the name of the same person, then you need to ensure that any changes to that person are applied to both tables to avoid data inconsistency.

In general, `RDBMS` normalization also has the following features:

an increase in the number of tables
a reduction in the number of rows in many/most tables
the user of `JOIN` statements can access data across multiple tables
slower performance due to the need for `JOIN` statements

In some cases, denormalization can improve performance, and it is a task that experienced database administrators should perform.

Edgar Codd is the inventor of the relational model for an `RDBMS`, which consists of the following sequence of normal forms that involve an increasing number of constraints:

- `1NF` (First Normal Form)
- `2NF` (Second Normal Form)

- 3NF (Third Normal Form)
- BCNF (Boyce-Codd Normal Form)
- 4NF (Fourth Normal Form)
- 5NF (Fifth Normal Form)
- 6NF (Sixth Normal Form)

As you progress through the preceding list of bullet items, each normal form is more restrictive than its predecessor. For example, second normal form (2NF) is more restrictive than first normal form (1NF), and 3NF is more restrictive than 2NF. In general, 3NF is suitable for applications that store data in an RDBMS.

An RDBMS is in 1NF if each attribute contains indivisible values. In fact, 1NF is an essential and minimal property of a relation in a RDBMS that ensures the following:

- the removal of repeating groups (if any) from tables
- creation of a separate table for each set of related data
- creation of a primary key for each table

If you look closely at the four database tables for our *mytools* Website, you can see that there are no repeated groups in any of the tables.

As mentioned earlier, the best situation for applications that involve an RDBMS is the third normal form.

WHAT ARE SCHEMAS?

A *schema* is somewhat analogous to a blueprint for a house or an apartment complex. However, there are three types of schemas in RDBMSes, ranging from an abstract representation of a database to a representation that involves the actual SQL statements to create a database:

- conceptual schema
- logical schema
- physical schema

A *conceptual schema* is the most abstract of the three types of schemas in the preceding list. This schema includes high-level data constructs. A conceptual schema does not contain any SQL statements. It's "agnostic" and can be used as a "blueprint" for implementation in any RDBMS.

A *logical schema* (also known as a logical data model) contains the entities (tables and views), the attributes of the entities, and relationships among entities. Although a logical schema is a problem-specific schema, it is still database "agnostic." A logical schema is limited to the entities (and their relationships) that represent a particular problem.

Finally, a *physical schema* includes the information in a logical schema, along with its validation rules, stored procedures, and constraints. In fact, a physical schema is a SQL script that contains the complete definition of every entity (and relationships) in a database. A physical schema is the simplest way to "clone" an existing database and recreate an exact copy in another location.

OTHER RDBMS TOPICS

Performance tuning is an important task that involves many factors. One example that might seem counter-intuitive is determining whether you can improve performance by de-normalizing a table. In situations involving small tables, you can "pin" their contents in memory, which can speed up the lookup time for those tables because you avoid searching through a table that is in secondary storage. Indexes are easy to create, but knowing which indexes will be most effective is not necessarily obvious in every case.

Optimization strategies have changed from rule-based optimization to cost-based optimization, where the latter involves collecting data from one or more tables to determine how frequently specific tables are accessed (i.e., to identity potential patterns of data access).

Another important task involves setting up a schedule to automatically perform database backups (e.g., via cron jobs). Moreover, you need to know how to manually restore data from a backup in cases of lost or corrupted data.

Database upgrades can be straightforward for minor releases of a database, but upgrading to a major release might involve changes to fields in table definitions in a database schema.

In general, a test environment is set up to fully test the upgrade, and if all goes well, the production system can be switched over to the new release.

If you are serious about performance tuning (whether by choice or as part of your job), some useful tips for database tuning are available online:

https://www.tecmint.com/mysql-mariadb-performance-tuning-and-optimization

WORKING WITH NOSQL

NoSQL refers to non-SQL or non-relational database design that provides an organized way of storing data but not in tabular form. Specifically, NoSQL databases use a "collection" that is similar to an RDBMS table and a "document" that is analogous to a row in a table. Each collection can store multiple documents, so collections and documents have a one-to-many relationship. In general, a document is a JSON-based file that consists of field-value pairs.

Unlike relational databases, a MongoDB collection does not involve a schema or a specification for the set of name/value pairs in documents that are inserted into a database.

Moreover, documents that are inserted into a collection can have a variable number of fields, and no modifications are required for the database.

However, the flexible manner in which you can insert documents also means that there is no way to describe the name/value pairs of all the documents.

For simplicity, the documents in the code samples contain the same attributes, with different values for the attributes. In general, though, you will probably have documents with differing attributes.

The next step involves creating the `cellphones` database and then inserting a row into the database, which is discussed in the next section.

Create MongoDB Cellphones Collection

Start `Mongo` by typing the following command in a command shell (which you can run in the background if you are on a `MacBook`):

```
Mongo
```

After some diagnostic-like text is displayed, you can enter the `Mongo` shell by typing this command in another command shell:

```
Mongo
```

The preceding command displays the following information (and some text that has been omitted) and the `Mongo` prompt:

```
MongoDB shell version v4.4.3
connecting to: mongodb://127.0.0.1:27017/?compressors=disab
led&gssapiServiceName=mongodb
Implicit session: session { "id" : UUID("86bb60c7-d685-
46e1-802d-9874ce87b06c") }
MongoDB server version: 4.4.3
>
```

To create a `Mongo` database such as `cellphones`, you need to invoke the command "use cellphones" and then insert a row into the database, after which you will see the database displayed. The step-by-step instructions are described below.

After making sure that `Mongo` is running on your system and from the `Mongo` prompt type the `show dbs` command to display the current databases and you will see something like this:

```
> show dbs;
abc      0.000GB
admin    0.000GB
config   0.000GB
local    0.000GB
temp     0.000GB
```

The cellphones database will not appear in the preceding list until after you insert a document in the cellphones database.

Sample Queries in MongoDB

For simplicity, all documents in `cellphones` contain the attributes `year`, `os`, `model`, `color`, and `price`. Moreover, the sample values for these attributes are only samples and not necessarily accurate values.

An example of values for these attributes is `2017`, `android`, `pixel2`, `black`, and `320`. Create and insert a document with the preceding values as follows:

```
use cellphones;
db.cellphones.insertOne( { year: 2017, os: "android",
model: "pixel2", color: "black", price: 320 } )
```

The preceding command inserted a row into the newly created `cellphones` database. You will see the following output:

```
{
        "acknowledged" : true,
        "insertedId" : ObjectId("60773e2f098364be587c5b45")
}
```

Display the databases to see the following output:

```
> show dbs;
abc             0.000GB
admin           0.000GB
cellphones      0.000GB
config          0.000GB
local           0.000GB
temp            0.000GB
test            0.000GB
```

Display the available collections in the cellphones database with the following command:

```
> show collections;
cellphones
```

Now insert two more documents with the following commands:

```
db.cellphones.insertOne( { year: 2018, os: "android",
model: "pixel3", color: "black", price: 400 } )
db.cellphones.insertOne( { year: 2018, os: "iOS", model:
"iphone_xr", color: "black", price: 700 } )
```

Example 1: Display all the documents in `cellphones` with the following command:

```
> db.cellphones.find();
{ "_id" : ObjectId("60774182098364be587c5b47"), "year"
: 2017, "os" : "android", "model" : "pixel2", "color" :
"black", "price" : 320 }
{ "_id" : ObjectId("607746dd84549580deeecf42"), "year" :
2018, "os" : "android", "model" : "pixel3", "color" :
"black", "price" : 400 }
```

```
{ "_id" : ObjectId("607746e284549580deeecf43"), "year" :
2020, "os" : "iOS", "model" : "iphone_xr", "color" :
"black", "price" : 700 }
```

Example 2: Display all the documents for Android phones in the cellphones collection:

db.cellphones.find({os: "android"}).limit(2).pretty();

```
The preceding command displays the following output:
{
    "_id" : ObjectId("60774182098364be587c5b47"),
    "year" : 2017,
    "os" : "android",
    "model" : "pixel2",
    "color" : "black",
    "price" : 320
}
{
    "_id" : ObjectId("607746dd84549580deeecf42"),
    "year" : 2018,
    "os" : "android",
    "model" : "pixel3",
    "color" : "black",
    "price" : 400
}
```

The limit() function limits the number of rows that are returned in a query.

The pretty() function displays the output in a more aesthetically pleasing manner.

Example 3: Display the documents with cellphones made by Android in 2018 by specifying multiple comma-separated conditions (which indicate an "and" logic on the specified conditions):

> db.cellphones.find({os: "android", year: "2018"}).pretty();

The preceding command displays the following output:

```
{
    "_id"   : ObjectId("607746dd84549580deeecf42"),
    "year"  : 2018,
    "os"    : "android",
    "model" : "pixel3",
    "color" : "black",
    "price" : 400
}
```

This concludes the introduction to MongoDB. There are numerous additional operations that you can perform in MongoDB, such as updating and deleting documents, collections, and databases.

SUMMARY

This chapter introduced you to SQL and various types of SQL commands, such as DCL, DDL, and DML. Next, you learned how to create and populate tables in MySQL and various SQL statements for retrieving data from tables.

Then you saw how to define a JOIN statement on two tables, which can be extended to multiple tables. You also learned about keys and indexes for relational tables. In addition, you saw how to join tables and create views, followed by a description of keys and indexes.

Then you learned about entity relationships, such as one-to-many, many-to-many, and self-referential relationships, along with code samples that illustrated some of these entity relationships.

Next, you learned about database normalization, and a brief description of six normal forms in RDBMSes. You saw examples of Python scripts that read the content of a table into a Pandas data frame and saved the data frame as an Excel spreadsheet.

You learned about MongoDB, which is a popular NoSQL database that involves collections (similar to tables) that contain documents (sort of like rows in a table).

## CHAPTER 10

DATA VISUALIZATION

This chapter introduces data visualization, along with a wide-ranging collection of Python-based code samples that use various visualization tools (including Matplotlib and Seaborn) to render charts and graphs. In addition, this chapter contains Python code samples that combine Pandas, Matplotlib, and Sklearn built-in datasets.

Since the title of the chapter is data visualization, you might be wondering why this chapter contains an introduction to Sklearn (also known as Scikit-learn). The reason is the introduction to some Sklearn functionality is possible without a more formal learning process. In addition, this knowledge is useful if you decide to delve into machine learning (and perhaps this section will provide additional motivation to do so). However, a thorough understanding of Sklearn involves significantly more time and effort, especially if you plan to learn the details of the Sklearn machine learning algorithms. If you are not interested in learning about Sklearn at this point in time, you can skip this section.

The first part of this chapter briefly discusses data visualization, with a short list of some data visualization tools, and a list of various types of visualization (such as bar graphs and pie charts).

The second part of this chapter introduces you to Matplotlib, which is an open-source Python library that is modeled after MATLAB. This section also provides the Python code samples for the line graphs (horizontal, vertical, and diagonal) in the Euclidean plane that you saw in a previous chapter.

The third part of the chapter introduces you to Sklearn, which is a powerful Python library that supports many machine learning algorithms and visualization. If you are new to machine learning, fear not. *This section does not require a background in machine learning to understand the Python code samples.*

The fourth part of the chapter introduces you to Seaborn for data visualization, which is a layer above Matplotlib. Although Seaborn does not have all of the features that are available in Matplotlib, Seaborn provides an easier set of APIs for rendering charts and graphs.

The final portion of this chapter contains a very short introduction to Bokeh, along with a code sample that illustrates how to create artistic graphics effect with it.

WHAT IS DATA VISUALIZATION?

Data visualization refers to presenting data in a graphical manner, such as bar charts, line graphs, and heat maps. Big Data comprises massive amounts of data, which leverages data visualization tools to assist in making better decisions.

A key role for good data visualization is to tell a meaningful story, which in turn focuses on useful information that resides in datasets that can contain many data points (i.e., billions of rows of data). Another aspect of data visualization is its effectiveness. How well does it convey the trends that might exist in the dataset?

There are many open-source data visualization tools available, some of which are listed here:

- Matplotlib
- Seaborn
- Bokeh
- YellowBrick
- Tableau
- D3.js (JavaScript and SVG)

If you have not already done so, install the following Python libraries (using pip3) on your computer so that you can launch the code samples in this chapter:

```
pip3 install matplotlib
pip3 install seaborn
pip3 install bokeh
```

Types of Data Visualization

Bar graphs, line graphs, and pie charts are common ways to present data, and yet many other types exist, some of which are listed as follows:

- 2D/3D Area Chart
- Bar Chart
- Gantt Chart
- Heat Map
- Histogram
- Polar Area
- Scatterplot (2D or 3D)
- Timeline

The Python code samples in the next several sections illustrate how to perform visualization via rudimentary APIs from Matplotlib.

WHAT IS MATPLOTLIB?

Matplotlib is a plotting library that supports NumPy, SciPy, and toolkits such as wxPython (among others). Matplotlib supports only version 3 of Python: support for version 2 of Python was available only through 2020. Matplotlib is a multi-platform library that is built on NumPy arrays.

The plotting-related code samples in this chapter use Pyplot, which is a Matplotlib module that provides a MATLAB-like interface. Here is an example of using Pyplot (copied from *https://www.biorxiv.org/content/10.1101/120378v1. full.pdf*) to plot a smooth curve based on negative powers of Euler's constant e:

```
import matplotlib.pyplot as plt
import numpy as np

a = np.linspace(0, 10, 100)
b = np.exp(-a)
plt.plot(a, b)
plt.show()
```

The Python code samples for visualization in this chapter use primarily Matplotlib, along with some code samples that use Seaborn. The code samples that plot line segments use the equation of a (nonvertical) line in the plane: $y = m*x + b$, where m is the slope and b is the y-intercept.

Some code samples use NumPy APIs, such as `np.linspace()`, `np.array()`, `np.random.rand()`, and `np.ones()`, which are discussed in Chapter 3.

HORIZONTAL LINES IN MATPLOTLIB

Listing 10.1 shows the contents of `hlines1.py` that illustrate how to plot horizontal lines using Matplotlib. Recall that the equation of a nonvertical line in the 2D plane is $y = m*x + b$, where m is the slope of the line and b is the y-intercept of the line.

LISTING 10.1: hlines1.py

```
import numpy as np
import matplotlib.pyplot as plt

# top line
x1 = np.linspace(-5,5,num=200)
y1 = 4 + 0*x1

# middle line
x2 = np.linspace(-5,5,num=200)
y2 = 0 + 0*x2
```

```
# bottom line
x3 = np.linspace(-5,5,num=200)
y3 = -3 + 0*x3

plt.axis([-5, 5, -5, 5])
plt.plot(x1,y1)
plt.plot(x2,y2)
plt.plot(x3,y3)
plt.show()
```

Listing 10.1 uses the `np.linspace()` API to generate a list of 200 equally spaced numbers for the horizontal axis, all of which are between -5 and 5. The three lines defined via the variables y1, y2, and y3 are defined in terms of the variables x1, x2, and x3, respectively.

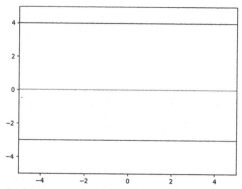

FIGURE 10.1 A graph of the three horizontal line segments whose equations are in Listing 10.1

SLANTED LINES IN MATPLOTLIB

Listing 10.2 shows the content of `diagonallines.py`, which illustrates how to plot slanted lines.

LISTING 10.2: diagonallines.py

```
import matplotlib.pyplot as plt
import numpy as np

x1 = np.linspace(-5,5,num=200)
y1 = x1

x2 = np.linspace(-5,5,num=200)
y2 = -x2

plt.axis([-5, 5, -5, 5])
plt.plot(x1,y1)
plt.plot(x2,y2)
plt.show()
```

Listing 10.2 defines two lines using the technique from Listing 10.1, except that these two lines define y1 = x1 and y2 = -x2, which produces slanted lines instead of horizontal lines.

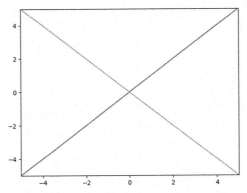

FIGURE 10.2: A graph of the two slanted line segments whose equations are in Listing 10.2

PARALLEL SLANTED LINES IN MATPLOTLIB

If two lines in the Euclidean plane have the same slope, then they are parallel. Listing 10.3 shows the contents of parallellines1.py that illustrate how to plot parallel slanted lines.

LISTING 10.3: parallellines1.py

```
import matplotlib.pyplot as plt
import numpy as np

# lower line
x1 = np.linspace(-5,5,num=200)
y1 = 2*x1

# upper line
x2 = np.linspace(-5,5,num=200)
y2 = 2*x2 + 3

# horizontal axis
x3 = np.linspace(-5,5,num=200)
y3 = 0*x3 + 0

# vertical axis
plt.axvline(x=0.0)

plt.axis([-5, 5, -10, 10])
plt.plot(x1,y1)
plt.plot(x2,y2)
plt.plot(x3,y3)
plt.show()
```

Listing 10.3 defines three lines using the technique that you saw in Listing 10.1, where these three lines are slanted and parallel to each other.

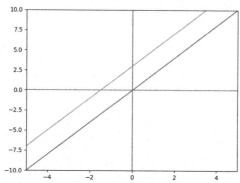

FIGURE 10.3: A graph of the two slanted, parallel line segments whose equations are in Listing 10.3

A GRID OF POINTS IN MATPLOTLIB

Listing 10.4 shows the contents of `plotgrid.py` that illustrate how to plot a simple grid.

LISTING 10.4: plotgrid.py

```
import numpy as np
from itertools import product
import matplotlib.pyplot as plt

points = np.array(list(product(range(3),range(4))))

plt.plot(points[:,0],points[:,1],'ro')
plt.show()
```

Listing 10.4 defines the NumPy variable `points` that defines a 2D list of points with three rows and four columns. The Pyplot API `plot()` uses the `points` variable to display a grid-like pattern.

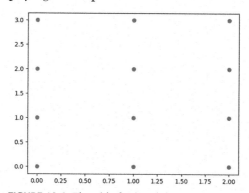

FIGURE 10.4: The grid of points defined in Listing 10.4

A DOTTED GRID IN MATPLOTLIB

Listing 10.5 shows the content of `plotdottedgrid1.py`, which illustrates how to plot a "dotted" grid pattern.

LISTING 10.5: plotdottedgrid1.py

```python
import numpy as np
import pylab
from itertools import product
import matplotlib.pyplot as plt

fig = pylab.figure()
ax = fig.add_subplot(1,1,1)

ax.grid(which='major', axis='both', linestyle='--')

[line.set_zorder(3) for line in ax.lines]
fig.show() # to update

plt.gca().xaxis.grid(True)
plt.show()
```

Listing 10.5 is similar to the code in Listing 10.4 in that both of them plot a grid-like pattern; however, Listing 10.5 renders a "dotted" grid pattern whereas Listing 10.4 renders a rectangular grid of points by specifying the value -- for the `linestyle` parameter.

The next portion of Listing 10.5 invokes the `set_zorder()` method that controls which items are displayed on top of other items, such as dots on top of lines or vice versa. The final portion of Listing 10.5 invokes the `gca().xaxis.grid(True)` chained methods to display the vertical grid lines.

You can also use the `plt.style` directive to specify a style for figures. The following code snippet specifies the classic style of Matplotlib:

```python
plt.style.use('classic')
```

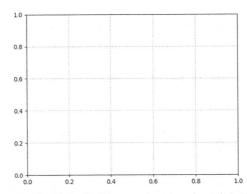

FIGURE 10.5: The "dashed" grid pattern based on the code in Listing 10.5

LINES IN A GRID IN MATPLOTLIB

Listing 10.6 shows the contents of `plotlinegrid2.py` that illustrate how to plot lines in a grid.

LISTING 10.6: plotlinegrid2.py

```
import numpy as np
import pylab
from itertools import product
import matplotlib.pyplot as plt

fig = plt.figure()
graph = fig.add_subplot(1,1,1)
graph.grid(which='major', linestyle='-', linewidth='0.5',
color='red')

x1 = np.linspace(-5,5,num=200)
y1 = 1*x1
graph.plot(x1,y1, 'r-o')

x2 = np.linspace(-5,5,num=200)
y2 = -x2
graph.plot(x2,y2, 'b-x')

fig.show() # to update
plt.show()
```

Listing 10.6 includes the NumPy variable `points` that defines a 2D list of points with three rows and four columns. The Pyplot API `plot()` uses the `points` variable to display a grid-like pattern.

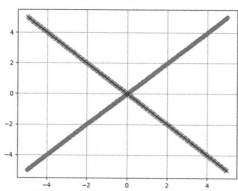

FIGURE 10.6: The set of "dashed" line segments whose equations are in Listing 10.6

A COLORED GRID IN MATPLOTLIB

Listing 10.7 shows the content of `plotgrid2.py`, which illustrates how to display a colored grid.

LISTING 10.7: plotgrid2.py

```
import matplotlib.pyplot as plt
from matplotlib import colors
import numpy as np

data = np.random.rand(10, 10) * 20

# create discrete colormap
cmap = colors.ListedColormap(['red', 'blue'])
bounds = [0,10,20]
norm = colors.BoundaryNorm(bounds, cmap.N)

fig, ax = plt.subplots()
ax.imshow(data, cmap=cmap, norm=norm)

# draw gridlines
ax.grid(which='major', axis='both', linestyle='-',
color='k', linewidth=2)
ax.set_xticks(np.arange(-.5, 10, 1));
ax.set_yticks(np.arange(-.5, 10, 1));

plt.show()
```

Listing 10.7 defines the NumPy variable `data` that defines a 2D set of points with ten rows and ten columns. The Pyplot API `plot()` uses the `data` variable to display a colored grid-like pattern.

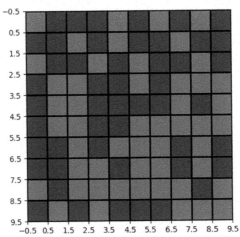

FIGURE 10.7: The colored grid whose equations are contained in Listing 10.7

A COLORED SQUARE IN AN UNLABELED GRID IN MATPLOTLIB

Listing 10.8 shows the contents of `plotgrid3.py` that illustrate how to display a colored square inside a grid.

LISTING 10.8: plotgrid3.py

```
import matplotlib.pyplot as plt
import numpy as np
from itertools import product
import Matplotlib.pyplot as plt
import Matplotlib.colors as colors

N = 15
# create an empty data set
data = np.ones((N, N)) * np.nan

# fill in some fake data
for j in range(3)[::-1]:
    data[N//2 - j : N//2 + j +1, N//2 - j : N//2 + j +1] = j

# make a figure + axes
fig, ax = plt.subplots(1, 1, tight_layout=True)

# make color map
my_cmap = colors.ListedColormap(['r', 'g', 'b'])

# set the 'bad' values (nan) to be white and transparent
my_cmap.set_bad(color='w', alpha=0)

# draw the grid
for x in range(N + 1):
    ax.axhline(x, lw=2, color='k', zorder=5)
    ax.axvline(x, lw=2, color='k', zorder=5)

# draw the boxes
ax.imshow(data, interpolation='none', cmap=my_cmap,
extent=[0, N, 0, N], zorder=0)

# turn off the axis labels
ax.axis('off')
plt.show()
```

Listing 10.8 defines the NumPy variable data that defines an N×N set of 2D points, followed by a for loop that initializes the variable data as a 15×15 array of NaN values. The Pyplot API plot() uses the data variable to display a colored square inside a grid-like pattern.

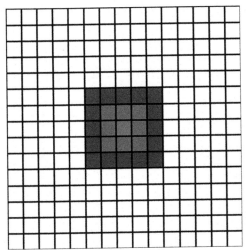

FIGURE 10.8: The colored square in a grid whose equations are in Listing 10.8

RANDOMIZED DATA POINTS IN MATPLOTLIB

Listing 10.9 shows the contents of lin_reg_plot.py that illustrate how to plot a graph of random points.

LISTING 10.9: lin_plot_reg.py

```
import numpy as np
import matplotlib.pyplot as plt

trX = np.linspace(-1, 1, 101) # Linear space of 101 and
[-1,1]

#Create the y function based on the x axis
trY = 2*trX + np.random.randn(*trX.shape)*0.4+0.2

#create figure and scatter plot of the random points
plt.figure()
plt.scatter(trX,trY)

# Draw one line with the line function
plt.plot (trX, .2 + 2 * trX)
plt.show()
```

Listing 10.9 defines the NumPy variable trX that contains 101 equally spaced numbers that are between -1 and 1 (inclusive). The variable trY is defined in two parts: The first part is 2*trX and the second part is a random value that is partially based on the length of the one-dimensional array trX. The variable trY is the sum of these two "parts," which creates a "fuzzy" line segment. The next portion of Listing 10.9 creates a scatterplot based on the values in trX and trY, followed by the Pyplot API plot() that renders a line segment.

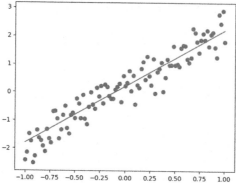

FIGURE 10.9 A random set of points based on the code in Listing 10.9

A HISTOGRAM IN MATPLOTLIB

Listing 10.10 shows the content of `histogram1.py`, which illustrates how to plot a histogram using Matplotlib.

LISTING 10.10: histogram1.py

```
import numpy as np
import Matplotlib.pyplot as plt

max1 = 500
max2 = 500

appl_count = 28 + 4 * np.random.randn(max1)
bana_count = 24 + 4 * np.random.randn(max2)

plt.hist([appl_count, appl_count],stacked=True,
color=['r','b'])
plt.show()
```

Listing 10.10 shows the NumPy variables `appl_count` and `bana_count` contain a random set of values whose upper bound is `max1` and `max2`, respectively. The Pyplot API `hist()` uses the points `appl_count` and `bana_count` in order to display a histogram.

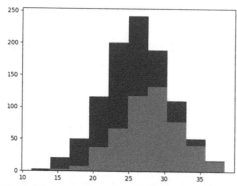

FIGURE 10.10: The histogram whose shape is based on the code in Listing 10.10

A SET OF LINE SEGMENTS IN MATPLOTLIB

Listing 10.11 shows the contents of line_segments.py that illustrate how to plot a set of connected line segments in Matplotlib.

LISTING 10.11: line_segments.py

```
import numpy as np
import matplotlib.pyplot as plt

x = [7,11,13,15,17,19,23,29,31,37]

plt.plot(x) # OR: plt.plot(x, 'ro-') or bo
plt.ylabel('Height')
plt.xlabel('Weight')
plt.show()
```

Listing 10.11 defines the array x that contains a hard-coded set of values. The Pyplot API plot() uses the variable x to display a set of connected line segments.

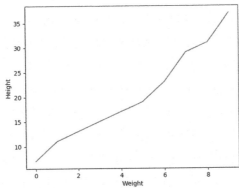

FIGURE 10.11: The set of connected line segments the result of launching the code in Listing 10.11

PLOTTING MULTIPLE LINES IN MATPLOTLIB

Listing 10.12 shows the contents of plt_array2.py that illustrate the ease with which you can plot multiple lines in Matplotlib.

LISTING 10.12: plt_array2.py

```
import matplotlib.pyplot as plt

x = [7,11,13,15,17,19,23,29,31,37]
data = [[8, 4, 1], [5, 3, 3], [6, 0, 2], [1, 7, 9]]
plt.plot(data, 'd-')
plt.show()
```

Listing 10.12 defines the array data that contains a hard-coded set of values. The Pyplot API plot() uses the variable data to display a line segment.

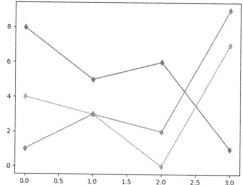

FIGURE 10.12: Multiple lines based on the code in Listing 10.12

TRIGONOMETRIC FUNCTIONS IN MATPLOTLIB

You can display the graph of trigonometric functions as easily as you can render "regular" graphs using Matplotlib. Listing 10.13 shows the contents of sincos.py that illustrate how to plot a sine function and a cosine function in Matplotlib.

LISTING 10.13: sincos.py

```
import numpy as np
import math

x = np.linspace(0, 2*math.pi, 101)
s = np.sin(x)
c = np.cos(x)

import matplotlib.pyplot as plt
plt.plot (s)
plt.plot (c)
plt.show ()
```

Listing 10.13 defines the NumPy variables x, s, and c using the NumPy APIs linspace(), sin(), and cos(), respectively. Next, the Pyplot API plot() uses these variables to display a sine function and a cosine function.

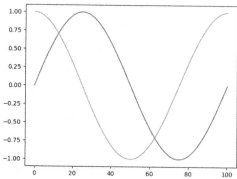

FIGURE 10.13: Sine and cosine functions based on the code in Listing 10.13

DISPLAY IQ SCORES IN MATPLOTLIB

Listing 10.14 shows the content of `iq_scores.py`, which illustrates how to plot a histogram that displays IQ scores (based on a normal distribution).

LISTING 10.14: iq_scores.py

```
import numpy as npf
import matplotlib.pyplot as plt

mu, sigma = 100, 15
x = mu + sigma * np.random.randn(10000)

# the histogram of the data
n, bins, patches = plt.hist(x, 50, normed=1, facecolor='g',
alpha=0.75)

plt.xlabel('Intelligence')
plt.ylabel('Probability')
plt.title('Histogram of IQ')
plt.text(60, .025, r'$\mu=100,\ \sigma=15$')
plt.axis([40, 160, 0, 0.03])
plt.grid(True)
plt.show()
```

Listing 10.14 defines the scalar variables `mu` and `sigma`, followed by the NumPy variable `x` that contains a random set of points. Next, the variables `n`, `bins`, and `patches` are initialized via the return values of the NumPy `hist()` API. Finally, these points are plotted via the usual `plot()` API to display a histogram.

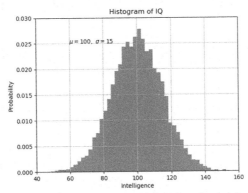

FIGURE 10.14: The histogram whose shape is based on the code in Listing 10.14

PLOT A BEST-FITTING LINE IN MATPLOTLIB

Listing 10.15 shows the contents of `plot_best_fit.py` that illustrate how to plot a best-fitting line in Matplotlib.

LISTING 10.15: plot_best_fit.py

```
import numpy as np

xs = np.array([1,2,3,4,5], dtype=np.float64)
ys = np.array([1,2,3,4,5], dtype=np.float64)

def best_fit_slope(xs,ys):
    m = (((np.mean(xs)*np.mean(ys))-np.mean(xs*ys)) /
         ((np.mean(xs)**2) - np.mean(xs**2)))
    b = np.mean(ys) - m * np.mean(xs)

    return m, b

m,b = best_fit_slope(xs,ys)
print('m:',m,'b:',b)

regression_line = [(m*x)+b for x in xs]

import matplotlib.pyplot as plt
from matplotlib import style
style.use('ggplot')

plt.scatter(xs,ys,color='#0000FF')
plt.plot(xs, regression_line)
plt.show()
```

Listing 10.15 defines the NumPy array variables xs and ys that are "fed" into the Python function best_fit_slope() that calculates the slope m and the y-intercept b for the best-fitting line. The Pyplot API scatter() displays a scatterplot of the points xs and ys, followed by the plot() API that displays the best-fitting line.

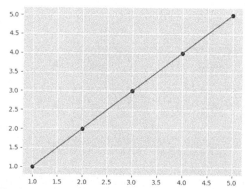

FIGURE 10.15: A simple line based on the code in Listing 10.15

This concludes the portion of the chapter regarding NumPy and Matplotlib. The next section introduces you to Sklearn, which is a powerful Python-based library that supports many algorithms for machine learning. After you have read the short introduction, subsequent sections contain Python code samples that combine Pandas, Matplotlib, and Sklearn built-in datasets.

INTRODUCTION TO SKLEARN (SCIKIT-LEARN)

Sklearn (which is installed as sklearn) is Python's premier general-purpose machine learning library:

https://scikit-learn.org/stable/

Sklearn is an immensely useful Python library that supports a number of machine learning algorithms. In particular, Sklearn supports many classification algorithms, such as logistic regression, naive Bayes, decision trees, random forests, and SVMs (support vector machines). Although entire books are available that are dedicated to Sklearn, this chapter contains only a few pages of Sklearn material. If you have "how to" questions involving Sklearn, you can almost always find suitable answers on stackoverflow.

Sklearn is well-suited for classification tasks as well as regression and clustering tasks in machine learning. Sklearn supports a vast collection of machine learning algorithms including linear regression, logistic regression, kNN ("K Nearest Neighbor"), kMeans, decision trees, random forests, MLPs (multi-layer perceptrons), and SVMs.

Moreover, Sklearn supports dimensionality reduction techniques such as PCA, "hyper parameter" tuning, and methods for scaling data; it is suitable for preprocessing data and cross-validation.

ML code samples often contain a combination of Sklearn, NumPy, Pandas, and Matplotlib. In addition, Sklearn provides various built-in datasets that we can display visually. One of those datasets is the Digits dataset, which is the topic of the next section.

The next section of this chapter provides several Python code samples that contain a combination of Pandas, Matplotlib, and the Sklearn built-in Digits dataset.

THE DIGITS DATASET IN SKLEARN

The Digits dataset in Sklearn comprises 1,797 small 8×8 images. Each image is a handwritten digit, which is also the case for the MNIST dataset. Listing 10.16 shows the content of load_digits1.py, which illustrates how to plot the Digits dataset.

LISTING 10.16: load_digits1.py

```
from sklearn import datasets

# Load in the 'digits' data
digits = datasets.load_digits()

# Print the 'digits' data
print(digits)
```

In Listing 10.16, after importing the `datasets` module, the variable `digits` is initialized with the contents of the Digits dataset. The `print()` statement displays the contents of the `digits` variable, which is displayed here:

```
{images': array(
        [[[0.,    0.,    5.,  ...,     1.,    0.,    0.],
          [0.,    0.,   13.,  ...,    15.,    5.,    0.],
          [0.,    3.,   15.,  ...,    11.,    8.,    0.],
          ...,
          [0.,    4.,   11.,  ...,    12.,    7.,    0.],
          [0.,    2.,   14.,  ...,    12.,    0.,    0.],
          [0.,    0.,    6.,  ...,     0.,    0.,    0.]]]),
'target': array([0, 1, 2,  ...,  8, 9, 8]), 'frame': None,
'feature_names': ['pixel_0_0', 'pixel_0_1', 'pixel_0_2',
'pixel_0_3', 'pixel_0_4', 'pixel_0_5', 'pixel_0_6',
'pixel_0_7', 'pixel_1_0', 'pixel_1_1', 'pixel_1_2',
'pixel_1_3', 'pixel_1_4', 'pixel_1_5', 'pixel_1_6',
'pixel_1_7', 'pixel_2_0', 'pixel_2_1', 'pixel_2_2',
'pixel_2_3', 'pixel_2_4', 'pixel_2_5', 'pixel_2_6',
'pixel_2_7', 'pixel_3_0', 'pixel_3_1', 'pixel_3_2',
'pixel_3_3', 'pixel_3_4', 'pixel_3_5', 'pixel_3_6',
'pixel_3_7', 'pixel_4_0', 'pixel_4_1', 'pixel_4_2',
'pixel_4_3', 'pixel_4_4', 'pixel_4_5', 'pixel_4_6',
'pixel_4_7', 'pixel_5_0', 'pixel_5_1', 'pixel_5_2',
'pixel_5_3', 'pixel_5_4', 'pixel_5_5', 'pixel_5_6',
'pixel_5_7', 'pixel_6_0', 'pixel_6_1', 'pixel_6_2',
'pixel_6_3', 'pixel_6_4', 'pixel_6_5', 'pixel_6_6',
'pixel_6_7', 'pixel_7_0', 'pixel_7_1', 'pixel_7_2',
'pixel_7_3', 'pixel_7_4', 'pixel_7_5', 'pixel_7_6',
'pixel_7_7'], 'target_names': array([0, 1, 2, 3, 4, 5, 6,
                7, 8, 9]), 'images': array([[[ 0.,    0.,    5.,
                ...,    1.,    0.,    0.],
        [ 0.,    0.,   13.,  ...,    15.,    5.,    0.],
        [ 0.,    3.,   15.,  ...,    11.,    8.,    0.],
// data omitted for brevity
])}
```

Listing 10.17 shows the contents of `load_digits2.py` that illustrates how to plot one of the `Digits` datasets (which you can change in order to display a different digit).

LISTING 10.17: load_digits2.py

```python
from sklearn.datasets import load_digits
from matplotlib import pyplot as plt

digits = load_digits()
#set interpolation='none'

fig = plt.figure(figsize=(3, 3))
plt.imshow(digits['images'][66], cmap="gray",
interpolation='none')
plt.show()
```

Listing 10.17 imports the `load_digits` class from Sklearn to initialize the variable `digits` with the contents of the Digits dataset. The next portion of Listing 10.17 initializes the variable `fig` and invokes the method `imshow()` of the `plt` class to display a number in the Digits dataset.

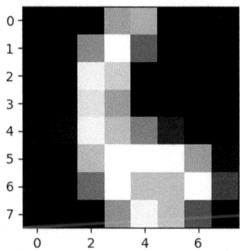

FIGURE 10.16: A plot of one of the digits in the Digits dataset based on the code in Listing 10.17

Listing 10.18 shows the content of `sklearn_digits.py`, which illustrates how to access the Digits dataset in Sklearn.

LISTING 10.18: sklearn_digits.py

```
from sklearn import datasets

digits = datasets.load_digits()
print("digits shape:",digits.images.shape)
print("data    shape:",digits.data.shape)

n_samples, n_features = digits.data.shape
print("(samples,features):", (n_samples, n_features))

import matplotlib.pyplot as plt
#plt.imshow(digits.images[-1], cmap=plt.cm.gray_r)
#plt.show()

plt.imshow(digits.images[0], cmap=plt.cm.binary,
interpolation='nearest')
plt.show()
```

Listing 10.18 starts with one `import` statement followed by the variable `digits` that contains the Digits dataset. The output from Listing 10.18 is here:

```
digits shape: (1797, 8, 8)
data    shape: (1797, 64)
(samples,features): (1797, 64)
```

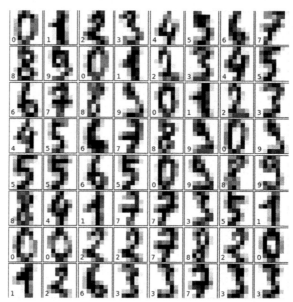

FIGURE 10.17: The images in the Digits dataset based on the code in Listing 10.18

THE IRIS DATASET IN SKLEARN (1)

Listing 10.19 shows the contents of `sklearn_iris.py` that illustrate how to access the Iris dataset in Sklearn.

In addition to support for machine learning algorithms, Sklearn provides various built-in datasets that you can access with one line of code. Listing 10.19 shows the contents of `sklearn_iris1.py` that illustrate how you can easily load the Iris dataset and display its contents.

LISTING 10.19: sklearn_iris1.py

```
import numpy as np
from sklearn.datasets import load_iris

iris = load_iris()

print("=> iris keys:")
for key in iris.keys():
  print(key)
print()

#print("iris dimensions:")
#print(iris.shape)
#print()

print("=> iris feature names:")
for feature in iris.feature_names:
  print(feature)
print()
```

```
X = iris.data[:, [2, 3]]
y = iris.target
print('=> Class labels:', np.unique(y))
print()

print("=> target:")
print(iris.target)
print()

print("=> all data:")
print(iris.data)
```

Listing 10.19 contains several import statements and then initializes the variable iris with the Iris dataset. Next, a for loop displays the keys in the dataset, followed by another for loop that displays the feature names.

The next portion of Listing 10.19 initializes the variable X with the feature values in columns 2 and 3, and then initializes the variable y with the values of the target column.

Launch the code in Listing 10.19 to see the following output (truncated to save space):

```
Pandas df1:

=> iris keys:
data
target
target_names
DESCR
feature_names
filename

=> iris feature names:
sepal length (cm)
sepal width (cm)
petal length (cm)
petal width (cm)

=> Class labels: [0 1 2]

=> x_min: 0.5 x_max: 7.4
=> y_min: -0.4 y_max: 3.0

=> target:
[0 0 0 0 0 0 0 0 0 0 0 0 0 0 0 0 0 0 0 0 0 0 0 0 0 0 0 0 0 0
 0 0 0 0 0 0 0 0
 0 0 0 0 0 0 0 0 0 0 0 0 1 1 1 1 1 1 1 1 1 1 1 1 1 1 1 1 1 1
 1 1 1 1 1 1 1 1
 1 1 1 1 1 1 1 1 1 1 1 1 1 1 1 1 1 1 1 1 1 1 1 1 1 1 1 2 2 2
 2 2 2 2 2 2 2 2
 2 2 2 2 2 2 2 2 2 2 2 2 2 2 2 2 2 2 2 2 2 2 2 2 2 2 2 2 2 2
 2 2 2 2 2 2 2 2 2 2]

=> all data:
[[5.1 3.5 1.4 0.2]
```

```
[4.9 3.  1.4 0.2]
[4.7 3.2 1.3 0.2]
// details omitted for brevity
[6.5 3.  5.2 2.0]
[6.2 3.4 5.4 2.3]
[5.9 3.  5.1 1.8]]
```

Sklearn, Pandas, and the Iris Dataset

Listing 10.20 shows the contents of pandas_iris.py that illustrate how to load the contents of the Iris dataset (from Sklearn) into a Pandas data frame.

LISTING 10.20: pandas_iris.py

```
import numpy as np
import pandas as pd
from sklearn.datasets import load_iris

iris = load_iris()

print("=> IRIS feature names:")
for feature in iris.feature_names:
  print(feature)
print()

# Create a dataframe with the feature variables
df = pd.DataFrame(iris.data, columns=iris.feature_names)

print("=> number of rows:")
print(len(df))
print()

print("=> number of columns:")
print(len(df.columns))
print()

print("=> number of rows and columns:")
print(df.shape)
print()

print("=> number of elements:")
print(df.size)
print()

print("=> IRIS details:")
print(df.info())
print()

print("=> top five rows:")
print(df.head())
print()

X = iris.data[:, [2, 3]]
y = iris.target
print('=> Class labels:', np.unique(y))
```

Listing 10.20 contains several `import` statements and then initializes the variable `iris` with the Iris dataset. Next, a `for` loop displays the feature names. The next code snippet initializes the variable `df` as a Pandas data frame that contains the data from the Iris dataset.

The next block of code invokes some attributes and methods of a Pandas `dataframe` to display the number of rows, columns, and elements in the `dataframe`, as well as the details of the Iris dataset, the first five rows, and the unique labels in the Iris dataset. Launch the code in Listing 10.20 to see the following output:

```
=> IRIS feature names:
sepal length (cm)
sepal width (cm)
petal length (cm)
petal width (cm)

=> number of rows:
150

=> number of columns:
4

=> number of rows and columns:
(150, 4)

=> number of elements:
600

=> IRIS details:
<class 'pandas.core.frame.DataFrame'>
RangeIndex: 150 entries, 0 to 149
Data columns (total 4 columns):
sepal length (cm)    150 non-null float64
sepal width (cm)     150 non-null float64
petal length (cm)    150 non-null float64
petal width (cm)     150 non-null float64
dtypes: float64(4)
memory usage: 4.8 KB
None

=> top five rows:
    sepal length (cm)  sepal width (cm)  petal length (cm)  petal width (cm)
0                 5.1               3.5                1.4                0.2
1                 4.9               3.0                1.4                0.2
2                 4.7               3.2                1.3                0.2
3                 4.6               3.1                1.5                0.2
4                 5.0               3.6                1.4                0.2

=> Class labels: [0 1 2]
```

THE IRIS DATASET IN SKLEARN (2)

The Iris dataset in Sklearn consists of the lengths of three different types of Iris-based petals and sepals: Setosa, Versicolor, and Virginica. These numeric values are stored in a 150×4 NumPy.ndarray.

Note that the rows in the Iris dataset are the sample images, and the columns consist of the values for the Sepal Length, Sepal Width, Petal Length, and Petal Width of each image. Listing 10.21 shows the contents of sklearn_iris2.py that illustrate how to display detailed information about the Iris dataset and a chart that displays the distributions of the four features.

LISTING 10.21: sklearn_iris2.py

```
from sklearn import datasets
from sklearn.model_selection import train_test_split

iris = datasets.load_iris()
data = iris.data

print("iris data shape:  ",data.shape)
print("iris target shape:",iris.target.shape)
print("first 5 rows iris:")
print(data[0:5])
print("keys:",iris.keys())
print("")

n_samples, n_features = iris.data.shape
print('Number of samples: ', n_samples)
print('Number of features:', n_features)
print("")

print("sepal length/width and petal length/width:")
print(iris.data[0])

import numpy as np
np.bincount(iris.target)

print("target names:",iris.target_names)

print("mean: %s " % data.mean(axis=0))
print("std:  %s " % data.std(axis=0))

#print("mean: %s " % data.mean(axis=1))
#print("std:  %s " % data.std(axis=1))

# load the data into train and test datasets:
X_train, X_test, y_train, y_test = train_test_split(iris.
data, iris.target, random_state=0)

from sklearn.preprocessing import StandardScaler
scaler = StandardScaler()
scaler.fit(X_train)
```

```
# rescale the train datasest:
X_train_scaled = scaler.transform(X_train)
print("X_train_scaled shape:",X_train_scaled.shape)

print("mean : %s " % X_train_scaled.mean(axis=0))
print("standard deviation : %s " % X_train_scaled.
std(axis=0))

import matplotlib.pyplot as plt

x_index = 3
colors = ['blue', 'red', 'green']

for label, color in zip(range(len(iris.target_names)),
colors):
  plt.hist(iris.data[iris.target==label, x_index],
          label=iris.target_names[label],
          color=color)

plt.xlabel(iris.feature_names[x_index])
plt.legend(loc='upper right')
plt.show()
```

Listing 10.21 starts with an `import` statement followed by the variables `iris` and `data`, where the latter contains the Iris dataset. The first half of Listing 10.21 consists of self-explanatory code, such as displaying the number of images and the number of features in the Iris dataset.

The second portion of Listing 10.21 imports the `StandardScaler` class in Sklearn, which rescales each value in `X_train` by subtracting the mean and then dividing by the standard deviation. The final block of code in Listing 10.21 generates a histogram that displays some of the images in the Iris dataset. The output from Listing 10.26 is as follows:

```
iris data shape:    (150, 4)
iris target shape: (150,)
first 5 rows iris:
[[5.1 3.5 1.4 0.2]
 [4.9 31.4 0.2]
 [4.7 3.2 1.3 0.2]
 [4.6 3.1 1.5 0.2]
 [53.6 1.4 0.2]]
keys: dict_keys(['target', 'target_names', 'data',
'feature_names', 'DESCR'])

Number of samples:  150
Number of features: 4

sepal length/width and petal length/width:
[5.1 3.5 1.4 0.2]
target names: ['setosa' 'versicolor' 'virginica']
mean: [5.84333333 3.054       3.75866667 1.19866667]
std:  [0.82530129 0.43214658 1.75852918 0.76061262]
X_train_scaled shape: (112, 4)
```

```
mean : [ 1.21331516e-15 -4.41115398e-17   7.13714802e-17
2.57730345e-17]
standard deviation : [1. 1. 1. 1.]
```

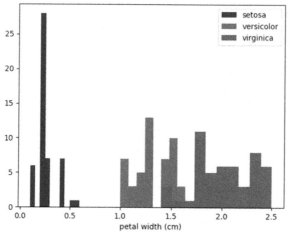

FIGURE 10.18: The images in the Iris dataset based on the code in Listing 10.21

THE FACES DATASET IN SKLEARN (OPTIONAL)

The Olivetti Faces dataset contains a set of face images that were taken between April 1992 and April 1994 at AT&T Laboratories Cambridge. As you will see in Listing 10.22, the `Sklearn.datasets.fetch_olivetti_faces` function is the data fetching and caching function that downloads the data archive from AT&T.

Listing 10.22 shows the code from `sklearn_faces.py` that displays the contents of the Faces dataset in Sklearn.

LISTING 10.22: sklearn_faces.py

```python
import sklearn
from sklearn.datasets import fetch_olivetti_faces

faces = fetch_olivetti_faces()

import matplotlib.pyplot as plt

# display figures in inches
fig = plt.figure(figsize=(6, 6))
fig.subplots_adjust(left=0, right=1, bottom=0, top=1,
hspace=0.05, wspace=0.05)

# plot the faces:
for i in range(64):
  ax = fig.add_subplot(8, 8, i + 1, xticks=[], yticks=[])
  ax.imshow(faces.images[i], cmap=plt.cm.bone,
interpolation='nearest')

plt.show()
```

Listing 10.22 starts with `import` statements and then initializes the variable `faces` with the contents of the Faces dataset. The next portion of Listing 10.22 contains some plot-related code, followed by a `for` loop that displays 64 images in an 8×8 grid pattern (similar to an earlier code sample).

Launch Listing 10.22 to see the image in Figure 10.19.

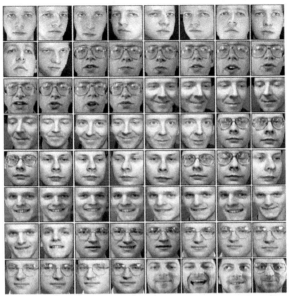

FIGURE 10.19: The plotted image from the Olivetti Faces dataset using the code from Listing 10.22

This concludes the portion of the chapter pertaining to Sklearn. Now let's turn our attention to Seaborn, which is a data visualization package for Python.

WORKING WITH SEABORN

Seaborn is a Python package for data visualization that provides a high-level interface to Matplotlib. Seaborn is easier to work with than Matplotlib, and actually extends Matplotlib, but Seaborn is not as powerful as Matplotlib.

Seaborn addresses two challenges of Matplotlib. The first involves the default Matplotlib parameters. Seaborn works with different parameters, which provide greater flexibility than the default rendering of Matplotlib plots. Seaborn addresses the limitations of the Matplotlib default values for features such as colors, tick marks on the upper and right axes, and style (among others).

In addition, Seaborn makes it easier to plot entire data frames (somewhat like Pandas) than doing so in Matplotlib. Nevertheless, since Seaborn extends Matplotlib, knowledge of the latter is advantageous and will simplify your learning curve.

Features of Seaborn

Some of the features of Seaborn include the following:

- scale Seaborn plots
- set the plot style
- set the figure size
- rotate label text
- set xlim or ylim
- set log scale
- add titles

Some very useful Seaborn methods are displayed below:

```
plt.xlabel()
plt.ylabel()
plt.annotate()
plt.legend()
plt.ylim()
plt.savefig()
```

Seaborn supports built-in datasets, just like NumPy and Pandas, including the Iris dataset and the Titanic dataset, both of which you will see in subsequent sections. As a starting point, the three-line code sample in the next section shows you how to display the rows in the built-in "Tips" dataset.

SEABORN BUILT-IN DATASETS

Listing 10.23 shows the contents of `seaborn_tips.py` that illustrate how to read the Tips dataset into a `dataframe` and display the first five rows of the dataset.

LISTING 10.23: seaborn_tips.py

```
import seaborn as sns
df = sns.load_dataset("tips")
print(df.head())
```

In Listing 10.23, after importing Seaborn, the variable `df` is initialized with the data in the built-in dataset Tips, and the `print()` statement displays the first five rows of `df`. Note that the `load_dataset()` API searches for online or built-in datasets. The output from Listing 10.23 is as follows:

```
   total_bill   tip     sex smoker  day    time  size
0       16.99  1.01  Female     No  Sun  Dinner     2
1       10.34  1.66    Male     No  Sun  Dinner     3
2       21.01  3.50    Male     No  Sun  Dinner     3
3       23.68  3.31    Male     No  Sun  Dinner     2
4       24.59  3.61  Female     No  Sun  Dinner     4
```

THE IRIS DATASET IN SEABORN

Listing 10.24 shows the contents of `seaborn_iris.py` that illustrate how to plot the Iris dataset.

LISTING 10.24: seaborn_iris.py

```
import seaborn as sns
import Matplotlib.pyplot as plt

# Load iris data
iris = sns.load_dataset("iris")

# Construct iris plot
sns.swarmplot(x="species", y="petal_length", data=iris)

# Show plot
plt.show()
```

Listing 10.24 imports `Seaborn` and `Matplotlib.pyplot` and then initializes the variable `iris` with the contents of the built-in `Iris` dataset. Next, the `swamplot()` API displays a graph with the horizontal axis labeled `species` and the vertical axis labeled `petal_length`, and the displayed points are from the Iris dataset.

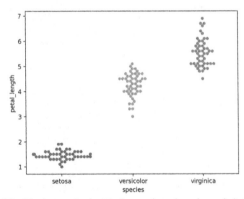

FIGURE 10.20: The images in the Iris dataset based on the code in Listing 10.24

THE TITANIC DATASET IN SEABORN

Listing 10.25 shows the contents of `seaborn_titanic_plot.py` that illustrate how to plot the Titanic dataset.

LISTING 10.25: seaborn_titanic_plot.py

```
import matplotlib.pyplot as plt
import seaborn as sns

titanic = sns.load_dataset("titanic")
```

```
g = sns.factorplot("class", "survived", "sex",
data=titanic, kind="bar", palette="muted", legend=False)

plt.show()
```

Listing 10.25 contains the same import statements as Listing 10.24, and then initializes the variable titanic with the contents of the built-in Titanic dataset. Next, the factorplot() API displays a graph with dataset attributes that are listed in the API invocation.

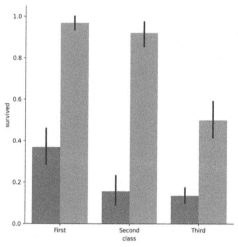

FIGURE 10.21: A plot of the data in the Titanic dataset based on the code in Listing 10.25

EXTRACTING DATA FROM THE TITANIC DATASET IN SEABORN (1)

Listing 10.26 shows the contents of seaborn_titanic.py that illustrate how to extract subsets of data from the Titanic dataset.

LISTING 10.26: seaborn_titanic.py

```
import matplotlib.pyplot as plt
import seaborn as sns

titanic = sns.load_dataset("titanic")
print("titanic info:")
titanic.info()

print("first five rows of titanic:")
print(titanic.head())

print("first four ages:")
print(titanic.loc[0:3,'age'])

print("fifth passenger:")
print(titanic.iloc[4])

#print("first five ages:")
```

```
#print(titanic['age'].head())

#print("first five ages and gender:")
#print(titanic[['age','sex']].head())

#print("descending ages:")
#print(titanic.sort_values('age', ascending = False).
head())

#print("older than 50:")
#print(titanic[titanic['age'] > 50])

#print("embarked (unique):")
#print(titanic['embarked'].unique())

#print("survivor counts:")
#print(titanic['survived'].value_counts())

#print("counts per class:")
#print(titanic['pclass'].value_counts())

#print("max/min/mean/median ages:")
#print(titanic['age'].max())
#print(titanic['age'].min())
#print(titanic['age'].mean())
#print(titanic['age'].median())
```

Listing 10.26 contains the same import statements as Listing 10.25, and then
initializes the variable titanic with the contents of the built-in Titanic dataset. The next portion of Listing 10.26 displays various aspects of the Titanic
dataset, such as its structure, the first five rows, the first four ages, and the
details of the fifth passenger.

There is a large block of "commented out" code that you can uncomment
to see the associated output, such as age, gender, persons over 50, and unique
rows. The output from Listing 10.26 is as follows:

```
#print(titanic['age'].mean())
titanic info:
<class 'pandas.core.frame.DataFrame'>
RangeIndex: 891 entries, 0 to 890
Data columns (total 15 columns):
survived       891 non-null int64
pclass         891 non-null int64
sex            891 non-null object
age            714 non-null float64
sibsp          891 non-null int64
parch          891 non-null int64
fare           891 non-null float64
embarked       889 non-null object
class          891 non-null category
who            891 non-null object
adult_male     891 non-null bool
deck           203 non-null category
embark_town    889 non-null object
```

```
alive               891 non-null object
alone               891 non-null bool
dtypes: bool(2), category(2), float64(2), int64(4), object(5)
memory usage: 80.6+ KB
first five rows of titanic:
   survived  pclass     sex   age  sibsp  parch     fare embarked  class \
0         0       3    male  22.0      1      0   7.2500        S  Third
1         1       1  female  38.0      1      0  71.2833        C  First
2         1       3  female  26.0      0      0   7.9250        S  Third
3         1       1  female  35.0      1      0  53.1000        S  First
4         0       3    male  35.0      0      0   8.0500        S  Third

     who  adult_male  deck  embark_town alive  alone
0    man        True   NaN  Southampton    no  False
1  woman       False     C    Cherbourg   yes  False
2  woman       False   NaN  Southampton   yes   True
3  woman       False     C  Southampton   yes  False
4    man        True   NaN  Southampton    no   True
first four ages:
0    22.0
1    38.0
2    26.0
3    35.0
Name: age, dtype: float64
fifth passenger:
survived                  0
pclass                    3
sex                    male
age                      35
sibsp                     0
parch                     0
fare                   8.05
embarked                  S
class                 Third
who                     man
adult_male             True
deck                    NaN
embark_town     Southampton
alive                    no
alone                  True
Name: 4, dtype: object
counts per class:
3    491
1    216
2    184
Name: pclass, dtype: int64
max/min/mean/median ages:
80.0
0.42
29.69911764705882
28.0
```

EXTRACTING DATA FROM THE TITANIC DATASET IN SEABORN (2)

Listing 10.27 shows the contents of seaborn_titanic2.py that illustrate how to extract subsets of data from the Titanic dataset.

LISTING 10.27: seaborn_titanic2.py

```
import matplotlib.pyplot as plt
import seaborn as sns

titanic = sns.load_dataset("titanic")

# Returns a scalar
# titanic.ix[4, 'age']
print("age:",titanic.at[4, 'age'])

# Returns a Series of name 'age', and the age values
associated
# to the index labels 4 and 5
# titanic.ix[[4, 5], 'age']
print("series:",titanic.loc[[4, 5], 'age'])

# Returns a Series of name '4', and the age and fare values
# associated to that row.
# titanic.ix[4, ['age', 'fare']]
print("series:",titanic.loc[4, ['age', 'fare']])

# Returns a DataFrame with rows 4 and 5, and columns 'age'
and 'fare'
# titanic.ix[[4, 5], ['age', 'fare']]
print("dataframe:",titanic.loc[[4, 5], ['age', 'fare']])

query = titanic[
    (titanic.sex == 'female')
    & (titanic['class'].isin(['First', 'Third']))
    & (titanic.age > 30)
    & (titanic.survived == 0)
]
print("query:",query)
```

Listing 10.27 contains the same import statements as Listing 10.26, and then initializes the variable titanic with the contents of the built-in Titanic dataset. The next code snippet displays the age of the passenger with index 4 in the dataset (which equals 35).

The following code snippet displays the ages of passengers with index values 4 and 5 in the dataset:

```
print("series:",titanic.loc[[4, 5], 'age'])
```

The next snippet displays the age and fare of the passenger with index 4 in the dataset, followed by another code snippet that displays the age and fare of the passengers with index 4 and index 5 in the dataset.

The final portion of Listing 10.27 defines the variable query:

```
query = titanic[
    (titanic.sex == 'female')
    & (titanic['class'].isin(['First', 'Third']))
    & (titanic.age > 30)
```

```
        & (titanic.survived == 0)
    ]
```

The preceding code block retrieves the female passengers who were in either first class or third class, were over 30, and did not survive the accident. The entire output from Listing 10.27 is as follows:

```
age: 35.0
series: 4      35.0
5       NaN
Name: age, dtype: float64
series: age         35
fare       8.05
Name: 4, dtype: object
dataframe:       age      fare
4    35.0   8.0500
5     NaN   8.4583
```

query:	survived	pclass	sex	age	sibsp	parch	fare	embarked	class \
18	0	3	female	31.0	1	0	18.0000	S	Third
40	0	3	female	40.0	1	0	9.4750	S	Third
132	0	3	female	47.0	1	0	14.5000	S	Third
167	0	3	female	45.0	1	4	27.9000	S	Third
177	0	1	female	50.0	0	0	28.7125	C	First
254	0	3	female	41.0	0	2	20.2125	S	Third
276	0	3	female	45.0	0	0	7.7500	S	Third
362	0	3	female	45.0	0	1	14.4542	C	Third
396	0	3	female	31.0	0	0	7.8542	S	Third
503	0	3	female	37.0	0	0	9.5875	S	Third
610	0	3	female	39.0	1	5	31.2750	S	Third
638	0	3	female	41.0	0	5	39.6875	S	Third
657	0	3	female	32.0	1	1	15.5000	Q	Third
678	0	3	female	43.0	1	6	46.9000	S	Third
736	0	3	female	48.0	1	3	34.3750	S	Third
767	0	3	female	30.5	0	0	7.7500	Q	Third
885	0	3	female	39.0	0	5	29.1250	Q	Third

VISUALIZING A PANDAS DATASET IN SEABORN

Listing 10.28 shows the contents of `pandas_seaborn.py` that illustrate how to display a Pandas dataset in Seaborn.

LISTING 10.28: pandas_seaborn.py

```python
import pandas as pd
import random
import matplotlib.pyplot as plt
import seaborn as sns

df = pd.DataFrame()

df['x'] = random.sample(range(1, 100), 25)
df['y'] = random.sample(range(1, 100), 25)

print("top five elements:")
```

```
print(df.head())

# display a density plot
#sns.kdeplot(df.y)

# display a density plot
#sns.kdeplot(df.y, df.x)

#sns.distplot(df.x)

# display a histogram
#plt.hist(df.x, alpha=.3)
#sns.rugplot(df.x)

# display a boxplot
#sns.boxplot([df.y, df.x])

# display a violin plot
#sns.violinplot([df.y, df.x])

# display a heatmap
#sns.heatmap([df.y, df.x], annot=True, fmt="d")

# display a cluster map
#sns.clustermap(df)

# display a scatterplot of the data points
sns.lmplot('x', 'y', data=df, fit_reg=False)
plt.show()
```

Listing 10.28 contains several familiar `import` statements, followed by the initialization of the Pandas variable `df` as a Pandas `dataframe`. The next two code snippets initialize the columns and rows of the `dataframe`, and the `print()` statement displays the first five rows.

For your convenience, Listing 10.28 contains an assortment of "commented out" code snippets that use Seaborn to render a density plot, a histogram, a boxplot, a violin plot, a heatmap, and a cluster. Uncomment the portions that interest you to see the associated plot. The output from Listing 10.28 is as follows:

```
top five elements:
    x    y
0   52   34
1   31   47
2   23   18
3   34   70
4   71    1
```

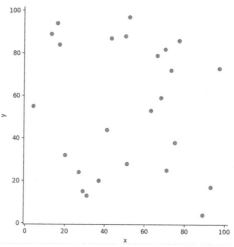

FIGURE 10.22: A plot of the data in the Titanic dataset based on the code in Listing 10.28

DATA VISUALIZATION IN PANDAS

Although Matplotlib and Seaborn are often the "go to" Python libraries for data visualization, you can also use Pandas for such tasks.

Listing 10.29 shows the contents `pandas_viz1.py` that illustrate how to render various types of charts and graphs using Pandas and Matplotlib.

LISTING 10.29: pandas_viz1.py

```
import pandas as pd
import numpy as np
import matplotlib.pyplot as plt

df = pd.DataFrame(np.random.rand(16,3),
columns=['X1','X2','X3'])
print("First 5 rows:")
print(df.head())
print()

print("Diff of first 5 rows:")
print(df.diff().head())
print()

# bar chart:
#ax = df.plot.bar()

# horizontal stacked bar chart:
#ax = df.plot.barh(stacked=True)

# vertical stacked bar chart:
ax = df.plot.bar(stacked=True)

# stacked area graph:
```

```
#ax = df.plot.area()

# non-stacked area graph:
#ax = df.plot.area(stacked=False)

#plt.show(ax)
```

Listing 10.29 initializes the dataframe df with a 16×3 matrix of random numbers, followed by the contents of df. The bulk of Listing 10.29 contains code snippets for generating a bar chart, a horizontal stacked bar chart, a vertical stacked bar chart, a stacked area graph, and a non-stacked area graph. You can uncomment the individual code snippet that displays the graph of your choice with the contents of df. Launch the code in Listing 10.29 to see the following output:

```
First 5 rows:
         X1        X2        X3
0   0.051089  0.357183  0.344414
1   0.800890  0.468372  0.800668
2   0.492981  0.505133  0.228399
3   0.461996  0.977895  0.471315
4   0.033209  0.411852  0.347165

Diff of first 5 rows:
         X1        X2        X3
0        NaN       NaN       NaN
1   0.749801  0.111189  0.456255
2  -0.307909  0.036760 -0.572269
3  -0.030984  0.472762  0.242916
4  -0.428787 -0.566043 -0.124150
```

WHAT IS BOKEH?

Bokeh is an open-source project that depends on Matplotlib and Sklearn. Bokeh generates an HTML Webpage based on Python code, and then launches that page in a browser. Bokeh and D3.js (which is a JavaScript layer of abstraction over SVG) both provide elegant visualization effects that support animation effects and user interaction.

Bokeh enables the rapid creation of statistical visualization, and it works with other tools with as Python Flask and Django. In addition to Python, Bokeh supports Julia, Lua, and R (JSON files are generated instead of HTML webpages).

Listing 10.30 shows the contents bokeh_gtrig.py that illustrate how to create a graphics effect using various Bokeh APIs.

LISTING 10.30: bokeh_trig.py

```
# pip3 install bokeh
from bokeh.plotting import figure, output_file, show
from bokeh.layouts import column
```

```
import bokeh.colors as colors
import numpy as np
import math

deltaY = 0.01
maxCount = 150
width  = 800
height = 400
band_width = maxCount/3

x = np.arange(0, math.pi*3, 0.05)
y1 = np.sin(x)
y2 = np.cos(x)

white = colors.RGB(255,255,255)

fig1 = figure(plot_width = width, plot_height = height)

for i in range(0,maxCount):
  rgb1 = colors.RGB(i*255/maxCount, 0, 0)
  rgb2 = colors.RGB(i*255/maxCount, i*255/maxCount, 0)
  fig1.line(x, y1-i*deltaY,line_width = 2, line_color = rgb1)
  fig1.line(x, y2-i*deltaY,line_width = 2, line_color = rgb2)

for i in range(0,maxCount):
  rgb1 = colors.RGB(0, 0, i*255/maxCount)
  rgb2 = colors.RGB(0, i*255/maxCount, 0)
  fig1.line(x, y1+i*deltaY,line_width = 2, line_color = rgb1)
  fig1.line(x, y2+i*deltaY,line_width = 2, line_color = rgb2)
  if (i % band_width == 0):
    fig1.line(x, y1+i*deltaY,line_width = 5,
              line_color = white)

show(fig1)
```

Listing 10.30 starts with a commented out `pip3` code snippet that you can launch from the command line to install Bokeh (in case you haven't done so already).

The next code block contains several Bokeh-related statements as well as NumPy and Math.

Notice that the variable `white` is defined as an (R,G,B) triple of integers, which represents the red, green, and blue components of a color. In particular, (255,255,255) represents the color white (check online if you are unfamiliar with RGB). The next portion of Listing 10.30 initializes some scalar variables that are used in the two `for` loops that are in the second half of Listing 10.30.

Next, the NumPy variable `x` is a range of values from 0 to `math.PI/3`, with an increment of 0.05 between successive values. Then the NumPy variables `y1` and `y2` are defined as the sine and cosine values, respectively, of the values in x. The next code snippet initializes the variable `fig1` that represents a context in which the graphics effects will be rendered. This completes the initialization of the variables that are used in the two `for` loops.

The next portion of Listing 10.30 contains the first `for` loop that creates a gradient-like effect by defining (R,G,B) triples whose values are based partially on the value of the loop variable `i`. For example, the variable `rgb1` ranges in a linear fashion from (0,0,0) to (255,0,0), which represent the colors black and red, respectively. The variable `rgb2` ranges in a linear fashion from (0,0,0) to (255,255,0), which represent the colors black and yellow, respectively. The next portion of the `for` loop contains two invocations of the `fig1.line()` API that renders a sine wave and a cosine wave in the context variable `fig1`.

The second `for` loop is similar to the first `for` loop: the main difference is that the variable `rgb1` varies from black to blue, and the variable `rgb2` varies from black to green. The final code snippet in Listing 10.30 invokes the `show()` method that generates an HTML Webpage (with the same prefix as the Python file) and then launches the Webpage in a browser.

Figure 10.23 displays the graphics effect based on the code in Listing 10.30. If this image is displayed as black and white, launch the code from the command line and you will see the gradient-like effects in the image.

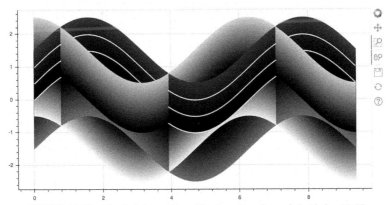

FIGURE 10.23: The Bokeh graphics effect based on the code in Listing 10.30

SUMMARY

This chapter started with some basic features of Matplotlib, along with examples of plotting lines, histograms, and simple trigonometric functions.

You also learned about Sklearn, including examples of working with the Digits and Iris datasets, and also how to process images. In addition, you saw how to perform linear regression with Sklearn.

Then you were introduced to Seaborn, which is an extension of Matplotlib, and saw examples of plotting lines and histograms, and also how to plot a Pandas `dataframe` using Seaborn. Finally, you saw an example of rendering graphics in Bokeh.

INDEX